PANJABI MANUAL AND GRAMMAR

PANJABI MANUAL
AND
GRAMMAR

A GUIDE TO THE
COLLOQUIAL PANJABI

T. GRAHAME BAILEY
T. CUMMINGS

GYAN

Published by

GYAN

Gyan Publishing House
5, Ansari Road
Daryaganj, New Delhi-110002
Phone: 011-47034999, 9811692060
E-mail: books@gyanbooks.com

Distribution Network
gyanbooks.com
India, USA, Canada, UK, Australia, France

ISBN : 978-81-212-3031-5 (PB)
First Published, 1912

2nd Impression 2020

Printed at: Gyan Press, Delhi.

Panjabi Manual and Grammar
Author: T. Grahame Bailey; T. Cummings

PREFACE.

This Grammar is intended as a Guide to the spoken Panjabi of the Northern Panjab, i.e. the Panjabi spoken in the districts of Sialkot, Gujranwala, Lahaur, Gujrat, Firozpur and to some extent in the adjoining districts. The language of the northern part of Gujranwala has been taken as the standard. It is a guide to spoken Panjabi, not to the Panjabi found in books, and in particular it is not meant to deal with the Panjabi of the Sikkhs, usually written in Gurmukkhi letters. The Panjabi treated of in this work is as a rule found printed in Persian letters.

It is now generally admitted that the old method of learning a language is unsatisfactory. To attempt to learn Panjabi as we learned Greek and Latin and Hebrew can only result in failure. In the following pages, therefore, great stress is laid on the modern oral method, and an exhaustive series of short questions and answers will be found in Part II, the Guide to Conversation, and of longer sentences in Part III, the Guide to Connected Speech.

The responsibility for the various parts of the work has been divided between us as follows :—Mr. Cummings has written the Introduction on the Right Method of learning a language; Part I, a Phonetic account of the Pronunciation; the English of Lessons I to XL in Part II on Conversation; Lessons I to XXI, with the English of XXII to XXXV, in Part III on Connected Speech; the Diversification Table.

I have written the Panjabi Grammar which forms the second section of this volume; the Preface, the Pronunciation Exercises; the Panjabi of the first forty lessons and the whole of the succeeding lessons in Part II, the Panjabi of Lessons XXII to XXXV in Part III; have revised the Panjabi of Lessons I to XXI at the request of Mr. Cummings, who has resided now for some time in America, and have corrected all the proofs of the work.

I should like to make grateful mention of the assistance

rendered by Lala Sundar Das, teacher in the Church of Scotland High School, Gujrat. He is particularly well acquainted with the niceties of his native language, and he has made many valuable suggestions.

Romanising. The values of the different letters will be found in the Phonetic Introduction, Part I. It will be useful here to draw attention to the difficulties of accurate Romanising. It is easy to transliterate from Persian or Gurmukkhi letters to Roman, for each letter in that case has its value, but when the standard is the spoken sound the difficulty is very great. Indeed to romanise accurately one would need new signs.

Sounds vary in different places, so that what is a correct representation for one district may not be quite correct for a neighbouring district. A teacher with Urduising tendencies may affect an Urdu pronunciation. Such a teacher would pedantically say **sāhib** for **sāhb**; **bīmār** for **bamār**, ill; **zamīn** for **jīwī̃**, land; **Arabī** for **Arbī**, Arabic.

In the following pages an effort has been made to avoid forms which are confined to illiterate villagers, to avoid also imitations of Urdu and to preserve the forms which are commonly used in daily speech amongst people of moderate education, such as schoolboys or shopkeepers. Thus for penknife **kācū** is avoided as illiterate, **cāqū** as Urdu, and **cakkū** is employed as the ordinary word; so also for road the word is not **sharak** or **saṛak, but sarak**. It follows that all special Arabic signs are rejected. Words like **haqq, huqqa, ta'rīf, liyāqat,** are changed to **hakk, hukkā, tarīf, liākat** and so on.

The determination of the length of vowels, especially unaccented vowels, is a matter of great difficulty. Thus **ā** is quite different from **a**, the former being generally considered long. Yet we have words like **sājē**, **sāsū**, **sāṇē** (see Pronom. Suffixes, pp. 84, 86), where the *a* is the same vowel as **ā**, but is quite short. Similarly the final unaccented **a in patā, bhijjṇā, tuhāḍḍā** is the vowel **ā**, but is shorter than an accented **ā**.

We find the same difficulty with **ē** and **e**, **ō** and **o**. Should we write **hōkē** or **hōke, hōeā** or **hoeā, kī ē** or **kī e**; is the second vowel in **tū̃ ē̃** short or long? A question arises also about words with short ai, paie or pae, lahe or laihe, baihe or bahe, gaie or gae.

Again there is a tendency in Panjabi to nasalize the vowel of every syllable containing n, and still more of every syllable containing ṇ. If we were to write all such syllables with the nasal sign we should produce very uncouth forms. The student will bear in mind this general tendency. **Sāṇē** might equally well be written **sāṇẽ**, **jāṇā** might be **jā̃ṇā̃**, **jaṇē** might be **jaṇẽ**.

Another tendency is to introduce a tonic h (i.e. an h which raises the tone of a syllable) in accented syllables at the end of sentences. It is common to hear **karhō** for **kā̃rō**, **jā̃h** for **jā̃**, **baṇāhā̃** for **baṇāā̃**, and so on. This h has not been written in these pages except in very marked cases such as **dēh**, **dēho**, **jāh**, **jāho**, instead of **de**, **deo**, **jā**, **jāo** (give, go).

On the other hand the deep guttural h is sometimes uttered especially after r, when there is a very strong accent, thus we hear **rhāṭh** for **rāṭh**, resolute: **Rhāṇō** for **Rāṇō**, girl's name: **rhātī̃** for **rātī**, by night.

There is a common tendency to double a consonant, other than ṇ, ḷ, ṛ, r and h, when an accented vowel precedes and an unaccented vowel follows. We sometimes hear **Panjābbī** for **Panjābī**, **tuhānnū̃** for **tuhānū̃**, to you, **māllī** for **mālī**, gardener. In other words, too, this difficulty arises, as in **calṇā** or **callṇā**.

Again g and g̱, kh and k̲h̲ are often interchangeable. It may be noticed that the sounds **kh**, **g**, **l**, **n**, tend to become either **kkh**, **gg**, **ll**, **nn** or **k̲h̲**, **g̱**, **ḷ**, **ṇ**. Thus **sikheā** is either **sikkheā** or **sik̲h̲eā**, **lagā**, is **lāgga** or **lagā**, and we find that n and l are rare undoubled unless when followed by a consonant which makes ṇ and ḷ hard to enunciate.

These varieties will occur in the declension of a single word. We may have **likkhā̃**, shall I write, but **lik̲h̲ẽā**, written, **sikkhẽgā**, you will learn, and **sik̲h̲ī** (f) learned, **wēkkhē**, he may see, **wēk̲h̲kē**, having seen. In a number of the above instances it has seemed better to allow both forms to appear and not to imply a uniformity which does not exist.

The reader will, therefore, expect to find some words written in two ways, and will moreover be prepared for somewhat unfamiliar spellings of words which occur in Urdu. It has hitherto been customary to romanise Urdu words as they are romanised in Urdu. This leads to mispronunciation. In the following pages words will be found written approximately as they are spoken. Thus **munsif** becomes **munsaf**, **hāzir** becomes **hāzar**, for **shaitān** we have **shatān**, and so with many others.

Owing to the habit of retaining the Urdu spelling one is in danger of overlooking the fact that even by educated speakers these words are not pronounced as they are in Urdu. In the interests of correctness it is clearly necessary to depart from the customary spelling.

Triple letters found in words like **cukkke**, **bhannnā**, **sadddā**, or with h added, in **bannhnā**, **nakhiddhdā**, are not easy to pronounce. Between them and double letters there is a difference which, if slight, is frequently quite perceptible See Pronun. Exx., p. xx.

In Parts II and III it should be noted that the translation is not always literal. It is important for the beginner early to realise that ideas and not words are to be translated. Thus if in a lesson on the use of Prepositions a Panjabi sentence is found containing no preposition, it is to be understood that in such a sentence Panjabi ordinarily does not need one. The student should, specially in Part III, make inquiries about the exact meaning of the words employed.

Some difficulty was felt in Part III with regard to the use of capitals for pronouns referring to the Persons of the Trinity As in a number of the sentences it is not clear from the actual words that any reference to the Divine Persons is intended, it seemed better to follow the practice of the Revised Version of the Bible and restrict capitals to nouns, printing the pronouns with small letters. The sentences founded on the Gospel according to St. John will be of special value to those who in their daily work experience a need for a religious vocabulary. It has been thought advisable to keep in a distinct section all the sentences directly bearing upon religious matters. They will be found in Part III.

In conclusion one may be permitted to express the hope that this Grammar will be found useful by those Europeans—missionaries,

Government servants and business men—who desire to acquire a knowledge of the language of the sturdy inhabitants of the Panjab. The avoidance of Persian and Gurmukkhi letters will have the double advantage of rendering the words easy to read and of securing greater correctness in the representation of sounds. As students will be spared the initial difficulty of learning a new script perhaps many will take courage and commence the study of this virile and fascinating tongue.

WAZIRĀBĀD: T. GRAHAME BAILEY.

February 20th. 1912

CONTENTS.

SYSTEM OF ROMANISING.

The approximate sounds of the letters employed may be given here, but fuller details should be sought in the Phonetic account of the pronunciation, pp. 11—25.

Consonants, **b, f, j, k, l, m, n, p, s, z** have nearly the same sound as in English, but great care should be taken not to aspirate **k** and **p**. English k and p are always slightly aspirated. This caution is required also for the letters c, t, ṭ, all of which a foreigner tends to aspirate.

c, like ch in child, but unaspirated.

d and t are the sounds we should make if we tried to say the English d and t with the tip *and sides* of the tongue against the front teeth, ḍ and ṭ are the same pronounced with the tip of the tongue against the soft palate. The difference between t and ṭ, and between d and ḍ, is very great.

g, like g in get. In Panjabi undoubled **g** between two vowels tends to become **g̲**.

g̲ is a voiced **k̲h̲**. One may learn to say **g̲** by repeating **ga-ga-ga** over and over again with extreme rapidity.

h, see Phonetics, p. 17, and Pronunc. Exx. pp. xvi—xxiv. In **ch, kh, ph, th, ṭh,** it resembles an English **h,** but must be forcibly enunciated without any vowel between it and the letter preceding it.

j, see above; when undoubled and followed and preceded by a vowel it tends to become **y**.

k̲h̲, like gh in Irish lough or ch in Scotch loch. **kh,** with **k** undoubled, preceded and followed by a vowel, tends to become **k̲h̲**.

ḷ, like l uttered with the tip of the tongue against the soft palate.

ṇ, like n with the tip of the tongue against the soft palate.

Nasal n is represented by a sign over the nasalized vowel as **ã, ẽ,** etc. It is like the n in the French mon, voyons.

ñ, like n in señor, cañon or the ni in lenient. **nj** tends to become **ñ**.

ṅ, like ng in sing.

r, like Scotch r well trilled, very unlike English, Irish or American r.

ṛ made from the soft palate, see Phonetics. It has no resemblance to the American or Irish r.

t, ṭ, see above under d.

w, see Phonetics. It is different from English w and v, but is nearer to v than to w. The lower lip must not touch the teeth in making Panjabi w.

y, like English consonantal y, but tends, especially when doubled, towards zh.

VOWELS.

ā, ī, ū, like Italian a, i, u; ē, ō, like French ê, ô.

a, e, i, o, u when not marked long are to be read short. Sometimes e and o have been marked short as a warning against the tendency to make them invariably long. But they are to be read long only when especially marked so.

a is like the first a in the word America or the u in plum.

e, o are like ē, ō shortened.

i is like English i in linen.

u like u in pull, but broad and unrounded.

ai; the pronunciation of ai heard from well-educated people is given on page 21 of Phonetics. Among ordinary people it has practically ceased to be diphthongal. If one says the vowel in *hand*, and while saying it lowers the jaw and spreads the lips one will get very near ai.

au is a combination of a and o made into a diphthong.

PRONUNCIATION EXERCISES.

The following sentences and words are given in the hope that they may suggest to the student the chief difficulties of pronunciation. They are merely suggestions. The list might be indefinitely extended; each day's study of the language will draw attention to new words which are hard to pronounce. There is perhaps nothing which students of language seem to find harder than to carry out a firm resolve to set apart a definite period of time every day for practice in pronunciation. Yet there is scarcely anything in language study so well worth acquiring as a good pronunciation. It is of far more value than a large vocabulary.

The following rules for the use of these and similar exercises may be of use:—

1. Set apart a definite time of at least 20 minutes every day for practice in pronunciation, and let nothing interfere with it.

2. During this time practise nothing but pronunciation. Do not get beguiled into a discussion of idioms or constructions or other points in connection with the language. They can wait for the Conversation hour.

3. Pay little or no attention to the Munshi's assurances that your pronunciation is practically correct. If you wish to test your pronunciation, do so by dictating to the Munshi a list of *imaginary* words and observing in how many cases he writes the sound which you intend. Dictate such sounds as these ṭā̃, ṭā, thā, ṭhā, tā, thā̃, tā̃, ṭhā̃, tāh, ṭāh, ṭā̃h, tā̃h. Then substitute for the initial ṭ or t the letters, ṛ, r, ḍ, d, p, b, c, ch, etc., and change all the vowels, and finally put all the consonants after the vowel instead of before it. Try them also doubled, e.g., atā attā, acā, accā, achā, acchā, etc. If the Munshi always knows what sounds you intend you have learned the pronunciation of the language well, but not of necessity perfectly, for the Munshi may come to recognise your method of making a particular sound.

Do not attempt all the sounds every day. A few are enough for each lesson. Sometimes one or two are sufficient, but do not go on too long at one sound, you will soon cease to be fresh enough to be able to make it.

5. Few instructors can teach pronunciation ; you will therefore have to teach yourself, by saying each word or sound after the teacher. Keep on doing this whether he says you have got it correctly or not. Do not, however, say a word twenty times after he has said it once, say it rather once, or perhaps twice, each time that he says it.

6. During conversation or reading do not spend much time on the niceties of pronunciation, for your conversation or reading will be unduly interrupted. This rule, No. 6, applies only if time is being set apart with unfailing regularity every day for practice in pronunciation.

7. Do not confine yourself to the words in the following sentences. Take up systematically all the sounds of the language, and be especially careful not to limit yourself to the sounds which are commonly considered difficult. *Pay great attention to vowels.* They are generally disregarded by students as being quite easy. The simplest vowels are often extremely difficult for a foreigner.

8. About once a week have dictation of sounds, using both real and imaginary words. For the purposes of this dictation words and sounds should be written in Roman letters. It need not occupy more than a very few minutes. Sometimes the student should dictate sounds to the Munshi, sometimes the Munshi should dictate them to the student. If the student is working at the Persian or Gurmukkhi character, he will have dictation, quite independent of this and at a different time, to test his knowledge of the letters.

The pronunciation of h. h is perhaps the most difficult letter in Panjabi. Its three pronunciations are dealt with under phonetics.

(*a*) The ordinary English pronunciation is found in only two or three words. It is probably merely softened down from k͟h, for it is quite common to hear āk͟hō for āhō, yes ; ēk͟hāī and ōk͟hāī for ēhāī and ōhāī, this very one, that very one.

(*b*) The tonic **h**, raising the tone of the syllable, occurs only in an accented syllable after the vowel, or before the vowel of the syllable following an accented syllable. It cannot occur before an accented vowel. As its only effect is to raise the tone it will be understood that from the point of view of pronunciation it is immaterial whether we write **ḍāḍhā** or **ḍāhḍā** (severe), **unnhīwā̃** or **unnīhwā̃**, nineteen, **wēhndā** or **wēndhā**, looking.

(*c*) The deep sound represented by **h** occurs always in an accented syllable before the vowel. It distantly resembles the Arabic ain, and can be enunciated only on a low tone. It strikes the ear as a deep guttural sound. It may accompany any consonant or vowel whatever, whether surd or sonant. In the majority of cases, **bh, jh, gh, dh, ḍh** when pronounced with this deep **h** are really pronounced as beginning with **p, c, k, t, ṭ**, but it is, of course, quite possible to have **b, j, g, d, ḍ**, also with this sound. The following examples show actual occurrences of it. The forms in brackets indicate the usual way of writing the words, the others the actual pronunciation. The sound is represented by (').

pr'ā (bhrā), brother.
p'ā, (bhā), price.
b'ā, (bahā), cause to sit.
ṭ'āī, (ḍhāī), 2½.
ḍ'āī, (ḍahāī), price of placing (beds, etc.).
s'āb, (hisāb), account.
S'āī, (Īsāī), Christian.
Z'āk (Izhāk), Isaac.
Sh'ābbā (Shahābā), a name.
pakh'ā, (pakhhā) fever, heat.
ph'ā (phahā), entanglement.
n'ērnī, (hanērnī), giddiness.
l'āī, (lahāī), descent.
waḷ'ēṭṇā, (waḷhēṭṇā), wrap up.
M'ammā (Mhammā), a name.
w'alā, (whalā), interj., well, etc.
laṅg'āṇā, (laṅghāṇā), cause to pass.
kaṭ'āṇā, (ghaṭāṇā), lesson.
kaḍ'āṇā, (kaḍhāṇā), turn out.
c'ajjar, (jhajjar), earthen pot.
J'ūrā (Hujūrā), a name.
ci'ūr, (jhiūr) waterman.
pale'āī, (bhaleāī), goodness
ch'attar (chihattar), 76.
panj'attar, (panjhattar), 75.
tar'āeā, (dharāeā), caused to be placed.
Wad'āwā, (Wadhāwā), a name.
kaṛ'āeā, (ghaṛāeā), caused to be engraved.
'īyyā̃, (hīyyā̃), sides of bed.
'ā̃, (hā̃) yes.

It is important to get a clear understanding of these sounds, to see for example the difference between **ḍhāī, the price of placing** beds, etc., and **ḍhāī, 2½ ; bhāī,** seated, and **bhāī,** brother. The first vowel 'a' usually written in **bahāī, seated,** and in **ḍahāī** price of placing, is not pronounced except by those who affect an Urdu pronunciation. The whole difference is in the initial letter. Note carefully the sounds in—

Kitthe bhāī bhāī, (kitthe b'āī, p'āī), where hast thou seated her, brother ?

ḍhāī ḍhāī ānē dittī (ḍ'āī ṭ'āī) he gave 2½ annas for placing the beds.

It will be seen, then, that the double letters **bh, gh, dh, ḍh, jh,** have two sounds for each pair. In one case the first letters are pronounced as sonants, **b, g, d, ḍ, j,** in the other case as surds, **p, k, t, ṭ, c.** It is somewhat difficult to know when to pronounce them as sonants and when as surds, but the following rules may be given :—

(1) When the combination **bh, gh,** etc., is the result of eliding a vowel between the **b** and the **h** or the **g** and the **h,** etc. the first letters are sonants. Thus in **bhānā,** pretence, for **bahānā ; jhāz,** ship, for **jahāz ; bhāī** for **bahāī,** seated (f), the initial letters are sonant, i e., are **b, j, b** and not **p, c, p.**

(2) Sometimes in the simplest form of a word one of these combinations, **bh, gh,** etc., occurs after the accented vowel and is, therefore, pronounced with the tone-raising **h,** yet in some of the words derived from the original simple form of the word the accent is thrown forward so as to follow **bh, gh,** etc. In this case the **h** naturally receives the deep guttural pronunciation and the **bh, gh,** etc., are pronounced with an initial sonant, **b, g,** etc.

This change of accent occurs chiefly in two cases, (*a*) in casual verbs and nouns formed from them and (*b*) in the organic passive heard in some districts. Thus we have such forms as the following—

	Causal.	Passive.
kaḍḍhṇā, turn out	**kaḍhāṇā**	**kaḍhīṇā**
waḍḍhṇā, cut	**waḍhāṇā**	**waḍhīṇā**
labbhṇā, find	**labhāṇā**	**labhīṇā**
ḍāhṇā, place	**ḍhāṇā (ḍahāṇā),** noun **ḍhāī (ḍahāī)**	

(3) When **jh** comes from an original **zh**, the **j** is always sonant. Thus in **Jhūrā**, for **Huzūrā**, **jhār** or **ajhār** for **hazār**, thousand, the first consonant is pronounced **j** not **c**.

In other cases these double letters usually have the first letter pronounced surd.

It follows from the above that while **bhiāī**, and **pihāī** are identical, (both being **pi'āī**), **bihāī** is different (**bi'āī**). Similarly **tihāī** and **dhiāī** are **ti'āī**, while **dihāī** is **di'āī** : **jhuārī**, **jhuhārī** and **cuhārī** are all **cu'ārī**, but **juhārī** is **ju'ārī**. (Most of these are imaginary words.) We find, too, that there is often doubt about the proper spelling of a Panjabi word. Thus some write **panjhāḷ**, others **bhanjāḷ**, partner. In either case the pronunciation is **panj'āḷ** ; **dhigāṇe**, meaning uselessly, could be written **tighāṇē** (**tig'āṇē**) ; **kahāṇī**, story, and **ghāṇī**, mud, are identical in pronunciation (**k'āṇī**).

Accent. It is difficult to give any useful rules for accent. The student will get most words right with care. One rule worth remembering is that the syllable of a word which has the accent will retain the accent through all declensions or conjugations of that word. Thus **dassṇā**, show, has the accent on **dass**, therefore all parts of that verb, such as **dassaṇwāḷā**, **dassaṇwāḷīā̃**, **dassā̃gā**, will have it on **dass**. Europeans often wrongly accent **wāḷā** in forms like **dassaṇwāḷā**. Similarly in **kaḍhāṇā**, cause to be turned out, the accent is on **ḍhā** and there remains through all parts of the verb.

An exception to this is found in the regular organic passive made by adding **īṇā** to the root. This passive in its complete form is not heard in north Gujranwala or Sialkot.

kaḍhīṇā́, be turned out, from **kaḍḍhṇā**, **waḍhīṇā**, be cut, from **waḍḍhṇā**, and all other such verbs, accent the **ī** of **īṇā**.

pailīā̃ waḍhīndīā̃ nē paiā̃, the fields are being cut.

Note however that the passive participle in **īdā** found in Gujranwala and Sialkot accents according to the ordinary rule ; thus **waḍḍhīdā**, **waḍḍhīdīā̃**, being cut, have the accent on **waḍḍh**.

Causative verbs are not really exceptions to the rule, for they are new words. Causative verbs formed regularly by adding **-ā**

or -wā to the root, always accent this added syllable. Hence kaḍhāṇā, cause to be turned out, waḍhāṇā, cause to be cut, and all others similarly formed accent the last syllable of the root.

PRONUNCIATION EXERCISES.

1.	**ēh paṭā e**	this is a lease.
	ēh patā e	this is the address.
	ēh Phattā e	this is Phatta.
	ēh patthā e	this is a piece of wood in a millstone.
	ēh paṭṭhā e	this is a young one.
2.	**ōh phāthā e**	that is entangled.
	ōh pāṭā e	that is torn.
3.	**kehṛe māṛe sāṇ**	which were feeble ?
	kehṛe māre sāṇ	which were beaten ?
4.	**ōh kaṛī e**	that is a bangle.
	ōh kharī e	that (f.) is good.
	ōh khaṛī e	she is standing.
5.	**ēh ḍāhḍā ē**	this is hard.
	ēh dāddā e	this is a grandfather.
	ēh dādā e	this is a professional singer.
6.	**jē ōh sadde**	if he calls.
	jē ōh saddde	if they had called.
	maĩ bhannā̃	shall I break ?
	maĩ bhannnā̃	I am breaking.
	maĩ bhannṇā e	I have to break.
	jē cukke jāṇ	if they are lifted.
	jē cukkke jāṇ	if they, having lifted it, go.
	maĩ bhajjā̃ ?	shall I run ?
	maĩ bhajj jā̃ ?	shall I run away ?
7.	**maḷeā hoeā**	ill.
	malleā hoeā	taken possession of.
	ēh gall e	this is an affair.
	ēh gallh e	this is a cheek.
	ēh gaḷ e	this is a neck.
	Pāllā e	that is Palla.
	pāḷā e	it is cold.

	hilleā hoeā	shaken.
	hiḷeā hoeā	accustomed.
	huṇ wēḷā e	now it is time.
	huṇ wēhlā e	now he is free.
	bāhḷe Shāh nū̃ mannde nẽ	many reverence the Shah.
	Bālle Shāh nū̃ mannde nẽ	they reverence Bale Shah.
	ikkō haḷ ī ?	have you only one yoke of oxen ?
	ikkō hall ī ?	have you only one plough ?
8.	**wacchā bannh**	tie up the calf.
	wacchā baṇ	become a calf.
	ōh sōhṇā e	he is beautiful.
	ōh sōnā e	that is gold.
	ēh saṇ māṛī e	this is bad flax.
	ēs sannh mārī e	he has committed a burglary.
	menū̃ pōṇā dēh	give me a cloth for bread.
	menū̃ pōnnā dēh	give me sugarcane.
	uṇ lai bhaiṇ	weave, sister.
	unn lai bhaiṇ	take wool, sister.
	ēh māṇī e	this is twelve maunds.
	ēh Māhṇī e	this is Mahni.
	ēh mānī e	this is a rope made of wheat stalks.
9.	**rōṛ dē sū**	give him kankar.
	rōṛh dē sū	pour it out.
	tū̃ baṛā kāḷā ẽ	you are very black.
	tū̃ baṛā kāhḷā ẽ	you are in a great hurry.
	ēh mērī kandh e	this is my wall.
	ēh mērī kaṇḍ e	this is my back.
	kis lāhiā nẽ	who has taken them down ?
	kis lāiā nẽ	who has attached them ?
	ōh banne nẽ	those are ridges.
	ōh bannhe nẽ	let him tie them ?
	ōh pīndiā nẽ	the women are drinking.
	ōh pīhndiā nẽ	the women are grinding.
	ēh sūā e	this is a big needle.
	eh sūhā e	this is red.

N.B.—The **h** in these sentences is not sounded. It merely raises the tone.

10.	**puḷ kitthe we**	where is the bridge ?
	phull kitthe we	where is the flower ?
	khōlī nẽ	open them.
	kōḷ ī nẽ	it is beside them.
	Kōhlī nẽ	they are Kohlis by caste.
	tattī e	it is warm (fem.).
	ṭhaṭṭī e	it is a low caste quarter (some say **ṭhaṭṭhī**).
	thatthī e	she stammers.
11.	**ẽh ghōṛī e**	this is a mare.
	ēh gōrī e	she is fair in colour, or red (of a cow).
	dũh bāīā̃ dī lakkaṛ	the wood of two doorposts.
	dũh bhāīā̃ dī lakkaṛ	the wood of two brothers.
	kaḍhāīā manjīā̃ dīā̃ hīyyā̃	had the side pieces of beds taken out.
	ku ḍhāīā manjīā̃ dīā̃ hīyyā̃	the side pieces of about two and a half beds.
	kī bhanneā sū	what did he break ?
	kī baṇeā sū	what was made for him ?
	mēz bhanāeā sū	he caused the table to be broken.
	mēz baṇāeā sū	he made the table.
	ēh bhārī (p'ārī) e	this is heavy (f.).
	ēh bhārī (b'ārī) e	this is a broom.

N.B.—The **h** in these words has a deep guttural sound (except in **dũh**).

12.	**huṇ jā**	now go.
	huṇ jā̃ ?	shall I now go ?
	jē ākhe	if he says.
	jē ākhẽ	if thou sayest.
	hāe	alas !
	hāẽ	now, now (threatening).
	hai whai ?	is it, my man ?

haĩ whai?	what did you say, my man?
bā mārie	O silly woman.
bā̃h māṛī e	the arm is weak.
ēh sau e	this is a hundred.
ēh saũh e	this an oath.
dẽh rātī̃	day and night
dē rātī̃	let him give at night.
dēṇ rātī̃	let them give at night.
dāṇā	grain.
dhāhṇā̂	parched barley grain.
13. ōh khaṛde nehī̃	they will not take away.
ōh khaṛde nẽ	they are taking away.
nũ	to.
nũh	daughter-in-law.
panjhī̃ rupaī̃	for twenty-five rupees.
panjī̃ rupaī̃	for five rupees.
14. uñ	without special reason.
unn	wool.
uṇ	weave.
aiñ we	it is thus.
aĩwê	without reason, anyhow.
sẽwiā̀	macaroni.
sai wihā̂	a hundred twenties.
15. ōh waggdā e	it is working (well), etc.
ōh wagdā e	it is leaking.
pagghardā e	it is melting. Cf. with following.
ragaṛdā e	he is rubbing.
16. maĩ wikā dēnnā̂	I will get it sold.
maĩ wikhā dēnnā̂	I will show it
likkheā hoeā, likheā hoeā	(two pronunciations) it is written.
rakkhā̂gā	I will place.
rakhāā̃gā	I will have it placed.

17. Practise all the words given above under Pronunciation of h.

18. Difficult combinations.

karṛ barṛe	grey hair.
bērṛā	wheat, barley and gram.
bhurṛiāṇ	smell of burning cloth, etc.
naṇān	husband's sister.
baṇaṇ	they may be made.
bannhaṇ	they may tie.
raḷaṇ	they may meet, etc.
ghṛam	noise of splashing.
ḍhōḍhā	bread made of maize or millet.
maḷāī	cream.
baḷā	misfortune.
tagrēṛā	rather strong.
wēkhke	having seen.
wagke	having leaked, etc.
waḷhēṭṇā	wrap up.
wikhāḷī dēṇī	show oneself.
wigaṛnā	be spoiled.
wigṛnwāḷā	one who is getting spoiled.

INTRODUCTION.

THE RIGHT METHOD OF LEARNING A LANGUAGE.

The right method of learning a language depends entirely on our definition of the terms *language* and *learning*. Language in its primary and fundamental sense is human speech. Writing, whether it be in alphabetic characters or in ideograms or picture writing, by hand or by printed type, is not really language. Language is speech. Writing and printing are by accommodation called language, but their appeal is to the eye, while language appeals to the ear. The spoken sound is what we must take as the basis of our study. But what is the unit of speech. Is it the word or the sentence ? The Encyclopædia Britannica says that it is now recognized that ' the sentence is the unit of speech, and that grammar should be taught inductively,' so we shall not need to argue the case further. Consequently in studying a language we must study the spoken sentence. As far as the *written form* of this spoken sentence enables us to study the *spoken form,* so far is writing an aid ; hence the value of writing a new language in a familiar character, such as Roman for Urdu or Panjabi : but as soon as the written or printed character interferes between us and the spoken form, it becomes a hindrance. It does thus interfere when it is wholly strange, as is at first Arabic, Hindi or Chinese writing, or when Roman, by its old familiar symbols, leads us to suppose that these well-known letters have the same value in Panjabi, as they have in English. If when we see a " ṭ," the dot under it conveys no significance to our mind and we pronounce it as we always do our English " t," then Roman has become a snare and not a help. It will be a help when we recognize the fact that these old symbols indicate sounds which are *only similar* to their corresponding values in English, and are not the identical sounds. In other words, one can learn the sound values of a foreign language not from the printed page, but only from the living tongue of the native or of the skilled fellow-countryman. Therefore the study of the sentence should be the study of the sounds of that sentence as they come from the mouth of the living teacher, and the writing or printing should be studied simply as an aid to remembering what we have already heard spoken. As, however, in beginning a new language, one only hears a babble of strange sounds, and as one quickly forgets the unfamiliar combinations of sounds, it is imperative that one's early teaching and study should be almost wholly by ear and therefore always with the teacher. Here is the greatest error of the scholastic method. It pretends to take in language through the eye. The ear is the natural receptive medium of language, which is speech and so audible. The eye is the medium of form and is necessary for writing and printing, which are not language, but only the conventional signs thereof.

It is here, in learning strange sound's that phonetic study is most valuable. In its broadest sense phonetics is the science of sounds, but as applied to linguistics, it is the science of the positions and movements of the vocal organs in the formation of speech sounds. Applied phonetics will teach how the sounds of Panjabi are made, and how they differ among themselves and from those of other languages. It is absolutely necessary that one should have had a previous training in phonetics, either practical, or technical and practical, to enable one to listen appreciatively and to remember correctly the sounds of any strange tongue.

But beyond the skill to pronounce the individual words is the ability to catch the rising and falling rhythm of the sentence with its changes of pitch and cadence, its movement and intonation. This, too, demands the study of the language in the sentence, since there alone can be found that vital rhythm, which is never present in the individual word. It is true, indeed, that this rhythm is found wholly and fully only in spoken living speech, where people mean what they say. It is seldom present in a teacher, and almost never in a reader, for very few read naturally. Hence the less one reads, in beginning the strange tongue, the better, and the more one can study the language right out among the people, talking with them, and above all listening to them talking among themselves, the sooner will one get the language in its rhythmic swing and natural beauty of intonation.

But it is not enough to say to some one, Go out and learn the language by association with the people. He must be taught to hear and to speak, that he may be able thus to learn. His whole education hitherto has been through the eye, and to thrust him out with untrained ear and expect success would be the sheerest folly. It is the aim of the Phonetic Inductive Method to impart such skill as will enable the pupil, after his first few months, to go out and get the language intelligently and successfully from the people. Languages are spoken rapidly. The slow hesitating utterance of the schoolroom is not found in house and street. So after a year, sometimes after years of study, by the old eye method, the student has to say, Do not speak so fast. Consequently a natural method must teach the pupils *to hear at the normal rate of utterance.*

Here should be defined the second term of our first sentence—"*learning.*" What is it to "learn"? It is safe to say that more people fail because they have not a true "standard of attainment"—have no measure to determine when they have really acquired a sentence, when they truly *know* a thing—than for any other reason. Let this be our standard—*To be able to express any given idea as readily, fluently and correctly in Panjabi as in English.* Having reached this standard we may consider that we are ready to pass on. Less than this does not suffice for the requirements of those who have to use Panjabi as the medium of their everyday work, for our ideal must be—*to hear so as to understand,* and *to speak so as to be understood.*

We note further, in this connection, that every language is made up of certain words, divisible into classes, which are called "parts of speech," and these form the elements of speech. In order to speak and understand we must be able to use and appreciate these various elements in all their different permutations and combinations. These word-changes are the facts of grammar, and "grammatical facts indicate logical processes." Hence, if one is to understand language as it is spoken naturally and rapidly, one must be a perfect master of all the endings, words, and auxiliaries which are used to show the interrelation of the different parts of sentences and paragraphs to one another.

It is perfectly evident from this that a man must know the grammar of any language which he pretends to use correctly, and, for this reason, most methods begin with the study of the grammar, for "grammar" to most of us means a book. But, in truth, grammar is only the codification of those forms of language which existed, and were correctly used by thousands of people, long before the "grammar" was written. Now, whether we can codify or not is of little practical importance in comparison with the ability to use these principles correctly. Correct speech is a product not of studying grammars, but of learning correct models of utterance. Thousands of Panjabis speak their language according to the best models, but are wholly unable to explain the underlying principles. A book of grammatical facts is a splendid thing to test yourself by to see whether you are getting into correct habits of speech, but mastery of grammatical principles is to be attained not by learning, for example, that "the adjective must agree with its noun in gender and number," and then thinking, when you wish to say "*the bread is black*," that *rōṭī* is feminine, and so you must say *kāḷī* not *kāḷā*, but rather through accustoming yourself to associating *kāḷī* and *rōṭī*. Ask a Panjabi the gender of noun and he is often unable to tell you, until he repeats to himself a sentence which demands the gender of the word in question, and then he will tell you. Yet he always uses it correctly. Let this then be our primary aim—to use correct speech, explaining it, if we can, but, if not, using it as the people do. Which of us can explain why we say in English, "We *had* better go"? Yet it is the accepted, classic phrase.

Let us note, also, some of the psychological principles involved in learning a language. "In learning a new language," says E. W. Scripture*, "one must learn to associate a new set of sensory and motor, auditory and speaking, sensations with the old ideas. It is the begetting of a new habit of thinking and speaking." Consequently, as we wish to form no bad habits,

* E. W. Scripture, Elements of Experimental Phonetics, p. 381.

we must give special attention, through phonetic study and by careful observation, to getting correct concepts of the sounds which we wish to reproduce. Only as our concept is accurate can our reproduction be exact, and, since many of the Panjabi sounds are very like our own, though still quite distinct, it requires trained and close observation to obtain a just and discriminating concept of these sounds. Yet it can and must be done, and the cultivation of the habit of careful listening to the exact character of the speech sounds and the exact forms of expression, is vital to a mastery of Panjabi.

But we forget so easily. Often it is because we have not really grasped the idea. One cannot expect to remember what one has not fully perceived, and the best way to correct a false impression, and strengthen a right one, is to have the exciting idea again brought before the mind. Have the sentence repeated. It has been determined that the memory normally loses more than 66 per cent. over night. So patience with one's memory is necessary, and frequent repetition must be resorted to, in order that the impression may be so deepened that the full 100 per cent. shall be retained.

All early study must be aloud with the teacher, and this careful hearing will fix the impression. For many the writing of the sounds in Roman is a great aid to remembering. Some find that by certain similarities of sounds they are able to aid their memory, as PANI-Pawnee-Indian-fire-water-WATER, and so to fix both sound and meaning. One should follow the bent of one's own mind, having once determined what that is, and learn to perfection whatever one attempts the first year. This involves, of course, the necessity of *attempting nothing save what must be learned*. Practice makes perfect, but it must be wide-awake, watchful practice. Repetition by a tired, worn-out mind is worse than useless.

It is also a matter of observation that words once learned are most economically learned again after an interval of twenty-four hours or at least a night. Peculiarly difficult subjects, such as new and strange sounds, should be taken up in the morning when one is thoroughly rested.

Another psychological principle is that "intense effort educates," and that is why this "Slip Study," demanding the attainment of a mathematically fixed standard of five syllables per second, is one of the most important parts of the Phonetic Inductive Method, for it requires ready, fluent and accurate utterance, not merely of one, but of many slips, in rapid succession. For this the mind must be alert and active, and so one is educated in the new speech. As one in using the slips is always trying to better, or at least equal, one's previous record for speed in the repetition of a given number of slips, it gives a zest to this study, which is the best earnest of success.

It is well, too, in accordance with psychological law, that impressions of one kind should not be dissipated by introduction of another set of impressions; when one is trying to learn Panjabi sounds, the introduction of English or even of Urdu, tends to break up the Panjabi associations and so weakens the resultant concept. It is a fundamental principle of the Phonetic Inductive Method that "*each language must be the medium of its own impartation.*" Consequently Panjabi must be begun at once, and after a month should be the sole medium of communication for both pupil and teacher.

Again, ordinary book study is hampered by that local memory which tries to recall what is "on the top of the left-hand page," or elsewhere, and get it from visualisation. Slip study breaks up all this local memory and compels one to go directly from the idea to the Panjabi expression of it.

So, too, the local and rote memory that plays so large a part in the paradigm study of the grammar, is quite supplanted. We no longer begin at the beginning and run through till we come to the required form, but, since we learn each form as a part of a sentence, disassociated from any particular paradigm, we are able to reproduce it at will.

Translation as an exercise for imparting skill in the language may be safely omitted from the first year's requirements, since one of the severest tests of ability i[illegible]nguage study is an idiomatic translation from one tongue into another. In slip study, the English expression is indeed given, but that is to impart the idea, and the Panjabi equivalent is required, not as an independent exercise of the mental faculties, but rather as a test of memory. Learning a language has all along been regarded too much as a task requiring great mental abilities, while, if one may draw a deduction from observation, ability to speak frequently goes with very little mental power. The truth is that learning a language is a mechanical process, wherein the muscles of speech are taught to work in new and unusual movements. It is like learning to knit. The process, slow at first, becomes more and more unconscious, until the skilled knitter, goes through the operation without a thought. It has taken many thousands of repetitions before such a result has been attained, but it has come at last, and the steel needles glide in and out as if they were a part of the living hand. So must it be with the tongue. Slowly at first, but, by careful and painstaking repetition, skill is attained, until at last, without any thought, the words run off without the least effort, and then, and not till then, one may learn *how* to speak. So long as one is engrossed with the tool, one's work is poorly done, but when the tool moves as a part of the workman, shape and shading will easily follow.

Slip study is, however, exhausting, and one consecutive hour of it is frequently too long. One should rest, on growing fatigued, by taking up some other branch of the study, such as grammatical forms, or copying out Panjabi, or reading along some other line, to rest the mind and organs of speech Such time should be used, if one intends to learn the Gurmukkhi character, by taking up S. Jno. iv, beginning with verse 7.

As to the length of time that one should study daily, it may be recalled that a gentleman who followed two children, of five and six years of age, during a whole day, and took note of their every word, ascertained that they each had made approximately 15,000 wordsutterances. Allowing 100 words to the minute in conversation, this would give two and one-half hours of steady talking and as much listening for each child. Doubtless if one gave the same time to using familiar words, both hearing and speaking within one's own vocabulary, and gradually extending it by introducing and using a few new words, one would get the language rapidly and accurately.

The number of new words that can be assimilated will vary according to the diligence and mental power of the student. A student of German learned fifty words a day for several months. His method, however, was wrong, as it was the word method, and he did not assimilate so many as this daily. It is better to take a few and thoroughly incorporate them into our sentences, so that we can use them, rather than merely to get the meaning of a large number. If we study twenty-five days in the month, and master ten words daily, we shall be able to use 1,500 in six months. When we realize that the Gospel of St. John has only 1,000 words, we see the possibilities of a well-chosen vocabulary of 1,500 words. By the end of the year we should be able to double or treble this number.

In the mastery of ten words daily it is implied that we distribute our effort over the various parts of speech, and learn not merely to employ ten nouns or verbs, but to use the new words in any sentence that we may have previously been able to say, substituting them for words of the same kind. It is possible that ten words would be too many for some students, but an earnest effort should be made to master at least this number. At first, say for the first two or three weeks, it may be allowable to count the variant forms of the verb 'to be' as different words, and so with variant forms of the noun, but the ambitious student will not do so. Hold yourself to not less than ten separate words, and if you do not get them thoroughly in mind, carry them along in review and add ten new words.

As you get out among the people, carry a book and pencil and enter words and phrases, then at home correct and enter them in ink, and if they are desirable expressions, learn them. At first, say for six months, confine your memorising very largely to the work outlined here. After that go as far afield as you choose, but always try to get your new words in phrases. Cultivate the habit of close and accurate noting of the exact forms of the words in every Panjabi sentence, and you will soon acquire a habit of correct speech, for the ear is the governor of the tongue, and as we hear so we speak. Avoid carefully all mongrel speech. When you talk Urdu, talk it, and when you talk Panjabi, talk it pure—no "khicaṛī."

It will be noted that the sentences of Part III are long and complex. The ordinary language method carefully avoids anything complex till later. But it is much easier to evolve the simple from the complex, than the complex from the simple. As mature students we are used to the complex in thought, and the difficulty of mastering an involved sentence of thirty words is little, if any more, than that of learning one of five or six words. Probably, because of the relation of thought, the complex will be found easier. So, too, the long and complex sentences, when mastered, give a command of idiomatic expression that is never learned from confining oneself to the simple, short sentences so commonly found. The adult student has been used to allowing his thoughts to roam in palaces of paragraphs and involved sentences, and when he is confined to the one-roomed cottage of the simple period, he feels straitened and oppressed.

The written compositions and translations of the ordinary methods will find their best substitute in what Prendergast calls "Diversification" and "Oral Composition." The already learned words are taken as the basis of new sentences. Changes of the subject are made by substituting the singular for the plural, nouns for pronouns, first person for second or third, past for present, future or perfect, feminine for masculine, and vice versa, until no ending, auxiliary or part of speech seems unfamiliar. Take the Diversification Table at the end of Part III, and practise one or more classes daily after the first two months, until all the changes involved by the use of any of the words come readily to mind. Mastery of these few forms will give the mastery of all.

"No one ever gained a fluent command over many words without first mastering a few at a time. Repetition of the same words in varied combinations, thus disclosing their various forms and uses, is the method whereby languages reveal their secrets." We learn to use a language as we learn to use the sword. How many times must one practise the thrust and stroke, the feint and parry before one is fit to cross swords with a foe. So, too, we must go over and over these thrusts and strokes of tongue and mind, before we can use our Panjabi in front of an audience.

Reading, as has already been said, should follow our ability to understand, and may be carried on as we memorise the sentences of the Manual. While resting, one might take up the Gurmukkhi character (beginning with S. John iv. 7). By having the Gurmukkhi written under the English of our slips, it is possible to learn the general outlines of the Gurmukkhi words, while we are memorising their sounds, and after the first lesson or two to begin an inductive study of the character, without the drudgery of the alphabet.

The true language method then, we may observe, by way of recapitulation, demands

1. A phonetic analysis of the sounds of the student's native tongue.

2. A phonetic analysis of Panjabi sounds.

3. A synthetic combination of Panjabi sounds in Pronunciation Exercises.

4. A study of Panjabi as spoken by a native Panjabi in complete sentences.

5. Memorising these sentences aloud, till the pupil can say them at a normal rate of utterance, five syllables per second.

6. A complete mastery of the changes which the various parts of speech undergo to indicate the logical interrelations of the various sentences and parts of sentences to one another.

7. The initial and continued use of Panjabi as a direct medium of communication and of teaching Panjabi itself.

PART I.—GUIDE TO PRONUNCIATION.

As a proof of the value of phonetics, one cannot do better than quote the opinion of Miss Mary Brebner, Gilchrist Scholar of the Cambridge (England) Training School for Women Teachers, who was sent abroad to investigate the teaching of modern languages in Germany. After six months' investigation she writes, "I am fully persuaded by all that I saw and heard, that phonetic drill is invaluable for giving the pupils a good pronunciation from the start. I often marvelled at the sure unhesitating way in which the pupils had mastered the English sounds."

Note also, in this connection, the deliverance of the World's Missionary Conference, Edinburgh, June 1910, Commission V, "The modern science of phonetics is without doubt of great use in the acquirement of a correct pronunciation and ought to be studied at home."

Were it not that this science is almost wholly neglected in both English and American schools and colleges, one might pass over a great deal of what follows. It will be a great advance toward linguistic perfection, too, when the advice of the Edinburgh Conference is followed and the subject is really studied at home. However, we must do the best we can on the field to make up for any lack of preparation at home, and so we shall treat the subject as if it were wholly strange to the student of Panjabi.

1. *Phonetics* is the science of sounds, but as applied to linguistics, it is the science of the positions and movements of the vocal organs in the production of speech-sounds. We shall endeavour to show the organic positions of Panjabi sounds, and show also how they differ from or resemble the corresponding Urdu and English sounds, so that the student may work intelligently and successfully toward acquiring a correct intonation in his use of Panjabi.

This drill in phonetics is indispensable for the adult, owing to the fixity of his organs of speech, and his tendency to hear according to his preconceived notions of what the sounds are

Not only will this educate him to hear, but he will be so trained that those who hear him will be able to tell with ease and certainty what he is saying and to recognize in his speech the distinctive Panjabi sounds. These are at first so much alike to the untutored ear that the ordinary beginner fails to distinguish them in his speaking or hearing, but a knowledge of them is absolutely necessary.

2. Speech is the original wireless telegraphy, and has as its medium the air. By means of the vocal organs certain wavelike movements are imparted to the air in the larynx and mouth, and these cause similar movements to radiate to the outer air. and thus they reach the ears of others. The lungs form the bellows from which the air of the chest is forced out through the larynx between the vocal chords, where it is so modified as to form the basis of articulate speech. The vocal chords, when brought close together, vibrate as do the lips, when one is blowing a trumpet. and by this vibration the vocal current becomes "sonant" whereas, if the approximation of the chords is slight, the vocal current is but little changed, and becomes "surd."

Just above the larynx or Adam's apple is the pharynx, the passage between the back of the mouth and the gullet and windpipe. By a contraction of the walls of the pharynx force is given to all explosives. It is at the upper part of the pharynx that the vocal current is deflected outward, either into the mouth or into the nasal passage. This deflection is determined by the velum, or soft palate. If it is raised, breath goes out through the mouth; if it is down, in the natural position, and so open, the current goes out through the nose.

Once the vocal current has passed the vocal chords, it may be modified by the pharynx, or by the soft palate and its pillars, or by its extremity, the uvula, or by the back, middle, front, or tip of the tongue, as it comes into more or less close or open relation with the organs above, and also by the teeth and by the lips. Sometimes through the modifications resulting from both mouth and nasal organs certain clicks and sniffs are produced.

3. *Sonant.*—Although there are many points in phonetic problems which have not been clearly settled, yet the action of

these modifiers, in their main features, can be easily ascertained. Lay your fingers on your larynx (putting a hand on the top of the head, or holding a finger in each ear, gives the same result) and say alternately z-z-z-z-z and s-s-s-s-s, but be careful not to call these letters by name, only hiss and buzz their sounds. As you do this, you will feel a vibration in your throat, ears or head. This arises from the vibration of the vocal current, produced by the action of the vocal chords. All sounds having this vibration are called "sonant," "voice," "vocal," or "sub-vocal," as l, m, b, v, g, a, o.

4. *Surd.*—When you pass from z-z-z to s-s-s, you will note a relaxation in the larynx, but when you pass from breathing with open mouth to the sound of h in one and the same breath, you will note a slight contraction of the larynx. This is at the basis of all letters which are not "sonant." Such are usually designated "breath," "aspirate," "voiceless," but the best designation is "surd." The English t, s, f, sh, p, k are surds.

5. *Vowels.*—When the mouth has a fixed, open position, the voiced current produces a sound that is called a vowel. We may have as many vowels as we have different positions of the mouth, and by gliding from one position into another we get an additional number of what are called dipthongs. The Panjabi vowel table is quite simple.

6. *Consonants.*—When the vocal current is cut off or constricted so that there is an evident stoppage or friction at the point of articulation, we get what is called a consonant. The name is false from an etymological standpoint, and is still defined by some grammars as "a sound that cannot be made alone." The name is too well settled for us to try to change it, but one should note that the sounds of s, sh, f, v, l, m and others, may be prolonged indefinitely without any vowel assistance.

7. *Consonant Varieties.*—Consonants are divided, according to the manner of articulation, into stops, continuants or fricatives, trills, nasals and laterals; and, according to the point of articulation, we have in Panjabi labials, dentals, palatals, cerebrals and gutturals. When stops end a syllable, they are called implosives, and when they begin it, they are called explosives. The

true explosive is explained later on. A combination of surd and sonant consonants is found under the term "blends." See Section 13.

Each point of articulation may have one pair of stops and one of continuants, with, in some positions, a pair of trills or flaps, and one of laterals. Out of all these possible sounds, there may be only one in use, but frequently there are two or three out of a possible six or eight.

8. *Alphabet.*—The Gurmukkhi alphabet, in common with the others derived from the Sanskrit, has a phonetic order superior to any of the western alphabets. It is probable that this alphabet came in along the south Arabian coast. It must have come into use long after the Sanskrit grammarians had classified their sounds, and, as a consequence, we have it arranged in good phonetic order, instead of in the topsy turvy way of our English letters.

9. *Phonetic Analysis.*—Any satisfactory study of phonetics must begin with an analysis of the sounds of English as spoken by the student. Let each one provide himself with a mirror and accustom himself to observe the actions of the vocal organs as they form the various speech sounds. Having observed, as before directed, the relation of, and difference between, s and z, let the same be noted in v and f, w and wh, sh and zh, th (thin) and th (thine).

Now say the sounds of p, b, t, d, ch, j, k, g, and, with fingers on larynx, note that p, t, ch, k are surd and b, d, j, g are sonant. Go from b to m, m to b, as in jab'm, jamb, and observe the vocal action. So with hind, hidden, kin, king, reversing the two latter to nik and ngik.

10. *Stops.*—Stops should be studied with the vowel ā (ah), as āp āb, pā bā, āt ād, tā dā, chā jā, āch āj, kā gā, āk āg, the exact point of articulation being noted. Say key, kay, kaw, gee, gay, gaw, and observe the change in point of articulation and in sound. Now say gaw, gay, gee, jee, and note that if we put the point of contact just a little further forward, the hard sound of gee becomes jee. In English, then, we have four distinct points of articulation, p, t, ch, k, but in Panjabi we have

five, owing to the fact that we have two different sets of t's. See 12.

11. *Continuants or Fricatives.*—Take the mirror and holding the mouth so that you can see up under the teeth, say mits, hits, and observe how the tongue which closes up tightly as you say hit, mit, opens at the point and allows the breath to escape over the tip for the s, and that the sounds of the two are quite different in length, the t being momentary, while the s is continuous, hence the term continuant. Owing to the fact that it and other similar letters take their character from friction of the vocal current passing between two approximated organs, the term *fricative* is also used. Each point for a stop will also give us continuants. Let us take up these sounds more in detail.

12. *Sound Table* (*a*)—

	Stops.	Explo-sives.	Frica-tives.		Nasals.	Trills.	Late-rals.	Blends.
Labials	p b	ph	"ph"	w	m			bh
Dentals	t d	th	s	z	n	r	l	dh
Palatals	c* j	ch	sh	zh	ñ			jh
Cerebrals	ṭ ḍ	ṭh			ṇ	ṛ	ḷ	ḍh
Gutturals	k g	kh	<u>Kh</u>		ṅ			gh
Sui generis			h h(ʻ)					

(*b*) It is to be observed that the only class in regard to which there is any dispute as to whether the sounds are simple or complex is that of the palatals. It is ordinarily taught that c is compounded of tsh and z of dsh, but this is incorrect for the following reasons. All alphabets have recognized it as a simple sound. Like other stop positions, it has its corresponding fricative, sh and nasal, ñ. It can be formed when the tip of the tongue is not involved, as it would be if there were a "t" in it.

It should also be noted that while our English "t" is called dental, it is really pre-palatal, since the tip of the tongue comes just above the upper gums.

(*c*) The labial fricatives "ph" and w are rather difficult for the beginner. The w is not the English w, which is rounded at

---

* c in Panjabi has the sound of ch in church.

lips and throat, but is a bilabial, made with lips drawn back at the corners, and sounds something like a v in English. The "ph" is the indigenous f of India, and is made by holding the lips flattened and quite close, and at the same time blowing between them. Our English f is made by placing the lower edge of the upper front teeth against the lower lip, rather toward the inner and upper part, and then making the sound by strong blowing. The sonant of f is English v, while the sonant of "ph" is Panjabi w. The English w is formed from English o, by making the lips a little more shut, and the English wh is the surd of the English w. The Panjabi w bears the same relation to Panjabi o that English w does to English o. But see secs. 21–23, vowels.

(*d*) The Panjabi palatals are, like many of the Panjabi sounds, farther to the front in the mouth than the corresponding English sounds. So, too, where the English make c, j, sh, zh, with lips protruding, Panjabis have their lips flattened. The y is also a palatal, but it has the front of the tongue much lower than the zh or sh. It sometimes has a sound like zh. y bears the same relation to i as w bears to o. So ñ bears the same relation to j as n does to d.

(*e*) Cerebrals are usually termed "hard." That they are "hard" to make correctly all foreigners will admit. Several elements enter into their formation: first, the throat must be well opened, the lips drawn back tensely, and the tongue also tensed and low in the back; second, the tensed tongue must be in a nearly perpendicular position, the sides spread out so as to fill completely the space between the upper teeth, from side to side, the tip being up against the hard palate for the ṭ ḍ ṭh ḍh ṇ ḷ, and must be widely open at the central tip for ṛ, though flapped down to normal position a moment after.

(*f*) The gutturals, so called from Latin *guttur*, throat, are formed at the back of the tongue, where it comes in contact with the soft palate. The stops k, g should give no difficulty, but the fricatives k̲h̲, g̲ may. Let it be noted that k̲h̲ bears the same relation to k as s does to t, or "ph" to p. Open the mouth widely and say ăk, then holding the tongue in the same position, which you will only do, if you are using the mirror, relax very slightly and then blow breath forcibly through between the tongue and soft palate. Now voice this kh and you get the g, for g has the same relation to kh as z has to s. The ng would more accurately be written ṅ, or have a different symbol entirely, for it has in it neither the sound of n nor that of g. To form it as a final is easy for us, but to get it as an initial, open the mouth widely and say āng, āng, āng. Note how the tongue is low in front. Keep it so and reverse the sounds and say ngā. If the tongue insists on rising in front, take a pencil and hold it down. If you say nā or nyā for ngā, it is simply because the tongue rises in front. Only a back contact will give ngā.

(*g*) The letter h is marked "sui generis," and has at least three values. It has the sound of the English h in home in the Panjabi āhō, hāe hāe, āḥā. In a certain class of words it is used to indicate a rise in pitch and gives no sound of its own, as in wēḷā, wēhlā, kāḷā kāhḷā. This corresponds to one of the Chinese "tones," a distinction which becomes more frequent as one proceeds toward east and south-east Asia. In most words it seems to be a sonant h, and should be carefully observed in the teacher's pronunciation. See Pronunciation Exercises.

13. *Blends.*—Whether it is on account of this "sonant h"

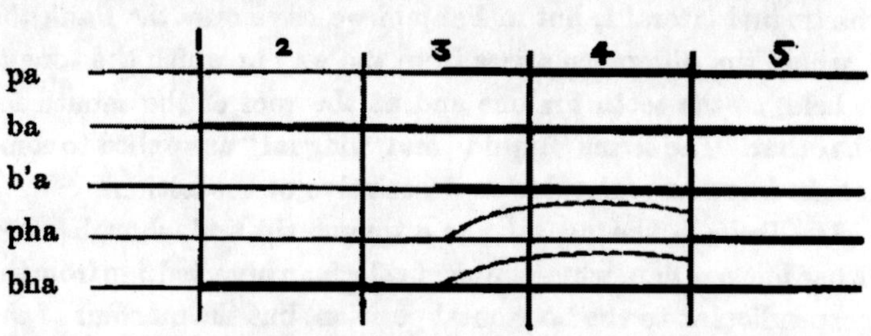

ERRATUM.—The heavy part of the top line for 'pa' should begin at the vertical line between 4 and 5, as for 'pha.'

that the letters bh, dh, jh, ḍh, gh have their peculiar character or not, is perhaps not known. Certain it is, however, that few Westerners master these sounds. An analysis on the kymagraph shows that the difference is like that of the German b, as compared with the English b. This same pronunciation is found across China and Tibet, right through to Korea. These letters bh, dh, jh, ḍh, and gh sometimes have their Urdu pronunciation, which is that of an explosive aspirated b, d, etc., but the regular Panjabi pronunciation is a blend of surd and sonant, in other words, bha, dha, jha, ḍha and gha are as if they were pba, tda, cja, ṭḍa, and kga.

In the diagram on preceding page, let 1 denote the point of closing the organs, 2 the duration of the closure, 3 the point of breaking the shut position, 4 the glide from the shut consonant position into the open vowel position, and 5 the vowel.

In these words pa, ba, b'a, pha and bha, the vowel, 5, is common, so also is the silent closure of the lips, 1. The difference therefore must be sought elsewhere. Between pa and ba, it is in the point where the vocal chords begin to sound, as indicated by the heavy line, that for ba beginning at once on the closure of the lips, and for pa not beginning till the vowel is reached. For pba (b'a), however, it begins at 3, immediately with the break. There is no aspiration with the blend pba, as there is with Urdu bha and pha. This aspiration begins with the break, 3, and runs to the vowel, as indicated by the dotted line.

14. *Laterals.*—In English we have the labio-dental laterals f and v and the dental laterals th (thin) and th (thine), and the lingual lateral l, but in Panjabi we have only the l and the ḷ, where the difference arises from the way in which the tongue is held, at the teeth for one and at the roof of the mouth for the other. The terms "liquid" and "lingual" as applied to some letters have no real value as descriptive of the action.

15. *Trills.*—The dental r is a tongue-tip trill, though often it has but one flap, while the cerebral ṛ is an inverted flap from the perpendicular to the horizontal position, but the murmur of the voice, as it passes over the tip of the perpendicular tongue, is an integral part of the sound, as is also that of the flap.

It should be noted that we have three or four r's in common use in English. Final r, as in are, is a back open guttural at most, while with some it is silent. Initial r, as in raw, is a front palatal flap, or it may be (with the Scotch it is) a tip trill.

Occasionally, however, initial r is "rounded," by protruding the lips. Tongue-tied persons then pronounce words like wrong, write, as wong, wite. It is probable that this w in write, which we call "silent," was formerly pronounced and written to distinguish write from rite. The tip trill r is the only one that can be used in Panjabi.

16. *Nasals.*—Each of the five stop positions give us a corresponding nasal. When the closure is held and the nasal veil opened, the vocal current, reverberating in the mouth as far forward as the closure will allow, passes out through the nasal chamber and gives us, corresponding to **b, d, j, ḍ, g**, the nasals **m, n, ñ, ṇ, ṅ**. The sound of **ñ** is usually Romanized **ny**, and occurs in cañon and onion. To get it initially take the word *Bunyan*, whisper the *Bu* and say the *nyan* aloud.

17. *Explosives.*—The letter **p** in English is usually called an explosive, but by many it is pronounced like the Panjabi **ph**. This ph and the th, ch, ṭh, kh are true explosives. The breath pent up behind the point of contact of the lips, or of the tongue and palate or teeth, rushes out sufficiently to cause the hand to feel a puff of air, if it is held close to the mouth; a slip of tissue paper or flock of cotton thus held will be driven away from the lips. One must practise until the **pa, pha, ta, tha**, etc., can be given alternately at will. See Pronunciation Exercises.

18. *Normal Pose.*—As a preliminary to discussing the vowels it will be well to note what is meant by "normal pose," "organic basis," or "basis of articulation," as it is variously termed. By this we mean that peculiar form and tension in which the vocal organs of the people of any given race are held as they speak their language. The points to be observed in determining this are whether the lips are neutral, forward or retracted, whether the throat is kept open or somewhat shut, and whether the organs are tense or lax.

19. *Spreading.*—This is the retraction of the lips at the corners, spreading the mouth and disclosing the teeth. It helps to produce the characteristic tone-quality of Panjabi.

20. *Tone Placing.*—Tone-quality, sometimes called "focus" or "placing" of the tone. The tone appears to be back in the

mouth, nasalized, or forward on the hard palate or even the teeth. This quality of the tone depends on the positions and tenseness of the organs. Spreading seems to carry with it the low back tongue, and tensed muscles of the throat, as may be felt by external pressure, and thus the tone is brought to the very front of the mouth and on the teeth, giving a ringing, metallic effect, which in singing is highly penetrating and unpleasant to Western ears.

There are many Americans and some Britons who carry their tongues very high in their mouths, and so smother their articulation that one understands them with difficulty, and when they add to this, as is frequently the case, the nasalization that comes from a lowered velum, it is highly unpleasant to the cultivated ear. It is likely that chronic catarrh tends to produce a nasal twang.

The best focus in English is on the hard palatal arch. This involves, of course, as do all good tones, a low back tongue. The normal Panjabi focus is against the upper front teeth, and this gives a voice of splendid carrying quality.

One of the best exercises to secure a lowered tongue, and the resulting open throat, is to practise yawning, and then learn to hold the throat in the position that it takes just before the yawn is relaxed. The position of the throat preparatory to coughing is much the same. Focus or tone quality is one of the most essential elements in audibility.

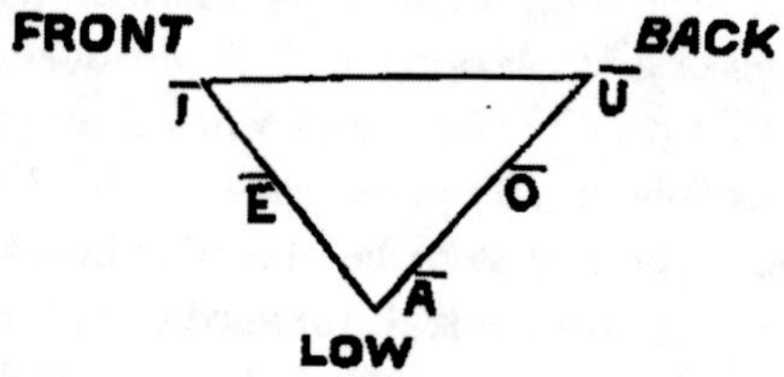

21. *Vowel Modifications.*—These arise from changes in the form of the oral cavity, which are made by varying shapes and tensions of the organs, as when the lips are passive, spread or rounded, when the tongue is highest at back, mid, front or tip, or when the velum (soft palate) is neutrally shut, open or rounded.

Further, all these organs may be in a lax or tense state, sometimes called "wide" or "narrow."

22. *Vowel Triangle.*—If you open your mouth widely and say **ā ē ī** (ah ey ee) you will note that the tongue moves forward, and when you say **ā ō ū** (ah o oo) the opening is made smaller and rounder, but if you keep your mouth wide open the rounding may be confined to the back of the tongue and palate. The short vowels **a e i o u** are made with organs more lax than they are when forming the corresponding long vowels.

23. *Rounding.*—There are two kinds of rounding, outer, at the lips, and inner, between the tongue and soft palate. English has both these, while Panjabi is characterised by inner rounding alone. If while saying English o, one inserts one's little fingers and draw the lips back at both corners, one will get an o with only inner rounding.

24. *Glides and Diphthongs.*—If you say the English vowels o, oo, as you look in the mirror, you will see the lips move slightly to a closer position at the end of the vowels o, oo. This is called the **w** glide. At the end of the English "long" a and e, there is the **y** glide. Perhaps this is why we spell day, they, bow, and wrongly explain the **y** and **w** as "silent." English "long i" is a diphthong composed of ah and i, though so often supposed to be a simple sound. It is difficult for the English tongue to pronounce a vowel without a glide. It is by gliding from one vowel position to another that we form diphthongs, the blending of two vowel sounds into one.

Panjabi vowels are level, without final glides, save the two diphthongs, usually romanized as **ai** and **au**. The former is composed of Panjabi **a + e**, both short, and **au** of Panjabi **a + o**, both short. Learn by imitation of the teacher and use of the mirror to say the Panjabi **ā ē ī ō ū** without any glide, and the diphthongs with their proper constituents. Some claim to hear **ai** as if it were the sound of **a** in English man, but it is really different.

25. *Nasal Vowels.*—Vowels in Panjabi are nasalized when the vowel is pronounced with the passage into the nasal chamber open; the sound reverberating in the nasal cavity gives it this peculiar

character. Nasalization forms the basis of some vital distinctions in meaning. This is more frequently true of Urdu than Panjabi, but is true of both.

The sign used to indicate the nasal is more properly a wave (ã) over the vowel, than n, since the latter implies that this "nūn gunna" is a separable sound, whereas it cannot be produced apart from a vowel.

26. *Intonation.*—Intonation is the peculiar melody which forms a part of the language, and differs in different localities, even though the language may be the same. The Panjabi intonation is characterized by a level and staccato movement and the front focus of tone. Intonation might be called the language "tune," and is more important than individual sounds. It is never acquired by those who study after the ordinary method of learning words. It is only as one gets the sentence as a whole, intonation and all, that one may hope to acquire this. Failure to give the proper intonation makes the foreigner always remain a foreigner in speech, and his best efforts in Panjabi are often the cause of the remark, "We do not understand English." It is because our fellow-countrymen retain the familiar language tune that we are able to understand their Panjabi so much better than that of the native, and because the foreigner speaks English to us with his own peculiar melody, we often fail to understand his meaning.

27. *Articulation.*—Articulation is the uniting of consonants and vowels so as to give each its proper value. Many students of Panjabi will need to cultivate a better articulation in Panjabi than they have in their native tongue. A valuable exercise to this end in any tongue is to practise reading in a whisper, so that a person some twenty or thirty feet distant can hear with ease. Rapid repetition of the letters p, t, c, ṭ, k, both forwards and backwards, will be of great assistance in cultivating a crisp, clear articulation. To do this one must know the exact point of contact, and, for vowel and consonant articulations, the exact positions of the organs, and then take such positions clearly and decidedly.

28. *Syllables.*—A syllable is a measure of speech determined by a single impulse of the voice. As a rule every syllable contains

a vowel. Syllables are closed when they end in a consonant, and open when ending in a vowel. According to Arabic grammatical rules, which have been imposed on India, every syllable begins with a consonant. This is not correct in Panjabi where we have likh-e-ā, baṛ-ā, etc.

29. *Doubled Consonants.*—While we have many double consonants in English spelling, we have them actually doubled only in compound words, as *head-dress*, *night-time*, *book-case*, where d, t, and k are doubled as we double them in Panjabi. In such words as *ripple* and *hitting* the *pp* and *tt* are used to indicate that the *i* is short. We ought, however, to distinguish beween such words as *holy* and *wholly*, by doubling the *l* of the latter. The Panjabi kaccā is often anglicised as "kutcha." The reason is that we are not used to hearing a syllable with a close "ch" such as we have in kaccā and acchā. In other words, the first consonant in such combinations as pakkā, pattar, kaccā, ḍabbī, is made as the organs close into position, and the second is made by a new impulse, as they open for the succeeding vowel. In such words as assī, the new impulse comes in while the continuant s is sounding, and this new impulse forms the second letter. It is probable that inability to distinguish between a closed "ch" and a "t" leads to the spelling watch, catch, etc.

30. *Recoil.*—A consonant properly consists of "a position, an action and a separation." This separation is the "recoil." In such words as *word*, *hit*, *back*, ending in stop consonants, the organs should recoil from the shut position, while the air of the mouth is at speech pressure. Such pressure should be non-vocal and thrown off immediately the break occurs, or we may hear a disagreeable aspiration, or in such words as *mud*, *rug*, one occasionally hears a final *uh*, which, of course, is to be avoided. One should note the exact character of this recoil in the teacher's pronunciation.

31. *Personal and National Difficulties.*—Occasionally a person is met with who through being tongue-tied is unable to articulate cerebral letters properly. A slight operation will cut the cord that binds the tongue and give it freedom, but it should be performed by a surgeon. Most difficulties arise from preconceived

notions of what the sounds are. So many on hearing a "t," think it is a t, and that settles it. To them an l is an l, an s is an s, and they do not recognize the difference between the Panjabi sounds and the similar sounds in English. Almost no Panjabi letter has the sound which it gets from an untutored Westerner.

Some English speakers are accustomed to omit or slur final r, or to give the lip rounded **r (wr)** at the beginning of words. Careful attention to eliminate both these peculiarities from one's Panjabi pronunciation will be required. If one has normally a nasal twang, one must learn to control it, to produce and eliminate it at will. If one habitually aspirates one's **p's, t's, k's, ch's** in English one must get the ability to hear the aspiration and master the unaspirated sounds as well.

If anyone finds that his words ending in l are not understood, it is probably because his final l sounds like his final **r.** Our English tendency to glide on all our long vowels must be thoroughly overcome.

32. *Analysis of Sounds.*—It is of great importance that the suggestions given here as to the manner in which sounds are formed be again, and yet again, reviewed, until perfectly understood, and the sounds mastered. An analytic study of one's own sounds must go along with the study of the Panjabi sounds. Whispering Panjabi sounds will often lay bare their secret. Sing them with "ā," preceding and following the consonants that are under investigation. A half-inch stick between the jaw teeth of the teacher will often assist one greatly in seeing organic positions.

33. *A Good Ear.*—Few adult foreigners are at first able to hear the differences between the Panjabi sounds and their own. A good ear can be cultivated by those born out of India, if they will take the trouble to practise the Pronunciation Exercises at the end of the Preface. The second or third term of mission service is not too late to mend any defects that may still exist. In training the ear it is well to know what sound the teacher is intending to make, so that we may listen for that, for one so often hears what one expects to hear, even though something else may be uttered.

34. *Gestures.*—No Panjabi ever speaks if gesticulations will serve his purpose. It is just as well to learn and use these, so the student should observe carefully their form and meaning.

35. *Clicks.*—The "smack" of a kiss is used to stop a horse in India, contrary to the custom in America where this sound is used to urge on an animal. In India they urge on the horse by a sucking sound with the tongue in the top of the mouth as for ṛ. A sharp explosive suction, made by drawing the tongue down and forward suddenly from the roof of the mouth, is also used for driving. There are others, also, but these are a few to excite attention and the student should observe and note any others.

36. *Pronunciation Exercises, Directions for Study.*—Let your teacher indicate by pointing, exactly which of the sounds he is about to make, so that you may not try to listen for something else. After you listen to him making that sound and then contrasting it with a similar sound, you should try to imitate him.

As far as possible observe carefully the position of his lips, teeth, tongue, etc., while he speaks, and try to imitate these.

At the same time as you are learning the sounds, learn also the meaning of the words and sentences.

After a time the teacher should give the catch phrases and require the pupil to distinguish which word was used.

Later on the pupil should say the words, previously making out a list, and make the teacher write them down. He can then tell by comparing lists whether he says what he intends to say.

These exercises should be practised 20 minutes twice daily for six months, and then once daily till perfection.

PART II.—GUIDE TO CONVERSATION.

To the Pupil.—This Guide is for the teacher. Unless he is thoroughly conversant with English, it must be, as it ought in any case to be, translated into the teacher's vernacular, Panjabi.

To the Teacher.—It has been definitely settled by those who have studied the subject, that the only way to teach a language is by means of that language itself. Hence several principles must be followed: First, in teaching this Part II your method must be entirely oral. You must give every thing by word of mouth, as a mother does, when she repeats and repeats till the child can say the word. Men are but children of a larger growth; so far as teaching to pronounce correctly is concerned, teach your pupil as you would a child that is just beginning to talk. When we teach children to pronounce we try to get them to speak fluently, even though they may not be able to pronounce all the sounds accurately. So you must teach your pupil to be fluent, going over and over the same sentences till he knows them perfectly. Of course you will give him a lesson every day, at some other time, in accuracy, but do not worry him by correcting him more than two or three times in other lessons for the same mistake. Perhaps he does not see where his mistake lies, and if you cannot point it out to him, or if he cannot perceive it when you do, it only irritates him to hear you say a thing again and again, and not to know wherein his failure lies.

Second, you must teach him to speak by teaching a complete sentence, and repeating this sentence, just as you would say it to a child, until he is able to hear it rapidly spoken, and then he will be able to repeat it rapidly himself. If he cannot hear it when you say it rapidly, he cannot repeat it fluently himself.

Third, Grammar, or use of correct idioms, is also to be taught in the same way. If your pupil learns correct idioms, so that he is able to use them, he will copy them in his other speaking, but if you permit him to learn from incorrect models, he will speak according to those incorrect models, and it will be his teacher's fault. A child speaks as he hears his father and mother speak, because their speech is his model.

Fourth, your pupil will speak what he hears spoken. IF YOU TEACH HIM TO HEAR and if he hears correct language, he will use it. If you do not teach him to hear, you are no teacher. If you hear him using a wrong expression, teach him the right one, and get him to repeat it ten, fifty, a hundred times, till it is firmly fixed in his memory. Never teach him words one by one, always teach them as they occur in sentences. If you think he has a very poor memory, that makes no difference, you must make him repeat till he cannot forget. Hence this is Rule IV. REPETITION IS THE SECRET OF SUCCESS.

Now in beginning you may think that you must speak English, but NO. Begin with the first question in the lessons, and say in your own Panjabi, What is this? as you point to some object, a chair, a table, or a book, and answer your own question, always in your own language, THIS IS A CHAIR, THIS IS A BOOK. When you have done this five or six times, then get him to point to the object and say, This is a chair, this is a book. When he can say it readily, let him answer you, as you point to the table, and ask, WHAT IS THIS? by saying to you, THIS IS A TABLE. Now ask the questions about the chair, the book, the table, and when he answers fluently, add another article, and ask about it, always reviewing the first familiar words. Ten new words are enough for one lesson, and count on it that in the next lesson he will forget or mix up half of the ten.

Keep a list of the words that you teach him day by day, and review them every day for the first two or three weeks. Then once in two weeks have a review, and if that is not often enough every week. No work must be left undone. No word not worth learning must be taught, and every word worth learning must be so well taught that it will come to mind at once. Make the pupil every now and then take the teacher's place and ask the questions. While he is learning the names of the common things about the room, articles of diet, clothing, furniture, of outdoor life, you may at the same time, and along with these, go on to

Lessons II, III, etc., and teach him ordinary action words such as eat, sleep, see, hear, smell, touch, catch, walk, sit, rise, etc., as detailed in the lessons.

These verbs will eventually be taught in three tenses, present past and future, but at first in only one.

You must teach the prepositions, the numerals, buying, selling, giving change, etc., for one or two hours daily. In fact, you should teach him the language by action and by pantomime.

Every day, before you come to teach, you must review the word lists and conversations of the preceding lessons, as well as those of the new lesson, so that you may recall the words that are familiar to him, and use them and them only, and may know exactly what is to be taught in the remaining lessons.

Ten new words daily will make 250 words a month. In six months he will have 1500 words, quite enough to enable a man to speak on all ordinary subjects. Of course he must get ten, fifteen, twenty thousand words to be a learned man in your language, but that is a matter of years, and all that is necessary for him the first year is to be able to use these 1500 words in their various forms according to the correct idiom. If he does this he will be able not only to converse but to address audiences.

Never discourage your pupil by telling him he cannot get a word, nor be discouraged about him. He has learned one language, as an ignorant child, surely he can learn another now that he has been educated. Learned men have proved that when someone is learning the words of a new language, which at first have no meaning to him, he will, in one hour, forget half of them, and over night he will forget two-thirds of them. So you must expect to repeat a word to him TEN times, before he is able to say it once, to have him repeat a sentence a hundred times before he can say it moderately well, to have him say his first sentences a thousand times, before they will come fluently, ten thousand times before he is able to make the difficult sounds smoothly and well. In teaching him pronunciation you must open your mouth widely to show him how and where the sounds are formed. Say them with the vowel " ā " rather than call them by name as, " āt, ag, āk" rather than "tē, gain, kāf," etc. Some sounds he will not be able to catch at first, but do not think him deaf. It is because he has never heard them before. Whisper these sounds to him or sing them for him. It may take him six months, or perhaps a year, of daily drill to learn them. First teach him to hear two similar sounds and to recognize the difference. Some people study English for five or ten years and cannot say some of our commonest sounds. In twelve months the student should be able to pronounce all the Panjabi sounds fluently and correctly.

Sometimes when you are teaching **kh, ch, ṭh, th, ph,** and he cannot distinguish them from **p, t, ṭ, c, k,** hold a bit of paper close to your lips and he will see the difference. Somehow, in some way, you must make him distinguish by the ear, and at the same time make him speak, so that even the old village women can understand what he is saying.

Get your pupil to memorise these sentences, which are just what people use in talking to one other. He should repeat them as rapidly as five syllables a second and keep this up for a month, and then he will not forget them. Do all this carefully and faithfully day by day, and soon people will say, How well this sahib is progressing.

You must use words so that he knows what you mean by them. Get him to use what he knows. If he knows something perfectly, he will be willing to use it. We learn to talk by talking. Follow the old adage, Practice makes perfect.

To the Pupil.—Ask your teacher to say the sentences, Did you catch that long whale? Did you catch that long wail? Did you catch that long veil? and perhaps he may appreciate your difficulty in apprehending some of the sounds he gives you.

The pupil ought to glance over the English of each lesson beforehand so that he may have a general idea of what is to come in it.

PART II.—SHORT SENTENCES.

Lesson I.

What is this?	This is a table.	Ēh kī e?	Ēh mēz e.
	This is a book.		Ēh kitāb e.
	This is a chair.		Ēh kursī e.
	This is a carpet.		Ēh darī e.
	This is a rug.		Ēh galīcā e.
	This is a floor.		Ēh farsh e.
	This is a door.		Ēh būhā e.
	This is a window.		Ēh bārī e.
	This is a room.		Ēh kamrā we.
	This is matting.		Ēh phūhṛ e.

The teacher will ask these questions; the pupil should give a full answer. Later on the pupil may answer by giving merely the name, as 'table,' mēz, 'carpet,' darī, but at first, he must reply, Ēh mēz e.

These things will probably be present, but if at any time they are not, either pictures or the names of the articles, written on cardboard slips, must be used, and the teacher can point as he asks the question.

Ten new words are enough for one lesson, yet Lesson I is not to be finished before II is taken up; it is rather to be carried on at the same time. These lists are not exhaustive, and anything missing may be added, only see to it that each list is kept and practised until perfection is attained.

List 2. Dish, plate, knife, spoon, fork, cup, glass, water, tea, coffee.

Fihrist 2. Ḍis, plēṭ, churī, cammac, kāṇṭā, piālā, gilās, pāṇī, cāh, kāfī.

List 3. House, verandah, dining-room, bed-room, bath-room, office, drawing-room, pantry, kitchen, store-room.

Fihrist 3. Ghar, barāṇḍā, khāṇā-kamrā, saũṇā-kamrā, gusl-k͟hānā, daftar, gōḷ-kamrā, bōtal-k͟hānā, bōarcī-k͟hānā, gudām.

List 4. Bread, butter, meat, rice, fruit, peas, vegetables, potatoes, onions, chicken, porridge.

Fihrist 4. **Rōṭī, makkhaṇ, mās, caul, phal, maṭar, sabzī, ālū, gaṇḍhe, kukkṛī, daḷīyā.**

List 5. Sugar, salt, black pepper, red pepper, sauce, vinegar, gravy, soup, curry, walnuts, sweets, rice cooked in milk.

Fihrist 5. **Khaṇḍ, lūṇ, kāḷī, marc, lāl marc, chaṭnī, sirkā, grēbi, shurbā, kārī, akhrōṭ, miṭhāī, khīr.**

List 6. Paper, ink, pen, post, newspaper, pencil, letter, post office, postman, stamp.

Fihrist 6. **Kāgaz, siāhī, par, ḍāk, akhbār, pinsal, ciṭṭhī, ḍāk-khānā, ḍāk-wāḷā, ṭikaṭ.**

List 7. Couch, curtain, wall, book-case, cup-board, box, luggage, bedding, handbag.

Fihrist 7. **manjī pardā, kandh, almārī, almārī, bakas, asbāb, bistrā, thailī.**

List 8. Broom, duster, shovel, tongs, brush, hat, clothes, dress, coat, shoes.

Fihrist 8. **Jhāṛū, jhāṛan, karch, uccā, burs, ṭōpī, kapṛē ḍrēs, kōṭ, juttī.**

List 9. Train, station, ticket, carriage, fare, railway, porter, guard, engine, luggage-van, booking-clerk, "class," luggage-receipt.

Fihrist 9. **Gaḍḍī, sṭēshan, ṭikaṭ, gaḍḍī, karāyā, laiṇ, kulī, gāḍ, iñaṇ, brēk, ṭikaṭ-wāḷā-bābū, darjā, bilṭī.**

List 10. Hand, foot, nose, mouth, eye, ear, head, arm, face, leg, finger, toe right, left.

Fihrist 10. **Hatth, pair, nakk, mū̃h, akkh, kann, sir, bā̃h, mū̃h, latt, uṅgaḷ, uṅgaḷ, sajjā, khabbā.**

List 11. Hair, beard, moustache, elbow, knee, ankle, joint, back, breast, shoulder, stomach, waist.

Fihrist 11. **Wāḷ, dāṛhī, mucchā̃, arak, gōḍḍā, giṭṭā, jōṛ, kaṇḍ, hikk, mōṇḍhā, ḍhiḍḍh, lakk.**

List 12. Man, woman, child, boy, girl, horse, mare, colt, cow, calf, ox.

Fihrist 12. **Jaṇā, janānī, baccā, muṇḍā, kuṛī, ghōṛā, ghōṛī, wachērā, gā̃, wacchā, ḍhaggā.**

List 13. Donkey, buffalo, mule, camel, sheep, cart, buggy,

Fihrist 13. **Khōtā, majjh, khaccar, ūṭh, bhēḍḍī, gaḍḍā,** coolie, wood, stone, coal, city, charcoal, shop.

bagghī, kulī, lakkaṛ, patthar, patthar dā kōḷā, shahr, kōḷā, haṭṭī.

List 14. Sheet, handkerchief, towel, pillow-case, blanket, mattress, pillow, shirt, undershirt, drawers, waistcoat, trousers, flannel, night-clothes, table-cloth, napkin, tray-cloth, cuffs, collar, skirt.

Fihrist 14. Palaṅg dī cādar, rumāl, tauliā, takīe-dā uchāṛ, kambaḷ, gadēlā, takīā, kamīz, banaiṇ, drāz, phutūhī, patlūṇ, falālaiṇ, rāt-dē-kapṛē, mēz-dī-cādar, mēz-dā-tauliā, trēl-dī-cādar, kafā, kālar, sāyā.

List 15. Servant, cook, scullion, water-man, groom, gardener, sweeper, table-servant, coachman, watchman, carpenter, blacksmith, pedlar.

Fihrist 15. Naukar, khansāmā, masālcī, māshkī, sahīs, mālī, mehtar, khidmatgār, sahis, caukīdār, tarkhāṇ, luhār, bakas-wāḷā.

List 16. Stable, cow-stable, garden, road, thatch, keys, organ (piano), picture, flowers, flower-pot, roof.

Fihrist 16. Astabal, kuṛh, bāg, saṛak, chappar, kunjīā, wājā, taswīr, phull, gamlā, chatt.

Lesson 11.

Teacher, holding up a book, says, What is this? Say, This is a book.

Munshī. Ēh kī e? Ākhō, ēh katāb e.

Pupil. This is a book.

Sāhb. Ēh katāb e.

T. That's right. Give me the book. I take the book from you.

M. Ṭhīk e, katāb menū deho. Maĩ tuhāḍḍe kōḷō katāb lainnā wā̃.

T. I give you the book. Now put the book on the table.

M. Maĩ tuhānū katāb dēnnā wā̃. Huṇ mēz utte rakkho.

P. I take the book from you. Now I put it on the table.

S. Maĩ tuhāḍḍe kōḷō katāb lainnā wā̃. Huṇ mēz utte rakkhnā wā̃.

T., as he successively holds up pen, ink, pencil, and paper, asks, What is this?

M. Ēh kī e? Kalam, shiāhi, pinsal, kāgat.

P. This is a pen, ink, paper, pencil.

S. **Ēh kalame, shiāhī, pinsal, kāg̲at.**

T. Give me the pen. That is right (as the pupil hands it). Now give me the paper, the book, the ink, the pencil.

M. **Menũ kalam deho. Ṭhīk e Huṇ kāg̲at deho, katāb, shiāhī, pinsal.**

P. says with each, I give you the pen, etc.

S. **Maĩ tuhānũ dēnnā wā̃.**

T. Where is the book? Say, The book is on the table.

M. **Katāb kitthe we? Ākhō, Katāb mēz utte we.**

P. The book is on the table.

S. **Katāb mēz utte we.**

T. Where is the pen?

M. **Kalam kitthe we?**

P. The pen is on the table.

S. **Kalam mēz utte we.**

T. Where is the ink?

M. **Shiāhī kitthe we?**

P. The ink is on the book.

S. **Shiāhī katāb utte we.**

T. Where is the paper?

M. **Kāg̲at kitthe we?**

P. The paper is on the table.

S. **Kāg̲at mēz te we.**

T. (putting it on the chair), Where is the pen now?

M. **Kalam huṇ kitthe we.**

P. The pen is now on the chair.

S. **Kalam huṇ kursī te we.**

T. And now?

M. **Te huṇ kitthe?**

P. Now it's on the carpet.

S. **Huṇ darī te we.**

T. Where is the table?

M. **Mēz kitthe we?**

P. The table is on the carpet

S. **Mēz darī te we.**

T. Where is the carpet?

M. **Darī kitthe we?**

P. The carpet is on the floor.

S. **Darī farsh utte we.**

T. Where is the ink? Now where?

M. **Shiāhī kitthe we? Huṇ kitthe?**

P. The ink is on the chair (the carpet, the floor, the table).

S. **Shiāhī kursī te we (darī, farsh, mēz).**

T. Where is the pencil? Where is the paper?

M. **Pinsal kitthe we? Kāg̲at kitthe we?**

P. The pencil is on the table. The paper is too.

S. Pinsal mēz te we. Kāgat wi mēz te we.

T. Where are the paper and pencil?

M. Pinsal te kāgat kitthe nẽ?

P. The paper and pencil are on the table.

S. Pinsal te kāgat mēz te nẽ.

T. Where are the pen and ink (bottle)?

M. Kalam dawāt kitthe we?

P. The pen and ink (bottle) are on the table.

S. Kalam dawāt mēz te we.

The teacher and pupil should exchange places, and the pupil should ask the questions.

Lesson III.

Teacher. Where is the chair (table, door, window, pen, carpet, hat, rug, etc., etc.)?

Munshi. Kursī kitthe we (mēz, būhā, darī, bārī, kalam, ṭōpī, galīcā)?

Pupil. This is the chair, etc. (pointing to each article in turn as the question is asked).

Sāhb. Ēh kursī e.

It is one great point of the teaching to get the pupil to understand when he is spoken to as rapidly as Panjabis speak to one another. Hence the pupil must be asked the questions until he can answer very rapidly, just as fast as the teacher can ask. It will need a great many reviews to attain this end, but it is imperative that it should be attained.

The teacher should prepare these lessons for teaching, since, although they are easy, it is not easy to teach them properly.

Lesson IV.

Teacher. Do you know what this is?

Munshī. Tuhānū patā e pai ēh kī e?

Pupil. A chair.

Sāhb. Kursī e.

T. Say: Yes, I know. It is a chair.

M. Āhō, āhō menū patā e, ēh kursī e.

P. Yes, I know. It is a chair.

S. Āhō, menū patā e, ēh kursī e.

T. Do you know what this is ? Say, Yes I know.	**M. Tuhānū patā e pai ēh kī e ? Ākhō, āhō, patā e.**
P. Yes, I know. It is a book.	**S. Āhō patā e. Ēh kitāb e.**
T. Madam, do you know what this is ?	**M. Mēmsāhb, tuhānū patā e pai ēh kī e ?**
P. Yes I know. It is a pen.	**S. Āhō patā e. Ēh kalame.**

T., in like manner, should ask about the other articles in the room, and require a complete answer from the pupil ; then get the pupil to ask about the same articles.

T. Do you know Panjabi ?	**M. Tuhānū Panjābī aundī e ?**
P. No, I do not know Panjabi. I know English.	**S. Nehī, menū Panjābī nehī aundī. Menū Aṅgrēzī aundī e.**
T. Do you speak English ? Say, I speak English.	**M. Aṅgrēzī bōl sakde o ? Ākhō, Aṅgrēzī bōl saknā wā̃.**
P. I speak English.	**S. Aṅgrēzī bōl saknā wā̃.**
T. You understand Panjabi don't you ?	**M. Tusī Panjābī samjhde o nā ?**
P. No, I do not understand Panjabi well.	**S. Nehī, maī caṅgī tarhā̃ nehī samjhda.**
T. Say it again. Did you understand the thing ?	**M. Phēr ākhō ; gall samajh leī e ?**
P. I did not understand.	**S. Nehī samjhī.**
T. Say again, I do not understand very well.	**M. Phēr ākhō, maī caṅgī tarhā̃ nehī samjhda.**
P. I do not understand very well.	**S. Maī caṅgī tarhā̃ nehī samjhdā.**
T. Well done. Now you understand.	**M. Shābāshi. Huṇ tā̃ samajh āī.**
P. Yes, I understand.	**S. Āhō mainū samajh āī.**
T. Do you know Persian ?	**M. Tuhānū Fārsī aundī e?**
P. No, I do not.	**S. Nehī, nehī aundī.**

Lesson V.

1. *T*. (Holding a book.) What is this? *P*. A book.	1. *M*. Ēh kī e? *S*, Katābe.
2. *T*. (Putting it on the table.) Where is the book? *P*. The book is on the table.	2. *M*. Katāb kitthe we? *S*. Katāb mēz utte we.
3. *T*. Where is the table? *P*. The table is in the room.	3. *M*. Mēz kitthe we? *S*. Mēz koṭhe wicc e.
4. *T*. What is the table on? *P*. The table is on the carpet.	4. *M*. Mēz kāh de utte we? *S*. Mēz darī utte we.
5. *T*. Well done! Now where is the carpet? *P*. The carpet is on the floor.	5. *M*. Bauht ṭhīk e. Acchā, darī kitthē e? *S*. Darī farsh utte e.
6. *T*. Right again, where is the door? *P*. The door is in the wall.	6. *M*. Ēh wī ṭhīk e. Būhā kitthē e? *S*. Būhā kandh wicc e.
7. *T*. What is this? (holding his hat). *P*. That is a hat.	7. *M*. Ēh kī e? *S*. Ōh ṭōpī e.
8. *T*. What is this? (holding his watch). *P*. That is a watch.	8. *M*. Ēh kī e? *S*. Ōh gharī e.
9. *T* Where is the watch? (putting it on the hat). *P*. The watch is on the hat.	9. *M*. Gharī kitthē we? *S*. Gharī ṭōpī uttē we.
10. *T*. Sir, give me the book. *P*. Sir, I take the book and give it to you.	10. *M*. Sāhb jī, menū katāb deho. *S*. Munshī jī, maī katāb laike tuhānū dēnnā wā.
11. *T*. Take the book and put it on the table. *P*. I take the book and put it on the table.	11. *M*. Katāb nū laike mēz utte rakkho. *S*. Maī katāb laike mēz uttē rakhnā wā.

12. *T*. Take it from the table and put it on the chair. *P*. I take it from the table and put it on the chair.	12. *M*. Ōhnū̃ mēz tō̃ laike kursī te rakkhē. *S*. Maī̃ ōhnū̃ mēz tō̃ laikē kursī te rakhnā wā̃.
13. *T*. Madam, you take the book from the chair and put it on the table. *P*. I take the book from the chair and put it on the table.	13. *M*. Miss Sāhb jī, katāb nū̃ kursī tō̃ laikē mēz utte rakkh dehō. *S*. Maī̃ katāb nū̃ kursī tō̃ laikē mēz utte rakhnī ā̃.
14. *T*. Madam, give the book to me, then take the book from me and give it to him. *P*. I take the book from you and give it to him	14. *M*. Miss Sāhb jī, menū̃ katāb dehō, phēr mērē kōḷō̃ laike ōhnū̃ dehō. *S*. Maī̃ tuhāḍḍē kōḷō̃ katāb laike ōhnū̃ dēnnī ā̃.
15. *T*. Sir, come here and take the book and put it on the bookcase. *P*. I put it on the bookcase.	15. *M*. Sāhb jī, ētthē ākē katāb laō te almārī tē rakkhō. *S*. Maī̃ ōhnū̃ almārī utte rakhnā wā̃.
16. *T*. Sir, give me the pen and ink. *P*. I give you the pen and ink.	16. *M*. Sāhb jī, mĕnū̃ kalam te shiāhī dehō. *S*. Maī̃ jī tuhānū̃ kalam te shiāhī dēnnā wā̃.
17. *T*. I now put the book on the floor. Where is it? *P*. It is on the floor.	17. *M*. Huṇ maī̃ katāb farsh tē rakhnā wā̃. Kitthe we? *S*. Farsh te we.
18. *T*. I put it on the table and I put the paper under the book. Where is the paper? *P*. It is under the book.	18. *M*. Maī̃ ōhnū̃ mēz te rakhnā wā̃, te katāb hēṭh kāgat rakhnā wā̃, kāgat kitthe we? *S*. kāgat katāb hēṭh e.
19. *T*. (As he puts the pen under the book.) Where	19. *M*. Kalam kitthe we? *S*. Kalam katāb hēṭh

is the pen? *P*. The pen is under the book. (Table, carpet, window, door, hat, watch, etc.)	**e. (Mēz, darī, bārī, būhā, ṭōpī, gharī.)**

Lesson VI.

1. *T*. Sir, give the book to Hira. *P*. I give the book to Hira.	1. *M*. **Sāhb jī, katāb Hīre nū̃ dehō.** *S*. **Maī katāb Hīre nū̃ dēnnā wā̃.**
2. *T*. Take the book from Hira and put it on the chair, then under the chair. *P*. I take the book from him and put it on the chair, now under it.	2. *M*. **Hīre kōḷõ katāb laikē kursī utte rakkhō, phēr kursī hēṭh rakkhō** *S*. **Maī ōhde kōḷõ katāb laikē kursī utte rakkhnā wā̃ te huṇ kursī hēṭh rakkhnā wā̃.**
3. *T*. Where is the book? *P*. It is under the chair.	3. *M*. **Katāb kitthē we?** *S*. **Kursī de hēṭh e.**
4. *T*. Put the book in the bookcase. *P*. I put the book in the book-case.	4. *M*. **Katāb nū̃ almārī wicc dharo.** *S*. **Maī ōhnū̃ almārī wicc dharnā wā̃.**
5. *T*. Put the paper in the book. *P*. does so. *T*. Now put it under the book.	5. **Kāgat katāb wicc rakkhō; huṇ katāb de hēṭh rakkho.**
6. *T*. Where is the book? *P*. I put it in the bookcase.	6. *M*. **Katāb kitthe we?** *S*. **Maī ōhnū̃ almārī wicc dhareā sī.**
7. *T*. Where is the paper? *P*. It is under the book.	7. *M*. **Kāgat kitthe we?** *S*. **Katāb hēṭh e.**
8. *T*. Give me the pen and	8. *M*. **Menū̃ kalam dawāt**

	ink and put the paper on the chair. *P*. Very well.		**dehō, te kāgat nū̃ kursī utte rakkhō.** *S*. **Caṅga. (Hala ji!) (Haccha)**
9.	*T*. What is this? *P*. It is a book.	9.	*M*. **Ēh kī e?** *S*. **Katāb e.**
10.	*T*. Right, and what is this? *P*. A book.	10.	*M*. **Ṭhīk e, ji, te āh kī ə?** *S*. **Katāb.**
11.	*T*. That is right, two books, one and one make two. Two books and one book make three books. Here are three books. What are these? *P*. These are books, three books.	11.	*M*. **Ṭhīk e, dō katābā̃. Ikk te ikk dō. Dō katābā̃ te ikk katāb trai katābā̃ hoīā̃. Āh wekhā̃ trai katābā̃ nē̃. Ēh kī nē̃?** *S*. **Ēh katābā̃ nē̃, trai katābā̃.**
12.	*T*. This is a chair. These are two chairs, these are three chairs. What are these; *P*. These are chairs.	12.	*M*. **Ēh kursī e, ēh dō kursīā̃ nē̃. Ēh trai kursīā̃ nē̃. Ēh kī nē̃?** *S*. **Ēh kursīā̃ nē̃.**
13.	*T*. One table, two tables, three tables. How do we say it? *P*. We say one table, two tables, three tables.	13.	*M*. **Ikk mēz, dō mēz, trai mēz. Asī̃ kis tarhā̃ āhnnē ā̃?** *S*. **Asī̃ āhnnē ā̃ ikk mēz, dō mēz, trai mēz.**
14.	*T*. (As he points to the chair.) What do we say? *P*. One chair, two chairs, three chairs.	14.	*M*. **Asī̃ kī āhnnē ā̃?** *S*. **Ikk kursī, dō kursīā̃, trai kursīā̃.**
15.	*T*. Pointing to his hat. What do we say? *P*. One hat, two hats, three hats.	15.	*M*. **Asī̃ kī ākhnē ā̃? Ikk ṭōpī, dō ṭōpīā̃, trai ṭōpīā̃.** *S*. **Ikk ṭōpī, dō ṭōpīā̃, trai ṭōpīā̃.**
16.	*T*. One watch, two watches, three watches.	16.	*M*. **Ikk ghaṛī, dō ghaṛīā̃, trai ghaṛīā̃.** *S*. **Asī̃**

P. We say one watch, two watches, three watches.	ākhnē ā̃ ikk ghaṛī, dō ghaṛīā̃, trai ghaṛīā̃.
17. *T.* This is one book, there is another. This is large, that is small.	17. *M.* Ēh ikk katāb e, ēh hōr katāb e. Ēh waḍḍī e, ōh nikkī e.
18. *P.* Where is the large book? *T.* This is the small book. So with chairs, watches, tables. Also with other adjec-	18. *S.* Waḍḍī katāb kitthe we. *M.* Nikki katāb ēh we. (kursī, ghaṛī, mēz, caṅgā, māṛā, waḍḍā, nikkā.)

tives good, bad, big, little, and other nouns to show the use of the adjective with the noun.

Lesson VII.

1. *T.* What is this? *P.* A chair.	1. *M.* Ēh kī e? *S.* Kursī.
2. *T.* (As he seats himself.) I sit on the chair, say "The teacher is sitting on the chair." *P.* The teacher is sitting on the chair.	2. *M.* Maĩ kursī te baih jānnā̃, ākhō munshī kursī te baiṭhā e. *S.* Munshī kursī te baiṭhā e.
3. *T.* Who is sitting on that chair (pointing to the one on which the Pupil is seated). *P.* I am sitting on this chair.	3. *M.* Ōs kursī te kauṇ baiṭhā e? Ēs kursī te maĩ baiṭhā wā̃.
4. *T.* What is Madam sitting on? *P.* Madam is sitting on a chair.	4. *M.* Miss sāhb kāhde te baiṭhē nē̃. *S.* Miss sāhb kursī te baiṭhē nē̃.
5. *T.* What are we all sitting on? *P.* We are all sitting on chairs.	5. *M.* Asī̃ sārē kāhde te baiṭhē ā̃. *S.* Asī̃ sārē kursīā̃ te baiṭhē ā̃.
6. *T.* Sir, what are you	6. *M.* Sāhb jī tusī̃ kāhde

sitting on? *P.* I am sitting on a chair.	te baiṭhē o. *S.* Maĩ kursī te baiṭhā wā̃.
7. *T.* What is the gentleman sitting on? *P.* He is sitting on a chair.	7. *M.* Sāhb kāhde te baiṭhē nē̃. *S.* Kursī te baiṭhe nē̃.
8. *T.* Who is sitting on that chair? *P.* Madam is sitting on that chair.	8. *M.* Ōs kursī te kauṇ baiṭhā e? *S.* Ōs kursī te Miss sāhb baiṭhē nē̃.
9. *T.* (As he rises) I rise from my chair, now I sit down, what do I do? *P.* Teacher rises from his chair. Teacher sits down on his chair.	9. *M.* Maĩ kursī tõ uṭṭhnā wā̃, huṇ maĩ baih jāṇnā̃. Maĩ kī karnā wā̃? *S.* Munshī horī kursī tõ uṭṭhdē nē, munshī horī kursī te baih jānde nē̃. (Grammar p. 27.)
10. *P.* You rise. *T.* I rise from my chair. *P.* Sit down. *T.* I sit down on my chair.	10. *S.* Tusī̃ uṭṭho. *M.* Maĩ kursī tõ uṭṭhnā wā̃. *S.* Baih jāō. *M.* Maĩ kursī te baih jānnā̃.
11. *P.* Rise and take the book. *T.* I rise and take the book.	11. *S.* Uṭṭhke katāb lĕllaō. *M.* Maĩ uṭṭhkē katāb lĕllainnā wā̃.
12. *P.* Give it to Madam and sit down. *T.* I give it to Madam and sit down.	12. *S.* Miss sāhb nū̃ de deō te baih jaō. *M.* Maĩ ōhnā̃ nū̃ dēnnā wā̃ te baih jānnā wā̃.
13. *T.* Is this a Panjabi or an English Book? *P.* It is an English book.	13. *M.* Ēh Panjābī katāb e ke Aṅgrēzī? *S.* Aṅgrēzī katāb e.
14. *T.* Is it a big or a little book? *P.* It is a little book.	14. *M.* Waḍḍī katāb e ke nikkī. *S.* Nikkī katāb e.
15. *T.* Is it a good book? *P.* Yes, it is a good book.	15. *M.* Caṅgī katāb e? *S.* Āhō, caṅgī katāb e.

16. *T*. Is that a bad book? *P*. No it is not a bad book, it is a good book.	**16.** *M*. **Ōh bhaiṛi katāb e?** *S*. **Nehī̃, bhaiṛi katāb nehī̃, caṅgī katāb e.**
17. *T*. Is this a good watch? *P*. No, it is not a *very* good watch.	**17.** *M*. **Ēh caṅgī ghaṛī e?** *S*. **Nehī̃, bauht caṅgī ghaṛī nehī̃.**
18. *T*. Is this a good chair? *P*. Yes, it is a good chair.	**18.** *M*. **Ēh caṅgī kursī e?** *S*. **Āhō caṅgī kursī e.**
19. *T*. Is this a good table? *P*. Yes, it is a good table.	**19.** *M*. **Ēh caṅgā mēz e?** *S*. **Āhō, caṅgā mēz e.**

The teacher should get the pupil to ask a lot of these questions and see to it that he is able to ask as well as to answer.

Lesson VIII.

1. *T*. I am sitting on my chair. Who is sitting on that chair? *P*. I am sitting on this chair.	**1.** *M*. **Maī apṇī kursī te baiṭhā wā̃. Ōs kursī te kauṇ baiṭhā ē?** *S*. **Ēs kursī te maī baiṭhā wā̃.**
2. *T*. Say we are sitting on our chairs. *P*. We are sitting on our chairs.	**2.** *M*. **Ākhō asī̃ apṇiā̃ kursiā̃ te baiṭhe ā̃.** *S*. **Asī̃ apṇiā̃ kursiā̃ te baiṭhe ā̃.**
3. *T*. You are sitting on your chair. *P*. You are sitting on your chair.	**3.** *M*. **Tusī apṇī kursī te baiṭhe ō.** *S*. **Tusī apṇī kursī te baiṭhe ō.**
4. *T*. He is sitting on his chair. *P*. Yes, he is sitting on his chair.	**4.** *M*. **Ōh apṇī kursī te baiṭhe nẽ.** *S*. **Āhō ōh apṇī kursī te baiṭhe nẽ.**
5. *T*. (Pointing to the lady.) She is sitting on her chair. *P*. Yes, she is sitting on her chair.	**5.** *M*. **Ōh apṇī kursī te baiṭhe nẽ.** *S*. **Āhō ōh apṇī kursī te baiṭhe nẽ.**

6. *T*. They are sitting on their chairs. *P*. Yes, they are sitting on their chairs.

6. *M*. **Ōh apṇiā̃ kursiā̃ te baiṭhe nē̃. *S*. Āho, ōh apṇiā̃ kursiā̃ te baiṭhe nē̃.**

7. *T*. You are sitting on your chair. *P*. Yes, you are sitting on your chair. The pupil should be able to say this conjugation easily and readily.

7. *M*. **Tusī̃ apṇī kursī te baiṭhe ō. *S*. Āhō tusī̃ apṇī kursī te baiṭhe ō.**

8. *T*. I rise from my chair and go to the door. Now you say it. *P*. I rise from my chair and go to the door.

6. *M*. **Maī̃ kursī tõ uṭṭhke būhē tīkar (or wall) jānnā wā̃. Huṇ tusī̃ ākhō. *S*. Maī̃ kursī tõ uṭṭhke būhē tīkar (or wall) jānnā wā̃.**

9. *T*. I open and shut the door and go and sit down on my chair. You say it. *P*. I open and shut the door and go and sit down on my chair.

9. *M*. **Maī̃ būhā lāhkē mārnā wā̃, tē kursī te jākē baih jānnā wā̃. Tusī̃ akhō. *S*. Maī̃ būhā lāhke mārnā wā̃, tē kursī te jākē baih jānnā wā̃.**

10. *T*. I take a book from the table and put it on the chair. *P*. I take a book and put it on the chair.

10. *M*. **Maī̃ mēz tõ katāb laike kursī te rakkhnā wā̃. *S*. Maī̃ mēz tõ katāb laike kursī te rakkhnā wā̃.**

11. *T*. I see a book. Do you see it ? *P*. Yes, I see it, it is a Panjabi book.

11. *M*. **Maī̃ ikk katāb wē<u>kh</u>nā wā̃. Tusī̃ ōh katāb wē<u>kh</u>dē ō? *S*. Āhō wē<u>kh</u>nā wā̃, Panjābī katāb e.**

12. *T*. (Pointing to the table.) Say I see the table. *P*. I see the table.

12. *M*. **Ākhō, maī̃ mēz nū̃ wēhnnā wā̃. *S*. Maī̃ mēz nū̃ wēhnnā wā̃.**

13. *T*. Now this (pointing to the chair). *P*. I see the chair.

13. *M*. **Huṇ ēh. *S*. Maĩ kursī nū̃ wēhnnā wā̃.**

T. Now this (pointing to the rug). *P*. I see the rug.

M. **Huṇ ēh *S*. Maĩ galīcā wēhnnā wā̃.**

14. *T*. And this, and this, (as he points to the door, window, watch, hat, etc.).

14. *M*. **Te ēh, tē ēh, (būhā bāri, ghaṛī, ṭōpī.)**

Lesson IX.

The teacher will get the following articles and so drill on them that the pupil cannot fail to remember the names.

Wood, fuel, fire, match, lamp, oil: also the words call, do, burn, for, from.

Lakkaṛ, bāllaṇ, agg, tīllī, battī, tēl. Saddṇā, karnā, baḷṇa, or ballṇa, laī, wāste, tõ.

1. *T*. (Showing the wood.) What is this? *P*. I do not know what they call it in Panjabi.

1. *M*. **Ēh kī e? *S*. Menū̃ patā nehĩ paī Panjābī wicc ōhnū̃ kī āhndē nẽ.**

2. *T*. We call it wood. *P*. We call it wood, it is wood.

2. *M*. **Asĩ ēhnū̃ lakkaṛ āhnnē ā̃. *S*. Asĩ ēhnū̃ lakkaṛ āhnnē ā̃, lakkaṛ e.**

3. *T*. (Showing a match.) We call this a match. What is it? *P*. We call it a match.

3. *M*. **Ēhnū̃ tīllī ākhnē ā̃. Kī e? *S*. Ēhnū̃ tīllī ākhnē ā̃.**

4. *T*. What is this? What do you call it? *P*. We call it a— *T*. A lamp. *P*. Yes, we call it a lamp.

4. *M*. **Ēh kī e? Ēhnū̃ kī āhndē ō? *S*. Ēhnū̃ asī āhnnē ā̃—*M*. battī. *S*. Āhō, ēhnū̃ asĩ battī āhnnē ā̃.**

5. *T*. Look in the lamp, that is oil. There is oil in the lamp. What

5. M. **Battī wicc wēkhō, ōh tēl e; battī wicc tēl e. Kī e? *S*.**

is it? *P.* We call it oil, there is oil in the lamp.

Ōhnū̃ tēl āhnnē ā̃, battī wicc tēl e.

6. *T.* I take a match and light it and set fire to the wick. I light the lamp. What do I do? *P.* You light the lamp.

6. *M.* Maĩ tīllī laikē bāḷnā wā̃, te battī nū̃ lānnā wā̃, maĩ battī bāḷnā wā̃. Maĩ kī karnā wā̃. *S.* Tusī̃ battī bāḷde ō.

7. *T.* Now you light the lamp. *P.* (Striking a match lights the lamp.) *T.* That is well done. What is this? *P.* Wood.

7. *M.* Huṇ tusī̃ bāḷō. Ēh caṅgā kītā e. Ēh kī e? *S.* Lakkaṛ.

8. *T.* Yes, I take the wood and hold it in the lamp and it burns. The wood burns, what does the wood do? *P.* The wood burns.

8. *M.* Āhō jī, maĩ lakkaṛ laikē battī utte phaṛī rakkhnā wā̃, tē ōh baḷ paindī e. Lakkaṛ baḷ paindī e, lakkaṛ kī kardī e? *S.* Lakkaṛ baḷ paindī e. (*See* Gram. pp. 67, 68.)

9. *T.* See the wood, it is burning. This we call fire or flame. What is it? *P.* This is fire.

9. *M.* Lakkaṛ nū̃ wēkhō, ōh baḷdī e paī. Ēh nū̃ asī̃ agg yā̃ lāṭ ākhnē ā̃. Kī e? *S.* Ēh agg we.

10. *T.* We say, too, the lamp is burning. *P.* The lamp is burning.

10. *M.* Ēh wī asī̃ ākhne ā̃ paī battī baḷdī e. *S.* Battī baḷdī e.

11. *T.* What is this? *P.* It is oil.

11. *M.* Ēh kī e? *S.* Ēh tēl e.

12. *T.* What is oil for? *P.* Oil is for burning.

12. *M.* Tēl kāh de wāstē hundā e? *S.* Tēl bāḷan wāstē hundā e.

13. *T.* Yes, it burns in the

13. *M.* Āhō jī, battī wicc

	lamp. *P.* What is the lamp for?		baḷdā e. *S.* Battī kāh de wāstē e?
14.	*T.* The lamp is for light. What is the wood for? *P.* The wood is for fuel.	14.	*M.* Battī lō wāstē e, lakkaṛ kehṛe kamm wāstē e? *S* Lakkaṛ bāḷan wāstē e (or bāllaṇ).
15.	*T.* Right, what is the match for? *P.* The match is to light the fire.	15.	*M.* Ṭhīk e, tīllī kāh de laī e? *S.* Tīllī agg bāḷan laī e.
16.	*T.* Yes, that is right, we strike a match and light the lamp for light. We either burn the wood for cooking or for heat. *P.* What is the chair for?	16.	*M.* Ṭhīk e, lō wāstē asī̃ tīllī bāḷkē battī bāḷnē ā̃. Lakkaṛ asī̃ yā̃ rōṭī pakāṇ wāstē yā̃ agg sēkkaṇ wāstē bāḷnē ā̃. *S.* Kursī kāh de wāstē we?
17.	*T.* The chair is for sitting on. What is the table for? *P.* We eat at the table.	17.	*M.* Kursī baihṇ wāstē we. Mēz kāhde wāstē we? *S.* Mēz te asī̃ rōṭī khānne ā̃.
18.	*T.* What is the door for? *P.* We go by way of the door.	18.	*M.* Būhā kāhde wāstē we? *S.* Asī̃ būhē rāh andar jānne ā̃.

(It may be necessary for the teacher to help in answering.) The teacher should ask this same question about all the articles with which the pupil is familiar. It is not necessary that the pupil should learn new words, rather he should use those he knows.

Lesson X.

The teacher should use pantomime to explain the words. We learn words in our own tongue by being able to understand them from their connection or by hearing them in connection with some action.

1. *T*. What is this? *P*. A room. *T*. Is the room clean? *P*. "Clean?" I do not understand.	1. *M*. **Ēh ki e? *S*. Kãwrā. *M*. Kãwrā sāf e? S. 'Sāf' dā nĕhĭ mĕnū̃ patā laggdā.**
2. *T*. (Soiling his finger with pencil, etc. and showing a clean and a soiled finger.) This finger is clean, this finger is not clean. (Showing handkerchiefs.) This handkerchief is clean, this is not clean. Now is the room clean? *P*. Yes, the room is clean.	2. *M*. **Ēh uṅgaḷ sāf e, ēh uṅgaḷ sāf nĕhĭ. Ēh ramāl sāf e, ēh sāf nĕhĭ. Huṇ, kãwrā sāf e? *S*. Āhō kãwrā sāf e.**
3. *T*. (Showing a book.) Is the book clean? *P*. Yes, the book is clean.	3. *M*. **Ēh katāb sāf e? *S*. Āhō katāb sāf e.**
4. *T*. Who cleans the room? I will tell you. The servant. Who? *P*. The servant. The servant cleans the room.	4. *M*. **Kãwre nū̃ sāf kauṇ kardā e? Maĭ tuhānū̃ dassnā̃, naukar. Kauṇ? *S*. Naukar. Naukar kãwre nū̃ sāf kardā e.**
5. *T*. How does he clean the room? I will tell you. He cleans it thus (imitates sweeping and dusting and says), He sweeps the floor and dusts the furniture—the chairs, table, doors, bookcase. Now is the room clean? *P*. Yes, the room is clean.	5. *M*. **Ōh kis tarhā̃ kãwrā sāf kardā e? Maĭ tuhānū̃ dassnā̃, es tarhā̃ kardā e. Darī te baukar phērdā e, te mēzā̃ kursīā̃ nū̃ jhāṛ pōc kardā e (kursīā̃, mēz būhē, almārī), huṇ kãwrā sāf e? *S*. Āhō kãwrā sāf e.**
6. *T*. How does he clean it? *P*. He cleans with a	6. *M* **Kis tarhā̃ sāf kardā ē? *S*. Bhārī te**

	English		Panjabi
	broom and duster. *P*. He cleans it with a broom and duster.		jhāṛan nāḷ sāf kardā e. (Inquire jhāṛū, bhārī.)
7.	*T*. You tell me. *P*. I will tell you. He sweeps the floor and dusts the chairs, tables, doors, windows.	7.	*M*. Tusī̃ mēnū̃ dassō. *S*. Maĩ tuhānū̃ dassnā̃. Ōh jhāṛū phērdā e te kursīā̃, mēzā̃, būhēā̃, bārīā̃ nū̃ jhāṛ pōc kardā e.
8.	*T*. What is on your shoes? *P* Dust.	8.	*M*. Tuhāḍḍī juttī te kī e? *S*. Dhūṛ.
9.	*T*. Who cleans your shoes? *P*. The servant cleans my shoes.	9.	*M*. Tuhāḍḍī juttī kauṇ sāf kardā e? *S*. Naukar juttī sāf kardā e.
10.	*T*. How does he clean them? *P*. He cleans them with a brush.	10.	*M*. Kis tarhā̃ sāf kardā e? *S*. Bursh nāḷ sāf kardā e.
11.	*T*. What is this? *P*. It is my hat.	11.	*M*. Ēh kī e? *S*. Mērī ṭōpī e.
12.	*T*. Who cleans your hat? *P*. I clean it with a brush.	12.	*M*. Tuhāḍḍī ṭōpī nū̃ kauṇ sāf kardā e? *S*. Maĩ ehnū̃ āpī bursh nāḷ sāf karnā wā̃.
13.	*T*. How are your clothes cleaned? *P*. Some we brush and some we have washed.	13.	*M*. Tuhāḍḍe kapṛe kikaṇ sāf karīde nẽ? *S*. Kise kise nū̃ bursh nāḷ sāf karne ā̃, kise kise nū̃ dhuānne ā̃.
14.	*T*. Who washes your clothes? *P*. A woman and her son.	14.	*M*. Tuhāḍḍe kapṛe kauṇ dhōndā e? *S*. Ikk dhōbaṇ te ōhdā puttar.
15.	*T*. This is a handkerchief. I give it to the washerman. He washes it with soap and water and makes it clean. He gives clean clothes to	15.	*M*. Ēh ramāl e. Maĩ dhōbē nū̃ dēnnā wā̃, ōh sabūṇ te pāṇī nāḷ dhōkē sāf kardā e. Sāf kapṛē ōh sānū̃ dēndā e, asī ōhnū̃

us and we give him money. *P*. Yes, he cleans our clothes and we give him money.	**paise dēnnē ā̃. *S*. Āhō ōh sāḍḍē kapṛē dhōndā e, te asī̃ ōhnū̃ paisē dēnnē ā̃.**
16 *T*. What do you eat from? *P*. We eat from plates.	**16. *M*. Tusī̃ rōṭī kāh de wicc khānde ō. *S*. Asī̃ bhāṇḍeā̃ wicc khānnē ā̃.**
17. *T*. Who washes the plates? *P*. The water-carrier washes the plates.	**17. *M*. Bhāṇḍeā̃ nū̃ kauṇ dhōndā e? *S*. Māshkī bhāṇḍeā̃ nū̃ dhōndā e.**
18. *T*. Who washes your face and hands? *P*. I wash my own face and hands.	**18. *M*. Tuhāḍḍā mū̃h hatth kauṇ dhōndā e? *S*. Mū̃h hatth maī̃ āpē dhōnnā wā̃.**

Lesson XI.

The teacher should procure a cup, saucer, knife, fork. spoon, plate, teapot, teaspoon, medium and large spoons, sugar.

1 *T*. (Showing a cup.) This is a vessel, (a saucer) this too is a vessel, (a plate) this also is a vessel, three vessels. What are these? *P*. Vessels.	**1. *M*. Eh bhāṇḍā e, ēh wī bhāṇḍā e, ēh wī bhāṇḍa e, trai bhāṇḍē. Ēh kī nē? *S*. Bhāṇḍē.**
2. *T*. Yes, they are vessels. This is a cup. What is it? *P*. It is a cup.	**2. *M*. Āhō ji, bhāṇḍē nē. Eh piālā we, kī e? *S*. Piālā we.**

So for the rest, though these should have been taught beforehand from the lists in Lesson I. Having reviewed them all to see that the pupil is familiar with them, and having set them all on the table,

3. *T*. I see a cup. This is a cup. I see a knife. This is a knife. Pupil	**3. *M*. Maī̃ piālā wēkhnā wā̃. Ēh piālā we, maī̃ churī wēkhna wā̃.**

points out each as it is asked for. Now show me a cup. (*P.* A knife).

Ẽh churī e. Huṇ mĕnū̃ piālā wakhāō. *S.* Mĕnū̃ churī wakhāō.

4. Teacher (pretending, or better actually performing). Here is the teapot, I put in some hot water, I throw it out, I put in tea, I pour in hot water; let it draw, the tea is made. I put tea into the cup. I drink the tea.

4. *M.* Ẽh cāhpōcī e, maĩ tattā pāṇī pānnā̃, maĩ ohnū̃ ḍōhl chaḍḍnā̃, maĩ cāh pānnā wā̃, maĩ tattā pāṇī pannā̃ wā̃; ēhnū̃ raṇg ā laiṇ dehō, cāh tiār e, maĩ piālē wicc cāh pānnā wā̃, maĩ cāh pī lennā wā̃. (*See* Gram. p. 112.)

The teacher should lead the pupil through these stages, then procuring some eatable and a plate should go through the process of eating, explaining each action.

5. *T.* (Taking up a teaspoon and a large spoon.) This spoon is large and this is small. *P.* This spoon is large and this is small.

5. *M.* Ẽh cammac waḍḍā e, ēh nikkā e. *S.* Ẽh cammac waḍḍā e, ēh nikkā e.

6. *T.* These are 3 spoons, this is large, this is smaller, this is medium.

6. *M.* Ẽh trai cammac nẽ, ēh waḍḍā e, ēh ōdū̃ nikkā e, ēh wishkārlē mēḷ dā e.

7. *T.* Is the cup small? *P.* Yes, the cup is small.

7. *M.* Piālā nikkā e? *S.* Āhō, piālā nikkā e.

8. *T.* Is the plate small? *P.* No, the plate is not small.

8. *M.* Plēṭ nikkī e? *S.* Nĕhī̃, plēṭ nikkī nĕhī̃.

9. *T.* Is this spoon small? *P.* No, that is large.

9. *M.* Ẽh cammac nikkā e? *S.* Nā, ōh waḍḍā e.

10. *T.* Is this book large? *P.* No, the book is small.

10. *M.* Ẽh katāb waḍḍī e? *S.* Nĕhī̃, katāb nikkī e.

11. *T*. Is the watch large ? *P*. No, my watch is small.	11. *M*. Gharī waḍḍī e? *S*. Nĕhī̃, mērī gharī nikkī e.
12. *T*. Is this chair large ? *P*. No, it is not large, that one is large.	12. *M*. Ēh kursī waḍḍī e? *S*. Nĕhī̃ ēh waḍḍī nehī̃, ōh waḍḍī e.
13. *T*. Is the table large ? *P*. Yes, it is large.	13. *M*. Mēz waḍḍā e? *S*. Āhō waḍḍā e.
14. *T*. Is the room large ? *P*. Yes, it is large.	14. *M*. Kamrā waḍḍā e? *S*. Āhō, waḍḍā e.

The teacher should get the pupil to ask these questions about the various articles in the room, seeing that the right gender of the adjective is used with each noun, and remembering that what the pupil needs is to learn how to use the words he already knows.

Lesson XII.

1. *T*. (Pointing to his eye.) What is this ? It is my eye. *P*. It is my eye.	1. *M*. Ēh kī ē? Mērī akkh e. *S*. Mērī ākkh e.
2. *T*. Oh no, you must not say it is my eye, but it is your eye. *P*. It is your eye.	2. *M*. Nā jī, 'mērī akkh' nā ākhō, aiñ ākhō 'tuhāḍḍī akkh e.' *S*. Tuhāḍḍī akkh e.
3. *T*. That's right, this is my eye, and that is your eye. I see with my eyes. What do you do with your eyes ? *P*. I see with my eyes.	3. *M*. Ṭhik e, ēh mērī akkh e, ōh tuhāḍḍī akkh e, maī akkhā̃ nāḷ we<u>kh</u>nā wā̃, tusī akkhā̃ nāḷ kī karde o? *S*. Maī akkhā̃ nāḷ wē<u>kh</u>nā wā̃.
4. *T*. Right, what do I do with my eyes ? *P*. You see with your eyes.	4. *M*. Ṭhik e, maī akkhā̃ nāḷ kī karnā wā̃? *S*. Tusī akkhā̃ nāḷ wēhndē ō.

5. *T*. I see with one eye, now I see with two eyes. You say it. *P*. I see with one eye, now I see with two eyes.

5. *M*. **Maĩ ikk akkh nāḷ wēhnnā wã, huṇ dūh akkhĩ wēhnnã. Tusĩ wī ākhō. *S*. Maĩ ikk akkh nāḷ wēhnnā wã, huṇ dūh akkhĩ wēhnnã.**

6. *T*. What does this woman do with her eyes? (It may be necessary to have clay figures). *P*. She sees with her eyes.

6. *M*. **Ēh janānī akkhã nāḷ kī kardī e? *S*. Akkhã nāḷ wēhndī e.**

7. *T*. What does this man do with his eyes? *P*. He sees with his eyes.

7. *M*. **Ēh jaṇā akkhã nāḷ kī kardā e? *S*. Akkhã nāḷ wēhndā ē.**

8. *T*. What do men do with their eyes? *P*. They see with their eyes.

8. *M*. **Jaṇē akkhã nāḷ kī kardē nẽ? *S*. Ōh akkhĩ wēkhdē nẽ.**

9. *T*. What do women do with their eyes? *P*. They see with their eyes.

9. *M*. **Janānīã akkhã nāḷ kī kardīã nẽ? *S*. Ōh akkhĩ wekhdīã nẽ.**

10. *T*. What do we all do with our eyes? *P*. We all see with our eyes.

10. *M*. **Asī sārē akkhã nāḷ kī karnē ã? *S*. Asī sārē akkhĩ wēkhnē ã.**

11. *T*. This is my right eye, this is my left eye. Which is this? *P*. That is your right eye and that is your left.

11. *M*. **Ēh mērī sajjī akkh e, tē ēh mērī khabbī e, ēh kēhṛī e? *S*. Ēh tuhāḍḍī sajjī akkh e, tē ōh tuhāḍḍā khabbī e.**

12. *T*. (Putting hand to ear.) What is this? *P*. That is your ear.

12. *M*. **Ēh kī e? *S*. Ōh tuhāḍḍā kann e.**

13. *T*. What do I do with my

13. *M*. **Mai kannã nāḷ kī**

	ears? I hear with my ears? What do you do with your ears? *P.* I hear with my ears.		karnā wā̃. Maĩ kannā̃ nāḷ suṇnā wā̃, tusĩ kannā̃ nāḷ kī kardē ō? *S.* Maĩ kannā̃ nāḷ suṇnā wā̃.
14.	*T.* How many ears have we? *P.* We have two ears.	14.	*M.* Sāḍḍē kinnē kann nē̃? *S.* Sāḍḍē dō kann nē̃.
15.	*T.* Which is your right ear, which is your left? What does the man do with his ears? *P.* He hears with his ears.	15.	*M.* Tuhāḍḍā sajjā kann kĕhṛā e? Khabbā kĕhṛā e? Ōh jaṇā kannā̃ nāḷ kī kardā e. *S.* Kannā̃ nāḷ suṇdā e.
16.	*T.* What does the woman do with her ears? *P.* She hears with her ears.	16.	*M.* Janānī kannā̃ nāḷ kī kardī e. *S.* Kannā̃ nāḷ suṇdī e.
17.	*T.* What do we all do with our ears? *P.* We all hear with our ears.	17.	*M.* Asĩ sārē kannā̃ nāḷ kī karnē ā̃. *S.* Asĩ sārē kannā̃ nāḷ suṇnē ā̃.
18.	*T.* This is my foot. I have two feet. What do I do with my feet? *P.* I walk with my feet.	18.	*M.* Ēh mērā pair e. Mērē dō pair nē̃. Maĩ pairā̃ nāḷ kī karnā wā̃. *S.* Maĩ pairā̃ nāḷ ṭurnā wā̃.
19.	*T.* You walk with your feet. What do I do with my feet? *P.* You walk with your feet. (So with man, men, woman, women.)	19.	*M.* Tusĩ pairā̃ nāḷ ṭurdē ō. Maĩ pairā̃ nāḷ kī karnā wā̃? *S.* Tusĩ pairā̃ nāḷ ṭurdē ō. (Jaṇā, janānī, jaṇē, janānīā̃.)
20.	*T.* (Pointing to his mouth.) What is this? It is my mouth. What is it? *P.* It is your mouth.	20.	*M.* Ēh kī e? Ēh mērā mũh e. Kī e? *S.* Tuhāḍḍā mũh e.

21. *T.* (Pointing to the pupil's mouth.) What is that? *P.* It is my mouth.	**21.** ***M.*** **Ōh kī e?** ***S.*** **Mērā mū̃h e.**
22. *T.* What do you do with your mouth? *P.* I speak with my mouth.	**22.** ***M.*** **Tusī̃ mū̃h nāḷ kī kardē ō** ***S.*** **Maī mū̃h nāḷ bōlnā wā̃.**
23. *T.* What does Jhanda do with his mouth? *P.* He speaks with his mouth.	**23.** ***M.*** **Jhaṇḍā mū̃h nāḷ kī kardā e.** ***S.*** **Ōh mū̃h nāḷ bōldā e.**
24 *T.* What does the woman do with her mouth? *P.* She speaks, etc. (Man, boy, girl, men, boys.) *T.* I eat with my mouth (showing), do you do that way? *P.* I eat with my mouth.	**24.** **Janānī mū̃h nāḷ kī kardī e.** ***S.*** **Ōh mū̃h nāḷ bōldī e (jaṇā, muṇḍā, kuṛī, jaṇe, muṇḍē.** ***M.*** **Maī mū̃h nāḷ khānnā wā̃. Tusī̃ wī ēs tarhā̃ kardē ō?** ***S.*** **Mā̃wī mū̃h nāḷ khānnā wā̃.**
25. *T.* (Showing from a cup.) I drink with my mouth. Do you? Yes, I drink with my mouth.	**25.** ***M.*** **Maī mū̃h nāḷ pīnnā wā̃. Tusī̃ wī ēs tarhā̃ kardē ō?** ***S.*** **Āhōḷ mā̃wī mū̃h nāḷ pīnnā wā̃.**
26. *T.* Jhanda eats and drinks with his mouth. Do we all do so? *P.* Yes, well all eat and drink with our mouths.	**26.** ***M.*** **Jhaṇḍā wī mū̃h nāḷ khāndā pīndā e. Asī̃ sārē ese tarhā̃ karnē ā̃?** ***S.*** **Āhō, asī̃ sārē mū̃h nāḷ khānnē pīnnē ā̃.**
27. *T.* I laugh (ha ha ha) with my mouth, and sing (la la la) with my mouth. Do you laugh and sing with your mouth? *P.* Yes, I laugh and sing with my mouth.	**27.** ***M.*** **Maī mū̃h nāḷ hasnā wī ā̃, te mū̃h naḷ gāunnā wī ā̃. Tusī̃ wī mū̃h nāḷ hasdē te gaundē ō?** ***S.*** **Āhō, mā̃wī mū̃h nāḷ hasnā te gaunnā wā̃.**
28. *T.* Does J. laugh and sing	**28.** ***M.*** **Jhaṇḍā wī mū̃h nā**

with his mouth? (Boys, girls, etc.). *T*. This is my nose, I breathe with it and smell with it. What do I do? *P*. You breathe and smell with your nose. (So boys, men, girls in pictures.)

hasdā te gaundā e? (Muṇḍē, kuṛīā̃, etc.). *M*. Ēh mērā nakk e, ēh de nāḷ maĩ sāh lennā wā̃ te suṅghnā wā̃. Maĩ kī karnā wā̃? *S*. Tusī̃ nakk nāḷ sāh lendē te suṅghdē ō.

29. *T*. This is my hand, I take and give with my hand. What do I do? *P*. You take and give with your hand.

29. *M*. Ēh mērā hatth e. Hatth nāḷ maĩ lennā te dēnnā wā̃. Kī karnā wā̃? *S*. Tusī̃ hatth nāḷ lendē te dēndē ō.

30. *T*. What else do you do with your hand? Say, I write and work with it. *P*. I write and work with my hand.

30. *M*. Tusī̃ hatth nāḷ hōr kī kardē ō? Ākhō maĩ ōh de nāḷ likkhnā te kamm karnā wā̃. *S*. Maĩ hatth nāḷ likkhnā te kamm karnā wā̃.

The teacher must keep a list of all new words and see that there are not too many.

Lesson XIII.

1. *T*. (Showing a book.) What is this? Take it. *P*. It is a book. I take it.

1. *M*. Ēh kī e? Lellaō. *S*. Katāb e. Maĩ lai lennā wā̃.

2. *T*. What do you take the book with? *P*. I take it with my hand.

2. *M*. Tusī̃ katāb kāhde nāḷ lendē ō? *S*. Maĩ hatth nāḷ lennā wā̃.

3. *T*. Do you see the table? what with? *P*. I see the table with my eyes.

3. *M*. Tusī̃ mēz nū̃ wēhnde ō? Kāhde naḷ wēhnde ō? *S*. Maĩ mēz nū̃ akkhīā̃ nāḷ wēhnnā wā̃.

4. *T.* I walk to the door. With what do you walk? *P.* I walk with my feet.

4. *M.* **Mai būhē tikar jānnā wā̃. Kāh de nāḷ ṭurde ō? *S.* Mai pairā̃ nāḷ ṭūrnā wā̃.**

5 *T.* With what do you open the door? *P.* I open the door with my hands.

5. *M.* **Būhā kāhde nāḷ lāhnde ō? *S.* Maī būhē nū̃ hatthā̃ nāḷ lāhnnā wā̃.**

6. *T.* Do you see the door? With what do you see the door? *P.* I see the door with my eyes.

6. *M.* **Būhe nū̃ wēhnde ō? Būhē nū̃ kāhde nāḷ wēhnde ō? *S.* Bū̃hē nū̃ akkhīā̃ nāḷ wēhnnā wā̃.**

7. *T.* Do you hear my words? *P.* Yes, I hear you speak.

7. *M.* **Tusī̃ mērīā̃ gallā̃ suṇde ō? *S.* Āhō, tuhāḍḍīā̃ gallā̃ suṇnā wā̃.**

8. *T.* With what do you hear my words? *P.* I hear you speak with my ears.

8. *M.* **Kāhde nāḷ mērīā̃ gallā̃ suṇde ō? *S.* tuhāḍḍīā̃ gallā̃ kannā̃ nāḷ suṇnā wā̃.**

9. *T.* Please smell this flower. With what do you smell it? *P.* I smell it with my nose.

9. *M.* **Mēhrbānī karkē es phull nū̃ suṅgho. Kāh de nāḷ suṅghde ō? *S.* Maí nakk nāḷ suṅghnā wā̃.**

10. *T.* Please speak louder, say it again. What do you speak with? *P.* I speak with my mouth. *T.* Asks about woman man, boy, boys, girl, girls, walk, hear, see, smell, speak.

10. *M.* **Zarā dabbke ākhō, phēr ākhō. Kāh de nāḷ kūnde ō? *S.* Mū̃h nāḷ kūnnā̃ wā̃. (Janānī, jaṇā, muṇḍā, muṇḍe, kuṛī, kuṛīā̃, ṭurnā, suṇnā, wēkhṇā, suṅghṇā, kūṇā.)**

It is not new words the pupil needs to learn, but how to use old ones.

Lesson XIV.

1. *T*. What is this? *P*. It is a book. *T*. Whose book is it? Is it mine? *P*. No, it is mine.	1. *M*. Ēh kī e. *S*. Katāb e. *M*. Kihdī katāb e? Mērī e? *S*. Nehī̃ mērī e.
2. *T*. Whose book is this, then? *P*. That is mine too. *T*. And this? *P*. That book is yours.	2. *M*. Ēh, pher, kihdī e? *S*. Ōh wī mērī e. *M*. Te ēh? *S*. Ōh katāb tuhāḍḍī e.
3. *T*. Whose chair is this, yours or mine? *P*. That is Mr. Smith's. *T*. Whose house is this? *P*. It is Mr. Smith's.	3. *M*. Ēh kihdi kursī e, tuhāḍḍī ke mērī? *S*. Ēh sāhb dī e. *M*. Ēh ghar kihdā e? *S*. Ēh Smith sāhb dā ghar e.
4. *T*. Whose books are these? *S*. They are his. (Cup-s, pen-s, hat-s, rug-s, coat-s, shoe-s, chair-s, picture-s, furniture.)	4. *M*. Ēh kihdīā̃ kītābā̃ nē̃? *S*. Ohdiā̃ nē̃ (piālā-e, kalam-ā̃, ṭōpī-ā̃, galicā-e, kōṭ, juttīā̃, kursī-ā̃, mūrat-ā̃, sabāb).
5. *T*. Have you a book? *P*. Yes, I have two books. *T*. Have you a chair? *P*. Yes, I have one chair.	5. *M*. Tuhāḍḍē kōḷ katāb e? *S*. Āhō Mērē kōḷ dō kitābā̃ nē̃. *M*. Tuhāḍḍē kōḷ kursī e? *S*. Āhō, mērē kōḷ ikk kursī e.
6. *T*. Have you a pen? *P*. Yes, I have a pen. *T*. Has Jhanḍa a hat? *P*. Yes, Jhanḍa has a hat.	6. *M*. Tuhāḍḍē kōḷ kalam e? *S*. Āhō mērē koḷ kalam e. *M*. Jhanḍē kōḷ ṭōpī e? *S*. Āhō Jhanḍē kōḷ ṭōpī e.
7. *T*. Have you all got pens? *P*. Yes, we all have pens. (Men, women, John, Mary,	7. *M*. Tuhāḍḍeā̃ sāreā̃ kōḷ kalamā̃ haiṇ? *S*. Āhō, sāḍḍeā̃ sāreā̃ kōḷ nē̃ (jaṇeā̃, janānīā̃, Jhan-

etc., chairs, pens, cups, shoes, etc.)

ḍē, Tābaṇ kōḷ kursīā̃, kalamā̃, piāle, juttīā̃ nē̃).

Lesson XV.

1. *T.* Here is a bag for books, what is it? *P.* A bag for books. *T.* What is in the bag? *P.* There are books in the bag.

1. *M.* Ēh katābā̃ wāstē bastā e, kī e? *S.* Katābā̃ wāstē bastā. *M.* Baste wicc kī e? *S.* Baste wicc katābā̃ nē̃.

2. *T.* How many books are in the bag? *P.* There are one big, two thin, three small ones. *T.* How many are there? *P.* There are six books.

2. *M.* Baste wicc kinnīā̃ katābā̃ nē? *S.* Ikk waḍḍī, dō patlīā̃, trai nikkīā̃. *M.* Kinnīā̃ nē̃? *S.* Chē katābā̃ nē̃.

3. *T.* How many chairs are there in the room? *P.* There are—chairs in the room. *T.* How many tables are there in the room? *P.* There are—tables in the room.

3. *M.* Kā̃wrē wicc kinnīā̃ kursīā̃ nē̃? *S.* Kā̃wrē wicc—kursīā̃ nē̃. *M.* Kā̃wre wicc kinnē mēz nē̃? *S.* Kamrē wicc—mēz nē̃.

4. *T.* How many carpets are there in the room? *P.* There is only one. *T.* How many rugs are there? *P.* There are —rugs in the room.

4. *M.* Kamrē wicc kinnīā̃ darīā̃ nē? *S.* Ikkoī e. *M.* G̱alīce kinnē nē̃? *S.* Kamrē wicc—g̱alīce nē̃.

5. *T.* How many hands have I? *P.* You have two hands. *T.* How many fingers on one hand? *P.* There are five fingers on each hand.

5. *M.* Mērē kinnē hatth nē̃? *S.* Tuhāḍḍē dō hatth nē̃. *M.* Ikk hatth dīā̃ kinnīā̃ uṅgḷā̃ nē? *S.* Dōhā̃ hatthā̃ dīā̃ panj panj uṅgḷā̃ nē̃.

6. *T.* How many fingers are

6. *M.* Dōhā̃ hatthā̃ dīā̃

there on both hands together? *P*. There are ten on both hands together. *T*. How many fingers am I showing? (rapidly holding up 1, 2, 3, 4, 5, 6, 7, 8, 9, 10 until the pupil can answer rapidly).	raḷākē kinnīā̃ uṅgḷā̃ nē̃? *S*. Dōhā̃ diā̃ raḷākē das uṅgḷā̃ nē̃. *M*. Maĩ kinnīā̃ uṅgḷā̃ peā wikẖānnā wā̃? Ikk, dō, trai, cār, panj, chē, satt, aṭṭh, naũ, das.
7. *T*. How many books are there on the table? *P*. There are 3, 7, 9 on the table. *T*. How many are there under the table? (as he puts them under).	7. *M*. Mēz utte kinnīā̃ katābā̃ nē̃? *S*. Mēz te trai, satt, naũ katābā̃ nē̃. *M*. Mēz dē hēṭh kinnīā̃ nē̃.
8. *T*. How many are there on the cushion? *P*. There are—on the cushion. *T*. On the chair, the paper, under the hat, by the hat?	8. *M*. Sarhāne kinnīā̃ nē̃? *S*. Sarhāne utte —nē̃? *M*. Kursī utte, kāgaz utte, ṭōpī hēṭh, ṭōpī dē kōḷ.
9. *T*. Where is the big book? (as he puts it into the bag). *P*. It is in the bag. *T*. Where is the little book? *P*. It is under the big book.	9. *M*. Waḍḍī katāb kitthē wē? *S*. Bastē wicc e. *M*. Nikkī katāb kitthē e? *S*. Waḍḍī katāb dē hēṭh e.
10. *T*. Now where is the little book? *P*. It is in the big book. *T*. How many persons are in this room? *P*. There are—persons in this room.	10. *M*. Huṇ nikki katāb kitthē wē? *S*. Waḍḍī katāb dē wicc e. *M*. Ēs kā̃wrē wicc kinnē bandē nē̃? *S*. Ēs Kā̃wre wicc—bandē nē̃.
11. *T*. How many eyes have we all? *P*. We all	11. *M*. Sāḍḍeā̃ sāreā̃ diā̃ kinnīā̃ akkhīā̃ nē̃? *S*

have two eyes. *T*. Yes, each has two eyes, but how many have all of us together ? *P*. We all have—eyes.	**Sāḍḍeā̃ sāreā̃ diā̃ dō akkhīā̃ nē̃.** *M*. **Āhō jī, sāreā̃ diā̃ dō dō akkhīā̃ nē̃, par sāḍḍeā̃ sāreā̃ diā̃ kull kinnīā̃ akkhīā̃ nē̃?** *S*. **Sāḍḍeā̃ sāreā̃ diā̃—akkhīā̃ nē̃.**
12 *T*. How many rupees have I ? Count them. *P*. Ten and one are—? *T*. Eleven. How many have you ? *P*. I have ten and five.	**12.** *M*. **Mērē koḷ kinnē rupae nē̃? Giṇ laō.** *S*. **Das te ikk kinnē hunde nē̃?** *M*. **Yārā̃; tuhāḍḍē kōḷ kinnē nē̃?** *S*. **Mērē kōḷ das te panj nē̃.**
13. *T*. Fifteen. Now here are ten, you give ten, how many have we now ? *P*. Twenty.	**13.** *M*. **Pandrā̃. Ētthē das nē̃, te tusī̃ das deō, huṇ sāḍḍē kōḷ kinnē nē̃?** *S*. **Wīh.**
14. *T*. Count after me 1, 2, 3, 4, 5, 6, 7, 8, 9, 10, 11, 12, 13 14, 15, 16, 17, 18, 19, 20.	**14.** *M*. **Mērē picchē picchē giṇō ikk, dō, trai, cār, panj, chē, satt, aṭṭh, naū̃, das, yārā̃, bārā̃, tērā̃, caudā̃, pandrā̃, sōḷā̃, satārā̃, ṭhārā̃, unnī, wīh.**

Lesson XVI.

1. *T*. Look at this watch, what is it ? *P*. It is a watch. *T*. What is that ? We call that a clock. *P*. It is a clock.	**1.** *M*. **Ēs gharī nū̃ wēkhō, kī e?** *S*. **Gharī e.** *M*. **Ōh kī e? Ōhnū̃ wī asī̃ gharī āhnne ā̃.** *S*. **Ōh wī gharī e.**
2. *P*. How many hours are on it ? Count. *P*. (As teacher points) 1, 2, 12 hours (as above).	**2.** *M*. **Ōh de kinnē ghaiṇṭe nē̃? giṇō jī.** *S*. **Ikk, dō, bārā̃ ghaiṇṭē.**

3. *T*. What time is it now? *P*. It is ten o'clock. *T*. And now? (There should be a drill on time till the pupil can readily tell the time. Sometimes the teacher may say it is 5-30, and he should set the time accordingly, etc.)

3. *M*. Huṇ kī wajeā e? *S*. Das wajē nẽ. *M*. Te huṇ?

Practise on the following numbers for a month or so. till they are perfectly familiar.

4. 1, $1\frac{1}{4}$, $1\frac{1}{2}$, $1\frac{3}{4}$, 2, $2\frac{1}{4}$, $2\frac{1}{2}$, $2\frac{3}{4}$, and so on up to 20, 25, 30, 40, 50, 60, 100. 1-35 A.M., 10 A.M., 8-30 A.M., 12 noon, 12 midnight, 2 A.M., 5 A.M., etc.

4. Ikk, sawā, ḍūḍh or ḍēḍh, pauṇē dō, dō, sawā dō, ḍhāī, pauṇē trai, trai, sawā trai, sāḍhe trai and so on with the numbers up to 12 as above, then **pauṇē tērā̃, terā̃, sawā tērā̃, sāḍhe tērā̃,** and so on with **caudā̃, pandrā̃, sōḷā̃, satārā̃, aṭhārā̃, unnī, wīh, panjhī, trīh, cāḷī, panjāh, sāṭṭh, sau, rāt dā ikk wajjkē paīntī minṭ, das wajē din dē, sāḍhē aṭṭh wajē din de, bārā̃ wajē dopaihr, bārā̃ wajē rāt dē, dō wajē rāt dē, panj wajē fajrī.**

5. 60 seconds make a minute, 60 minutes make an hour, 3 hours make a watch, 8 watches or 24 hours make a day, 7 days make a week, 4 weeks or 30 days make a month, 12 months a year

5. Saṭṭhā̃ sikinṭā̃ dā minṭ hundā e, saṭṭhā̃ minṭā̃ dā ghainṭā hundā e, tinnā̃ ghainṭeā̃ dā ikk paihr, aṭṭhā̃ paihrā̃ yā̃ cawhīā̃ ghainṭeā̃ dā din, sattā̃ dihāṛeā̃ dā haftā, caūh hafteā̃ yā̃ trīhā̃ dihāṛeā̃ dā mahīnā, bārā̃ mahīneā̃ dā sāl (warhā).

Lesson XVII.

1. *T*. What is this? *P*. A book. *T*. And this? *P*. That too, is a book. *T*. And these? *P*. They are all books.	1. *M*. **Ēh kī e? *S*. Katāb e. *M*. Te ōh? Ōh wī katāb e? *M*. Te eh? *S*. Sārīā̃ katābā̃ nē̃.**
2. *T*. Yes, it is a book-shop. I will sell the books. Will you buy a book? *P*. How many rupees will it cost?	2. *M*. **Āhō jī, katābā̃ dī haṭṭī ē. Maĩ katābā̃ wēcā̃gā, tusī̃ katāb laōge? *S*. Kinnē rupaē lagganġē?**
3. *T*. Say what is the price? *P*. How much is it?	3. *M*. **Aiñ ākhō, kī mull e? *S*. Kī mull e?**
4. *T*. It is very cheap. The price is only Rs. 2. *P*. That is very expensive. I will give you 8 annas. *T*. All right, give me 8 annas.	4. *M*. **Bauht sastī e, dō rupaē mull e. *S*. Bauht waddh e, maĩ tuhānū̃ dhēlī deā̃gā. *M*. Halā jī, dhēlī hī dē deō.**
5. *P*. Here are 4 annas, give me this book for 4 annas. *T*. No, that is very little, it is worth a whole rupee. *P*. All right. I do not want it.	5. *S*. **Āh wēkhā̃ pauḷī e. Menū̃ ōh katāb pauḷī tō̃ dē deō. *M*. Ēh bauht ghaṭṭ e, ēh pūrē rupaē dī e. *S*. Acchā, whaĩ, maĩ nehī̃ laindā.**

The pupil should be taught to understand current coinage and local measures and usage in the purchase of cloth, food, fuel, furniture, building materials and whatever the pupil will need. It will need much practice, but it may as well be done in the study as in the market at the expense of one's pocket-book.

Lesson XVIII.

1. *T*. See what I do. I take my seat on	1. *M*. **Tusī̃ wēkhō pāī maĩ kī karnā wā̃ peā. Maĩ**

this chair, I sit down, I rise from my chair and walk to the door and open it. I am standing by the opened door, I shut it and walk back again to my chair.

ēs kursī te baih jānnā wā̃. Maī baih jānnā wā̃, maī kursī tō̃ uṭṭhkē te būhē tīkar jākē būhā lāhnnā wā̃. Latthē būhē dē kōḷ maī khlōtā wā̃, būhā mārkē maī phēr kursī kōḷ jānnā wā̃.

2. Now I will tell you what I did. I sat down in my chair, I rose and went to the door and then shut it and opened it again. I stood by the opened door. I shut it and walked back to my chair and sat down. Now I will do it again. (Goes through every movement and after each movement asks, what do I do ?)

2. *M.* Huṇ maī tūhānū̃ dassā̃gā paī maī kī kītā sī. Maī̃ kūrsī te baih geā, maī kursī tō̃ uṭṭhkē būhē wall geā, phēr būhā mārkē phēr lāheā ; latthē būhē kōḷ khlō geā, phēr kursī kōḷ ākē ōh de te baih geā ; huṇ maī̃ phēr karnā wā̃.

3. *P.* You sit down, you rise from the chair, you walk to the door, you open it, you stand by the open door, you shut the door and walk back again to your chair.

3. *S.* Tusī̃ baih jānde ō, kursī tō̃ uṭṭhde ō, būhē tīkar jānde ō, ohnū̃ lāhnde ō, latthē būhē de kōḷ khlōnde ō, būhā mārde ō, te phēr apṇī kursī tīkar part aunde ō.

4. *T.* (Doing it again) what did I do ? *P.* You sat down. *T.* (Rising) what did I do ? *P.* You rose from your chair.

4. *M.* Maī kī kītā sī ? *S.* Tusī̃ baih gaē. *T.* Maī kih kita si ? *S.* Tusī̃ kursī tō̃ uṭṭhē.

5. *T.* What am I doing now ? *P.* You are

5. *M.* Huṇ maī kī peā karnā wā̃ ? *S.* Tusī̃

standing. *T*. (After walking to the door) what did I do? *P*. You walked to the door. *T*. (After opening door) what did I do?	**khlōtē ō. *M*. Huṇ maĩ kī kītā e? *S*. Tusī̃ būhē kōḷ gaē. *T*. Maĩ kih kītā e?**
6. *P*. You opened the door. *T*. (After standing by opened door a few moments) what did I do? *P*. You stood by the opened door. *T*. (Shutting door and walking back to chair) what did I do?	6. **_S_. Tusā̃ būhā lāh dittā. *T*. Maĩ kī kītā? *S*. Tusī̃ latthē hoē būhē dē kōḷ khlōtē sau. *T*. Maĩ kī kītā e?**
7. *P*. You shut the door and returned to your chair. *T*. (After sitting down), what did I do? *P*. You sat down. *T*.	7. **_S_. Tusī̃ būhā mārkē kursī tīkar part āe. *T*. Main kī kītā e? *S*. Tusī̃ baih gaē. *M*. Huṇ tusī̃ sārā muṇḍhō̃ kar laō.**

Now you do it all from the beginning. Pupil goes through movements and describes them in present and past tenses.

Lesson XIX.

1. ***T*. What is this? *P*. A book. *T*. What are these? *P*. They are books.**	1. **_M_. Ēh kī e? *S*. Katāb. *M*. Ēh kī nē? *S*. Katābā̃.**
2. ***T*. See this book and this, one is big and one little. This is the big one. This book is bigger than that one. Which is bigger? *P*. That book is bigger than this one, this is smaller than that.**	2. **_M_. Ēs katāb nū̃ te ēs nū̃ wēkhō, ikk waḍḍī e te ikk nikkī. Waḍḍī ēh we. Ēh katāb ōh de nāḷō̃ waḍḍī e. Waḍḍī kēhṛī e? *S*. Ōh katāb ēh de nāḷō̃ waḍḍī e. Ēh ōh de naḷō̃ nikkī e.**

3. *T*. This book is little, very little, this book is large very large. Which book is larger? *P*. This book is larger.	3. *M*. **Ēh katāb nikkī e, bauht nikkī, ēh katāb waḍḍī e, bauht waḍḍī, dohā̃ wiccō̃ waḍḍī kehṛī e? *S* Ēh katāb waḍḍī e.**
4. *T*. This is a large book, that is larger, this is largest. You say it. *P*. This book is large, that is larger, that is largest.	4. *M*. **Ēh waḍḍī katāb e, ōh edū̃ waḍḍī e, ēh sāriā̃ tō̃ waḍḍī e. Tusī̃ ākhō. *S*. Ēh katāb waḍḍī e, ōh edū̃ waḍḍī e, ēh sāriā̃ tō̃ waḍḍī e.**
5. *T*. Look at these rupees, they are round and flat. This book, too, is flat. Say it. *P*. The book is flat, the rupee, too, is flat.	5. *M*. **Ēhnā̃ rupayyā̃ nū̃ wēkhō, gōḷ te capṭē nē̃, ēh katāb wī capṭī e. Tusī̃ ākhō. *S*. Katāb capṭī e, rupayyā wī capṭā e.**
6. *T*. The book is thin, the rupee is thin, which is thinner? *P*. The book is thin, but the rupee is thinner, it is very thin.	6. *M*. **Katāb patlī e, rupayyā wī patlā e, bauhtā patlā kehṛā e? *S*. Katāb patlī e, par rupayyā ōdū̃ patlā e, ōh bauht patlā e.**
7. *T*. Yes, the rupee is the thinnest of all. See these two-anna, four-anna bits, now tell me which is small. *P*. That one is small, this one smaller, this is smallest.	7. *M*. **Āhō jī, rupayyā sāreā̃ nāḷō̃ patlā we. Ēhnā̃ pauḷiā̃, duanniā̃ nū̃ wēkho, menū̃ dassō kēhṛī nikkī e. *S*. Ōh nikkī e, ēh ōdū̃ nikkī e, ēh sārīā̃ nāḷō̃ nikkī e.**
8. *T*. This is a pencil, is it large? *P*. No, it is small. *T*. Here is an-	8. *M*. **Ēh pinsal e, waḍḍī e? *S*. Nehī̃, nikkī e. *M*. Ēh hōr pinsal e,**

	English		Panjabi
	other pencil, is it small? *P.* No, it is larger.		nikki e? *S.* Nehī, odū waḍḍī e.
9.	*T.* We say long and short for pencils, this is long and this is short. P. I am short, John is shorter than I. Is that right?	9.	*M.* Pinsalā̃ nū̃ asī lammīā̃n te nikkīā̃ āhnnē ā̃, ēh lammī e tē ōh nikkī e. *S.* Maĩ madhrā wā̃, Jhaṇḍā mērē nāḷõ madhrā e. Ṭhīk e?
10.	*T.* Yes you are taller than I, and I am shorter than you. The pencil is long, the stick is longer, the rope is longest. I am tall, Jhaṇḍa is taller than Hira, the tree is tallest.	10.	*M.* Jī āh, maĩ tuhāḍḍe nāḷõ madhrā wā̃, tusī mērē nāḷõ ucce ō. Pinsal lammī e, sōṭī ōhde nāḷõ lammī e, rassā sabbhnā̃ tõ lammā e. Maĩ lammā wā̃, Jhaṇḍā Hirē nāḷo uccā e, rukkh sāreā̃ tõ uccā e.
11.	*P.* I am taller than Jhaṇḍa, is that right? *T.* Yes, that is right, Jhaṇḍa is not so tall as you are, and I am shorter than you, you are tallest.	11.	*S.* Maĩ Jhaṇḍē nāḷõ uccā wā̃, ṭhīk e? *M.* Jī āh, ṭhīk e. Jhaṇḍā tuhāḍḍē jēḍḍā uccā nēhī, te maī tuhāḍḍē nāḷō maddhrā wā̃. tusī sāreā̃ tõ uccē o.
12.	*T.* This chair is high, that is not so high, this is higher and that is highest. This paper is good, that is better, this is best. Which is best?	12.	*M.* Ēh kursī uccī e, ōh innī uccī nehī, ēh waddh uccī e, ōh sārīā̃ tõ uccī e. Ēh kāgat caṅgā e, ōh ehde nāḷõ caṅgā e, ōh sāreā̃ tõ caṅgā e. Sāreā̃ tõ caṅgā kēhṛā e?
13.	*T.* I have some money in this hand, I have more	13.	*M.* Ēs hatth wicc kujjh rupae paise nẽ, te ēs

in this hand, I have most in my purse. Now they are all on the table.	hatth wicc waddh nẽ, sāreā̃ tõ waddh baṭūē wicc nẽ. Huṇ sārē mez te nẽ.

Let the teacher take the various articles in the room and compare them. and ask for comparison as to size, height, length, thickness, goodness. Many repetitions will be necessary.

Lesson XX.

1. *T*. What is this? It is a ball, what is it? *P*. It is a ball.	1. *M*. Ēh kī e? ēh khēhnū̃ (gēnd) e, kī e? *S*. Khēhnū̃ e (gēnd).
2. *T*. Is it long? *P*. It is not long a bit. It is—. *T*. Round. *P*. It is round.	2. *M*. Lammā e? *S*. Ōh lammā hai ī nehī̃, ōh ——. *M*. Gōḷ e. *S*. Gōḷ e.
3. *T*. Here is another ball, is it round? *P*. Yes, it is round too.	3. *M*. Ēh ikk hōr khēhnū̃ e, ēh wī gōḷ e? *S*. Āhō, ēh wī gōḷ e.
4. *T*. Is this ball larger or smaller than that one? *P*. It is larger. *T*. Yes, it is larger than that. Is it rounder than that? *P*. No, both are round.	4. *M*. Ēh ōh de nāḷõ waḍḍā e ke nikkā? *S*. Ēh oh de nalõ waḍḍā e. *M*. Ōh de nāḷõ waḍḍā te hai we, ōh de nāḷõ gōḷ wī e? *S*. Nehī̃ dōwẽ gōḷ nẽ.
5. *T*. Here is a rupee, is it round? *P*. Yes the rupee is round, but it is flat.	5. *M*. Ēh wekhō, rupayyā e. Gōḷ e? S. Āhō gōḷ e, par capṭā e.
6. *T*. Is the ball flat? *P*. No the ball is round every way.	6. *M*. Gēnd capṭā e? *S*. Nā, gend sabbhnī pāsī̃ gōḷ e. (*See* Grammar, pp. 77 and 78.)
7. *T*. Here is my pencil. Is it round? *P*. Yes, it is round and long.	7. *M*. Ēh mērī pinsal e, ēh gōḷ e? *S*. Āh, gōḷ e te lammī.

8. *T*. Are these things all round? *P*. A ball is only round, a rupee is round and flat, a pencil is round and long.	8. *M*. Ēh sāriā̃ cīzā̃ gōḷ nẽ? *S*. Gēnd nirā gōḷ e, rupayyā gōḷ tē capṭā e, pinsal gōḷ te lammī e.
9. *T*. See this orange. Is it round like a ball? *P*. The ball is rounder than the orange.	9. *M*. Ēs santare nū̃ wēkh-ō, ēh khēhnū̃ wāṅgar gōḷ e? *S*. Khēhnū̃ san-tare nāḷō̃ waddh gōḷ e.
10. *T*. Is the rupee rounder than the orange? *P*. No, the orange is rounder than the rupee.	10. *M*. Rupayyā santarē nāḷō̃ gōḷ e? *S*. Nĕhī̃, santarā rupayye nāḷō̃ gōḷ e.
11. *T*. What do we do with the ball? *P*. We do thus (showing by pan-tomime throwing, catch-ing, hitting, and saying) what do you call this?	11. *M*. Gēnd nāḷ kī karnē hunnē ā̃? *S*. Aiñ karnē ā̃, ēh nū̃ kī ākhdē ō?
12. *T*. We call this—throw-ing, and this catching, and this hitting. Can you throw? *P*. Yes, give me the ball, catch it.	12. *M*. Asī̃ eh nū̃ suṭṭṇā ahnnē ā̃, te ehnū̃ jhōp-ṇā; eh nū̃ ṭallā marna; tusī̃ suṭṭ sakde ō? *S*. Āhō, mĕnū̃ gēnd dehō, huṇ jhōp laō.
13. *T*. Can you catch a ball? *P*. Yes, and I play tennis a little.	13. *M*. Tusī̃ gēnd jhop sak-dē ō? *S*. Aho, te ṭenis thōṛā bāhḷā khēḍnā wā̃.
14 *T*. What is tennis? We do not play it. Is it like cricket? *P*. No it is another game.	14. *M*. Ṭenis kī e? asī̃ nĕhī̃ ṭenis khēḍdē, kirkaṭ wāṅgar e? *S*. Nĕhī̃ hōr khēḍ e.
15. *T*. Here is a book, is it round? No, it is not, what shape is it? *P*.	15. *M*. Ēh katāb e, ēh gōḷ e? Nĕhī̃ gōḷ nĕhī̃ e, kī shakl e? *S*. Cauṛī

It is flat, but not like the rupee. That is round and flat, this is—.	e, par rupayye wāṅgū̃ nĕhī̃, ōh gōḷ te cauṛā e, ĕh—.
16. *T*. Square and flat. It is thin, too, but the paper is thinner. (Introduce heavy, light, big, little, long, round, some, more, most, all.)	16. *M*. Cauras te capṭā e, nāḷē patlī e, par kāgat edū̃ wī patlā e. (Bhārā, hauḷā, waḍḍā, nikkā, lammā, goḷ, kujjh, waddh, sāreā̃ tō̃ waddh, sāre.)

Lesson XXI.

1. *T*. Here is a penknife, what is it? *P*. It is a penknife. *T*. Take the penknife and put it on the table. *P*. It is now on the table.	1. *M*. Ĕh cakkū e, kī e? *S*. Cakkū e. *M*. Cakkū nū̃ laike mēz tē rakkhō. *S*. Huṇ mēz te wē.
2. *T*. Put it under the chair. *P*. It is under the chair.	2. *M*. Kursī dē hēṭh rakkhō. *S*. Kursī de hēṭh e.
3. *T*. Now under the rug. *P*. It is under the rug.	3. *M*. Huṇ gallcē hēṭh rakkhō. *S*. Galicē hēṭh e.
4. *T*. Take the knife and give it to the lady. *P*. I have given it to her.	4. *M*. Cakkū nū̃ laikē mēmsāhb nū̃ dehō. *S*. Mai mēmsāhb nū̃ dē chaḍḍĕā e.
5. *T*. Madam, who gave you the penknife? *P*. The gentleman gave me the knife.	5. *M*. Mēmsāhb jī, tuhānū̃ kis cakkū dittā? *S*. Sāhb horā̃ menū̃ dittā.
6. *T*. I go and open the door. The door is open, how is the door? *P*. The door is open.	6. *M*. Mai jākē būhā lāhnnā wā̃. Būhā latthā e, būhā kis tarā̃ e? *S*. Būhā latthā e.
7. *T*. I shut it, now how	7. *M*. Mai ōhnū̃ mārnā

is it ? *P.* It is shut.

wā̃. Huṇ kis tarā̃ e? *S.* Mārĕā hōĕā.

8. *T.* Right, who opened the door ? *P.* You opened it. *T.* Who shut the door ? *P.* You shut it.

8. *M.* Ṭhīk e, būhā kis lāhĕā sī? *S.* Tusā̃ lāhĕā sī. *M.* Būhā kis mārĕā sī? *S.* Tūsā̃ mārĕā sī.

9. Who gave you the penknife ? *P.* You gave me the knife. *T.* To whom did you give it ? *P.* I gave the knife to Madam.

9. *M.* Tūhānū̃ cakkū kis dittā? *S.* Tusā̃ mēnū̃ dittā. *M.* Tusā̃ kih nū̃ dittā? *S.* Maī cakkū mēmsāhb nū̃ dittā.

10. *T.* Who went to the door ? *P.* You went. *T.* Why did I go to the door ? *P.* You said, I am going to the door.

10. *M.* Būhē kōḷ kauṇ gēā? *S.* Tusī̃ gaē sao. *M.* Maī kāh de laī būhē kōḷ geā? *S.* Tusā̃ ākhĕā sī paī būhē kōḷ jānnā wā̃.

11. *T.* What did I do at the door ? P. You opened the door and then you shut it. (Long, short, coarse, fine, heavy, light, old, new, weak, strong, young, good, very, bad, cloth, leather, thin, thick.)

11. *M.* Maī būhē kōḷ kī kītā? *S.* Paihlē būhā lāhĕā sājē te magarō̃ mārĕā sājē. [Lammā, nikkā, mōṭā, mahīn, bhārā, hauḷā, purāṇā, nawā̃, māṛā, tagṛā, thōṛī umr dā, umdā, bauht, burā (māṛā nikammā, etc.), kapṛā, cam, patlā, mōṭā.]

Lesson XXII.

1. *T.* I have two books, this is old and that is new. Which is this? *P.* That is the old book. The other is new.

1. *M.* Mērē kōḷ dō katābā̃ nĕ̃, ēh purāṇī e, te ēh nawī̃, ēh kĕhṛī e? *S.* Ōh purāṇī katāb e, dujjī nawī̃ e.

2. *T*. One is thick and one is thin. Which is which ? *P*. The new one is thick, the old one thin.	2. *M*. Ikk mōṭī e, ikk patlī. Kehṛī mōṭī e, te kehṛī patlī? *S*. Nawī̃ mōṭī e te purāṇī patlī.
3. *T*. Yes, the old one is thinner, which is heavier ? (Lifting it.) *P*. The new one is heavier, for it is thicker.	3. *M*. Jī āh, purāṇī bauhtī (edū̃) patlī. e, bauhtī bhārī kĕhṛī e? *S*. Nawī̃ bauhti bhārī e, mōṭī jō hōī.
4. *T*. Right, the thick one is heavier, the thin one is light. What is this one ? *P*. That is thinner and lighter. It is very thin.	4. *M*. Ṭhīk e, mōṭī katāb bauhtī bhārī e, patlī katāb hauḷī e. Āh kis tarā̃ di e? *S*. Ēh ōh de nāḷō̃ patlī te hauḷī e, ēh baṛī patlī e.
5. *T*. How is this compared with the large book ? *P*. It is not so thick or so heavy.	5. *M*. Ēh waḍḍī de mukāble wicc kehōjehī e? *S*. Ēh ōḍḍī mōṭī nĕhī̃, te nā ōḍḍī bhārī.
6. *T*. Here are two pieces of cloth, one is good. Are both good ? *P*. No, one is good and one is bad.	6. *M*. Ēh kapṛō de dō ṭōṭē nē̃, ikk caṅgā e. Dōwē̃ caṅgē nē̃? *S*. Nehī̃ ikk caṅgā e, te ikk māṛā.
7. *T*. Yes, it is bad, it was good, but it is old. This piece is new. *P*. The new is better than the old.	7. *M*. Jī āhō, māṛā e, caṅgā sī, par purāṇā e; ēh ṭukṛā nawā̃ e. *S*. Purāṇē nāḷō̃ nawā̃ caṅgā e.
8. *T*. Yes, the new is strong, the old is weak. *P*. Is this old book weak ?	8. *M*. Āhō jī, nawā̃ ḍāhḍā e, purāṇā kamzōr e. *S*. Ēh purāṇī katāb kamzōr e?
9. *T*. No, books are not strong and weak, they	9. *M*. Nĕhī̃ katābā̃ tagrīā̃ te kamzōr nĕhī̃ hun-

are good and bad. Old books are often the best. *P.* The old cloth is weaker than the new cloth, but the old book is better than the new book. Is that right?

diã, ōh caṅgiā te buriā hundiā nẽ; kinnī wārī purāṇiā katābā sabbhnā tõ caṅgiā hundiā nẽ. *S.* Purāṇā kapṛā nawẽ nāḷõ kamzōr e, par purāṇī katāb nawī nāḷõ caṇgī e, ēh ṭhīk e?

10. *T.* Yes, that is right in this case, it is not always true. *P.* Is Gaṇḍū strong or weak?

10. *M.* Jī āh, huṇ te gall ṭhīk e, kadī kadāī ṭhīk nĕhī hundī. *S.* Gaṇḍū tagṛā e ke māṛā.

11. *T.* Yes, we say men are strong or weak. Gaṇḍū is strong. *P.* Is Gaṇḍū stronger than Nūr?

11. *M.* Āhō asī ākh saknē ā pai jaṇē tagṛē nẽ yā māṛē. Gaṇḍū tagṛā e. *S.* Gaṇḍū Nūre nāḷõ tagṛā e?

12. *T.* Yes. but Jummā is the strongest of all. *P.* Is Pira older than his brothers?

12. *M.* Āhō jī, par Jummā sāreā nāḷõ tagṛā e. *S.* Umr wicc Pīrā apneā bhrāwā nāḷõ waḍḍā e?

13. *T.* Gaṇḍū is older than all his brothers. *P.* Is Jummā younger than Karmū?

13. *M.* Gaṇḍū sāreā bhrāwā wiccõ waḍḍā e. *S.* Jummā Karmū nāḷõ nikkā e?

14. *T.* No, he is not younger, they are twins. This cloth is coarse, it is strong, too, is this coarse? *P.* No, it is not coarse, it is weak, too.

14. *M.* Nehī jī, nikkā nehī e, jauṛē nẽ. Ēh kapṛā mōṭā we, ḍāhḍā wī e; ēh mōṭā e? *S.* Nĕhī mōṭā nĕhī e, nāḷē kamzōr e.

15. *T.* Yes, it is very fine cloth, and not very

15. *M.* Jī āh, baṛā mahīn kapṛā e, bauht ḍāhḍā

strong. *P*. Here is some strong cloth. It, too, is coarse.	nohī. *S*. Ēh ḍāhḍā kapṛā e, ēh wī mōṭā e.
16. *T*. Who is stronger, Jummā or Shamsū? *P*. Shamsū is stronger, he is the strongest of all.	16. *M*. Tagṛā kehṛā we, Jummā ke Shamsū? *S*. Shamsū tagṛā e sārĕā bandĕā wiccō̃ ōhī tagṛā e.
17. *T*. Is cloth or leather stronger (showing leather). *P*. Do you call this leather?	17. *M*. Kapṛā ḍāhḍā hondā e ke camm? *S*. Ēhnū̃ camm āhnde ō?
18. *T*. Yes, we call it cow (leather). *P*. Good leather is stronger than this cloth. Some cloth is stronger than leather.	18. *M*. Jī āhō, ēhnū̃ gōkā (camm) āhnnē ā̃. *S*. Caṅgā camṛā ēs kapṛē nāḷō̃ ḍāhḍā hondā e, kōī kapṛā camṛē nāḷō̃ ḍahḍā hondā e.
19. *T*. Yes, but the strongest leather is stronger than the strongest paper.	19. *M*. Jēhṛā sāreā̃ tō̃ ḍāhḍā camṛā e, ōh ḍāhḍē tō̃ ḍāhḍē kāgat nāḷō̃ ḍāhḍā hondā e.

Lesson XXIII.

Colours, red. white, blue, green, fiery red, yellow, black.	Raṅg, lāl (sūhā), ciṭṭā or (bagga), līlā (dark blue), asmānī (light blue), harā, guṭai, pīḷā, kāḷā.

Get some strips of cloth, paper and some beads or other articles of these colours and ask questions till the pupil can instantly answer for all the colours.

P. This is a black bead, that is a white piece of cloth, that is a red paper.	*S*. Ēh kāḷā maṇkā e, ōh ciṭṭē kapṛē dā ṭōṭā e, ēh lāl kāgad e.
T. Show me a green bead, show me a yellow cloth, etc., etc.	*M*. Mēnū̃ ikk harā maṇkā wakhāō, menū̃ pīḷā kapṛā wakhāo.

Lesson XXIV.

1. *T*. This is my hand, here are both hands, where is your hand? *P*. This is my hand, here are both hands.	1. *M*. **Ēh mērā hatth e, ēh dōwẽ hatth nẽ, tuhāḍḍā hatth kitthē wē? *S*. Ēh mērā hatth e, ēh dōwẽ hatth nẽ.**
2. *T*. Tell him to show his hand. *P*. Where is your hand? *A*. Here is my hand, here are both my hands.	2. *M*. **Ōh nū̃ ākhṇā pai hatth wikhāē. *S*. Tērā hatth kitthe wē? *A*. Ēh mērā hatth e, ēh dōwẽ hatth nẽ.**
3. *T*. All have two hands, altogether we have two, four, six, eight hands. *P*. One hand, two hands, three hands, four hands, five hands. Is that right?	3. *M*. **Sārēā̃ de dō dō hatth hunde nẽ. Sāḍḍēā̃ sārēā̃ de dō, cār, chē, aṭṭh hatth nẽ. *S*. Ikk hatth, dō hatth, trai hatth, cār hatth, panj hatth, ṭhīk e?**
4. *T*. Yes, that is the way we say it. This is my right hand, I tell you, this is my left, I tell you. *P*. This is my right hand, this is my left. Is this my right——?	4. *M*. **Jī āh, esē tarhā̃ āhnnē ā̃, ēh mērā sajjā hatth jē, ēh mērā khabbā jē. *S*. Ēh mērā sajjā hatth e, ēh mērā khabbā je. Ēh mērā sajjā——?**
5. *T*. Foot, yes, that is your right foot, and that is your left foot. This is my ear. *P*. This is my right ear, this is my left ear. I have two ears.	5. *M*. **Pair, āhō ōh tuhāḍḍā sajjā pair e, te ōh tuhāḍḍā khabbā pair e, ēh mērā kann e. *S*. Ēh mērā sajjā kann e, ēh mērā khabbā kann e, mērē dō kann nẽ.**
6. *T*. Have you two of any other member? *P*.	6. *M*. **Hōr wī kujjh tuhāḍḍē badan wicc dō**

English	Panjabi
Yes, I have two hands, two feet, two eyes (one ear, two ears, three ears).	dō hunde nẽ? *S.* Āhō, mērē dō hatth, dō pair, dō akkhīā̃ nẽ (ikk kann, dō kann, trai kann).
7. *T.* Yes, so one foot, two feet, three feet, one eye, two eyes, three eyes. *P.* We all have two eyes, two ears, two hands, two feet.	7. *M.* Jī āh, te esē tarhā̃ ikk pair, dō pair, trai pair, ikk akkh, dō akkhīā̃, trai akkhīā̃. *S.* Sāḍḍēā̃ sārēā̃ dīā̃ dō dō akkhīā̃, dō dō kann, dō dō hatth, dō dō pair hundē nẽ.
8. *T.* This is my right arm, this is my left. *P.* Here is my right arm, here is my left, what is this?	8. *M.* Ēh mēri sajjī bā̃h e, te ēh mērī khabbī bā̃h e. *S.* Ēh mērī sajjī bā̃h e, te ēh mērī khabbī bā̃h e, ēh kī e?
9. *T.* That is your right leg, that your left, now I will keep pointing out and you go on telling the name, or I will keep naming and you go on pointing out. Which is your right foot, left arm, right ear, left eye, right hand, left leg, both hands, both eyes, both ears? Touch your right ear with your left hand, your right eye with your right hand. Put your left hand on your right arm, put your right foot on your left foot. Now	9. *M.* Ēh tuhāḍḍī sajjī latt e, te ōh tuhāḍḍī khabbī latt e, huṇ maī ishārā karā̃gā te tusī nā̃ dassde jāō, yā̃ maī nā̃ lāā̃gā te tusī ishārā kardē jāō. Kēhṛā e tuhāḍḍā sajjā pair, khabbī bā̃h, sajjā kann, khabbī akkh, sajjā hatth, khabbī latt, dōwẽ hatth, dōwẽ akkhā̃, dōwẽ kann, sajjē kann nū̃ khabbā hatth lāō, sajjī akkh nū̃ sajjā hatth lāō, sajjī bā̃h uttē khabbā

I will go on putting my hand on and you keep on naming.	hatth rakkhō, sajjā pair khabbē pair uttē rakkho. Huṇ maĩ hatth lāndā jāãgā, tusĩ nā̃ lendē jāō.

Lesson XXV.

1. *T*. What have I in my hand? *P*. A book. *T*. Where is the book? *P*. It is in your hand.	1. *M*. Mērē hatth wicc kī e? *S*. Katāb. *M*. Katāb kitthe e? *S*. Tuhāḍḍē hatth wicc.
2. *T*. What are these? (I tell you) We call them fingers, one finger, two fingers, three fingers, how many are there? Count them. *P*. 1, 2, 3, 4, 5, 6, 7, 8, 9, 10.	2. *M*. Ēh kī nē? ehnā̃ nū̃ asī̃ uṅgḷā̃ āhndē jē (*see* App., p. 124), ikk uṅgaḷ, dō uṅgḷā̃, trai uṅgḷā̃, kinnīā̃ nē? Giṇ laō nē. *S*. Ikk, dō, trai, cār, panj, chē, satt, aṭṭh, naū̃, das.
3. *T*. Right, we have each ten fingers, how many fingers have you? *P*. I have ten fingers.	3. *M*. Ṭhik ē, sāḍḍīā̃ das das uṅgḷā̃ nē, tuhāḍḍīā̃ kinnīā̃ nē? *S*. Mērīā̃ das uṅgḷā̃ nē.
4. *T*. What have you on your feet? Toes. *P*. I have ten toes on my two feet.	4. *M*. Pairā̃ dīā̃ kī je? Uṅgḷā̃? *S*. Mēreā̃ dū̃h pairā̃ dīā̃ das uṅgḷā̃ nē.
5. *T*. How many fingers are there on one hand? *P*. I have five fingers on one hand.	5. *M*. Ikk hatth dīā̃ kinnīā̃ uṅgḷā̃ nē? *S*. Ikk hatth dīā̃ panj uṅgḷā̃ nē.
6. *T*. How many books are here? *P*. One, two.. six books. *T*. How many books have I? *P*. You have six books.	6. *M*. Ētthe kinnīā̃ katābā̃ nē? *S*. Ikk, dō,—chē katābā̃. *M*. Mērē kōḷ kinnīā̃ katābā̃ nē? *S*. Tuhāḍḍē kōḷ chē katābā̃ nē.

7. *T.* How many have you? *P.* I have very many. *T.* How many have you here? *P.* I have three here.

7. *M.* Tuhāḍḍē kōḷ kinnīā̃ nē̃? *S.* Mērē kōḷ bauht sārīā̃ nē̃. *M.* Ētthē tuhāḍḍīā̃ kinnīā̃ nē̃? *S.* Ētthē mērē kōḷ trai nē̃.

8. *T.* (I ask you) Have you a pencil here? *P.* Yes, I have three here. *T.* (I ask you) Have you a pen? *P.* Yes, I have one and madam has oṇe. We have two pens.

8. *M.* Ētthē pinsal hai je? *S.* Āhō, trai nē̃. *M.* Kalam hai je? *S.* Āhō, mērē kōḷ ikk e, te mēmsāhb kōḷ ikk. sāḍḍē kōḷ dō kalamā̃ nē̃.

9. *T.* Is this your pen? *P.* No, that is madam's pen. *T.* Has Hira a pen? *P.* Yes, Hira has four pens.

9. *M.* Ēh tuhāḍḍī kalam e? *S.* Nĕhī̃, ōh mēmsāhb dī e. *M.* Hīrē kōḷ kalam e? *S.* Āhō, Hīrē kōḷcār kalamā̃ nē̃.

10. *T.* Is this your chair? *P.* No, that is not my chair, this is my chair. *T.* Have you any tables? *P.* We have none. We have no dining table, there is a study-table.

10. *M.* Ēh tuhāḍḍī kursī e? *S.* Nĕhī̃, ōh mērī kursī nĕhī̃ e, mērī kursī ēh we. *M.* Tuhāḍḍe kōḷ mēz haiṇ? *S.* Kōī nĕhī̃, sāḍḍā khāṇe dā kōī mēz nĕhī̃ e, daftar dā ikk mēz hai we.

11. *T.* Have you a house? *P.* No, we have no house. This is a mission house.

11. *M.* Tuhāḍḍī kōī kōṭhī e? *S.* Nehī̃, sāḍḍī kōī nĕhī, ēh kōṭhī mishan dī e.

12. *T.* Have you a rug, buggy, cow, horse, book, coat, hat? etc., etc., changing the form of the question thus, Has Mr. Smith a cow, have

12. *M.* Tuhāḍḍē kōḷ galīcā e? (bagghī, gā̃, ghōṛā, kōṭ, ṭōpī), Smit sāhb de kōḷ kōī gā̃ hai? Tuhāḍḍe te mēmsāhb kōḷ ghōṛā e? Nehī̃,

you and madam a horse, etc., requiring a fuller answer thus, No, Mr. Smith has not a cow, yes, madam and I have two horses, etc.

Smit sāhb kōḷ kōī gā̃ nehī̃. Āhō, mēre te mēmsāhb kōḷ dō ghōṛe nẽ.

Lesson XXVI.

The ordinary form of the imperative, so that the pupil may not use honorifics in addressing servants.

1. *T.* Here is a servant. Tell him to do these things for you. *P.* Go and get that book. *S.* Very well, sir.

1. **M. Ēh ikk naukar e, ēh nū̃ hukm dēhō pai eh kamm tuhāḍe lai kare. S. Ōh katāb jākē lai ā. N. Caṅga jī.**

2. *P.* Put that book on the table, no, do not put it on the table, put it on the chair. Do not steal my money. *S.* No sir, I will not.

2. **S. Ōh katāb mēz utte rakkh, nehī̃, mēz te nā rakkh, kursī te rakkh. M. Mēre paise nā curāṇe. N. Taubā jī, maī nehī̃ kujjh curāndā.**

3. Sit down, get up, go to the door, shut it, open it, open the window, shut it, order the buggy, order dinner, call the cook, bring the post.

3. **Baih jā, uṭṭh khlō, būhē tikar jāh, mār sū, lāh sū, bārī lāh, mār sū, bagghī jōṇ dā hukm dē, khāṇē dā hukm dē, khā̃sāmē̃ nū̃ kuā, ḍāk lai ā.**

4. Post this letter, go and get meat, bring bread, bring six loaves of bread, bring good butter, ask for good flour to-day, bring a bag of coal.

4. **Ēh ciṭṭhī ḍāk wicc pāī̃, jākē gōsht lĕāwī̃, rōṭī lai ā, chē rōṭīā̃ lai ā, caṅgā makkhaṇ lai ā, ajj caṇgā āṭā maṅgī̃, kōḷeā̃ dī bōrī lai ā.**

5. Call me a good cook, where

5. **Mērē lai caṇgā khā̃sāmā̃**

is the waterman? Bring a workman to mend the broken table, and one to repair the chimney, go out and buy a book.	bulāī, māshkī kitthe wē, tuṭṭe hoe mēz nū̃ baṇāṇ wāstē ikk tarkhāṇ nū̃ sadd, te dhū̃kash nū̃ baṇāṇ wāstē rāj lai ā. Jākē katāb mull lai.
6. Write a letter to your brother, beat that dog, do not beat the donkey. Tell me your name, take this letter and give it to Mr. Jones and come back quickly.	6. Apṇē bhrā nū̃ ciṭṭhī likkh, ōs kuttē nū̃ mārī̃, khōtē nū̃ nā mār. Apṇā nā̃ dass, ēh ciṭṭhī laike Jones sāhb nū̃ dēī̃ te hallke part āwī.
7. Cut this paper with a knife, cut this cloth with these scissors, call a barber to cut my hair, cook the potatoes with the meat, boil the water.	7. Ēh kāgad cakkū nāḷ waḍḍhī̃, ēh kapṛā kaincī nāḷ katar, nāī nū̃ sadd pai mērē wāḷ katrē, ālūā̃ nū̃ gōsht de nāḷ rinnhī̃, paṇī kāṛh.
8. Make tea quickly, rise early and bake the bread, go to the other room and make the bed, hear what I say, run to the doctor's and call him here quickly.	8. Cāh chētī baṇā, sawērē uṭṭhkē. rōṭī pakā, dujjē kamre jākē bistrā kar, mērī gall suṇ, ḍākdār sāhb de koḷ bhajjke jā tē ohnā̃ nū̃ shitābī etthe kuā.
9. Show me your hand, send your son to bring the vegetables to-day, wait here till the postman comes, go and find the boy's ball, bring the baby's coat.	9. Hatth wakhā, ajj apṇē puttar nū̃ ghallkē sabzī maṅgā, ētthē ḍāk wāḷē nū̃ uḍīk, jā, muṇḍēā̃ de khēhnū̃ nū̃ labbh lai, nikkē bāwē dā kōṭ lēā.
10. Give me madam's hat, do	10. Mēmsāhb dī ṭōpī mēnū̃

this work quickly, stand up, sit down.	dēh, ēh kamm chētī kar, uṭṭh khlō, baih jā.

Lesson XXVII.

1. *Doctor*. Good morning, what is the matter with you? *P*. I am ill, so I have come. *D*. How long have you been ill? *P*. For a long time.	1. *D*. Salām, kī hōĕā ī? *B*. Maī bamār ā̃, tā̃ karke āĕā. *D*. Kadō̃ tō̃ bamār ē̃? *B*. Cōkhē cir tō̃.
2. *D*. Well, what is the matter then? Have you fever too? *P*. A little, sometimes it comes daily and sometimes it misses two days. *D*. Had you fever yesterday and to-day? *P*. No, but to-day is the turn.	2. *D*. Halā, kī pher hōĕā? Kass wī hai ī? *B*. Jī āh, thōṛī e, kadī rōz caṛhdī ē, kadī dō din chaḍḍkē. *D*. Kall kass hai sī? te ajj? *B*. Nēhī̃ jī, par ajj wārī e.
3. *D*. All right, here is medicine, take it in a swallow of water and when it operates take these four pills, two in the morning and two in the evening. *P*. Thank you, shall I come again?	3. *D*. Caṇgā, ēh dawāī e, pāṇī dē ghuṭṭ nāḷ khā, te jad asr hōwē ēh cār gōḷīā̃ khā, dō waḍḍē wēḷē, te dō shāmī̃. *B*. Tūhāḍḍī mĕhrbānī e, maī phēr āwā̃?
4. *D*. Yes, if you are not well after taking the pills.	4. *D*. Āhō jē gōḷīā̃ khākē wall nā hōwē̃, tā̃ āwī̃.
5. *D*. Well, what is your trouble? Sore eyes, how long? *P*. Three months.	5. *D*. Hachchā̃ tēnū̃ kī hōĕā, akkhīā̃ āīā̃ hōīā̃ nī? Kadō̃ dī gall e? *B*. Trai mahīnē hoē nē̃.

6. Three months! Why didn't you come sooner? Take this medicine and continue to drop it into your eyes for three days, four times a day, and then put on this yellow ointment.	6. *D*. Trai mahīnē! paihlē kyū̃ nēhī ō āeā? Ēh dawāī lēllai te tinnā̃ dinā̃ tīkar akkhīā̃ wicc pāndā jā, cār wērī dihāṛē wicc, te ōh de picche ēh pīḷī malham lā. (*See* Appdix. p. 124.)
7. *D*. Well, mother, what can I do for you? Oh, it is the little girl that is ill, is it? *P*. She has an enlarged spleen. She has had fever off and on for three months.	7. *D*. Kyū̃ māī, tērē wāstē kī karā̃, acchā, kuṛī maḷī hōī e? *B*. Ohnū̃ tiḷī e, tinn mahīnē tō̃ kass caṛhdī rēhī e.
8. *D*. Poor child, has she still fever? I see her pulse shows she has still some. Put out your tongue, little girl, that's right. Keep giving her goat's milk three times a day and along with it keep giving this medicine.	8. *D*. Ōhō wacārī, aje wī kass caṛhdī sū? Hatth wēkkhaṇ tō̃ patā laggdā e pai ajē wī e, jībh kaḍḍh kākīē, bas ṭhīk e, ēhnū̃ bākrā duddh rōz trai wērī piāī̃ karī̃, te ēh dawāī wī nāḷō nāḷ dēndī jā.

Lesson XXVIII.

1. *T*. We must write to-day, let us get pens, paper and ink, and let us write. *P*. Very well, we have pens, ink and paper.	1. *M*. Ajj asā̃ zarūr likkhṇā e, kalam te shiāhī te kāgat lēllēīyē te likkhīye. *S*. Caṅgā jī, sāḍḍē kōḷ par te shiāhī te kāgat haiṇ.
2. *T*. Write now, I am writing, what am I doing? *P*. You are writing. I, too, am	2. *M*. Huṇ likkhō, maī peā likkhnā wā̃, maī̃ kī peā karnā wā̃? *S*. Tusī̃ pae likkhde ō,

writing.	maĩ wī likkhnā wā̃ peā.
3. *T*. You write very well. Do you write Panjabi as well as you write English? *P*. No, I have been writing English for many years and I am only now beginning to write Panjabi.	3. *M*. Baṛā hacchā likkhde ō, jikaṇ Aṅgrēzī likkhde o, ose tarhā̃ Panjābī wī likhde o? *S*. Nehī̃, Aṅgrēzī te maī bauht warhēā̃ tõ likhnā wā̃ te Panjābī te aje huṇe shurū kītī.
4. *T*. Madam writes very well. She writes better than some others. *P*. Yes, she writes better than I do, she writes very well.	4. *M*. Mēmsāhb horī baṛā hacchā likkhdē nẽ, kaiā̃ tõ canga likhde nẽ. *S*. Āho, ōh mērē nāḷō wall likhde nẽ, ōh baṛā sōhṇā likhde nẽ.
5. *T*. Did she write this letter? *P*. Yes, she wrote this letter yesterday. *T*. Who wrote this letter yesterday? *P*. Madam wrote that letter yesterday.	5. *M*. Ēh ciṭṭhī ōhnā̃ likkhī? *S*. Āhō kall likkhī sāṇē. *M*. Ēh ciṭṭhī kall kis likkhī? *S*. Mēmsāhb horā̃ ōh ciṭṭhī kall likkhī sī.
6. *T*. When did you come here? *P*. I came at nine o'clock. When did you come?	6. *M*. Tusī̃ kadõ ētthē āē saō? *S*. Maī naū wajē āēā, tusī̃ kadõ āē?
7. *T*. I came at nine too. When did you eat breakfast? *P*. At eight o'clock. *T*. When did you get up? *P*. I got up this morning at half past six.	7. *M*. Maī wī naū wajē āēā, tusā̃ hāzrī kadõ khādhī? *S*. Aṭṭh wajē. *M*. Uṭṭhe kadõ saō? *S*. Ajj fajrī̃ maī sāḍhē chē wajē uṭṭhēā.
8. *T*. I got up at five.	8. *M*. Maī panj waje uṭ-

When do you retire? *P.* About ten, and you?	ṭhēā sā, tusī̃ saundē kadō̃ o? *S.* Kōī das wajē dē nēṛē trēṛē, te tusī̃?
9. *T.* I, too, go to bed at ten, what time did the teacher go home yesterday? *P.* He went home at four.	9. *M.* Maĩ wī das wajē saunnā wā̃, kall astād kēhṛē wēḷē ghar geā sī? *S.* Ōh cār waje ghar gēā.
10. *T.* Did you get your foreign mail yesterday? *P.* Yes, it came in the morning.	10. *M.* Kall wilaitī ḍāk miḷī sājē? *S.* Āhō, sawere āī sī.
11. *T.* How many letters did you get? *P.* I got three and Madam got five. Did you get anything else? *P.* Yes, we got books, papers and cards.	11. *M.* Kinnīā̃ ciṭṭhīā̃ miḷīā̃ sājē? *S.* Mēnū̃ trai, te mēmsāhb horā̃ nū̃ panj. *M.* Hōrwī kujjh miḷēā sājē? *S.* Jī āh, sanū̃ katābā̃ te akhbārā̃ te kāṭ mile saṇ.
12. *T.* Where did they come from? *P.* Some from England, some from America, and some of them from Italy. Two were from my home.	12. *M.* Uh kitthō̃ āē sāṇ? *S.* Kujjh Inglistānō̃, kujjh Amrīka tō̃ te kujjh Iṭalī tō̃; dō mērē gharō̃ āē saṇ.
13. *T.* Were there no Indian letters? *P.* Yes, there were two. *T.* Who brought them? *P.* The postman brought them.	13. *M.* Ēs mulkh diā̃ kōī ciṭṭhīā̃ nehī̃ saṇ? *S.* Āhō, dō saṇ. *M.* Kis āndīā̃ saṇ? *S.* Ḍākwāḷē lēāndīā̃ saṇ.
14. *T.* Did he bring any for me? *P.* No, he gave me none for you. *T.* Did you ask him? *P.* Yes, I did, but he	14. *M.* Mērē wāstē wī kōī lēāndiā̃? *S.* Nēhī̃, tuhāḍḍē wāstē mēnū̃ kōī nēhī̃ dittī. *M.* Tusā̃ puccheā sī? *S.*

said there were none for you.	Āhō pucchēā sī, par ōs ākhēā ōhnā dī kōī nēhī, akhē. (*See* Gram. p. 74.)
15. *T*. Write these letters, hold your pen thus, make that letter straight, make this letter round. Put the dots under that letter, put the points over those letters. The ink is too thick, I will put some water in it. Let us get some blotting paper next time. Now that is enough for to-day.	15. *M*. Ēh harf likkhō, kalam aiñ phaṛō, ōh harf siddhā baṇāō, jī, ēh harf gōḷ baṇāō, ōs harf hēṭh nukte pāō, ohnā harfā dē utte dande baṇāō. Shiāhī saṅhṇi e, maī pāṇī pāṇnā; aglī wārī kujjh blāṭiṅ (siāhī-caṭṭ) lēāwīyē, huṇ ajj wāste baṛa e.

Lesson XXIX.

1. *T*. Good morning. *P*. Good morning, is it nine o'clock? *T*. Yes, nine comes quickly. Let us write again to-day. *P*. Here are pen and paper. Show me how to write "swad."	1. *M*. Salām jī. *S*. Salām, naū wajj gaē nē? *M*. Jī āh, naū jaldī wajj jāndē nē, ajj asī phēr likkhīyē. *S*. Ah wēkhā kalam te kāgaz. Menū suād dassō.
2. *T*. Do you wish to learn it now? *P*. Yes, I want to learn to write, but still more to talk. Talking first and then writing.	2. *M*. Huṇ sikkhṇā cāhnde o? *S*. Āhō, par likkhṇā sikkhaṇ nāḷō, maī bōlṇā waddh sikkhṇā cāhnnā wā, paihle bōlṇā, magarō likkhṇā.
3. *T*. Good, let us write the things that you know already. *P*. Yes, that will be right.	3. *M*. Caṅgā jī, asī ōhī gallā likkhīye jēhṛiā tuhanū aggē aundiā nē. *S*. Āhō esē tarhā ṭhīk e.

4. *T.* This is a good pen, hold it thus and write. *P.* It is hard to write this language.

4. *M.* **Ēh kalam caṅgi e, aiñ phaṛkē likkhō. *S.* Ēs zabān dā likkhṇā aukkhā e.**

5. *T.* First write these simple words, and then the harder ones. Madam writes nicely, she will write Panjabi well. *P.* Yes, she writes well.

5. *M.* **Paihle ēh sukhalle lafs likkho, te picchē jehṛe aukkhe nẽ, mēmsāhb baṛā acchā likhdē nẽ, ōh Panjābi ṭhīk likkhaṇgē. *S.* Āhō, hacchā likhdē nẽ.**

6. *T.* You will write one hour to-day. *P.* Shall we write an hour tomorrow?

6. *M.* **Ajj ikk ghaiṇṭā likkhōgē. *S.* Bhalke wī ghaiṇṭā likkhīyē?**

7. *T.* Yes, I will come at nine and we shall write till ten. *P.* It is hard to learn to speak and write Panjabi.

7. *M.* **Āhō jī, maī naū waje āwāgā, te das waje tīkar likkhāgē. *S.* Baṛī muskal nāḷ asī Panjābī bōlṇī te likkhṇī sikkh sakne ā.**

8. *T.* Yes, it takes a great many days of hard work. Is this ink good? I got it from a good shop. *P.* It does not seem to me good.

8. *M.* **Āhō jī, bauht dinā tīkar sakht mehnat karnī paindī e, ēh shiāhī caṅgi e? Maī caṇgī haṭṭī tō leī sī. *S.* Mēnū caṇgī nehī jāpdī.**

9. *T.* It is too thick. *P.* Shall I put water in? *T.* Yes, it needs more water, put some in.

9. *M.* **Baṛī saṅhṇī e. *S.* Maī pāṇī pā? *M.* Āhō jī, pāṇī dī lōṛ e, thōṛā jehā pāō.**

10. *T.* Is this English ink? *S.* No, it is country ink. *P.* Who makes

10. *M.* **Ēh Aṇgrēzī shiāhī e? *S.* Nehī, dēsī shiāhī e. *S.* Baṇāndā kauṇ**

it ? *T*. I do not know. I always get it at the shop.	e? *M*. Mēnū̃ nēhī̃ patā, maī hatṭī tō̃ lennā hunnā wā̃.
11. *T*. Write slowly, now write this word again. That letter is well made, this is crooked, see, there are points over this letter. That letter has points under it. There are two points over that letter. Make this part of this letter straight. This is a curve.	11. *M*. Zarā hauḷī hauḷī likkhō ēh lafz phēr likkhō, ōh harf caṅgā baṇēā hōēā e, ēh harf ḍiṅgā e, wēkhō ēs harf de uttē nukte nē̃, te ōh de hēṭh nukte nē̃, ōs harf de utte dō nukte nē̃. Harf de ēs hissē nū̃ siddhā baṇāō, ēh gōḷ e.
12. *P*. Now we ought to stop, let us talk. *T*. Yes, it is ten o'clock now, we must read.	12. *S*. Huṇ chaḍḍṇā cāhīdā e, huṇ gallā̃ kariyē. *M*. Āhō jī, huṇ das waj gaē nē̃, huṇ paṛhnā cāhīdā e.
13. *P*. No, let us talk first. First talking, then reading. *T*. Yes, children learn to talk before they learn to read, so you do the same.	13. *S*. Nēhī̃ paihlē gallā̃ kariyē, paṛhn tō̃ paihle gallā̃ karīdiā̃ nē̃. *M*. Añāṇē paihlē bōlṇā sikhdē nē̃, te magarō̃ paṛhnā, tussī̃ wī esē tarhā̃ karēō.

Lesson XXX.

1. *T*. Can you read English ? *P*. Yes, I read English easily, but not Panjabi.	1. *M*. Tusī̃ Aṅgrēzī paṛh sakde ō? *S*. Aṅgrēzī tē maī asānī nāḷ paṛh saknā wā̃, par Panjābī nēhī̃ paṛh sakdā.
2. *T*. Did you learn to speak English from reading	2. *M*. Tusā̃ paṛh paṛhke Aṅgrēzī sikkhī? *S*.

it? *P.* No, I learned it from my parents by talking.	**Nĕhĩ, māpeā̃ kōḷō̃ bōldĕā̃ bōldĕā̃ sikkhī sī.**
3. *T.* All languages ought to be learned this way—by the ear. No one can get a language through the eye from a book. *P.* Oh yes, we learn Latin and Greek from our books.	3. *M.* **Sārīā̃ bōlīā̃ esē tarhā̃ sikkhṇīā̃ cāhīdīā̃ nĕ, suṇ suṇke. Kōī katābā̃ paṛh paṛhke rehī sikkh sakdā. *S.* Ahō asī̃ Lātīnī te Yunānī paṛh paṛhke sikhnē ā̃.**
4. *T.* Do you speak Latin and Greek? *P.* No, but we learn lessons from our books.	4. *M.* **Lātīnī Yunānī bōl sakdē ō? *S.* Nĕhĩ, par sabak katābā̃ tō̃ yād karnē ā̃.**
5. *T.* Yes, lots of people study lessons from books, but no one can learn to speak this way. You must hear the sound of the words. You learned English from your mother. You learn Panjabi from Panjabis.	5. *M.* **Bauht sārē lōk katābā̃ tō̃ sabak yād kardē nĕ, par kōī bōlṇā ēs tarhā̃ nĕhī̃ sikkh sakdā. Gallā̃ suṇṇīā̃ cāhīdīā̃ nĕ. Aṅgrēzī tusā̃ apṇī mā̃ kōḷō̃ sikkhī, Panjābī Panjābīā̃ kōḷō̃ sikhde o.**
6. *T.* Can you open the door? Say it this way. I can open the door. *T.* Can you shut the door? *P.* I can shut the door.	6. *M.* **Būhā lāh sakde ō? aiṅ ākhō, maī būhā lāh saknā wā̃. *S.* Maī būhā lāh saknā wā̃. *M.* Būhā mār sakde ō? *S.* Maī būhā mār saknā wā̃.**
7. *T.* Can you sit on this chair? *P.* Yes, I can sit on this chair.	7. *M.* **Ēs kursī utte baih sakde ō? *S.* Āhō, ēs kursī te baih saknā wā̃.**

8. *T*. Can I take a book off the table and put it on the chair? *P*. Yes, you can take a book off the table and put it on the chair.

8. *M*. Maĩ kitāb mēz tõ cukkkē kursī utte rakkh saknā wā̃? *S*. Āhō, tusī̃ katāb mēz tõ cukkkē kursī utte rakkh sakdē ō.

9. *T*. Can a boy sit all day on a chair? *P*. No, a boy cannot sit all day on a chair.

9. *M*. Sārā din muṇḍā kursī te baih sakdā e? *S*. Nĕhī̃, sārā din muṇḍā kursī te nĕhī̃ baih sakdā.

10. *T*. Can you tell the time by the clock? *P*. Yes, it is eleven o'clock.

10. *M*. Tusī̃ gharī wēkhke wakat dass sakde ō? *S*. Āhō, yārā̃ waje nẽ.

11. *T*. Can you play bat and ball? *P*. Yes, I can.

11. *M*. Khēhnũ ṭallā khēḍ sakde ō? *S*. Āhō khēhnũ ṭallā khēḍ saknā wā̃.

12. *T*. Can all Americans play bat and ball? *P*. No, not all can play. Madam is an American and she cannot play. Most boys play bat and ball at school.

12. *M*. Sārē Amrīkṇiē khēhnũ ṭallā khēḍ sakde nẽ? *S*. Nĕhī̃ sārē nĕhī̃ khēḍ sakdē, mēmsāhb Amrīkā de nẽ, te ōh nĕhī̃ khēḍ sakdē, muṇḍē te askhar skūle khēhnũ ṭallā khēḍdē nẽ.

13. *T*. Can you see what is in my hand? *P*. Yes, it is a watch. *T*. Can you hear it tick? *P*. Yes, it says tick, tick, tick.

13. *M*. Tusī̃ wēkh sakde ō paī mere hatth wicc kī e? *S*. Jī āh, gharī e. *S*. Ṭik ṭik suṇ sakde ō? *S*. Āhō, ṭik ṭik kardī e.

14. *T*. Can you see its hands? *P*. Yes, I see its hands. It has three

14. *M*. Sūīā̃ dissdīā̃ je? *S*. Āhō, trai sūīā̃ sū. *M* Kĕhṛī caldī e? *S*.

hands. *T.* Which one is moving? *P.* The little one appears to be moving.	Nikkī caldī dissdī e.
15. *T.* Do you write to America? *P.* Yes, I write to America every week.	15. *M.* Tusī̃ Amrīke nū̃ likhde ō? *S.* Āhō jī, aṭṭhī̃ dinī̃ likhnā wā̃.
16 *T.* Can you throw and catch a ball? *P.* Yes, I can throw and catch a ball.	16. *M.* Khēhnū̃ suṭṭ sakde ō te jhōp sakdē ō? *S.* Āhō khēhnū̃ suṭṭ wī te jhōp wī sakknā wā̃.
17. *T.* Can a cow write? *P.* No, a cow cannot write. *T.* Can a horse drink? *P.* Yes, a horse and a cow can eat and drink.	17. *M.* Gā̃ likkh sakdī e? *S.* Nĕhī̃, gā̃ nehī̃ likkh sakdī. *M.* Ghōṛā pī sakdā e? *S.* Āhō, ghōṛā te gā̃ khā pī sakdē nĕ̃.
18. *T.* Do horses drink tea or liquor? *P.* Horses drink water. *T.* What do cows eat? Cows eat hay, grass and grain.	18. *M.* Ghōṛē cāh yā̃ sharāb pī sakde nĕ̃? *S.* Ghōṛē pāṇī pīndē nĕ̃. *M.* Gāīā̃ kī khāndīā̃ nĕ̃? *S.* Gāīā̃ bhōh, ghāh, dāṇā khāndīā̃ nĕ̃.
19. *T.* What do you eat? Can you eat ghi? *P.* No, I eat meat, flour, and vegetables, but not ghi.	19. *M.* Tusī̃ kī khānde ō? Gheō khā sakde ō? *S.* Nĕhī̃, maĩ gōsht, āṭā te sabzī khānnā hunnā wā̃, gheō nĕhī̃ khāndā.

Lesson XXXI.

1. *T.* Good morning, may I come in? *P.* Yes, certainly. Come in. Good morning.	1. *M.* Salām sāhb, main andar āwā̃? *S.* Āho jī zarur langē ā jāo, salām.
2. *T.* Please take your pen and ink and write. *P.*	2. *M.* Mehrbānī karke kalam dawāt laike

Shall I write yesterday's lesson ?	likkho. *S.* Maī kall dā sabak likkhā̃ ?
3. *T.* Yes, you may write that and a new one too. *P.* May I write the old lesson first ?	3. *M.* Jī āh, ōh wī likkho te ikk nawā̃ wī likkho. *S.* Maī pishlā sabak paihle likkhā̃ ?
4. *T.* Yes, and take this paper to write on if you wish. *P.* May I sit by the door ?	4. *M.* Jī āh, te ēh kāgat wī bhāwē̃ likkhaṇ wāste lellō. *S.* Maī būhe kōḷ bawhā̃ ?
5. *T.* Yes, there is more light there. Madam may write too. *P.* May we put these chairs and table by the door ? *T.* I will place them.	5. *M.* Jī āh, ōtthe lō waddh e. Mēmsāhb wī likkhaṇ. *S.* Asī̃ mēz te kursīā̃ būhe kōḷ rakkhīye ? *M.* Maī rakkh dennā̃.
6. *P.* May I take these books off the table ? *T.* Yes, if they are in your way.	6. *S.* Ēh kitābā̃ maī mēz tō̃ cukkā̃ ? *M.* Āhō jī, jē taklīf dēndīā̃ nē̃ te.
7. *P.* May I stop writing now ? It is ten o'clock. *T.* Yes, you stop now.	7. *S.* Huṇ maī likkhṇā chaḍḍ deā̃ ? Das waj gae nē̃. *M.* Āhō jī, huṇ chaḍḍ deō.
8. *P.* May we go to the market to-day ? Will you go with us ? *T.* Yes, if you wish.	8. *S.* Ajj asī̃ bazār jālye ? Tusī̃ wī nāḷ jāōde ? *M.* Jē ākho te.

They go to the market and the teacher describes the various things, or it may be better to use pictures to describe from.

Lesson XXXII.

1. *T.* We must write more to-day than we did yesterday. *P.* Indeed !	1. *M.* Ajj sānū̃ kall nāḷō̃ waddh likkhṇā pawēgā. *S.* Halā, merā

I thought that we wrote enough last time.	khiāl sī kall coōkhā likkheā.
2. *T*. But you should write more and more every day so that you may learn to write nicely. *P*. Yes, I must learn to write and read well so that I may read and write letters.	2. *M*. Par rōz waddh likkhṇā cāhidā e, pai tusī caṅgā likkhṇā sikkho. *S*. Menū ṭhīk likkhṇā paṛhnā sīkkhṇā cāhidā e, pai maī ciṭṭhiā likkhā te paṛhā.
3. *T*. Yes, you must write me a letter soon. I will show you a copy. *P*. Let us not write too long for I must go to the bookshop and get a copy-book.	3. *M*. Āhō jī, thōṛe cir picche tuhānū mere wall ciṭṭhī likkhṇī cāhidī e, maī tuhānū namūnā dassāgā. *S*. Bauht cir nā likkhīye, maī haṭṭī te jāke nawī kāpī laiṇī e.
4. *T*. Is the old book full? *P*. It is almost full.	4. *M*. Purāṇi mukk geī e? *S*. Karīb karīb mukk geī e.
5. *T*. What did you pay for it? Six pence? That is too dear. We must go to another shop. *P*. Find a good shop. *T*. I think I know a place that sells cheap.	5. *M*. Kinnī paisī leī je? Chī anī? chē ānē waddh nē, kisē hōr haṭṭī te jāāge. *S*. Kōī caṅgi haṭṭī labbh lao. *M*. Ikk mēnū, shait dukān yād e, jitthe sastā wēcde nē.
6. *T*. You must write more slowly. This is not so good. *P*. It is better than the first.	6. *M*. Hōr hauḷī hauḷī likkho, ēh ōnnā wall nehī e. *S*. Paihle nāḷō wall e.
7. *T*. True, but you must make great progress both in writing and speaking. *P*. Right!	7. *M*. Ēh te gall ṭhīk e, par huṇ likkhaṇ wicc te bōlaṇ wicc baṛī tarakkī karnī cāhīdī

We will have to speak more every day.

8. *T.* You make a practice of speaking the hard words rapidly. *P.* Well, you must teach us.

9. *T.* I ought to come earlier in the morning, so that we can do more. *P.* Oh no, do not come any earlier than this, for we should have some time for other things.

10. *T.* Very well, I must go now. *P.* Must you? Is the time up? *T.* I must go a little early today. May I go now? *P.* Yes, you can go and we will go somewhere and take a walk. We ought to walk more.

e. *S.* Ṭhik e, sānū̃ rōz waddh bolṇa pawēgā e.

8. *M.* Tusī̃ aukhe aukhe lafs chēti bōlea karō. *S.* Halā tusī̃ sānū̃ dassō.

9. *M.* Mĕnū̃ sawēḷe auṇā cāhīdā e, tā̃ asī̃ waddh kamm kar sakiye. *S.* Nehī̃, edū̃ sawēḷe nā āo, sānū̃ hōrnā̃ kammā wāste wēḷā cāhīdā e.

10. *M.* Bauht acchā, huṇ, jī, mĕnū̃ jāṇā e. *S.* Halā, wēḷā hō geā e? *M.* Ajj mĕnū̃ zarā sawēre jāṇā e, huṇ mai jāwā̃? *S.* Hacchā jī, jāo, te asī̃ kitle jāke sair karā̃ge, sair waddh karnā cāhīdā e.

Lesson XXXIII.

1. *T.* Here is a book. Whose is it? *P.* It is mine. This, too, is my book. *T.* Are these, too, your books? *P.* Yes, these are our books, but these are yours.

2. *T.* Jhaṇḍa said that these books were his. Is it true? *P.* Yes, they are his. *T.* Have you any books like Jhaṇḍa's? *P.* Yes, there are some like his.

1. *M.* Āh wēkhā̃ katāb e, kih dī e? *S.* Mērī e, ēh wī mērī e. Ēh wī tuhāḍḍīā̃ katābā̃ nē̃? *S.* Āhō, ēh sāḍḍīā̃ ne, par ōh tuhāḍḍīā̃ nē̃.

2. *M.* Jhaṇḍe ākheā ēh mērīā̃ katābā̃ nē̃, saccī gall e? *S.* Āhō, osē dīā̃ nē̃. *M.* Tuhāḍḍe koḷ kujjh Jhaṇḍē dīā̃ katābā̃ jehīā̃ haiṇ? *S.* Jī āh, kujjh te haiṇ ne. (*See* Gram., p. 56.)

3. *T*. Pira and Jhaṇḍā gave me their books yesterday Here they are. *P*. Those? Those books are not theirs. I beg your pardon, those are mine. These are their books.	3. *M*. **Pīre te Jhaṇḍe kall mēnū̃ apṇiā̃ katābā̃ dittiā̃, ēh nẽ. *S*. Ōh? muāf karnā, ōh ohnā̃ diā̃ nehī̃, ōh meriā nẽ, ohnā̃ diā̃ ēh nẽ.**
4. *T*. Yes, I was mistaken. That is right. These belong to you and those are theirs. This is Amar's book. *P*. Yes, and that is Pirā's.	4. *M*. **Āhō, mai galti kiti sī, ṭhīk e, ēh tuhāḍḍiā̃ nẽ, te ōh ohnā̃ diā̃, ēh Amar dī kitāb e. *S*. Āhō, te ēh Pīre dī e.**
5. *T*. Give me Pira's book and Jhaṇḍa's pen and I will give them to them. *P*. Never mind, I will give them back myself.	5. *M*. **Mēnū̃ Pīrē dī katāb te Jhaṇḍe dā par dē deo, mai ohnā̃ nū̃ dē chaḍḍā̃gā. *S*. Khair mihr e, mai āpe dē deā̃gā.**
6. *T*. All right, you may return them. *P*. Shall I go now and return them?	6. *M*. **Caṅgā jī, tusī̃ dē deo. *S*. Mai huṇe jāke partā deā̃?**
7. *T*. No, not now. Make another sentence like that. *P*. May I come and get the book?	7. *M*. **Aje nehī̃. Ehojehā ikk hōr fikra baṇāo. *S*. Mai huṇe āke katāb lellā̃?**
8. *T*. Now make another sentence still. *P*. Let Peter come and I will give him the book. *T*. Another. *P*. Let me sit on this chair. Let me take the book from the table and then I will put it on the chair.	8. *M*. **Aje wī ikk hōr baṇāo. *S*. Pire nū̃ ā laiṇ dēho, te mai ohnū̃ katāb dē deā̃gā. *M*. Aje ikk hōr. *S*. Mainū̃ ēs kursī te baihṇ dēō. Menū̃ mēz tõ katāb cukkaṇ deo, te tā̃ mai kursī te rakkhā̃gā.**

9. *P.* May I walk to the door and open it? May I go to the door and shut it? Let me have your pencil. Let me write a letter. Let me eat this bread. Let Peter drink this water.	9. *S.* **Maī būhā jāke lāhā̃? Maī būhā jāke mārā̃? Mĕnū̃ apṇī rūl wikhāo. Mainū̃ ciṭṭhī likkhaṇ dēō. Mainū̃ēh rōṭī khaṇ dēō. Pīrā ōh pāṇī pie?**
10. *T.* Very well, again. *P.* Throw the ball and let me catch it. Let us go and play ball. Let us go to school. Let us write Arabic to-morrow. Let us read Arabic again. Let us talk Panjabi the whole time. Let us go to the city and get books for writing. Let the boys and girls go home. Let the girls write a letter to their teacher.	10. *M.* **Bauht acchā, ikk hōr.** *S.* **Gēnd suṭṭo te maī jhōp lā̃. Asī̃ jāke gēnd nāḷ khēḍ-īyē. Asī̃ skūle calīye, bhaḷke asī̃ Arbī likk-hīye. Asī̃ Arbī phēr paṛhīye. Asī̃ sārā wakat Panjābī bōlīye. Asī̃ shaihr jāke likkhaṇwāḷīā̃ katābā̃ leāwīye. Muṇḍē kuṛīā̃ ghar jāṇ, kuṛīā̃ apṇe ustād wall ciṭṭhī likkhaṇ.**

Lesson XXXIV.

1. *T.* Let us make some more sentences. I want you to say what I say. *P.* You do what I do.	1. *M.* **Asī̃ hor fikre baṇāīye. Maī cāhnnā wā̃ pai jō kujjh maī ākhā̃ tusī ākho.** *S.* **Jo kujjh maī karā̃, tusī karō.**

(Begin all the following sentences with the words "**maī cāhnnā wā̃ pai,**" which are, however, generally omitted in Panjabi unless both nominatives are of the third person.)

2. *T.* That is right, I want you to take what I	2. *M.* **Ṭhīk e, jō kujjh maī lā̃, tusī lao.** *S.*

take. *P*. I want you to give what I give.	Jō kujjh maī deā̃, tusī deo.
3. *T*. I want her to give what I give. *P*. I want her to drink what I drink.	3. *M*. Jō kujjh maī deā̃, ōh dē. *S*. Jō kujjh maī piā̃ ōh pīe.
4. *T* I want her to eat what I eat. *P*. I want her to buy what he buys.	4. *M*. Jō kujjh maī khā̃wā̃ ōh khāe. *S*. Maī cāhnnā wā̃ pai jō kujjh ōh mull lae, ōh wī mull lae.
5. *T*. I want him to eat what I eat. *P*. I want him to sell what I sell.	5. *M*. Jō kujjh maī khā̃wā̃, ōh khāe. *S*. Jō kujjh maī wēcā̃, ōh wēcē.
6. *T*. I want him to teach what I teach. *P*. I want the girls to do what I do.	6. *M*. Jō kujjh maī sikhānnā̃, ōh sikhāe. *S*. Jō kujjh maī karā̃, kuṛiā̃ wī karn.
7. *T*. Now another kind of sentence. I want him to go where I go. *P*. I I want her to go where you go. *T*. I want the boys to sit where I sit.	7. *M*. Huṇ hōr tarā̃ dā fikrā. Maī cāhnnā wā̃ pai jitthē maī jā̃, ōh wī jāe. *S*. Jitthē tusī jāō, ōh wī jāe. *M*. Jitthe maī bawhā̃, ōtthe muṇḍē wī baihṇ.
8. *T*. I want them to stay where I stay. *P*. I want you to sleep where I sleep. *T*. He wants me to work where you work. *P*. I want them to eat where I eat.	8. *M*. Jiṭthe maī rahā̃, ōtthe ōh raihṇ. *S*. jitthe maī sawā̃, ōtthe tusī saṇwo. *M*. Ōh cāhndā e pai maī ōtthe kamm karā̃ jitthe tusī karde ō. *S*. Maī cāhnnā wā̃ pai jitthe maī khā̃, ōtthe ōh khāṇ.

9. *T.* I want Jhaṇḍa to play where I play. *P.* I want Pira to play where the boys play.	9. *M.* **Maī cāhnnā wā̃ paī jitthe maī khēḍḍā̃, ōtthe Jhaṇḍā khēḍ-ḍe.** *S.* **Maī cāhnnā wā̃ paī jitthe muṇḍē khēḍḍaṇ, ōtthe Pīrā khēḍḍe.**
10. *T.* Now another kind. I want him to eat as much as I eat. *P.* I want her to do as much as I do. *T.* I want her to take as much as I take. *P.* She wants to take as much as I take.	10. *M.* **Huṇ ikk hōr kism. Maī cāhnnā wā̃ paī jinnā maī khā̃, ōnnā ōh khāe.** *S.* **Maī cāhnnā wā̃ paī jinnā maī karnā wā̃, ōnnā ōh kare.** *M.* **Maī cāhnnā wā̃ paī jinnā maī lā̃ ōnnā ōh laie.** *S.* **Ōh cāhndī e paī jinnā maī lā̃, ōnnā ōh laie.**
11. *T.* Good. I want them to give as much as I give. *P.* I give as much as you do.	11. *M.* **Bauht acchā, maī cāhnnā wā̃ paī jinnā maī deā̃, ōnnā ōh dēṇ.** *S.* **Jinnā tusī dēnde ō, ōnnā maī dēnnā wā̃.**
12 *T.* He sells as much you sell. *P.* He buys as much as I buy. *T.* She drinks as much as a man. *P.* They (fem.) eat as much as men.	12. *M.* **Jinnā tusī wēcdē ō, ōnnā ōh wēcdā e.** *S.* **Jinnā maī mull lāinnā wā̃, ōnnā ōh mull lendā e.** *M.* **Ōh jaṇe jinnā pīndī e.** *S.* **Ōh jaṇeā̃ jinnā khāndīā̃ nē̃.**
13. *T.* The boys read as much as the girls. *P.* They write as much as the girls. *T.* We want	13. *M.* **Jinnā kuṛīā̃ paṛh-dīā̃ nē̃, ōnnā muṇḍē paṛhdē nē̃.** *S.* **Jinnā kuṛīā̃ likhdīā̃ nē̃,**

as many books as they have. *P*. They want as many books as we have.

ōnnā̃ ōh li<u>kh</u>dē nẽ. *M*. Jinniā̃ katābā̃ ohnā̃ kōḷ nẽ, ōnniā̃ asī̃ cāhnne ā̃. *S*. Jinniā̃ katābā̃ sāḍḍē kōḷ nẽ, ōnniā̃ ōh cāhnde nẽ.

14. *T*. I want as many books as you have. *P*. You want as many books as she has. *T*. He wants as many chairs as I have. *P*. You want as many dogs as he has.

14. *M*. Jinniā̃ katābā̃ tuhāḍ-ḍe kōḷ nẽ mai cāhnnā wā̃. *S*. Jinniā̃ katābā̃ ohde kōḷ nẽ, ōnniā̃ tusī̃ cāhnde ō. *M*. Jinniā̃ kursiā̃ mēre kōḷ nẽ, ōnniā̃ ōh cāhndā e. *S*. Jinne kutte ōhde kōḷ nẽ, ōnne tusī̃ cāhnde ō.

15. *T*. They (m.) want as many boys as he has. *P*. They (f.) want as many girls as I have. *T*. Thou wantest as many pens as they have. *P*. Thou wantest as many rugs as I have.

15. *M*. Jinne muṇḍe ōhde kōḷ nẽ, ōnne ōh cāhn-de nẽ. *S*. Jinniā̃ kuṛiā̃ mēre kōḷ nẽ, ōnniā̃ ōh cāhndiā̃ nẽ. *M*. Jinniā̃ kalamā̃ ohnā̃ de kōḷ nẽ, ōnniā̃ tū̃ cāhnnā ẽ. *S*. Jinne galīce mēre kōḷ nẽ, ōnne tū̃ cāhnnā ẽ.

16. *T*. Bring me as many letters as he has. *P*. Take as many as Jhanḍa has. *T*. Is this book as thick as yours? *P*. No, it is as thick as Jhanḍa's.

16. *M*. Jinniā̃ ōhde kōḷ ciṭṭhiā̃ nẽ, ōnniā̃ mēre kōḷ leāo. *S*. Jinniā̃ Jhanḍe kōḷ nẽ, ōnniā̃ lellao. *M*. Ēh katāb tuhāḍḍī jēḍḍī mōṭī e? *S*. Nehī̃, Jhanḍe dī jēḍḍī mōṭī e.

17. *T*. Does Jhanḍa run as fast as Pira? *P*. Jhanḍa

17. *M*. Jhanḍā Pīrē jinnā bhajj sakdā e? *S*.

runs as fast as, or faster than Pira. *T.* You may sleep as late as Amar does. *P.* As late as Amar does? Never!

Jhaṇḍā Pirē jinnā bhajjdā e yā̃ waddh. *M.* Jinnā cir Amar saundā e tusī̃ wī saũ sakde o. *S.* Jinnā cir Amar saundā we? Taubā jī.

18. *T.* This cloth is as fine as silk? *P.* As fine as silk? Is it not silk? *T.* He is as black as ink. *P.* She is as white as snow (ice).

18. *M.* Ēh kapṛā paṭṭ jehā mahīn e. *S.* Paṭṭ jehā? āpe paṭṭ nehī̃ e? *M.* Ōh siāhī jehā kāḷā e. *S.* Ōh barf (warf) jehī ciṭṭī.

19. *T.* This chair is not as high as the table. The table is higher than the chair. *P.* This rug is not as large as the carpet. The carpet is larger than the rug. (Door, small, window. Window, high, roof. Coat, big, yours. Hand, large, mine. Bed, small, yours. Book, black, red, yours. Bread, good, Pira's. Cloth, fine, that. Horse, good, cow.)

19. *M.* Ēh kursī mēz jinnī uccī nehī̃. Mēz kursī nāḷõ uccā e. *S.* Ēh galīcā darī jēḍḍā nehī̃. Darī galīce nāḷõ waḍḍī e. (Būhā, nikkā, bārī. Bārī, uccī, chatt. Kōṭ, waḍḍā, tuhāḍḍā. Hatth, waḍḍā, mērā. Manjī, nikkī, tuhāḍḍī. Katāb, kāḷī, lāl, tuhāḍḍī. Rōṭī, caṅgī, Pīrē dī. Kapṛā, mahīn, ōh. Ghōṛā, caṅgā, gā̃.)

Change the pronouns of the first person in the first dozen sentences, to other persons.

Lesson XXXV.

Future (complicated in Panjabi).

1. *T.* I am going to teach a new lesson now. *P.*

1. *M.* Huṇ maī̃ nawā̃ sabak sikhāṇ laggā

I am going to learn a new lesson.	wā̃. *S*. **Maĩ nawā̃ sabak sikkhaṇ laggā wā̃.**
2. *T*. I am going to go to the city soon. *P*. I am going to go to the church soon.	2. *M*. **Zarā ku nū̃ maĩ shaihr jāṇ lagā̃.** *S*. **Maĩ zarā ku nū̃ girje jāṇ lagā̃.**
3. *T*. I am going to go to the market to-day. *P*. I am going to the Post Office	3. *M*. **Ajj maĩ bazār jā-ā̃gā.** *S*. **Maĩ ḍāk-k͟hāne jaṇ laggā wā̃.**
4. *T*. I am going to send a letter home to-day. *P*. I am going to write home to-day.	4. *M*. **Maĩ ajj ghar chiṭṭhi lik͟haṇ laggā wā̃.** *S*. **Maĩ ajj ghar chiṭṭhī lik͟haṇ laggā wā̃.**
5. *T*. I am going to write a letter to the bookseller to-morrow. *P*. I am going to bring you a letter from the Post Office to-morrow. I am going to send a letter by you now.	5. *M*. **Bhaḷkē maĩ katābā̃ wēccaṇ wāḷe nū̃ ciṭṭhī likkhā̃gā.** *S*. **Maĩ bhaḷkē tuhāḍḍē wāstē ḍāk-k͟hāneõ ciṭṭhī leāwā̃gā, huṇ maĩ tuhāḍḍē hatth ciṭṭhī ghallaṇ laggā wā̃.**
6. *T*. I am going to take your letter to the Post Office. I am going to buy some books for you. *P*. I am going to let you buy some books for me.	6. *M*. **Maĩ tuhāḍḍī ciṭṭhī ḍāk-k͟hānē lai jāṇ lagā̃. Maĩ tuhāḍḍē laī katābā̃ k͟harīdā̃gā.** *S*. **Maĩ tuhānū̃ apṇe jōgīā̃ katābā̃ k͟harīdaṇ deā̃gā.**
7. *T*. Why are you going to buy books? *P*. I am going to read some Panjabi stories.	7. *M*. **Tusī̃ kyū̃ katābā̃ mull laiṇ lagge ō.** *S*. **Maĩ kōī Panjābī kahāṇīā̃ paṛhā̃gā.**

(The teacher should change all these pronouns to second and third persons, of both numbers.)

8. *T*. It is going to rain to-	8. *M*. **Bhaḷkē mī̃h wassēgā**

morrow, is it not? *P.* I do not know.

ke nehī̃? *S.* Menū̃ k̲h̲abarē?

9. *T.* Are you going to the mountains this year, or to the seashore? *P.* We are not going anywhere this summer, I think; but we may go to the mountains.

9. *M.* Aitkīpahāṛjāōgēke samundar dē kōḷ? *S.* Aitkī asī̃ garmīā̃ wicc kitale nehī̃ jāṇ laggē, par shait pahāṛ jāā̃gē. (*See* Gram., p 113.)

10. *T.* Will you go to the city with me to-morrow? *P.* I shall not be able to go. *T.* Why can't you go? *P.* I shall be writing letters to America to-morrow.

10. *M.* Bhaḷke mērē nāḷ shaihr callōgē? *S.* Bhaḷkē nehī̃ jā sakā̃gā. *M.* Kyū̃ nehī̃ jā sakde ō? *S.* Bhaḷkē maī̃ wilaitī ḍāk lik̲h̲ṇī e.

11. *T.* Jhanḍa is going with me to buy clothes. Will you go too? *P.* No, I am going to be busy with letter writing, as I told you. Will you put this letter in the box for me?

11. *M.* Jhaṇḍā mērē nāḷ kapṛē mull laiṇ jāēgā. Tusī̃ wī nāḷ callōge? *S.* Nehī̃ maī̃ te ākh baiṭhā wā̃, maī te ciṭṭhīā̃ lik̲h̲ṇīā̃ nē. Ēh ciṭṭhī mērē wastē ḍākē pāōgē?

12. *T.* Certainly. I am going out anyway and will do it for you. *P.* Will you take this book and put it on the chair? *T.* Certainly, with pleasure.

12. *M.* Baṛī k̲h̲ushī nāḷ (or Beshakk), maī ū̃ wī bannē jāṇā e. *S.* Ēh katāb laikē kursī te rakkhōgē? *M.* Baṛī k̲h̲ushī nāḷ.

13. *T.* I have to write a letter home every day. *P.* Have you to write every day? Why?

13. *M.* Mēnū̃ rōz ciṭṭhī ghar lik̲h̲ṇī paindī e. *S.* Tuhānū̃ rōz lik̲h̲ṇā paindā e? Kī sababb e?

14. *T.* I have to give word to my mother daily, or she is worried as to

14. *M.* Bēbbē nū̃ rōz k̲h̲abar dēṇī paindī e, nehī̃ te ghābbar jāndī

whether I am well or not. So I have to get up early and write to her. Jhaṇḍa, too, has to write daily.	e, paī khabrē wall e ke nēhī, tā̃ karke mĕnū̃ rōz sawērē uṭṭhkē likkhṇā paindā e. Jhaṇḍē nū̃ wī rōz likhṇā paindā e.
15. *P.* Do you keep cows? *T.* Yes, we have to milk them twice daily.	15. *S.* Tusī̃ gāīā̃ rakhde o? *M.* Jī āh, ohnā̃ nū̃ rōz dō wārī cōṇā paindā e.
16. *T.* I have to go. I must go. I am compelled to go. It is necessary for me to go. I have got to go.	16. *M.* Maī jāṇā e, maī zarūr jāṇā e, menū̃ jāṇā paindā e, (or jāṇā peā). Maī te majbūr hōeā, jāṇā te pawēgā.

Lesson XXXVI.

1. *T.* Good morning. What day is this? Is it Monday? *P.* It is Monday. *T.* What will it be to-morrow? Tuesday? *P.* To-morrow will be Tuesday.	1. *M.* Salām ji, ajj kehṛā wār e? Ajj suār e? *S.* Ajj suār e. *M.* Bhalke kehṛā wār e, maṅgaḷ? *S.* Bhalkē maṅgaḷ e.
2. *T.* Is the next day Wednesday? *P.* Yes, the next day is Wednesday. *T.* Is the day after Wednesday, Thursday? *P.* Yes, after Wednesday comes Thursday.	2. *M.* Te aglē din buddh? *S.* Āhō aglē din buddh e. *M.* Te Buddh de aggē Jumerāt. *S.* Jī āh, Buddh de aggē Jumerāt e.
3. *T.* Then what day? Friday? *P.* After Thursday comes Friday. *T.* Is the seventh day Saturday? *P.* Yes, it is	3. *M.* Te phēr kēhṛā din e? Jumā? *S.* Jumerāt de picche Jumā aundā e. *M.* Sattwā̃ din haftā e? *S.* Āhō,

	Saturday. Sunday or Sabbath, Monday, Tuesday, Wednesday, Thursday, Friday, Saturday.		haftā e. Aitwār yā̃ Sabbat, Suār, Mangaḷ, Buddh, Jumerāt, Jumā, Haftā.
4.	*T*. How many days are there in the week? *P*. There are seven days in the week.	4.	*M*. Hafte wicc kinnē wār hunde nẽ? *S*. Hafte wicc satt wār hunde nẽ.
5.	*T*. Learn this table of time: 60 seconds make one minute, 60 minutes make one hour, 3 hours make one watch, 8 watches or 24 hours make one day, 7 days make one week, 4 weeks or 30 days make one month, 12 months make one year, 100 years make a century. What century is this? *P*. This is the 20th Century.	5.	*M* Ēh wakat dā hisāb yād karnā cahīdā e. Saṭṭhā̃ sikiṇṭā̃ dā ikk miṇṭ hundā e, saṭṭhā̃ miṇṭā̃ dā ikk ghaiṇṭā, triũh ghaiṇṭeā̃ dā ikk paihr, aṭṭhā̃ paihrā̃ yā̃ cawhiā̃ ghaiṇṭeā̃ dā ikk din, sattā̃ dinā̃ dā ikk haftā, caũh hafteā̃ yā̃ trīhā̃ dihāṛeā̃ dā ikk mahīnā, bāhrā̃ mahineā̃ dā ikk sāl, sau sālā̃ dī ikk sadī. Huṇ kehṛī sadī e? *S*. Huṇ wīhwī̃ sadī e.
6.	*T*. How long have you been in this country? *P*. I have been here four months. *T*. Is your father living? *P*. Yes, he is about 55 years old.	6.	*M*. Tuhānū̃ ēs mulkh wicc āeā̃ kinnā cir hōeā e? *S*. Menū̃ cār mahīnē hoē nẽ. *M* Tuhāḍḍē wālid horī jiūndē nẽ? *S*. Āhō, ōh kōī pacwanjhā̃ sālā̃ dī umr dē nẽ. (*See* Gram., p. 79.)
7.	*T*. Your mother? *P*. No, she died when I was a boy. *T*. How	7.	*M*. Te tuhāḍḍī bebbe hōrī? *S*. Nĕhī̃, mērī mā̃ mērē nikkĕā̃ hundeā̃

old were you? *P.* I was 16. Teach me some other expressions of time.	mar gei. *M.* Tusī kēḍḍē ku saō? *S.* Maī sōhḷā̃ warhēā̃ dā sā̃. Wakat dīā̃ hōr kōī gallā̃ dassō.
8. *T.* Very well, I will give some. I will come in ten days. This child is ten months old. This calf is four days old. This woman is thirty years old. How old is this horse? He is five years. seven months and fifteen days What is the age of this girl? Six years, three months and two days.	8. *M.* Caṅgā jī, hōr dass dēnnā̃, maī dasā̃ dinā̃ picche āwā̃gā, ēh bāl dasā̃ mahīneā̃ dā e, ēh wacchā caũh dihāṛeā̃ dā e. Ēh janānī trīhā̃ waṛheā dī e. Ēh ghōṛā kinnī umr dā e? Ōh dī umr panj warhe satt mahīnē, pandrā̃ dihāṛē we. Ēh kuṛī kinnī umr dī e. Chē warhē tinn mahīne, dō dihāṛe ēh dī umr e.
9. How long did Christ live in Palestine? About thirty-three years. How long did he teach? About three years.	9. Masīh Kanān de mulkh kinnē warhē rehā? Kōī tētti warhē. Kinnā cir sikhāndā rehā? Kōī trai warhē.
10. How long does it take to make bread? It takes two or three hours. In what time did you learn to read? It took three or four years.	10. Rōṭī pakāṇ wicc kinnā cir laggdā e? Dō tinn ghaiṇṭē. Tusā̃ paṛhnā kinnē cir wicc sikheā? Trai cār warhe lagge sāṇ.
11. How long does it take to boil potatoes? It takes twenty minutes. How long does it take to come here from New	11. Ālū rinnhaṇ wicc kinnā cir laggdā e? Wīh minṭ laggdē nē. New York shaihrō ētthē tīkar auṇ wāstē

York ? About four weeks.

kinnā cir laggdā e? Kōi cār hafte.

12. How old was Moses when he died ? One hundred and twenty years old. How old was Adam when he died ? Nine hundred and thirty years old.

12. Mūsā dī kinnī umr sī jad mōeā? Ikk sau wīh warhē. Ādam kinnē dā sī jad mōeā? Naũ sau trīhā̃ dā.

13. How old was Noah when the flood came ? Six hundred years old. What was the age of Noah when he died ? Nine hundred and fifty years.

13. Nūh kinnē dā sī jad nūh-nadī āi sī? Cheā̃ saiā̃ dā. Te jad Nūh mōeā sī, kinnī umr sāsū? Sāḍhē naũ sau.

14. Whose age was greatest of all ? Methusaleh, nine hundred and sixty-nine. Where did Moses spend forty years ? He spent 40 years in Egypt.

14. Sāreā̃ nāḷō̃ waddh kihdī umr hoī? Matūsalāh dī umr naũ sau anattar warhē sī jad mōeā. Mūsā cāḷī warhē kitthe rehā? Misr wicc cāḷī warhe rehā.

Lesson XXXVII.

1. *T*. Let us take a walk. Look what is that man doing ? *P*. He is working. Let us go and ask him.

1. *M*. Asī̃ sair karīye, wēkhō jī, ōh jaṇā kī peā kardā e? *S*. Ōh kamm peā kardā e, asī̃ calkē ōhnū̃ pucchīye.

2. *T*. Well, what are you making ? *Workman*. I am making a chair out of wood. *P*.

2. *M*. Kyū̃ whai, kī peā baṇānnā ē̃? *T*. Lakkaṛ dī kursī. *M*. Kinne ku mull dī e?

What price is it worth? *W*. It will be worth Rs. 9.	*T*. Naũ rupae dī.
3. *T*. That is very dear. *W*. Wait till it is done, then when you see it you will call it cheap.	3. *M*. Baṛī maihṅgī e. *T*. Jad mukk jāe, tā̃ wēkkhō, tā̃ sastī ākkhōgē.
4. *T*. What is that wood for? *W*. For burning. *T*. And that? *W*. That is for my work.	4. *M*. Ōh lakkaṛ kāh dē wāstē e? *T*. Bāḷaṇ wāste. *M*. Te ōh? *T*. Mērē kamm wāstē.
5. *P*. Why do they burn wood? *T*. For cooking and for warmth. Do you not burn it?	5. *S*. Lakkaṛ kāhnū̃ bāḷdē nē̃? *M*. Pakāṇ wāstē te sekkaṇ wāstē. Tusī̃ nehī̃ bāḷde?
6. *P*. We? No, we burn coal or gas. Some people burn wood, but most people burn coal. *T*. Where is gas found? *P*. Some is natural and some is made from coal.	6. *S*. Asī̃? Nehī̃, asī̃ yā̃ kōḷe bāḷne ā̃ yā̃ gais, kōī kōī lakkaṛ bāḷdā e, par bauhtē kōḷe bāḷdē nē̃. *M*. Gais kitthō̃ labbhdā e. *S*. Kujjh te aiwē̃ wā wiccō̃ miḷdā e, te kujjh kōḷē bāḷkē baṇāndē nē̃.
7. *T*. Is it dearer than coal? *P*. No, it is about the same, or perhaps cheaper	7. *M*. Kōḷeā̃ nāḷō̃ maihṅgā e? *S*. Nehī̃, ōnnā ī hōwēdā yā̃ kujjh sastā hōwēdā.
8. *T*. Of the two which is better. coal or gas? *P*. Gas is better because it is cleaner and leaves no ashes.	8. *M*. Caṅgā dohā̃ wiccō̃ kehṛā e? *S*. Gais caṅgā e, kyū̃ jō sāf e te ōh dī sāh nehī̃ koī hundī.
9. *T*. Why do people make fires in the winter? *P*. It is very cold. One cannot sit in the house without a fire.	9. *M*. Siāḷ wicc lōk agg kāhnū̃ bāḷdē nē̃? *S*. Pāḷā bauhtā hundā e, agg binā ghar wicc baihṇ nehī̃ hundā.

10. *T*. Do people everywhere make fires in winter to keep warm? *P*. No, in some places they put on more clothes and keep warm without a fire.

10. *M*. **Sabbhnī̃ pāsī̃ lōk agg bāḷ bāḷke niṅghē raihndē nẽ? *S*. Nehī̃, kitale kitale kapṛē waddh pākē agg binā niṅghē raihndē nẽ.**

11. *T*. Can they keep warm without a fire? *P*. Yes, making clothes of skins or quilted garments, keeps out the cold.

11. *M*. **Agg binā niṅgheā̃ rawhīdā e? *S*. Jatt de kapṛē baṇākē yā̃ rū̃ wicc pākē pāḷā ḍhakkidā hundā e.**

12. *T*. What do you do in America? *P*. We keep our houses as warm in winter as in summer.

12. *M*. **Tusī̃ Amrīkā wicc kī karde hunde o? *S*. Asī̃ siāḷ wicc gharā̃ nū̃ ōnnā garm ra<u>kh</u>ne ā̃ jinnā garmīā̃ wicc.**

13. *T*. How do you keep them so warm? *P*. We burn a lot of hard coal, gas and wood. What do you burn? *T*. We burn wood, charcoal, and cow-dung. Some burn hard coal.

13. *M*. **Innā garm kīkkaṇ ra<u>kh</u>de o? *S*. Asī̃ bauht patthar dā kōḷā te gais te lakkṛīā̃ bāḷne ā̃, tusī̃ kī bāḷde o? *M*. Asī̃ lakkṛīā̃ te kōḷē te gōhē bāḷne ā̃, kōī kōī patthar dā kōḷā bāḷdā e.**

14. *P*. Why do you not use wood or charcoal instead of cow-dung? *T*. Wood and coal are dear and hard to get. Cow-dung is cheap.

14. *S*. **Gōhē dē thā̃ tusī̃ lakkaṛ yā̃ kọḷē kyū̃ nehī̃ bāḷde o? *M*. Lakṛī te kōḷē maihṅgē nẽ te aukhē labbhdē nẽ; gōhē sastē hundē nẽ.**

15. *P*. Is it clean? *T*. Clean? Certainly, it is the nicest of fuels. It does not give off much heat in "sum-

15. *S*. **Gōhē sā̃f hundē nẽ? *M*. Zarūr, ōh sabbhnā̃ nāḷō̃ acche hundē nẽ, hāṛ wicc ohnā̃ dī innī garmī**

mer" (or 'Hār').

nehī̃ hondī. (*See* Grammar, p. 114.)

16. *P.* What grains do you eat? *T.* We eat rice, wheat, maize, millet, barley, and pulse. We grind some of them for bread. Some we cook whole.

16. *S.* **Tusī̃ kāhde dāṇē khānde ō? *M.* Asī̃ cauḷ, kaṇak, makaī, bājrā, jaū̃ te dāḷ khānne ā̃, kisē kisē nū̃ pīhke āṭā baṇānne ā̃, kisē kisē nū̃ samūcha pakaunnē ā̃.**

17. *P.* What meat do you eat? *T.* We eat mutton, fowls, almost everything. *P.* Are there any meats that are forbidden you to eat?

17. *S.* **Gōsht kāhdā khānde ō? *M.* Asī̃ nikkī tarkārī khānne ā̃, kukkṛīā̃ wī, karīb karīb sabbho kujjh. *S.* Kisē gōsht dī tuhāḍḍī saūh e?**

18. *T.* Yes, we are not allowed to eat pig's flesh (beef). Are any forbidden to you? *P.* No, we eat what we wish.

18. *M.* **Āhōjī, bāhrlē (waḍḍe mās) dī sāḍḍī saūh e. Tuhāḍḍī wī kōī saūh e? *S.* Nehī̃, asī̃ jō marzī e khā lainne ā̃.**

19. *T.* Does not your religion forbid you to eat certain things? *P.* All good meat we eat. God made it all.

19. *M.* **Tuhāḍḍē dīn wicc kise shai dī saūh nehī̃ e? *S.* Nehī̃, jehṛā mās caṅgā e khā lainne ā̃, sārā Khudā i baṇāeā sī.**

Lesson XXXVIII.

(Work and Wages.)

1. *T.* The men have come to do the work, sir. *P.* Why have they come so late?

1. *M.* **Mazdūr kamm wāste ā gae nē. *S.* Innā cir kyū̃ lāeā nē?**

2. *T.* They have been here for some time. *P.* In-

2. *M.* **Ōh cirōkṇe āē hoe nē. *S.* Halā? Ākheo**

deed? Tell them to begin at once and to do good work today. What are their wages?	nē huṇē shurū karn, ajj caṅgā kamm karn, diāṛī kī miḷdā ne?
3. *T.* The masons get Re. 1-4, the coolies 8 annas. *P.* You must see to it that they work well.	3. *M.* Rājjā nū̃ sawā sawā rupeā diāṛī, mazdūrā̃ nū̃ dhēlī dhēlī. *S.* Zarā dhiān karnā, kamm te caṅgā karn.
4. *T.* It is hard to get them to do their work well. *P.* Are they stupid? *T.* No, they are lazy.	4. *M.* Ohnā̃ kōḷō̃ caṅgā kamm karāṇā mushkil e. *S.* Akl ghaṭṭ nē̃? *M.* Nehī̃ jī, sust nē̃.
5. *P.* When must we pay them? *T.* They will want their pay every evening at sundown. *P.* What do they do with their money? *T.* They pay it out for food and clothes.	5. *S.* Sānū̃ mazdūri kadō̃ dēṇī pawēgī? *M.* Rōz din ḍubbē maṅgaṇgē. *S.* Mazdūrī dē paiseā̃ nāḷ kī karde nē̃? *M.* Rōṭī kapṛē wāstē kharc kardē nē̃.
6. *P.* How much do they give for food and how much for clothes? *T.* Let us ask them. Men, how much do you give for rent, for fuel, for food, for clothes? *Men.* We give nothing for rent and fuel, but have to pay for food and clothes.	6. *S.* Rōṭī wāste kinnā dēnde nē̃ tē kapṛeā̃ wāstē kinnā? *M.* Asī̃ pucch leīye. Kyū̃, whaī, karāē wastē te bāllaṇ te rōṭī kapṛē wāstē kinnā dēnde o. *J.* Karāe te bāllaṇ wāstē asī̃ kujjh nehī̃ dēnne ā̃, rōṭī kapṛe dā k͟harc hundā e.
7. *P.* Have you large families? *M.* Some have and some have	7. *S.* Bauht sāre bāl bacce je? *J.* Kisē dē bauhte nē̃, kisē dē

not. How many hast thou? *M*. I have three boys, little fellows.	thōṛē. *S*. Tērē kinnē nē̃? *J*. Mērē, jī, trai puttar nē̃, aje añāṇē nē̃.
8. *P*. How many has that man? *M*. He has two boys and four girls. *P*. How many has that man there? *M*. He is not married yet.	8. *S*. Ohdē kinnē nē̃? Ohdē dō jātak nē̃ te cār kākīā̃. *S*. Te ōs jaṇē dē kinne nē̃? Ōh aje kuārā ī e.
9. *P*. What are thy wages? (eight annas) and thine? (seven and a half annas). What do you pay for food for one day? We do not know.	9. *S*. Tērī kinnī mazdūrī e? (aṭṭh ānnē), tē terī? (sāḍhē satt ānnē). *S*. Rōz rōṭī wāstē kī dēnde o? Sānū̃ patā e?
10. *P*. If they give grain how much do they give as one day's wages? One load, What do you eat? Chapatis and pulse, sometimes rice.	10. *S*. Jē dāṇē dēṇ tā̃ dihāṛī kī dēndē nē̃? Ikk bharī. *S*. Khānde kī hunde o? Dāḷ rōṭī, kadī kadāī̃ cauḷ.
11. *P*. What do you eat with your bread (some vegetable, etc.) or rice (sugar)? Do you keep a cow?	11. *S*. Rōṭī nāḷ kī khānde o? (kōī salūṇā), te cauḷā̃ nāḷ? (khaṇḍ) Tuhāḍḍe kōḷ gā̃ we?
12. Do you use milk? (Yes, if we get it.) Do you eat butter?	12. Duddh pīnde o? (Labbhe te pī lainne ā̃.) Makkhaṇ khānde o?
13. What do you pay for sugar? What do you pay for salt? Does the shop-keeper take cash or give credit? (loan.)	13. Khaṇḍ dā kī bhā we? Te lūṇ dā? *S*. Haṭṭiwāḷā nakd laindā e yā̃ udhār (hadār) dēndā ē?

14. Does he charge interest? What is the price of the dearest wheat? How much does it cost to get enough vegetables for one day?	14. Biāj laindā e? Maihṇgī tõ maihṅgī kaṇak dā kī bhā hundā e? Salūṇē (inquire exact meaning) dā kī rōz laggdā e?
15. Do you drink tea? Do you use tobacco, liquor? Do you eat opium? How much daily?	15. Cāh pīnde o? Hukkā yā sharāb pīnde o? Afīm khānde o? Rōz kinnī khānde o?
16. How much would that be in a year? Would it not be a good thing to give it up entirely?	16. Sāl wicc kinnī baṇdī e? Jē ukkā mukkā chaḍḍ deo caṅgī gall nehī̃?

Lesson XXXIX.

1. *T.* Come, we will play a game of "giving out the washing." I will be the washerman and you give me the clothes. *P.* Very well, you be washerman and I will give out the clothes to wash.	1. *M.* Huṇ asī̃ jugān dī khēḍ khēḍīye, mai dhōbā hōwā̃gā, te tusī̃ menū̃ kapṛē deo, *S.* Bauht acchā, tusī̃ dhōbā baṇō te mai kapṛe dhōṇē deā̃gā.
2. *T.* Sir, have you any soiled clothes? *P.* Yes, I have, come in and take them. *T.* All right, I will take and wash the clothes. *P.* Where will you wash them?	2. *M.* Tuhāḍḍē kōḷ maiḷē kapṛē haiṇ? *S.* Haiṇ nē̃, andar laṅgh-e-ā te lellai. *M.* Bauht acchā mai laike dhō chaḍḍā̃gā. *S.* Kitthe dhōwẽgā?
3. *T.* At the river or well, as you wish. *P.* Wherever you please,	3. *M.* Yā̃ daryā̃ te yā̃ khūh te, jīkaṇ ākhō. *S.* Bhāwē̃ jitthe cāhē̃.

but make them clean. *T*. Very well. I will count them and you write them down.	par ṭhīk sāf karnā. *M*. Bauht acchā mai giṇā̃gā, tusī̃ likkhde jāō.
4. *T*. Trousers, one pair; coats, two; vests (waistcoats), three; shirts, four; cuffs, four pairs; collars, five; neckties, six; handkerchiefs, seven; towels, eight; drawers, three pairs, undershirts, three; dusters, nine; hat-cover, one; turban, one; bags, ten; table-cloths, four; napkins, eleven, no, twelve; white dresses, four; flannel dresses, two; pillow-cases, five; sheets, three; blankets, five; petticoats, four; socks, six pairs; stockings, three pairs; pieces of lace, four; curtains, three; tray-cloth, one, and one carpet. That is all.	4. *M*. Ikk patlūṇ, do kōṭ, trai phutūhīā̃, cār kamīzā̃, cār jōṛī kafā̃, panj kālar, chē nakṭāīā̃, satt rumāl, aṭṭh nahāuṇ de taulīē, tinn drāzā̃, trai bañaiṇā̃, naũ jhāṛan, ṭōpī dā achāṛ ikk, ikk pagg, das thailīā̃, cār mēz dīā̃ cādarā̃, yārā̃ mēz dē taulīē, nā bārā̃, cār ciṭṭe ḍrēs, dō falālaiṇ de ḍrēs, takīe de uchāṛ panj, trai palaṇ dīā̃ cādarā̃, panj kambaḷ, cār pēṭīkōṭ, chē jōṛī mōze or jurābā̃ (jalābā̃), lammīā̃ jalābā̃ (lamme mōze) trai jōṛī, lēs de cār ṭōṭe, tinn paṛde, ikk trēl dī cādar, ikk darī, bas hōr kujjh nehī̃.
5. *P*. These are very dirty and you must wash them thoroughly. *T*. Very well, sir, I will wash them well.	5. *S*. Ēh kapṛe baṛe maiḷe nē̃, baṛī hacchī tarhā̃ dhōṇe. *M*. Hacchā ji, ṭhīk dhōā̃gā. (*See* Gram., p. 86.)
6. *P*. Put plenty of starch in the white clothes, but	6. *S*. Ciṭṭeā̃ kapṛeā̃ nū̃ cōkhī kalf lāṇī, par

do not starch the flannel. *T*. No sir, I never starch woollen garments.	falālaiṇ deā nū̃ kalf nā lāṇī. *M*. Nehī̃ jī, unn de kapṛeā nū̃ maī nehī̃ kalf lāndā.
7. *P*. Iron them well too. Now, what will you take? *T*. I will leave that to you, sir.	7. *S*. Istrī wī ṭhīk karī̃. Kī laoge? *M*. Maī̃ tuhāḍḍē tē chhaḍnā, jī.
8. *P*. Yes? I will give you Rs. 3 a hundred. *T*. That is very little. I always get five.	8. *S*. Halā, maī tuhānū̃ trai rupayye saikṛā deā̃gā. *M*. Bauht ghaṭṭ e, menū̃ panj rupeā saikṛā miḷdā hundā e.
9. *P*. Well, we'll see. If you do your work well, I will give you four. *T*. That is kind of you or Thank you. (I will do it for four.)	9. *S*. Acchā, whaī, wēkhī jāpēgī, je kamm caṅgā kītō ī cār rupae dēā̃gā. *M*. Tuhāḍḍī mehrbānī e. (*See* Gram., p. 105.)
10. *P*. Do you do this work alone? *T*. No, my wife and boys help me. *P*. Have you a machine to wash in? *T*. No, we beat the clothes on a stone.	10. *S*. Ēh kamm kallā karnā ē̃? *M*. Nehī̃ jī, mērī wauhṭī te muṇḍe wī madad dēnde nē̃. *M*. Dhōṇwāḷī mashīn hai ī? *M*. Nehī̃ jī, asī̃ patthar te mār mār ke dhōnne ā̃.
11. *P*. That must tear them. *T*. Yes, you have to make new ones. *P*. Do you put on the buttons. *T*. No, the tailor will do that.	11. *S*. Tā̃ te pāṭ jānde hōṇge. *M*. Jī āh, tuhānū̃ nawē̃ baṇāṇē painde nē̃. *S*. Biṛē tusī̃ lāndē hundē o? *M*. Nehī̃ jī, darzī lāndā hundā e.

Lesson XL.

1. *T*. I will be the servant and you tell me to do the work of the house. *P*. Very well, look at my boots. They are dirty. Clean them.

1. *M*. Maĩ naukar baṇ-ãgā, te tusĩ menū̃ ghar dā kamm dassō. *S*. Acchā, whaī, mērā būṭ wēkh lai, maiḷā we, ohnū̃ sāf kar.

2. *T*. Very well, shall I clean them now? *P*. No, make the bed now. *T*. All right, I will make it now. *P*. Sweep the room and dust it. *T*. Yes, sir.

2. *M*. Bauht acchā jī, huṇē ūhnā̃ sāf karā̃? *S*. Nehĩ, hāli bistrā kar. *M*. Huṇē kar dēnnā̃. *S*. Kamrē wicc bhārī phēr, te jhāṛ pōc kar. *M*. Bauht acchā jī.

3. *P*. Make this water warm. *T*. I have warmed it. Shall I make it warmer? *P*. Yes, make it warmer.

3. *S*. Ēs pāṇī nū̃ tattā kar. *M*. Tattā te maĩ kar leā e, aje hōr wī tattā karā̃? *S*. Āhō, hōr wī tattā kar.

4. *P*. Do we use long, short, big, small, white, black, red, sweet with 'make'? *T*. Yes, we say, make it long. Make it shorter. Make it big, bigger. Make it smaller. Make it white, make it red, make it black. Make it sweet or make it sweeter. We say, too, make it better. When a coat is too small, we say, let it out a little. If too big, take it in.

4. *P*. Jehṛā fēl "karnā" e, ohde nāḷ asĩ lammā, nikkā, waḍḍā, nikkā, ciṭṭā kāḷā, lāl, miṭṭhā ākh sakne ā̃? *M*. Āhō jī, asĩ āhnne ā̃ lammā kar, nikkā kar, waḍḍā kar, ĕdū̃ waḍḍā kar, ĕdū̃ nikkā kar, ehnū̃ ciṭṭā kar, lāl kar, kāḷā kar, miṭṭhā kar, edū̃ miṭṭhā kar, ēh wī āhnne ā̃ ĕdū̃ caṇgā kar (or frequently baṇā). Jē kōṭ nikkā hōwe asĩ āhnnē ā̃

ehnũ zarā waḍḍā kar, jē waḍḍā howe tā̃ āhnnē ī̃ ehnũ nikkā baṇā.

5. *T.* Now tell me what I do. Walks, runs, tastes, smells, catches, holds, lifts, throws, picks up, drops, places, looks and cuts paper (as with scissors), eats, drinks, chews, listens, sleeps, touches, knocks, pulls, turns, falls, sits, rises, shuts his eyes, yawns, whistles, and performs any other action that he thinks worth while teaching, going over and over the actions till the pupil is able to give the name readily.

5. *M.* Huṇ tusī̃ dassō pai maī kī karnā wā̃ peā—ṭurnā, bhajjṇā, cakkhṇā, sunghṇā, jhōpṇā, phaṛnā, cukkṇā, suṭṭṇā, cukkṇā, ḍēgṇā, rakkhṇā, wēkhṇā, waḍḍhṇā, khāṇā, pīṇā, cabbṇā, suṇṇā, saũṇā, hatth lāṇā, khaṛkāṇā, khiccṇā, bhaũṇā, ḍiggṇā, baihṇā, uṭṭhṇā, akkhī̃ mīṭṇiā̃, ubāsī laiṇī, sīṭī mārnī.

The teacher should take the words that have become familiar in one tense, the present, and change them with the words "tomorrow" and "yesterday" into future and past, until the pupil understands all these three tenses.

The teacher will work in ordinary changes in number so that the pupil may become an adept in noun changes So, too, he will use prepositions and degrees of comparison with the adjectives till the words are familiar.

The teacher must realise that whatever the pupil learns, he must learn so well that it is as familiar to him as his mother-tongue. If he begins with a few words at first, and thus gains familiarity with them, they will form a good foundation for following work, but if he does nothing thoroughly, he will make poor progress. Half a dozen repetitions are not enough to teach a sentence. Hundreds of repetitions are necessary to enable one to say a foreign sentence readily and easily.

The remaining lessons are either to be found in the latter portion of the Grammar in Section II of this volume or are directly founded upon it.

If the student will familiarise himself thoroughly with the sentences which go to make up Lessons XLI to L he will gain a considerable knowledge of the rules of Grammar which they illustrate. Some of these rules will be made the subjects of succeeding lessons, but they cannot be gone over too frequently or illustrated too fully. For the purpose of these lessons it is better to omit all phrases which do not form complete sentences. Such phrases occur here and there alongside of the sentences, but attention should at present be fixed more particularly on the complete sentences. The briefer phrases can be learned when the Grammar is being directly studied.

Lesson XLI.

PRONOMINAL SUFFIXES AND INFIXES.

Use for this lesson the sentences on pages 350–353, they are 58 in number. Special attention should be paid to them, for the idioms illustrated in them are peculiarly difficult for Europeans.

Lesson XLII.

THE INFINITIVE.

Go over the 63 sentences on pages 368–372.

Lesson XLIII.

THE CASES.

Use similarly the sentences exemplifying the Cases, 43 on pages 341–347 and 11 on pages 273–275, 54 sentences in all.

Lesson XLIV.

PARTICIPLES, PRESENT CONDITIONAL, PRESENT INDICATIVE, IMPERFECT.

See pages 374–377, 33 sentences.

Lesson XLV.

PREPOSITIONS.

36 sentences, 26 on pages 365-366 and 10 on pages 300–303.

Lesson XLVI.

PRONOUNS: PERSONAL, INTERROGATIVE, INDEFINITE, REFLEXIVE, ETC.

See pages 347–349, 360–362; 30 sentences: pages 292, 293; 5 sentences, altogether 35.

Lesson XLVII.

ORDER OF WORDS, REPETITION OF WORDS, AGREEMENT OF THE VERB, DIRECT AND INDIRECT SPEECH, EUPHEMISMS.

See pages 337–341, 389–390; 35 sentences.

Lesson XLVIII.

COMPOUND VERBS.

These are of great importance. The student should thoroughly master the 73 sentences on pages 332–337, 384–386.

Lesson XLIX.

ADJECTIVES AND ADVERBS.

32 sentences, on pages 283, 284, 288, 299, 300, 364–368.

Lesson L.

CONDITIONAL SENTENCES.

It is difficult to acquire a fluent and correct use of these. Those which are given under the heading of -o forms are not so common as the others. Yet they are all used. Pages 377–381, 44 sentences.

DIVERSIFICATION TABLE.

I.	Horse, horses, mare, mares, water, father, mother, sister, brother, boy, boys, girl, girls, book,	I.	**Ghōṛā, ghōṛe, ghōṛī, ghōṛīā̃, pāṇī, peō, mā̃, bhaiṇ, bhrā, muṇḍā, muṇḍe, kuṛī, kuṛīā̃, katāb, ka-**

	books, box, boxes, tear, tears, night, nights, day, days.		tābā̃, sandūk, sandūk, atthar, atthrā̃, rāt, rātā̃, dihāṛā, dihāṛe.
II.	I, me, from me, we, us; you (sing.), you, you, you; he, him, she, her, it, from it; they, them.	II.	Maī, menū̃, methõ, asī, sānū̃, tū̃, tenū̃, tusī, tuhānū̃; ōh, ohnū̃, ōsnū̃, ōsthõ; ōh, ohnā̃ nū̃.
III.	My, mine, our, ours; you, yours (sing.), you, yours; his, her, its; their, theirs.	III.	Mērā, mēre, mērī, mērīā̃, sāḍḍā, -e, -ī, -iā̃, tērā, -e, -ī, -iā̃, tuhāḍḍā, -e, -ī, -īā̃; ohdā, -e, -ī, -īā̃; ohnā̃ dā, de, dī, dīā̃.
IV.	Who? which? what? where? when? why? which one? whatsort of? how big? how much?	IV.	Kauṇ? kehṛā, -e, -ī, -iā̃? kī? kitthe? kadõ? kyū̃? kehṛā? kehojehā? koḍḍā? kinnā?
V.	Who, whom; which, or what; this, these; that, those, some one; several.	V.	Jehṛā, jehṛī, jehṛe, jehṛiā̃, jisnū̃, or jihnū̃, jihnā̃ nū̃; jehṛā, jis nū̃; ēh, ēsnū̃, ēh, ehnā̃ nū̃; ōh, ōsnū̃, ōh, ōhnā̃ nū̃; kōī, kise nū̃; kaī.
VI.	Go, come, run, drive, be, eat, drink, know, say, sleep, speak, die, do, make, see, give, take, send.	VI.	Jāṇā, auṇā, bhajjṇā, calāṇā, hōṇā, khāṇā, piṇā, jāṇṇā, ākhṇā, saũṇā, kūṇā, marnā, karnā, baṇāṇā, wēkhṇā, dēṇā, laiṇā, ghallṇā.
a.	Pres. and pres. continuative.	*a.*	Jāndā e, and lagā jāndā e, peā jāndā e.

b.	Past. went, came, became, drank, knew, said, slept, spoke, died, did, made, saw, gave, took, sent.	*b.*	**Geā, āeā, hoeā, pītā, jātā, ākkheā, suttā, koeā, moeā, kītā, baṇāeā, wēkkheā, dittā, leā, ghalleā.**
c.	Perf. Has gone, come, become, drunk, known, said, slept, spoken, died, done, made, seen, given, taken, sent.	*c.*	**Geā e, āeā, hoeā, pītā, jātā, ākkheā, suttā, koeā, moeā, kītā, baṇāeā, ḍiṭṭhā, dittā, leā, ghalleā,** *all with* **e.**
d.	Future. Shall or will go, come, run, etc.	*d.*	**Jāẫgā, āwẫgā, bhajjẫgā, etc.**
e.	Imperative. Go, come.	*e.*	**Jāh, jāho, jāeō je; ā, āo, āweā je, āwī. etc.**
f.	Can, was able, will be able.	*f.*	**Sakdā e, sakeā, sakēgā.**
g.	Let; may; must, may, must.	*g.*	**Jāṇ deho, auṇ deho, karn de sū, etc.; jẫ, āwẫ, bhajje, calāīye, karn; maī jāṇā e, etc.**
h.	I want to go, come, etc.	*h.*	**Maī jāṇā cāhnnā wẫ, ōh auṇā cāhndā e, etc.**
i.	To go, come, as a rule, etc.	*i.*	**Jāṇā karnā, auṇā karnā, bhajjṇā karnā, etc.**
j.	Interrogatives. Is he going? Is he coming? Did he run? Can he drive? Was he able to drink? May I speak? Shall I do this? etc., etc.	*j.*	**Ōh lagā jāndā e? Ōh aundā e? Ōh bhajjā sī? Ōh calā sakdā e? Pāṇī pī sakeā? Maī ākkhẫ? Maī ēh kamm karẫ?**
VII.	Simple and Causative	**VII.**	**Ṭuṭṭṇā, ṭrōṛnā; ḍigg-**

	Roots. To be broken, to break; to fall, fell, make fall; to die, kill, have killed; fall down, put down, have put down; to be made, make, have made; to be sold, sell, have sold; to burn, to make burn; to graze, make graze; to go up, put up; to go, to make go, or drive; to drink, to give drink; to be fastened or planted, fasten, or plant, cause to fasten or plant.		ṇā, ḍēgṇā, ḍigāṇā; marnā; mārnā, marwāṇā; paiṇā, pāṇā, puāṇā; baṇṇā, baṇāṇā, baṇwāṇā; wikṇā, wēcṇā, wikāṇā; saṛnā, sāṛnā; carnā, cārnā; caṛhnā, cāṛhnā; calṇā, calāṇā; pīṇā, piāṇā; laggṇā, lāṇā, lawāṇā.
VIII.	Passives in various forms, he was killed, etc.	VIII.	Mār ghatteā, māreā geā, mārīdā; etc., etc.
IX.	Participles. Going, coming, running, eating, drinking, giving, taking, breaking, seated; goer, comer, runner, givers, a taker, giver, relinquisher; on falling, on giving.	IX.	Jāndeā̃, aundeā̃, bhajjdeā̃, khāndeā̃, pīndeā̃, dēndeā̃ lendeā̃, trōṛdeā̃, baiṭheā̃; jāṇwāḷā, auṇwāḷā, bhajjaṇwāḷā, dēṇwāḷe; leū, dēū, chaḍḍū; ḍiggdeā̃ sār, dēndeā̃ sār.
X.	Adjectives. Predicate. To be good, hot, white, black, small, large; To make good, hot, white, black, small, large; To be better, best; bad, worse,	X.	Caṅgā hōṇā, tattā, ciṭṭā, kāḷā, nikkā, waḍḍā; Caṅgeā, tatteā, ciṭṭeā, kāḷeā, nikkā, waḍḍā, karnā; edū̃ caṅgā, hōṇā, sabbhnā̃ thō̃

	worst; long, longer, longest; big, bigger, biggest; young, younger, youngest; straight, straighter, straightest. More or less.		caṅgā hōṇā, burā lammā, waḍḍā, nikkā, siddhā. Edū, sabbhnā̃ thō̃, nāḷō̃, -ērā. Waddh ghaṭṭ.
XI.	Numerals. Cardinals. First, second, third, etc. About ten, about five.	XI.	Ikk, dō trai, cār, panj, chē, satt, aṭṭh, nāū, das, wīh, panjhī, panjāh, sau, hazār. Paihlā, dujjā, trījjā, cauthā, panjwā̃, sattwā̃, aṭṭhwā̃, nauwā̃, daswā̃, dasku, panjku, etc.
XII.	Adverbs. Now, just now, to-day, yet, hither, near, here, there; with difficulty, not at all, quickly, speedily, thus, that way, this way, yesterday, day before yesterday, day before that, to-morrow, early, this time, month, or year, yes, no, not, very, then, indeed, forcibly, before, behind.	XII.	Huṇ, huṇe, ajj, aje, ure, nēṛe, ētthe, ōtthe, masā̃, ukkā nā, chētī, shitābī, aiñ, uñ, ōs tarhā̃, ēs tarhā̃, kall, parsō̃, cauth, bhaḷke, sawēḷe, aitkā̃, āhō, nehī̃, nā, hī, tā̃, te, bado badī, agge, pioche.
XIII.	Prepositions. To, from, by, in, toward, under, for, like, equal to, for sake of, about, before, behind, till, up to, from, from out	XIII.	Nū̃, thō̃, de kōḷō, (de) wicc, (de) wall, (de) hēṭh, (de) wāste, (de) wāngū̃, de barābar, dī khātar, dī bābat, (de) agge,

	of, inside, with, compared with, from.		(de) picche, tōṛī, taĩ, -õ, (de) wiccõ, (de) wishkār, (de) nāḷ, (de) nāḷõ, (de) wallõ.
XIV.	Conjunctions. If, if, and, then, or, though, rather, but, lest, also, even, then, whether . . or, for this reason, for which reason, wherefore? when, when, because, so that, since.	XIV.	Jē, jēkar, te, tā̃, yā̃, bhāwẽ, sagõ, par, mate, bī, tā̃mī, cāhe . . cāhe, ēs karke, jis karke, kis karke. Jadõ, jadõ dā, kyũjō, tā̃jō, jicir.

Fluent and ready command of the XIV classes of these words will insure the correct use of the whole language.

PART III.

[For summary of principal grammatical contents, see p. 265.]

Lesson I.

Directions for Study.[1]

The student should take one of his slips[2] and write on it major clause I*a*, in English only. If, however, he is carrying on at the same time the study of the native script, the letters should be inscribed just beneath the English, and the eye, unconsciously falling on them as it rests on the English, will become accustomed to them, and will be ready later on for an inductive study of the character. As the student rests his eye on the English, the teacher should repeat the Panjabi, and if a picture of the scene of "The Woman at the Well" can be used, it will be best to point to persons and things so that, as soon as possible, the words may begin to *function*, i.e., to convey meaning directly without translation. After the teacher has repeated, six or eight times, **ikk janāni shahrõ pāṇī bharn āī**, he should break it into two breath-groups **ikk janānī shahrõ** and **pāṇī bharn āī**, and the pupil should repeat them thus, learning to say the first three words before taking up the second three. When he can repeat the second three he should say the whole six words, alternately with the teacher, till he can say them without hesitation. It is important that this repetition be alternate, and not in concert with the teacher.

Once the pupil can say the whole sentence fairly well, it may be written on the reverse of the slip, with the English equivalent under each Panjabi word.

Ikk janānī shahrõ pāṇī bharn āī.

One woman city-from water draw-to came.

---

[1] These principles are to be followed with all lessons in Part III.

[2] Get 800 or 1,000 slips of cardboard or paper, stiff enough to shuffle nicely, about 2 in. wide and 4 or 5 in. long, for "slip study," and a 100 paper-clips for holding sets of slips together. The paper may be had in large sheets and cut to size by the dealer.

This reverse side will do as the basis of the second lesson, but if the student is tired, he should rest from work on the *major* and take up the *minors*, the "derived sentences." In these the familiar words, cast into new combinations, are used to reveal the secrets of the language. New uses of familiar words allow the student to give his attention to the grammatical form of the words and sentences, instead of having his whole attention engrossed with the meanings.

So, too, working over old words in new combinations fixes the words more firmly in the memory, and assists in the memorising of the as yet imperfectly mastered major.

After taking up I*a* and mastering it so as to be able to repeat it five times in twelve seconds, the pupil may write clause *b* on the slip in English (while under it, if he is learning the character, should be written the Panjabi letters) in this order *and Jesus, Who was sitting on the well, said to her, Give me to drink.* In order, however, to teach this simply and easily the teacher should say the last clause first, and it would be well for the student to lay his slip *b* aside temporarily, while he writes three new temporary slips and learns them in this order, *Give me to drink*, then *and Jesus said to her*, and finally *Who was sitting on the well.* Now having mastered the three in this form, he must recombine them into the first form, *and Jesus, Who was sitting on the well, said to her, Give me to drink.* When he has so far learned any clause that he can repeat it after the teacher, he should have the Roman-Panjabi, with underlined English meaning, written on the reverse of his slip **te Yesū, Jehṛā khūh te baiṭhā sī, ohnū̃ ākheā, Menū̃ pāṇī piā de,** and Jesus, Who well on seated was her-to said, Me-to water make-drink give. When he can say clause *b* in the regular order, he should alternate it with clause *a*, until he can say both in seven seconds. When this speed has been reached, or sooner, if wearied, he may take up the derived sentences of I*b* and master them, noting the grammatical forms and changes.

Now write Ic in English and let the teacher say it in three breath-groups—

shahr gae hoe saṇ.	**city gone been were.**
kyũjō ohdē cēlē.	**why-that him-of disciples.**
rōṭī mull laiṇ.	**bread buy take-for.**

When able to repeat this, write it with English interlined on the reverse and memorise clause to speed. Now, with eyes on the English slips, recite *a b c* in any and every order up to required speed of 5 syllables per second, or all in 13 seconds.

When speed has been attained, write I *d* and get the teacher to give it in four-breath groups, **Jadõ ōh muṛ āe—tad kise ohnū̃ nā ākheā—ēh kauṇ ẽ? yā̃, Tū̃ kī cāhnnā ẽ?** When able to say them fairly well first separately and then together, write them on the reverse and link up with *a b c* by repeating from the English slips in the order *a d, b d, c d, d a, d c, d b,* until the four clauses *a b c d* can be said in any order in 17 seconds.

During the mastery of these major sentences the minors will richly repay careful study, for thus an inductive acquaintance with grammatical principles, and the practical mastery of the same, will be easily attained—easily as compared with the scholastic method, but still it will require exacting application to fix all these forms in mind.

The succeeding idioms grouped under Lesson I will in the same manner give an insight into the structure of the Panjabi language. Not one of them can safely be omitted. See remark at end of Lesson I.

A note of warning.

There is a danger that in acquiring facility of utterance, accuracy of pronunciation, especially as regards giving full value and distinctive character to the unaccented medial and final vowels, particularly ā, e, ī, may be overlooked. It is very characteristic of English to pronounce the final vowel in *fir, her, fur, honour, beggar*, with the same sound, but in Panjabi each vowel has its own distinct sound. So in Panjabi some Westerners are inclined to pronounce alike words ending in e and ī. English words like *villa, America,* should not induce us to shorten the final a of Panjabi words, such as **bābbā, kākkā.**

Lesson I(a).

A woman came from the city to draw water.	**Ikk janānī shahrō̃ pāṇī bharn āī.**

Derived Sentences.

1.	A woman came.	**Ikk janānī āī.**
2.	A woman came from the city.	**Ikk janānī shahrō̃ āī.**
3.	A woman came to draw water.	**Ikk janānī pāṇī bharn āī.**
4.	Did the woman come?	**Janānī āī?**
5.	Yes, she came.	**Āhō, āī.**
6.	Is there water?	**Pāṇī hai we?**
7.	Yes, there is.	**Āhō, hai we.**
8.	Did he come from the city?	**Shahrō̃ āeā?**
9.	Yes, he came from the city.	**Āhō, shahrō̃ āeā.**
10.	Did the gentleman come?	**Sāhb āeā?**
11.	Yes and his wife too.	**Āhō, āeā, te Mēmsāhb wī āī.**
12.	Draw water.	**Pāṇī kaḍḍh.**
13.	Come and draw water.	**Ā, pāṇī kaḍḍh.**
14.	Come to the city.	**Shahr ā.**

Lesson I(b).

And Jesus who was sitting on the well said to her, give me to drink.	(*b*) **Te Yesū, jeḥrā khūh te baiṭhā sī ohnū̃ ākheā, Menū̃ pāṇī piāḷdē.**

Derived Sentences.

1.	Jesus came to the well.	1.	**Yesū khūh te āeā.**
2.	Jesus sat on the well.	2.	**Yesū khūh te baiṭhā.**
3.	Jesus came and sat on the well.	3.	**Yesū khūh te ā baiṭhā.**
4.	The woman came to the well.	4.	**Janānī khūh te āī.**
5.	Jesus was at the well. and the woman came.	5.	**Yesū khūh te sī, te janānī āī.**
6.	The woman came from the	6.	**Janānī shahrō̃ āī, te ikk**

	city and a man was sitting on the well.		**jaṇā khūh te baiṭhā sī.**
7.	This man was the Lord Jesus.	7.	**Ēh jaṇā <u>Kh</u>udāwand Yesū sī.**
8.	A man said to the woman, give water.	8.	**Ikkī jaṇe janānī nū̃ ākh-eā, pāṇī dēh.** (*See* Gram., p. 286.)
9.	Give the man a drink.	9.	**Jaṇē nū̃ pāṇī piyāḷ.**
10.	Give the man water.	10.	**Jaṇē nū̃ pāṇī deh.**
11.	Give the woman water.	11.	**Janānī nū̃ pāṇī deh.**
12.	Draw water and give it to me.	12.	**Menū̃ pāṇī bhar dē.**
13.	The woman came to draw water from the well.	13.	**Janānī khūhō̃ pāṇī bharn āī.**
14.	The woman who was in the city came to draw water.	14.	**Ōh janānī, jehṛī shahr wicc sī, pāṇī bharn āī sī.**
15.	The man who was in the city came to draw water.	15.	**Ōh jaṇā, jehṛā shahr wicc sī, pāṇī bharn āeā sī.**
16.	Put the woman out of the city.	16.	**Janānī nū̃ shahrō̃ kaḍḍh.**
17.	Pull the man out of the water.	17.	**Jaṇē nū̃ pāṇī wiccō̃ kaḍḍh.**
18.	Take me out of the well.	18.	**Menū̃ khūh wiccō̃ kaḍḍh.**
19.	Give him a drink.	19.	**Ohnū̃ pāṇī piyāḷ.**
20.	Two women came from the city.	20.	**Dō janānīā̃ shahrō̃ āīā̃.**
21.	Two men came to the well.	21.	**Dō bande khūh te āe.**
22.	Eight men and women came to the city.	22.	**Aṭṭh jaṇe janānīā̃ shahr āe.**
23.	He was at the well.	23.	**Ōh khūh te sī.**
24.	Five men were at the well.	24.	**Panj bande khūh te sāṇ.**

Lesson I(c).

For his disciples had gone to the city to buy bread.	(*c*) **kyū̃jō ohdē cēlē rōṭī mull laiṇ wāste shahr gae hoe sāṇ.**

DERIVED SENTENCES.

1.	Why did they come ?	1.	**Ōh kyũ āe ?**
2.	They came for bread (food).	2.	**Ōh rōṭī wāste āe.**
3.	Why did they go to the city ?	3.	**Ōh shahr kyũ gae ?**
4.	They went to get water.	4.	**Ōh pāṇī laiṇ gae.**
5	His disciples came to the well.	5.	**Ohde cēlē khūh te āe sāṇ.**
6.	He went to draw water.	6.	**Ōh pāṇī bharn wāste geā.**
7.	She went to get bread (food).	7.	**Ōh rōṭī laiṇ geī.**
8.	They went to get the woman.	8.	**Ōh janānī nũ laiṇ gae.**
9.	The men, who went to the city, were his disciples.	9.	**Ōh bandē, jehṛē shahr gae, ohde cēlē sāṇ.**
10.	Buy food (bread), brother.	10.	**Rōṭī mull lai, bhāī.**
11.	Give bread to the disciple, sir.	11.	**Rōṭī cēlē nũ dehō, jī.**
12.	Give water to the disciples, sir.	12.	**Pāṇī cēleā̃ nũ dehō, jī.**
13.	Take bread for the Master, sir.	13.	**<u>Kh</u>udāwand wāste rōṭī lao, jī.**
14.	Have you come to buy (take) bread ?	14.	**Rōṭī laiṇ āe o ?**
15.	They went to give bread to the disciples.	15.	**Ōh cēleā̃ nũ rōṭī dēṇ gae.**
16.	He was seated at the well.	16.	**Ōh khūh te baiṭhā hoeā sī.**
17.	She was seated at the well.	17.	**Ōh khūh te baiṭhī hoī sī.**
18.	They were seated at the well.	18.	**Ōh khūh te baiṭhe hoe sāṇ.**
19.	They (fem.) were seated at the well.	19.	**Ōh khūh te baiṭhiā̃ hoiā̃ sāṇ.**
20.	Buy bread from the city.	20.	**Shahrō̃ rōṭī mull lai**

21. Give the bread that came from the city.	21. **Jehṛī rōṭī shahrō̃ āī, ōh dehō.**
22. The woman who came to draw water, give her bread.	22. **Jehṛī janānī pāṇī bharn wāste āī, ohnū̃ rōṭī deho.**
23. The water which you drew from the well, give it.	23. **Jehṛā pāṇī tū̃ khūhō̃ kaḍḍheā, ōh dēh.**
24. Have you been to the city (and come back)?	24. **Shahrō̃ hō āe o?**

Lesson I(d).

When they came back no one said to him, who is this? or what do you want?	**Jadō̃ muṛ āe, tā̃ kise ohnū̃ nā ākheā, eh kauṇ e? yā̃, tū̃ kī cāhnnā ẽ?**

DERIVED SENTENCES.

1. What is this?	1. **Ēh kī e?**
2. Stop (doing that) brother.	2. **Muṛ, bhāī.**
3. Come again, brother.	3. **Muṛ āwī̃, bhāī.**
4. Who are you (familiar or to a servant)?	4. **Tū̃ kauṇ ẽ?**
5. Who are you (polite)?	5. **Tusī̃ kauṇ o?**
6. When she came he said, give me a drink.	6. **Jadō̃ āī, ōs ākheā, pāṇī piā.**
7. They went back to get bread.	7. **Rōṭi laiṇ muṛ gae.**
8. Say it again.	8. **Muṛ ākhō.**
9. Come again.	9. **Muṛ āō.**
10. Stop doing that.	10. **Muṛ jāō.**
11. Do you wish for food?	11. **Tū̃ rōṭī cāhnnā ẽ?**
12. He wishes for food.	12. **Ōh rōṭī cahndā e.**
13. I want water.	13. **Maī pāṇī cāhnnā wā̃.**
14. What did you say?	14. **Tū̃ kī ākheā?**
15. What did he say?	15. **Ōs kī ākheā?**
16. What did you (polite) say?	16. **Tusā̃ kī ākheā?**
17. What did the disciples say?	17. **Cēleā̃ kī ākheā?**

18.	Did I say it right ?	18.	**Māī ṭhīk ākheā ?**
19.	Yes, you said it right.	19.	**Āhõ, tusā̃ ṭhīk ākheā ?**
20.	Did he say it correctly ?	20.	**Ōs ṭhīk ākheā sī ?**
21.	No, he did not say it correctly.	21.	**Nehī̃, ōs ṭhīk nehī̃ sī ākheā.**
22.	Did you say it right ?	22.	**Tusā̃ ṭhīk ākheā ?**
23.	Yes, I said it correctly.	23.	**Āhõ, maī ṭhīk ākheā.**
24.	Who said it ?	24.	**Kis ākheā ?**
25.	No one at all said it.	25.	**Kise wī nā ākheā.**

Lesson I(e).

DERIVED SENTENCES.

1	What is this ? It is a well.	1.	**Ēh kī e ? Ēh khūh e.**
2.	Who came to the well ? The Lord Jesus came to the well.	2.	**Khūh te kauṇ āeā ? Khudāwand Yesū khūh te āeā.**
3	Who came to the well from the city ?	3.	**Shahrõ kauṇ khūh te āī ?**
4.	A woman came to the well from the city.	4.	**Ikk janānī shahrõ khūh te āī.**
5.	Who was sitting on the well ? The Lord was.	5.	**Khūh te kauṇ baiṭhā sī ? Khūdāwand baiṭhā sī.**
6.	What did he say to her ? He said, give to drink.	6.	**Ohnū̃ kī ākheā sū ? Ākheā sū pāṇī piā.**
7.	Who had gone to the city ? His disciples had gone.	7.	**Kauṇ shahr gae hoe sāṇ ? Ohdē cēlē gae hoe sāṇ.**
8.	What had they gone to get ? They had gone to get bread.	8.	**Ōh kī laiṇ gae hoe sāṇ ? Rōṭī laiṇ gae hoe sāṇ.**
9.	Who is this woman ? She is a Samaritan.	9.	**Ēh janānī, kauṇ e ? Ēh Sāmaran e.**
10.	Who is this man ? He is a Jew.	10.	**Ēh bandā kauṇ e ? Ōh Yahūdī e.**

English	Panjabi
11. Who are these men? They are his disciples.	11. Ēh bandē kauṇ nē̃? Ohdē cēlē nē̃.
12. Are his disciples, too, Jews? They, too, are Jews.	12. Ohdē cēlē wī Yahūdī nē̃? Āhō, ōh wī Yahūdī nē̃.
13. Who are these women? They are city women.	13. Ēh buḍḍhīā̃ kauṇ nē̃? Ēh shahr dīā̃ buḍḍhīā̃ nē̃.
14. Who is coming from the city? Some woman.	14. Shahrō̃ kauṇ aundī e? Kōī janānī aundī e.
15. Who are going to the city? The disciples are going.	15. Shahr nū̃ kauṇ paē jānde nē̃? Cēlē jāndē nē̃.
16. Why are they going to the city? They are going to get bread.	16. Ōh shahr nū̃ kyū̃ jānde nē̃? Rōṭī laiṇ jānde nē̃.
17. Are they coming back now? Yes, when they buy food, they will come back.	17. Huṇē muṛ auṇgē? Āhō, jadō̃ rōṭī lellaiṇgē tā̃ muṛ auṇgē.
18. When did Jesus say to the woman, Give me a drink? When she came to draw water he said it.	18. Yesū janānī nū̃ kadō̃ ākheā, Menū̃ pāṇī piā? jādō̃ ōh pāṇī bharn āī, tadō̃ ākheā.
19. Woman, what dost thou want?	19. Buḍḍhīye, tū̃ kī cāhnnī ē̃?
20. Sir, I want to draw water from this well.	20. Janāb, maī ēs khūhō̃ pāṇī kaḍḍhṇā cāhnniā̃.
21. My man, what have you come for? or how have you come?	21. Jaṇeā, tū̃ kis tarhā̃ āeā ē̃?
22. Sir, I have come to buy food from the city.	22. Hazūr, maī tā̃ shahrō̃ rōṭī mull laiṇ āeā wā̃.
23. Men, what do you wish? We want water to drink.	23. Jaṇeō, tusī kī cāhnde o? Asī pīṇ jōgā pāṇī cāhnne ā̃.

24. Sisters, what do you wish? We came to get bread.	24. **Bhaiṇō, tusī̃ kī cāhndīā̃ o? Asī̃ rōṭī laiṇ āīā̃ ā̃.**
25. What do his disciples want? They want to say something to him.	25. **Ohdē cēlē kī cāhndē nē̃? Ohnū̃ kujjh ākhṇā cāhndē nē̃.**
26. Madam, where are you going? I am going to the city.	26. **Mēmsāhb, tusī̃ kitthē jāndē o? Maĩ shahr jānnī ā̃.**
27. My boy, where are you going? I am going to the city for bread.	27. **Muṇḍeā, tū̃ kitthē jānnā ē̃? Rōṭī wāstē shahr jānnā wā̃.**
28. Old man, you are going to the well, aren't you?	28. **Buḍḍheā, tū̃ khūh te jānnā ē̃ nā?**
29. No, but I am going to the city by way of the well.	29. **Nehī̃, par maĩ khūhō̃ hōkē shahr jānnā wā̃.**
30. Disciples, you are going to get bread, are you not? Yes, sir.	30. **Cēleō, tusī̃ rōṭī laiṇ jānde o nā? Janāb.**
31. Where is the woman going? To the well, sir.	31. **Ōh janānī kitthē jāndī e? Khūh te, janāb.**
32. Where is that man going? He, too, is going to the well.	32. **Ōh bandā kitthē jāndā e? Ōh wī khūh te jāndā e.**
33. Where are the disciples going? To draw water.	33. **Ōh cēlē kitthē jāndē nē̃? Pāṇī bharn.**
34. Where are the women going? They are going to the city.	34. **Janānīā̃ kitthē jāndīā̃ nē̃? Shahr jāndīā̃ nē̃.**

Lesson I(f).

Negative, Interrogative and Assertive Forms.

It would be well to have a picture of this incident and to learn, by pointing to the objects, to pass directly from the object to the Panjabi name.

1. What is this? It is a well. (a city, a man, a woman, water, a water-pot).	1. Ēh kī e? Ēh khūh e, [shahr, bandā, janānī, pāṇī, ghaṛā].
What are these? These are men, (women, water-pots).	Ēh kī nẽ? Ēh bande nẽ, [janānīā̃, ghaṛē].
2. It is not a well.	2. Ēh khūh nehī̃ e.
Is it a water-pot? It is.	Ēh ghaṛā we? Aho, hai ghaṛa.
This is a water-pot, isn't it?	Ēh ghaṛā we nā?
This is not a water-pot, is it?	Ēh tā̃ ghaṛā nehī̃ nā?

3. Each "person" in 3 *a*, *b*, etc., should be written on a separate slip and learned to speed, and that in connection with the other persons, for thus learned, it is instantly available for use.

(*a*) I am going to buy bread.	Mai rōṭī laiṇ jānnā wā̃ [fem. jānnī ā̃].
You (s.) are going to buy bread.	Tū̃ rōṭī laiṇ jānnā ẽ [fem. jānnī ẽ].
He is going to buy bread.	Ōh rōṭī laiṇ jāndā e [fem. jāndī e].
We are going to buy bread.	Asī̃ rōṭī laiṇ jānne ā̃ [fem. jānnīā̃ ā̃].
You are going to buy bread.	Tusī̃ rōṭī laiṇ jānde o [fem. jāndīā̃ o].
They are going to buy bread	Ōh rōṭī laiṇ jānde nẽ [fem. jāndīā̃ nẽ].
(*b*) I am not going to draw water.	Maī̃ pāṇī bharn nehī̃ jāndā [fem. jāndī].
You are not going to draw water.	Tū̃ pāṇī bharn nehī̃ jāndā [fem. jāndī].
He (she) is not going to draw water.	Ōh pāṇī bharn nehī̃ jāndā [fem. jāndī].
We are not going to draw water.	Asī̃ pāṇī bharn nehī̃ jānde [fem. jāndīā̃].
You are not going to draw water.	Tusī̃ pāṇī bharn nehī̃ jānde [fem. jāndīā̃].

They are not going to draw water.	Ōh pāṇī bharn nehī̃ jānde [fem. jāndiā̃].
(*c*) I came for a water-pot.	Maĩ ghaṛē wāste āeā [āī].
You came for a water-pot.	Tū ghaṛē wāste āeā [āī].
He (she) came for a water-pot.	Ōh ghaṛē wāste āeā [āī].
We came for water-pots.	Asī̃ ghaṛeā̃ wāste āe [āīā̃].
You came for water-pots.	Tusī̃ ghaṛeā̃ wāste āe [āīā̃].
They came for water-pots.	Ōh ghaṛeā̃ wāste āe [āīā̃].
(*d*) I did not come for a water-pot.	Maĩ ghaṛe wāste nā āeā [āī].
You did not come for a water-pot.	Tū̃ ghaṛe wāste nā āeā [āī].
He did not come for a water-pot.	Ōh ghaṛe wāste nā āeā [āī].
We did not come for water-pots.	Asī̃ ghaṛeā̃ wāste nā āe [āīā̃].
You did not come for water-pots.	Tusī̃ ghaṛeā̃ wāste nā āe [āīā̃].
They did not come for water-pots.	Ōh ghaṛeā̃ wāste nā āe [āīā̃].
(*e*) I have come from the city.	Maĩ shahrō̃ āeā wā̃ (āī ā̃).
You have come from the city.	Tū̃ shahrō̃ āeā [āī] ē̃.
He (she) has come from the city.	Ōh shahrō̃ āeā [āī] e.
We have come from the city.	Asī̃ shahrō̃ āe [āīā̃] ā̃.
You have come from the city.	Tusī̃ shahrō̃ āē [āīā̃] o.
They have come from the city.	Ōh shahrō̃ āe [āīā̃] nē̃.
(*f*) I have not come from the city.	Maĩ shahrō̃ nehī̃ āeā [āī].
You have not come from the city.	Tū̃ shahrō̃ nehī̃ āeā [āī].

	English	Panjabi
	He (she) has not come from the city.	**Ōh shahrō̃ nehī̃ āeā [āī].**
	We have not come from the city.	**Asī̃ shahrō̃ nehī̃ āe [āīā̃].**
	You have not come from the city.	**Tusī̃ shahrō̃ nehī̃ āe [āīā̃].**
	They have not come from the city.	**Ōh shahrō̃ nehī̃ āe [āīā̃].**
(g)	I eat bread daily.	**Maī̃ rōz rōṭī khā̃nnā wā̃ [khā̃nnī ā̃].**
	You eat bread and butter daily.	**Tū̃ rōz rōṭī makkhaṇ khā̃nnā ē̃ [khā̃nnī ē̃].**
	He eats meat daily.	**Ōh rōz mā̃s khā̃ndā we [khā̃ndī e].**
	We drink water daily.	**Asī̃ rōz pāṇī pīnne ā̃ [pīnnīā̃ ā̃].**
	You drink milk daily.	**Tusī̃ rōz duddh pīnde o [pīndīā̃ o].**
	They drink tea daily.	**Ōh rōz cāh pīnde nē̃ [pīndīā̃ nē̃].**

(h) INTERROGATIVE WHO OR WHAT?

English	Panjabi
Who am I? You are a Panjabi.	**Maī̃ kauṇ ā̃? Tū̃ Panjābī ē̃.**
Who are you? I am a carpenter?	**Tū̃ kauṇ ē̃? Maī̃ tarkhāṇ wā̃.**
Who is he? she? He is a teacher, she, etc.	**Ōh kauṇ e? Ōh astād wē. Ōh astānnī e. (In villages astādnī.)**
Who are we? You are farmers.	**Asī̃ kauṇ ā̃? Tusī̃ jaṭṭ o (inquire meaning.)**
Who are you? We are strangers.	**Tusī̃ kauṇ o? Asī̃ ōpare ā̃.**
Who are they? They are beggars.	**Ōh kauṇ nē̃? Ōh maṅgaṇwāḷe nē̃ (Maṅgaṇwāḷīā̃ nē̃.)**
Is she drawing water? No, she's not.	**Ōh pāṇī bhardī e? Nehī̃, pāṇī nehī̃ bhardī.**

Is he sitting on the well? No, he is not.	Ōh khūh te baiṭhā we? Nehī, khūh te nehī baiṭhā.
Are the men going to the city? No, they are not going.	Ōh shahr jānde nẽ? Nehī, ōh shahr nehī jānde.
Are the women drawing water? No, they are not drawing water.	Ōh pāṇī bhardiā̃ nẽ? Nehī, ōh pāṇī nehī bhardiā̃.
What are you doing?	Tusī kī karde o?
What is he doing?	Ōh ki kardā e?
What is she doing?	Ōh kī kardī e?
What are the women doing?	Ōh kī kardiā̃ nẽ?
What are the men doing?	Ōh kī karde nẽ?
What are you doing?	Tū̃ kī karnā ẽ?
What are you (f) doing.	Tū̃ kī karnī ẽ?

INTERROGATIVE FORM.

What did he say? He said, give me a drink.	Ōs kī ākheā? Ōs ākheā, pāṇī piāḷ.
What did she say? She, too, said, give me a drink.	Ōs kī ākheā? Ōs wī ākheā, menū̃ pāṇī piāḷ.
What did they say? They said, who is this woman?	Ohnā̃ kī ākheā? Ohnā̃ ākheā, eh janānī kauṇ e?
What did they (f.) say? They said, give us a drink.	Ohnā̃ kī ākheā? Ohnā̃ ākheā, sānū̃ pāṇī piāō.
What did you (s.) say? I said, give them a drink.	Tū̃ kī ākheā? Maī ākheā, ohnā̃ nū̃ pāṇī piāḷ.
What did you (pl.) say? We said, give us some tea.	Tusā̃ kī ākheā? Asā̃ ākheā sānū̃ cāh piāo.
What did I say? You said, give the cooly two pice.	Maī kī ākheā? Tusā̃ ākheā, kulī nū̃ dō paise deho.
What did we say? You said, give the boy bread.	Asā̃ kī ākheā? Tusā̃ ākheā, muṇḍe nū̃ rōṭī deho.

(*i*) IMPERATIVES.

Sit on the well.	**Khūh te bauh, or khūh te bauho.**
Sit on this chair.	**Ēs kursī te bauho, jī.**
Sit here.	**Ētthe bauh.**
Go to the city and buy bread, and bring it back.	**Shahr jāke rōṭī mull leā.**
Come here.	**Ure ā.**
Tell him to go quickly.	**Ohnū̃ ākh, chētī jāh.**
Tell him to come quickly.	**Ohnū̃ ākh, shatābī ā.**
Come back quickly.	**Chētī muṛe ā.**
Go and give this letter to Mr. Smith.	**Ēh ciṭṭhī Smit sāhb nū̃ de ā.**
Go and tell the cook to get bread from the city.	**Jāke khā̃sāmẽ nū̃ ākho, Shahrō̃ rōṭī mull leā.**

If the pupil compels himself to master the sentences of Lesson I, so that he is ready, accurate and fluent in their use, he will have laid a sure foundation for a good part of the language.

It may be that he will find it convenient to go on to the next lesson before completing this one. This is allowable, but there is nothing in this first lesson that should be passed over without being mastered. If he goes on, let him not fail to come back and get every expression, so that it is on the tip of his tongue. How long will it take? Do not be surprised if it takes a month of hard work entailing thousands of repetitions. Pay the price, even if it should be ten thousand, and you will find that succeeding lessons will come much easier.

Lesson II.

a When they asked, What shall we do	**Jadō̃ ohnā̃ puccheā, Asī̃ kī karīye**
b that we may work the works of God	**paī Khudā de kamm karīye**
c then he gave answer (answered),	**tad ōs jawāb dittā**
d This is the work of God	**Khudā dā kamm ēh we**

e that ye believe on him whom God hath sent.	pai tusī ōs te imān leāo, jihnū̃ Khudā ghalleā e.

[Directions for memorising. Learn according to clauses *a*, *b*, *c*, *d*, *e*, writing each on a slip, in the manner indicated for Lesson I.]

Derived Sentences.

1. What shall I do?	1. Maĩ kī karā̃?
2. What work shall I do?	2. Maĩ kī kamm karā̃?
3. Shall I go to the city for bread?	3. Maĩ rōṭī wāste shahr jāwā̃?
4. Where shall we go to buy bread?	4. Kitthe jākē roṭī mull laīye?
Where........meat, milk, wood, fuel, stamps?	Kitthe........mās, duddh, lakkaṛ, bāllaṇ, ṭikaṭ?
5. Where shall he go to get water?	5. Ōh kitthe jākē pāṇī lae?
6. Where shall she go to get milk?	6. Ōh kitthe jākē duddh lae?
7. Where shall I send him to buy meat?	7. Maĩ ohnū̃ tarkārī wāste kitthe ghallā̃?
8. When shall I go to buy wood?	8. Maĩ lakkaṛ mull laiṇ wāste kadȭ jāwā̃?
9. When shall he go to the city to give you the fuel?	9. Tuhānū̃ bāllaṇ dēṇ wāste shahr kadȭ jāē?
10. When shall they come back from the city to give you the letters?	10. Tuhānū̃ ciṭṭhīā̃ dēṇ wāste shahrȭ kadȭ muṛ auṇ?
11. Shall I send two women to him for water?	11. Maĩ ohde kōḷ dō janānīā̃ pāṇī wāste ghallā̃?
12. Shall we send her to the city?	12. Ohnū̃ shahr ghallīye?
13. Shall we draw water from the well in this city?	13. Ēs shahr de khūhȭ pāṇī kaḍḍhīye?
14. Who asked you to do this work?	14. Kis tenū̃ ākheā, ēh kamm kar?

	English		Panjabi
15.	Mrs. Smith told me to.	15.	Smit sāhb dī mēm menū̃ ākheā.
16.	Shall we give you tea?	16.	Tuhānū̃ cāh piāīye?
17.	May I go to the city? Yes, you may go.	17.	Maī shahr jā̃? Āhō, jāho.
18.	Shall I take your boy with me to the city?	18.	Maī tuhāḍḍe munḍe nū̃ nāḷ shahr laī jāwā̃?
19	May I ask her to draw water for two men?	19.	Maī ehnū̃ ākhā̃, dō bandeā̃ wāste pāṇī kaḍḍh?
20.	Shall we go to work?	20.	Kamm karn jāīye? (Kamm te jāīye?)
21.	Come, let us go to the city to work.	21.	Āō, kamm karn shahr calīye.
22.	What is the work of God?	22.	Khudā dā kamm kī e?
23.	Believe me this is the work of God.	23.	Merā jakīn karō, Khudā dā kamm ēh we.
24.	Who said, believe on him whom God sent?	24.	Kis ākheā Khudā de ghalle hōe te imān leāō?
25.	Go, work the works of God in this city.	25.	Jāho te ēs shahr wicc Khudā de kamm karō.
26.	The disciples of Jesus do the works of God.	26.	Yesū dē cēle Khudā dē kamm karde nẽ.
27.	The woman said, I believe on God.	27.	Janānī jawāb dittā, maī Khudā nū̃ manniā̃.
28.	We believe on him whom God sent.	28.	Āsī̃ ōs te imān leaunne ā̃, jihnū̃ Khudā ghalleā e.
29.	Shall we not believe on God?	29.	Khudā te imān nā leā̃wīye?
30.	We believe that thou camest from God.	30.	Sānū̃ yakīn e paī tū̃ Khudā kōḷō̃ āeā ẽ.
31.	Jesus answered them, do ye now believe?	31.	Yesū jawāb dittā paī tusī̃ huṇ yakīn karde o?
32.	I work a work which ye will not believe.	32.	Maī ōh kamm karnā wā̃ jihdā tusī̃ yakīn nā karōgē.

33. He told the truth that ye may believe.	33. Ōs sacc ākheā tā̃ jō tusī̃ imān leāō.
34. When they saw the works that Christ did, they believed.	34. Jadō̃ ohnā̃ oh kamm wēkh lae jehṛe Masīh kītē, ohnā̃ imān leāndā.
35. On whom do you believe? I believe on the Lord Jesus Christ.	35. Tuhāḍḍā imān kis utte we? or Tusī̃ Kihnū̃ mannde ō? Merā imān Khudāwand Yesū Māsīh utte we.
36. He has sent me so that the disciples may believe.	36. Ōs menū̃ ēs karkē ghalleā pai cēlē imān leauṇ.

Present Subjunctive and Future.

What good work shall I do that I may inherit eternal life?	Maĩ kehṛā nēk kamm karā̃ pai maĩ hamēshā dī zindagī dā [dī] wāris baṇā̃.
What good work canst thou do that thou mayest inherit eternal life?	Tū̃ kehṛā nēk kamm karē̃ pai tū̃ hamēshā dī zindagī̃ dā [di] wāris baṇē̃.
What good work can he do that he may inherit eternal life?	Ōh kehṛā bhalā kamm kare pai ōh hamēshā dī zindagī dā [dī] wāris baṇē.
What good works shall we do that we may inherit eternal life?	Asī̃ kehṛe nēk kamm karīye pai asī̃ sadā dī zindagī dē (dīā̃) wāris baṇīye?
What good works will you do that you may inherit eternal life?	Tusī̃ kehṛe nēk kamm karōgē pai tusī̃ sadā dī zindagī dē wāris baṇō?
What good works can they do that they may inherit eternal life?	Ōh kehṛe bhale kamm karn pai ōh sadā dī zindagī dē (dīā̃) wāris hōṇ?
Where shall I go?	Maĩ kitthe jāwā̃?
Where will you (s.) go?	Tū̃ kitthe jāẽgā?
Where shall he go?	Ōh kitthe jāē?
Where shall she go?	Ōh kitthe jāē?

Where shall we go?	Asī̃ kitthe jāīye?
Where will you go?	Tusī̃ kitthe jāōgē?
Where shall they go?	Ōh kitthe jāṇ?
Where will they go?	Ōh kitthe jāṇgē?
When shall I come?	Maĩ kadõ āwā̃?
When wilt thou come?	Tū̃ kadõ āwẽdā?
When shall he come?	Ōh kadõ āwē?
When shall we come?	Asī̃ kadõ āwīye?
When will you come?	Tusī̃ kadõ āode?
When will they come?	Ōh kadõ auṇde?
Ask me.	Methõ pucchō.
Ask him.	Ōsthõ pucchō.
Work here.	Ētthe kamm kar.
Do your work there.	Ōtthe apṇā kamm kar.
Give it to me, brother.	Menū̃ deh, bhrā.
Give it to him.	Ohnū̃ dē chaḍḍō.
Bring it quickly, my boy.	Chētī leā, puttar.
Bring it to me.	Menū̃ leā dē.
Send it at once.	Huṇē ghallō.
Send it to-morrow.	Bhaḷkē ghall deō.
I believe on him whom God sent.	Jihnū̃ Khudā ghalleā e, maĩ ōste imān leaunnā ā̃.
You (s.) believe on him whom God sent.	Jihnū̃ Khudā ghalleā e, tū̃ ōste imān leaunnā ẽ.
He believes on him whom God sent.	Jihnū̃ Khudā ghalleā e, oh ōste imān leaundā e.
We believe on him whom God sent.	Jihnū̃ Khudā ghalleā e, asī̃ ōste imān leaunne ā̃.
You believe on him whom God sent.	Jihnū̃ Khudā ghalleā e, tusī̃ ōste imān leaunde o.
They believe on him whom God sent.	Jihnū̃ Khudā ghalleā e, ōh ōste imān leaunde nẽ.
I sent him [her, them, you, you (s.)] to draw water.	Maĩ ohnū̃ [ohnū̃, ohnā̃nū̃, tuhā̃nū̃, tenū̃], pāṇī bharn ghalleā.
You (s.) sent him [her, us, me, them] to buy bread.	Tū̃ ohnū̃ [ohnū̃, sānū̃, menū̃ ohnā̃nū̃], rōṭī laiṇ ghalleā.

He sent us [me, you (s.), you, her, them] to get milk.	**Ōs sānū̃ [menū̃, tenū̃, tuhānū̃, ohnū̃, ohnā̃nū̃], duddh laiṇ ghalleā.**
We sent him, (her, them, you (s.), you) to get food.	**Asā̃ ohnū̃ [ohnū̃, ohnā̃nū̃, tenū̃, tuhānū̃], roṭī laiṇ ghalleā.**
You sent him [her, me, us, them] to work.	**Tusā̃ ohnū̃ [ohnū̃, menū̃, sānū̃, ohnā̃nū̃], kamm karn ghalleā.**
They sent him [her, them, you (s.), you, me, us] to work.	**Ohnā̃ ohnū̃, [ohnū̃, ohnā̃nū̃, tenū̃, tuhānū̃, menū̃, sānū̃] kamm karn ghalleā.**

The model sentence should be written on a large page at first in Panjabi and later on in English, and the personal pronouns at one side. The teacher should point to a different person for subject and object each time, until the pupil can go over the whole list with perfect ease and readiness. Hesitating, deliberating, repetition of the sentences was all right for the Latin classroom, perhaps, but it will not do in actual life.

I am doing my own work.	**Maĩ apṇā kamm karnā ā̃.**
You (s.) are doing your own work.	**Tū̃ apṇā kamm karnā ē̃.**
He is doing his.	**Ōh apṇā kardā e.**
We are doing our own work.	**Asī̃ apṇā kamm karne ā̃.**
You are doing your own work.	**Tusī̃ apṇā kamm karde o.**
They are doing their own work.	**Ōh apṇā kamm karde nē̃.**
She is doing her own work.	**Ōh apṇā kamm kardī e.**
The women are doing their own work.	**Ōh apṇā kamm kardīā̃ nē̃.**
The girl is doing her own work.	**Kuṛī apṇā kamm kardī e.**
The men are doing their own work.	**Ōh apṇā kamm karde nē̃.**

Write each sentence on a separate slip and memorise to speed.

Lesson III. (Future.)

*a.** He who drinks of this water shall thirst again,	**Eh pāṇī jehṛā pīe ohnū̃ phēr treh laggēgī,**
*b.** but whoever drinks of the water that I shall give,	**par jō kōī ōh pāṇī pīe jehṛā maĩ ohnū̃ dēā̃gā,**
*c** he shall never thirst,	**ohnū̃ kadī treh nā laggēgī,**
*d** but the water that I shall give,	**par jēhṛā pāṇī maĩ dēā̃gā,**
*e.** it shall become in him a spring of water, flowing for ever.	**ōh ohdē wicc paṇī dā sōtā baṇ jāēgā jehṛā hamēshā tīkar wagdā rahēgā.**

Derived Sentences.

1. This water will make you sick. (You will get sick from this water.)	**1. Tū̃ ēs pāṇī thõ bamār hō jāẽgā.**
2. It will never make me sick. (I, indeed, shall never get sick from drinking the water.)	**2. Maĩ tā̃ ēh pāṇī piṇ nāḷ kadī bamār nā hāwā̃gā.**
3. I shall never drink water from this well again.	**3. Maĩ phēr ēs khūh thõ pāṇī kadī nā piā̃gā.**
4. Jesus said, I will give you the bread of life and whoever will eat this bread shall not become hungry and shall not die.	**4. Yesū ākheā, Maĩ tuhānū̃ zindagī dī rōṭī deā̃gā te jō kōī ēh rōṭī khāēgā nā ohnū̃ bhukkh laggēgī te nā ōh marēgā.**
5. The one you give drink to will thirst again, but the one Christ gives drink to shall never thirst.	**5. Jihnū̃ tū̃ piyāḷēgī ohnū̃ phēr treh laggēgī, par jihnū̃ Masīh piāēgā ohnū̃ phēr nā laggēgī.**

* Memorise a clause at a time as indicated in Less. I.

6. Who believes on my name shall not die.	6. Jehṛā Mērē nā̃ utte imān leaundā e, ōh nā marēgā.
7. I will come again and take you with me.	7. Maĩ muṛ āṇkē tuhāṇū̃ Apṇe nāḷ khaṛā̃gā.
8. The Father will send the Holy Spirit in my name.	8. Bāp Mērē nā̃ utte Pāk Rūh nū̃ ghallēgā.
9. When the Comforter will come, whom I will send to you from the Father, he will teach you.	9. Jad Tasallī-dēṇwāḷā āwēgā, Jihnū̃ Maĩ Bāp wallō̃ tuhāḍḍe kōḷ ghallā̃gā, Ōh tuhānū̃ sikhāēgā.
10. Then among the brethern was this thing said, This disciple will not die.	10. Tad bhāīā̃ wicc ēh gall ākhī geī, Ēh cēlā nā marēgā.
11. They will send you to do this work.	11. Ōh tuhānū̃ ēh kamm karn wāste ghallaṇge.
12. When will the chair be ready? It will be made by to-morrow, sir.	12. Kursī kadō̃ teār hōwēgī? Bhaḷak tōṛī baṇ jāēgī, janāb.
13. The women will draw water from this well to-day.	13. Janānīā̃ ajj ēs khūhō pāṇī kaḍḍhaṇgīā̃.
14. When will you come [my] girl? I shall come tomorrow, mother.	14. Kadō̃ āwẽgī, kuṛīye? Bēbbē, bhaḷkē āwā̃gī.
15 Your servant will give it to-morrow, won't he? He will.	15. Tuhāḍḍā naukar fajrī dēwēgā nā? Dēwēgā.
16. We'll say to him: You will sit here.	16. Asī̃ ohnū̃ ākhā̃ge. pai tusī̃ ētthe baiṭhōgē.
17. The women will come back the day after to-morrow and bring you the bread.	17. Buḍḍhīā̃ parsō̃ muṛ auṇgīā̃ te rōṭī tenū̃ leā dēṇgīā̃.
18. They asked the women to	18. Ohnā̃ janānīā̃ nū̃ puccheā

	sit down; but they said, We'll come early to-morrow and sit.		paī bawhōgiā̃? par ohnā̃ ākheā; Bhaḷkē sawēḷē ākē bawhā̃giā̃.
19.	When will you send it? I will send it the day after to-morrow.	19.	Kadõ ghallōgē? Parsõ ghall deā̃gā.
20.	He will never be hungry and thirsty.	20.	Ohnū̃ kadī bhukkh treh nā laggēgī.
21.	When they drew the water, all the boys became thirsty.	21.	Jadõ ohnā̃ pāṇī kaḍḍh leā tad sāreā̃ muṇḍeā̃ nū̃ treh laggī.
22.	When the boy asked, Shall I draw water here, the gentleman said, By all means, my son.	22.	Jadõ ōs muṇḍe puccheā, Janāb, maī̃ pāṇī ētthõ kaḍḍhā̃; sāhb ākheā, Jam jam kaḍḍh, puttar.
23.	She came to draw water, for all the boys and girls were thirsty.	23.	Ōh pāṇī bharn āī si, kyū̃jō sāre muṇḍe kuṛīā̃ trihāe sāṇ.
24.	I'll give the one who goes to the city a rupee.	24.	Jō kōī shahr jāe, ohnū̃ rupayyā deā̃gī.
25.	The man who came from the city yesterday is a waterman.	25.	Jehṛā bandā kall shahrõ āeā si, ōh te māshki si.
26.	Waterman! What's a waterman? He is a drawer of water.	26.	Māshkī! Māshkī kī e? Ōh tā̃ pāṇī bharnwāḷā e.
27.	When he sent the men to the gentleman, he [pl. respect] asked them, Are you the disciples of the guru? No. Who then?	27.	Jadõ ōs sāhb kōḷ bande ghalle, ohnā̃ puccheā, tusī̃ gurū de cēlē o? Nehī̃. Tā̃ kauṇ o?
28.	They will send you and you will give this word to all the men.	28.	Ōh tuhānū̃ ghallaṇgē te tusī̃ ēh khabar sāreā̃ bandeā̃ nū̃ dēōgē.
29.	Don't come here again	29.	Ētthe muṛ nā āweō.

30. Don't get sick.	30. **Bamār nā hōweō.**
31. Don't do this work.	31. **Ēh kamm nā kar [pl. karō].**
32. Don't drink from this well.	32. **Ēs khūhō pāṇī nā pī [pīō].**
33. Don't ask him to-day.	33. **Ajj ōs thō̃ nā pucch [pucchō].**
34. Send the bread the day after to-morrow.	34. **Rōṭī parsō̃ ghallī̃ [ghalleo].**
35. Don't bring the letter to-morrow.	35. **Bhaḷkē ciṭṭhī na leāwī̃. (leāweō).**

FUTURE OF SEND. Be sure to master your tenses by the Slip method.

I shall send the book to you to-morrow.	**Maĩ bhaḷkē tenū̃ katāb ghall deā̃gā [deā̃gī].**
You (s.) will send the book to me to-morrow.	**Tū̃ bhaḷke menū̃ katāb ghall dē̃gā [dē̃gī].**
He (she) will send the book to us to-morrow.	**Ōh bhaḷkē sānū̃ katāb ghall dēgā [dē̃gī].**
We shall send the book to you to-morrow.	**Asī̃ bhaḷkē tuhā̃nū̃ katāb ghall deā̃gē [deā̃giā̃].**
You will send the book to my boy to-morrow.	**Tusī fajrī̃ mērē muṇḍē nū̃ katāb ghallōgē.**
They will send your girls the book to-day.	**Ōh ajj tuhāḍḍiā̃ kuṛiā̃ nū̃ katāb ghall dēṇgē [dēṇgiā̃.]**
I shall not go to the city with this man.	**Maĩ ēs bandē nāḷ shahr nā jāwā̃gā [jāwā̃gī].**
You will not go to the city with me.	**Tū̃ mērē nāḷ shahr nā jāē̃gā [jāē̃gī].**
He (she) will not go to the village with us.	**Ōh sāḍḍē nāḷ piṇḍ nā jāēgā [jāēgī].**
We shall never go with you.	**Asī̃ tērē nāḷ kadī nā jāā̃ge [jāā̃giā̃].**
You will not go with him.	**Tusī̃ ohdē nāḷ nā jāōgē [fem. jāōgiā̃].**
They will not go with you.	**Ōh tuhāḍḍē nāḷ nā jāṇge [jāṇgiā̃].**

I shall be sick in the morning.	**Maĩ fajrī bamār hōwẫgā [hōwẫgī].**
You will be present the day after to-morrow.	**Tū̃ parsõ hāzar hōwẽgā [hōwẽīg].**
He will be well in a moment.	**Ōh huṇē caṅgā hōjāēgā [caṅgī hōjāēgī].**
We shall be big.	**Asī̃ waḍḍe hōwẫgē [waḍḍiā̃ hōwẫgiā̃].**
You will be fat [thick].	**Tusī̃ mōṭē hōwōgē. (fem. moṭiā̃ hōwāgiā̃)**
They will be good.	**Ōh caṅgē hōṇgē (caṅgiā̃ hōṇgiā̃).**

Do not neglect to time yourself, see that you can repeat these with perfect readiness and fluency, alternating the repetition, as you learn them, with your teacher. Make haste slowly, and leave nothing half done.

Lesson IV.

a. Come, see a man who told me all that I ever did (whatever I did told me all).	*a.* **Āō ikk ādmī nū̃ wēkhō, jis sabbho kujjh menū̃ dass dittā jō kujjh maĩ kītā e.**
b. Is not this the Messiah?	*b.* **Bhalā ehī Masīh nā hōwēgā?**
c. For this reason people went out of the village and came to him (having gone out began to come to him).	*c.* **Ēs karkē lōk naggarõ nikaḷke ohdē kōḷ auṇ laggē.**

DERIVED SENTENCES.

1. He told me everything you did.	1. **Jō kujjh tusā̃ kītā ōs menū̃ dasseā̃ e.**
2. See these men who told the gentleman everything that you did.	2. **Ehnā̃ bandeā̃ nū̃ wēkhō, jihnā̃ sāhb nū̃ sabbho kujjh dass dittā jō kujjh tū̃ kītā e.**

3. We went out of the city to him.	3. **Asī̃ shahrõ nikḷkē ohdē kōḷ gae.**
4. As we saw some men going out of the city, we said, Aren't these the disciples of our "guru"? (Hindu religious teacher).	4. **Dũh caũh ādmīā̃ nū̃ shahrõ nikḷdeā̃ wēkhkē asā̃ ākheā, ēh sāḍḍē gurū dē cēlē nehī̃?**
5. That man's followers came and told all that he did.	5. **Jō kujjh ōs ādmī kītā ohdeā̃ cēleā̃ āṇkē dass dittā.**
6. The disciples came to me and asked, Did some servant of yours go out of the village and go to the city yesterday?	6. **Cēle mērē kōḷ āṇkē pucchaṇ lagge, Kall tuhāḍḍā kōī naukar naggarõ nikḷkē shahr geā?**
7. Whatever you desire, is yours.	7. **Jō kujjh tusī̃ cāhnde o, tuhāḍḍā ī e.**
8. Tell me everything that he ever did.	8. **Jō kujjh ōs kadī kītā ōh menū̃ dass dē.**
9. This is my food, that I may fulfil the work of my sender.	9. **Mērā khāṇā ēh we, pai maī̃ apṇe ghallaṇwāḷē dā kamm pūrā karā̃.**
10. When they sent the boys to the teacher then he asked them, Are you the guru's followers?	10. **Jad ohnā̃ muṇḍeā nū̃ astād kōḷ ghalleā, tad ōs ohnā̃ kōḷõ puccheā, tusī̃ gurū dē cēlē o?**
11. Who told you? He told me.	11. **Kis tenū̃ dasseā? Ōs menū̃ dasseā.**
12. I came for this reason, to tell God's works that people might believe on Him.	12. **Maī̃ ēs karke āeā pai <u>Kh</u>udā de kamm dassā̃ te lōk ohde utte imān leauṇ.**
13. They will send you to do this work that you should tell people of Christ.	13. **Ōh tuhānū̃ ēh kamm karn wāste ghallaṇge pai tusī̃ Masīh dī <u>kh</u>abar lōkā̃ nū̃ deho.**

14. He came to the city, so I went away.	14. Ōh shahr āeā, tā̃iẽ maĩ ṭur geā.
15 People came and asked, when did you come out ?	15. Lōk ohdē kōḷ āṇke pucchaṇ lagge, Kadõ nikḷe sao ?
16. Why did they draw water from the village well ?	16. Ohnā̃ naggar dē khūh thõ pāṇī kāhnū̃ bhareā.
17. They drew it so that they might give a drink of water to those who were thirsty.	17. Ēs karke bhareā paī jinhā̃ lōkā̃ nū̃ treh laggī hōī sī, piyāḷaṇ.
18. Whatever he did, he did well.	18. Jō kujjh ōs kita caṅgā kītā.
19. Tell exactly what he did.	19. Ṭhīk ṭhīk dasso, ōs kī kītā si ?
20. All the water has run out of this well.	20. Ēs khūhõ sārā pāṇī nikḷ geā we.
21. I saw you by the village yesterday.	21. Maī kall tuhānū̃ piṇḍ kōḷ wēkheā.
22. The women will tell everything (all things) to us.	22. Ōh sārīā̃ gallā̃ sānū̃ dassaṇgīā̃.

INTERROGATIVES.

You went to the city yesterday, didn't you ?	Tusī kall shahr gae sao nā ?
You will go to the city to-morrow, won't you ?	Tusī bhaḷkē shahr jāōgē nā ?
He came from the city yesterday, didn't he ?	Ōh kall shahrõ āeā sī nā ?
He told you, didn't he ?	Ōs tuhānū̃ dasseā sī nā ?
Did they do it, or did you ?	Ohnā̃ kītā sī, ke tusā̃ ?
She went to draw water towards evening, didn't she ?	Ōh lauḍhēwēḷē pāṇī bharn gaī sī nā ?
Did the women go out of the village early or not ?	Oh fajrwēḷē naggarõ nikḷ geīā̃ ke nā ?
They went to you at noon, didn't they ?	Oh dopaihr tuhāḍḍe kōḷ gae na ?

Did the man who told me go to you also ?	**Jis menū̃ dasseā, ōh tērē koḷ wī geā si ?**

Imperatives.	Amr.
Give me the book.	**Menū̃ katāb deh.**
Hand him the book.	**Ohnū̃ katab phaṛa deh.**
Give the basket to the boy.	**Muṇḍe nū̃ ṭōkra deh.**
Give the baskets to the boys.	**Mundeā̃ nū̃ ṭōkrē deh.**
Give me the little basket, sir.	**Sānū̃ ṭōkrī deho, jī.**
Give the books to my son, sir.	**Mērē puttar nū̃ katābā̃ deho, jī.**
Get the baskets from my sons, sir.	**Mērēā̃ puttarā̃ kōḷō ṭōkrīā̃ lao, jī.**
[My] girl, hand me that water-jar.	**Kuṛīye, ōh ghaṛā menū̃ phaṛā de.**
[My] boy, get out the water-jars.	**Muṇḍeā, ghaṛē kaḍḍh leā.**
Sir, get out a water-jar (for me) (to a shop-keeper).	**Shāh jī, (or Lālā Jī) kōī ghaṛā kaḍḍh deo.**
Give these jars to his servants.	**Eh ghaṛe ohdeā naukarā̃ nū̃ dē deo.**

Past Tenses.

What did he tell you ?	**Ōs tuhānū̃ kī dassēā ?**
He told us this.	**Ōs sānū̃ ēh gall dassī.**
They told us this only.	**Ohnā̃ ihōī dasseā.**
Did you tell anything else ?	**Tusā̃ kōī hōr gall wī dassī.**
I told many things.	**Maī tā̃ bathērīā̃ dassīā̃.**
We told everything.	**Asā̃ sabbh kujjh dasseā.**
You did not tell anything at all.	**Tū̃ tā̃ kujjh wī nā dasseā.**
He went to the city yesterday.	**Ōh kall shahr geā.**
She went to the city yesterday.	**Ōh kall shahr geī.**
They went to the village yesterday.	**Ōh kall piṇḍ gae.**
The women went to the village only to-day.	**Ōh ajj hī piṇḍ geīā̃**
He gave me the book.	**Ōs menū̃ katāb dittī.**

They gave me three books.	Ohnā̃ menū̃ trai katābā̃ dittīā̃.
The gentleman gave you a water-jar.	Sāhb tenū̃ ghaṛā dittā.
Mr.——gave the boy four jars.	Sāhb muṇḍe nū̃ cār ghaṛē dittē.
They gave us books, baskets, jars, and also one rupee.	Ohnā̃ sānū̃ katābā̃ dittīā̃, ṭōkrīā̃ dittīā̃, ghaṛe ditte te ikk rūpayyā wī dittā.

Lesson V.	*Panjwā̃ Sabak.*
a. When the teacher said to her,	*a.* Jadō̃ ustād ohnū̃ ākheā,
b. Go and call thy husband,	*b.* Jā apṇē gharwāḷē nū̃ sadd leā,
c. She answered, I have no husband,	*c.* Ōs jawāb dittā, Mērā kōī gharwāḷā nehī̃,
d but he knew her whole history, so he said,	*d.* par ohnū̃ sārē hāl dā patā sī ēs karke ōs ākheā.
e. You said right, I have no husband,	*e.* Tū̃ ṭhīk ākheā e, Mērā kōī k͟hasm nehī̃,
f. for you have had five husbands,	*f.* kyū̃jō tū̃ te panj k͟hasm kītē nē̃,
g. and he whom you now have is not your husband.	*g.* te jihnū̃ tū̃ huṇ rakkheā hōeā e, ōh tērā k͟hasm nehī̃.
h. You told the truth this time.	*h.* Ēh tū̃ sacc ākheā e.

Derived Sentences.

(Imperatives. Ḥave, possessive.)

1. Go and call the syce and bring him back.	1. Sahīs nū̃ sadd leā.
2. Go and call a cook and bring him for me.	2. Jā mērē wāstē kōī khansāmā̃ sadd leā.
3. Call some sweeper and waterman.	3. Kōī mehtar māshkī sadd lao.

	English		Panjabi
4.	Call a tailor and a carpenter for madam.	4.	Mēmsāhb wāstē kōī darzī te kōī tarkhāṇ sadd lao.
5.	Tell the truth.	5.	Sacc ākho.
6.	Tell the exact truth.	6.	Sacc sacc ākh.
7.	Tell the teacher to come here.	7.	Ustād nū mērā salām deho, Ustād nū ākhō, Sāhb bulānde nē, Ustad nū etthē sadd lāo.
8.	Answer at once.	8.	Jawāb jhaṭ paṭ deho.
9.	He said it to himself.	9.	Ōs Dil wicc ākheā sī.
10.	When she saw that "He knows my past life," then she said, Sir, you are a prophet.	10.	Jadō ōs diṭṭhā paī Ēh mērī picchlī zindagī nū jāṇdā e, tad ohnū ākheā, Janāb, tusī nabī o.
11.	When he understood her past life, then he said to her I will give you living water.	11.	Jadō ōs ohdī picchlī zindagī dā hawāl samajh leā tad ōsnū ākheā, Maī tenū jiūndā pāṇī deāgā.
12.	When the woman said, I have no husband, he said, You have had five, and the present one is not yours.	12.	Jad ōs aurat ākheā, Mērā kōī khasm nehī, ōs ākheā, Tērē tā panj hoe nē, par jehṛā huṇ e ōh tērā khasm nehī.
13.	The Lord said to his church, I am thy husband.	13.	Khudāwand āpṇī kalīsiā nū ākheā, Maī tērā shauhr ā.
14.	I have two boys and three girls.	14.	Mērē dō muṇḍē te trai kuṛīā nē.
15.	How many boys have you?	15.	Tuhāḍḍē kinnē bālak nē?
16.	We have no boys, only four girls.	16.	Sāḍḍā kōī muṇḍā nehī, nirīā cār kuṛīā nē.
17.	I have no girl, only five boys.	17.	Mērī kōī kuṛī nehī, nirē panj muṇḍē.
18.	They have eight half-acres	18.	Ohnā dī aṭṭh wige jīwī

of land and nine large houses.	te naũ hawēlīā̃ nē̃.
19. You have six cows and seven oxen.	19. Tuhāḍḍīā̃ chē gāīā̃ te satt ḍhaggē nē̃.
20. Have you a penknife? a pen?	20. Tuhāḍḍē kōḷ kōī cakkū e? kōī kalam?
21. You have my books. Have you my books?	21. Mērīā̃ katābā̃ tērē kōḷ nē̃.
22. I have neither book nor pen, nor paper, nothing at all.	22. Nā katāb, nā kalam, nā kāgad, kujjh wī nehī̃.
23. Have you any word of the post?	23. Tuhānū̃ kōī ḍāk dā patā e?
24. Has each boy in this class pen and ink?	24. Ēs jamāt dē har ikk muṇḍē kōḷ kalam dawāt e?
25. Why have you no shoes on to-day?	25. Terī pairī̃ ajj juttī kyū̃ nehī̃?
26. Had you the book yesterday?	26. Katāb kall tērē kōḷ sī.
27. Had the girls their (other people's) book to-day?	27. Ajj ohnā̃ dī katāb kuṛīā̃ kōḷ sī?
28. No, only the boys had books to-day.	28. Nehī̃, ajj sirf muṇḍeā̃ kōḷ katābā̃ sān.

Pasts, Imperatives, and Possessive Interrogatives.

Change "I" to thou, we, you, he, they, the boy, the girl, the boys, the girls.	Instead of "Maĩ" substitute tū̃, asā̃, tusā̃, os, ohnā̃, muṇḍe, kākī, muṇḍeā̃, kākīā̃, leaving the rest of the sentence unchanged.
I gave you my book.	Maĩ apṇī katāb tenū̃ dittī.
I gave him my house.	Maĩ apṇā ghar ōsnū̃ dittā.
I gave you my watch.	Maĩ apṇī ghaṛī tuhānū̃ dittī.
I gave them my jars.	Maĩ apṇē ghaṛē ohnā̃ nū̃ dittē.

I gave the boy my jar.	Maĩ apṇā ghaṛā muṇḍe nū̃ dittā.
I gave you my watches.	Maĩ apṇīā̃ ghaṛīā̃ tuhānū̃ dittīā̃.
I gave the girl my books.	Maĩ apṇīā̃ kitābā̃ kākī nū̃ dittīā̃.
I saw the boy yesterday.	Maĩ kall muṇḍe nū̃ ḍiṭṭhā.
I saw the girl yesterday.	Maĩ kall kuṛī nū̃ ḍiṭṭhā.
I saw the horses yesterday.	Maĩ kall ghōṛeā̃ nū̃ ḍiṭṭhā.
I saw all the mares.	Maĩ sārīā̃ ghōṛīā̃ nū̃ ḍiṭṭhā.
Did they say this ?	Ohnā̃ ēh gall ākhī sī?
They did.	Āhō, īhōī ākhī si.
Who sent you this watch ?	Ēh ghaṛī tenū̃ kis ghallī?
That boy sent it.	Ōs muṇḍē ghallī.
Where did you buy the baskets ?	Ṭōkrīā̃ kitthō̃ mull leīā̃ jē.
I got the baskets from that shop.	Mai tokrīā̃ ōs haṭṭīō leīā̃ nē̃.
Whom did they ask ?	Kihdē kōḷō̃ puccheā nē?
They asked the teacher.	Ohnā̃ ustād kōḷō̃ puccheā.
Did they send the jars ?	Ohnā̃ ghaṛē ghall dittē?
Yes, they sent them.	Āhō, ghall dittē.
No, they have not yet sent them.	Nehī̃, ajē nehī̃ ghallē.

Take the verbs of the following list and put them into appropriate imperatives sing. and pl. with predicate modifiers from the nouns of the next list :—

Come, go, ask, give, take, drink, do. sit, send, speak.	Ā, jā, pucch, dēh, lai, pī, kar, baiṭh, ghall, ākh.
Has the man a dog ? Yes, he has.	Ōs bandē kōḷ kutta we? Ahō, hai we.
Have they dogs ? They have.	Ohnā̃ kōḷ kuttē nē̃? Haiṇ nē̃.

As subjects use he, she, they, you, boy, girl, woman, girls, boys, cook, teacher. As objects, use dogs, horses, mare, mares, book-s, pen-s, pencil-s, jar-s, watch-es.

Lesson VI (Conditional).

a.	If thou knewest the gift of God,	*a.*	Jē tū̃ Khudā dī bakhshīsh nū̃ jāṇdīō̃,
b.	and Him that saith to thee, Give drink,	*b.*	te ohnū̃ jehṛā tenū̃ āhndā e pāṇī piā,
c.	then thou from him wouldst ask,	*c.*	tā̃ tū̃ ohdē kōḷō̃ maṅgdīō̃,
d.	and he would give thee living water.	*d.*	te Ōh tenū̃ jiūndā pāṇī dēndā.

Derived Sentences.

1.	If you had known the woman, you would not have asked water from her.	1.	Jē tū̃ zanānī nū̃ jāṇdō̃, tā̃ tū̃ ohdē kōḷō̃ pāṇī na maṅgdō̃.
2.	If you had known that man you would not have given him money.	2.	Jē tū̃ ōs bande nū̃ jāṇdō̃, tā̃ ōsnū̃ rupayye nā dēndō̃.
3.	If he had been a Jew, would he have asked water of a Samaritan woman ?	3.	Jē ōh Yahūdī hondā, tā̃ Sāmaran kōḷō̃ pāṇī maṇgdā ?
4.	To whom does God give living water ?	4.	Khudā jiūndā pāṇī kihnū̃ dēndā e ?
5.	If any one asks for living water, then God gives it through the Lord Jesus Christ.	5.	Jē kōī jiūndā pāṇī maṅgē, tā̃ Khudā ōsnū̃ Khudāwand Yesū Masīh dī rāhī̃ dēndā e.
6.	If you had asked of him, he would have given you living water.	6.	Jē tusī̃ ohdē kōḷō̃ maṅgdē, tā̃ ōh tuhānū̃ jiūndā pāṇī dēndā.
7.	If he had asked me for this living water, I should have said to him, Believe on Christ.	7.	Jē ōh mērē kōḷō̃ ēh jiūndā pāṇī maṇgdā, maĩ ohnū̃ āhndā, Masīh te imān leāō̃.

English	Panjabi
8. If you believe on the man who was seated on Jacob's well, he will give you living water.	8. Jē tū̃ ōs bandē te jehṛā Yakūb dē khūh te baiṭhā si imān leāwẽ ōh tenū̃ jiūnda pāṇī dēwēgā.
9. If any one drinks the water of this well, he will be thirsty again, but he who drinks the water of life shall never thirst again.	9. Jē kōī ēs khūh dā pāṇī pīwē, tā̃ muṛ treh laggsūgī, par jehṛā zindagī dā pāṇī pīegā, ohnū̃ muṛ kadī treh nā laggegī.
10. If any one drinks this spiritual water, it shall be made in his heart a spring of life eternal.	10. Jē kōī eh rūhānī pāṇī pīē, ēh ohdē dil wicc hamēshā dī zindagī dā sōtā baṇ jāēgā.
11. If the woman had not come to the well, then Christ would not have told her past life's history.	11. Jē zanānī khūh te nā aundī, tā̃ Masīh ohdī guzrī zindagī dā hawāl ohnū̃ nā dassdā.
12. If the disciples had not gone to get bread, then Christ would not have been left alone.	12. Jē cēlē rōṭī laiṇ nā jāndē, tā̃ Masīh akallā nā rahndā.
13. When people said, Show us the works of God, he said, Believe on his messenger.	13 Jadō̃ lōk āhndē sāṇ, Khudā de kamm sānū̃ wikhā, tad ōs ākheā, Tusī̃ ōsdē paikambar te imān leāō.
14. If any one will give information about your past life, then is he not a prophet?	14. Je kōī tērī picchlī zindagī dī khabar dē, tā̃ ōh nabī nēhī̃?
15. She said to the people, If you go out of the city and go to the well, then you will see a	15. Ōs lōkā̃ nū̃ ākheā, Jē tusī̃ shahrō̃ nikaḷkē khūh te jāō, tā̃ ikk nabī khūh te baiṭhā

	prophet seated on the well.		hoeā wēkhōgē.
16.	If you will call your husband here, then I will explain the meaning of the water of life.	16.	Jē tū̃ apṇe shauhr nū̃ sadd leāwẽgī, tā̃ maĩ zindagī de pāṇī dā matlab samjhā̃gā.
17.	If you have had five husbands, then why is not this man your husband ?	17.	Jē tērē panj shauhr hoe nẽ, tā̃ ēh bandā terā shauhr kyū̃ nehī̃ ?
18.	If he knew her past history, why did he talk to her ?	18.	Jē ōsnū̃ ohdē picchlē hal dā patā hai sī, tā̃ phēr ohdē nāḷ gall kyū̃ kītī ?
19.	For this reason he talked to her, that he might show her the need of the water of life.	19.	Ēs karkē gall kītī paī ohnū̃ zindagī de pāṇī dī lōṛ dassē.
20.	God gives it to those who ask it.	20.	Khudā ohnā̃ nū̃ dēndā e jehṛē maṇgdē nẽ.
21.	What is this living water ?	21.	Ēh jiūndā pāṇī kī e ?
22.	This gift of God is his Holy Spirit, is it not ?	22.	Ēh Khudā dī bakhshish, ohdā Pāk Rūh hai nā ?
23.	To what different ones does God give this gift of his ?	23.	Khudā kihnū̃ kihnū̃ Apṇī ēh bakhshish dēndā e ?
24.	If any one asks, God gives it freely.	24.	Jē kōī maṇge tā̃ Khudā aīwẽ dēndā e.
25.	When she said, This man is the Messiah, all the people went out of the city to see him.	25.	Jad ōs ākheā, Ēh bandā Masīh e, tā̃ sārē lōk shahrõ nikaḷkē ohnū̃ wēkhkhaṇ gaē.
26.	If he tells my past life, then I shall know that	26.	Jē ōh mērī picchlī zindagī dā patā dassē,

he is a prophet of God.	tā̃ maĩ jāṇā̃gī pai ēh Khudā dā nabī e.
27. If this were my jar, I would give it you.	27. Jē ēh mērā ghaṛā hondā tā̃ maĩ tuhānū̃ dēndā.
28. If this were my chair I'd give it thee.	28. Jē ēh mērī kursī hondī, tā̃ maĩ tenū̃ dēndā.
29. If you know where cloth is sold, I will go and bring some for you.	29. Jē tenū̃ patā e pai kapṛā kitthē wikdā e, tā̃ maĩ tērē lai leāwā̃gā.
30. If you are going to learn a Panjabi sentence, learn it thoroughly.	30. Jē tusī̃ kōī Panjābī fikrā sikkhaṇ laggē o, tā̃ pūrī tarhā̃ nāḷ sikkhō.
31. Who told you that we were sitting at the well?	31. Kis tuhānū̃ ākheā pai Asī̃ khūh te baiṭhē hoē sā̃?
32. Who told you the cow is in the garden?	32. Kis tenū̃ ākheā pai Gā̃ bagice wicc e?
33. Who told you the men have gone for oxen?	33. Kinhā̃ tuhānū̃ ākheā Bandē ḍhaggē laiṇ gae nē̃?
34. Who gave you the chair? Did Mr. Blank?	34. Kis tenū̃ kursī dittī? Sāhb dittī?
35. Who gave you boys the chairs?	35. Tuhānū̃ muṇḍeā̃ nū̃ kis kursīā̃ dittīā̃?

Diversification Exercises.

Take sentence 27 and learn it to speed, then write it on a sheet of paper so as to have it prominently before your eyes.

Now take the words for substitution and write them out on slips of paper or cardboard and take one from the list of "subjects" and substitute it, giving the sentence in full. Suppose you have laid down the word "horse," then you will say, Jē ēh mērā ghōṛā hondā, tā̃ maĩ tuhānū̃ dēndā. So on with "chair-s, book-s, mare-s, dog-s, basket-s, house-s, jar-s."

In like manner substitute the possessive pronouns for "**mērī**," and the above nouns one at a time for "**kursī**," in the sentence, **Ēh mērī kursī e**, writing them on slips or else on a sheet and getting the teacher to point now to one, now to another: "thy, your, his, her, their, our, the boy's, the girl's, the man's, the men's, the women's till fluency is secured. **Tērā-ī, tuhāḍḍā-ī, ohdā-ī, ohdā-ī, ohnā̃ dā-ī, muṇḍe dā-ī, kākī dā-ī, ādmī dā-ī, ādmīā̃ dā-dī, janānī dā-ī, janānīā̃ dā-ī.**

Kursī-ā̃, kitāb-ā̃, ghōṛī-ā̃, kuttā-ī, kuttē-īā̃, ṭōkrā-ī, ṭōkre-īā̃ ghar, ghaṛā, ghaṛē.

If an hour's daily practice is kept up for a week or two, the facility acquired will make all such work easier for the future, and establish a correct grammatical foundation for such sentences.

Lesson VII.

a. Though not the Lord Jesus himself, but rather his disciples gave baptism,	*a.* **Bhāwē̃ Khudāwand Yesū āpe nehī̃, sagō̃ ohdē cēlē baptismā dēndē sāṇ,**
b. yet the Pharisees heard that Jesus was making and baptising more disciples than John.	*b.* **tā̃mī Farīsīā̃ suṇeā pai Yesū Yuhannā nāḷō̃ waddh cēlē baṇāndā te baptismā dēndā e.**
c. Consequently when the Lord knew this, he left there and went to another place.	*c.* **Ēs karkē jadō̃ Khudāwand nū̃ ēh khabar hoī ōh otthō̃ ṭurkē hōr kite caleā gēā.** (*See* Gram. p. 29.)

Derived Sentences.

1. Although they saw, they did not believe, for they loved the world greatly.	1. **Bhāwē̃ ohnā̃ ḍiṭṭhā tā̃mī imān * nā leāndā, kyū̃jō dunyā nāḷ ohnā̃ dā piār bauht sī.**
2. Though the report is true, they will not believe it.	2. **Bhāwē̃ gall saccī e, tā̃mī ōh yakīn nā karngē.**

* **imān** is faith. **yakīn** belief of an ordinary fact.

3. Whoever believeth on me, though he die, yet shall he live.	3. **Jō mērē te imān leāwē, bhāwē̃ ōh mar wī jāe, tā̃mī ōh jīwēgā.**
4. Though she said, I have no husband, he did not believe [it] for he knew that she had had five husbands.	4. **Bhāwē ōs ākheā, Mērā kōī shauhr nehī̃, ōs yakīn nā kītā, kyū̃jō ohnū̃ patā sī paī ēh panj shauhr kar baiṭhī e.**
5. Though the Lord showed many signs to the Jews, yet they did not believe.	5. **Bhāwē̃ Khudāwand baṭhērīā̃ nishānīā̃ Yahūdīā̃ nū̃ wikhāḷīā̃ tā̃mī ohnā̃ imān nā leāndā.**
6. When he heard this, he left the city and went home.	6. **Jadō̃ eh gall suṇī sū, tā̃ shahr chaḍḍkē ghar nū̃ ṭur geā.**
7. I heard that you were baptising many men and women.	7. **Maī̃ suṇeā paī tusī̃ bathērē jaṇēā̃ janānīā̃ nū̃ baptismā dēndē o.**
8. It was not the teacher, but rather his disciples that were giving baptism.	8. **Ustād tā̃ nehī̃, sagō̃ ohdē cēlē baptishmā dēndē sāṇ.**
9. We heard that the Christians were making more followers than the Moslems.	9. **Asā̃ suṇeā paī Muslmānā̃ nāḷō̃ Isāī waddh cēlē baṇāndē nē̃.**
10. They heard that at Jacob's well a man was declaring himself as Messiah, so the people went out to see him.	10. **Ohnā̃ suṇeā paī Yakūb dē khūh te ikk bandā apṇē āp nū̃ Masīh karke ākhdā e, ēs wāste lōk ohnū̃ wēkkhaṇ laī nikḷe.**
11. We heard that people come to you more or less (i.e. hardly at all).	11. **Asā̃ suṇeā paī lōk tuhāḍḍē kōḷ ghaṭṭ waddh aundē nē̃.**

12. You heard that many people gave us the message of the Gospel.	12. Tusā̃ suṇeā̃ paī sānū̃ bathēreā̃ lōkā̃ Injīl dī k͟habar dittī.
13. Although she had come for water, she left her water-jar and returned to the city.	13. Bhāwē̃ pāṇī bharn āī sī, tā̃mī gharā chaḍḍkē shahr nū̃ muṛ geī.
14. Though they were wanting more money, I gave them only the nine rupees.	14. Bhāwē̃ ōh hōr paise maṅgdē sāṇ, maī̃ nire ōh nau̯ rupae dittē.
15. Although there are many more birds in that country than in this, yet the people do not eat them.	15. Bhāwē̃ ēs dēs nāḷō̃ ōs mulk͟h wicc janaur bauht nē̃, ōh lōk khānde nehī̃.
16. Although he asked, Who are you, they gave no reply.	16. Bhāwē̃ ōs puccheā Tusī̃ kauṇ o? ohnā̃ jawāb nā dittā.
17. Though I gave the money for buying eatables from the market, the cook did not bring a thing.	17. Bhāwē̃ maī bazārō̃ khāṇ dīā̃ cīzā̃ mull laiṇ wāste paise ditte khansāmā̃ koī cīz nā leāeā.
18. He gave all the rupees to the poor boys and girls who were sitting at the nearer city gate.	18. Jehṛē garīb muṇḍē kuṛīā̃ shahr dē urlē darwāzē te baiṭhē hoē sāṇ, ohnā̃ nū̃ sārē rupayye dē dittē.
19. I have more money than you.	19. Tuhāḍḍē nāḷō̃ mērē kōḷ rupayye waddh nē̃.
20. Have you more money than Buddhu?	20. Buddhū nāḷō̃ tērē kōḷ waddh rupayye nē̃?
21. Hassan makes more advance than Rajan.	21. Ḥassū Rājaṇ nāḷō̃ waddh tarakkī kardā e.

ū or ā for a man and ō, ā̃ or aṇ for a woman are the familiar endings of proper names like "ie" in English Willie.

22.	Did you hear this? Yes, sir, two days ago.	22.	Tusā̃ ēh gall suṇī? Āhō, janāb, parsō̃ suṇī.
23.	What are you making? I'm making chairs.	23.	Tusī̃ kī baṇānde o? Kursīā̃ baṇānnā wā̃.
24.	Go hence, I'm going with you.	24.	Ētthō̃ ṭur cal, maī̃ nāḷ calnā̃.
25.	Gave three rupees? He gave ten.	25.	Trai rupae dittē? Sagō̃ das dittē.
26.	Tell the woman yourself.	26.	Tū̃ āp janānī nū̃ khabar dēh.
27.	Kashmir is cooler than this country.	27.	Ēs dēs nāḷō̃ Kashmīr ṭhaṇḍā mulkh e.
28.	Although Bakhshi should ask, I will never give my father's book to him.	28.	Bhāwē̃ Bakhshī mangē wī, maī̃ apṇe peō dī katāb kadī ohnū̃ nā deā̃gā.
29	Though you learn many words one by one, you will not thus learn to talk.	29.	Bhāwē̃ ikk ikk karkē tusī̃ bathēre lafz sikkho tā̃mī ēs tarhā̃ gall karnī nehī̃ āwēgī.
30.	If you want to talk, memorise different new sentences thoroughly and say them again and again.	30.	Jē gallā̃ karnīā̃ chāhō tā̃ nawē̃ nawē̃ fikre cangī tarhā̃ nāḷ yād karkē muṛ muṛ ākhēā karo.

Forms of "was" and "be."	*Forms of "sī" and "hōṇā."*
I was ill yesterday.	Maī̃ kall bamār sā̃.
You were ill two days ago.	Tū̃ parsō̃ bamār saī̃.
He was ill three days ago (lit. on the fourth).	Ōh cauth bamār sī.
We were present yesterday.	Asī̃ kall hāzar sā̃.
You were ill last year.	Tusī̃ par bamār sau.
They were good two years ago.	Ōh parār cangē sāṇ.

Do not read these over and say, Yes, I know them, but write the English off on slips and test yourself to see whether your watch says that you have mastered them; you should say 5 syllables per second.

I am distressed daily.	**Maĩ rōz aukhā hunnā wā̃.**
You daily get ill at this time.	**Tū̃ rōz ēs wēḷē bamār hunnā ẽ.**
She is always distressed at this hour.	**Ōh rōz ēs wēḷē aukhī hundī e.**
We get hungry daily at noon.	**Asī̃ rōz dopaihr nū̃ bhukkhe hunne ā̃.**
You get distressed daily.	**Tusī̃ rōz aukhe hunde o.**
They become happy at this.	**Ōh ēs thō̃ khush hunde nē̃.**
What's the matter? Nothing at all.	**Kī hoeā? Kujjh wī nehī̃ hoeā.**
It seems that these things occurred last night.	**Malūm hundā e pai ēh gallā̃ rātī̃ hoīā̃.**
When did he get ill?	**Ōh kadō̃ bamār hoeā?**
The girl got ill three days ago.	**Kākī cauth bamār hoī.**
We became at ease that day.	**Asī̃ ōs dihāṛe saukhē hoe.**
Why have you become so thin.	**Tusī̃ māṛē kyū̃ hoe?**
She has been ill since last year.	**Ōh par dī bamār e.**
The women came yesterday.	**Ōh janānīā̃ kall hāzar hoīā̃.**
She became ill last year.	**Ōh par bamār hoī.**

Lesson VIII.	*Aṭṭhwā̃ Sabak.*
a. We perceive the love of God;	a. **Asī̃ Khudā dī mhabbat malūm karne ā̃;**
b. For God so loved the world	b. **kyū̃jō Khudā dunyā nū̃ ajehā piār kītā**
c. that he gave his only begotten Son	c. **pai Ōs Apṇe iklaute Bēṭē nū̃ bakhsheā**
d. that whoever believeth on him should not perish	d. **tā̃jō jehṛā Ōste imān leāwe ohdā nās nā hōwe**
e. but [rather] have eternal life.	e. **sagō̃ ohnū̃ sadā dī zindagī miḷe.**

Derived Sentences.

1. We have found this thing out.	1. **Asā̃ ēh gall malūm kītī e.**

2. Do you know when Mr. —will come ?	2. **Tuhānū̃ malūm e paī sāhb kadõ āwēgā ?**
3. He loved me greatly.	3. **Ohdā mērē nāḷ bauht piār sī.**
4. Mother and son love each other much.	4. **Mā̃ puttar dā āpe wicc baṛā piār e.**
5. They loved each other greatly.	5. **Ohnā̃ nū̃ ikk dūjje nāḷ baṛī mhabbat sī.**
6 Their home will be destroyed by this.	6. **Ēs kamm thõ ohnā̃ de ghar dā nās hōwēgā.**
7. The father gave each of his sons a house that they might know their father's love.	7. **Peō apṇeā̃ puttarā̃ nū̃ ikk ikk kōṭhā bak͟hsheā tā̃jō ohnā̃ nū̃ peō dī mhabbat malūm hōwē.**
8. Who gave you a watch ? Father did.	8. **Kis tuhānū̃ ghaṛī dittī ? Mērē cāccē dittī.**
9. Father gave me all his money lest his grandson should become poor.	9. **Lālle apṇē sāre rupae paise menū̃ dittē paī ohdā pōtrā garīb nā hō jāwē.**
10. Tell him, make the coat right for the gentleman lest he refuse it.	10. **Ohnū̃ ākh, Sāhb wāste kōṭ ṭhīk karō mate mōṛ dēṇ.**
11. Make one sheet long and one short.	11. **Ikk cādar lammī te ikk nikkī karō.**
12. Make either this short or that. Make either.	12. **Bhāwē̃ ēsnū̃ chōṭā karo bhāwē̃ ōsnū̃. Kise nū̃ karō.**
13. Don't go with such women, my girl, you will become bad.	13. **Ajehiā̃ janānīā̃ nāḷ nā miḷeā juḷeā kar, kuṛīyē, tū̃ k͟harāb hō jāẽgī.**
14. The teacher beat my boy so that—what shall I say ? He's a perfect wreck.	14. **Munshī mērē muṇḍē nū̃ ajehā māreā paī kī dassīye ? Ōhdā nās hō geā we.**
15. Where is such love as this found ?	15. **Ajehī mhabbat kitthē labbhdī e ?**

16. Don't say such things, lest the teacher hear them and turn you out of school.	16. Ajehīā̃ gallā̃ nā ākhō, matē ustād suṇkē tenū̃ skūlō̃ kaḍḍhē.
17. The mother is fondling her son and daughter.	17. Mā̃ apṇē dhī puttar nū̃ piār dēndī e.
18. It is a Panjabi saying. This world is sweet, who has seen the next ?	18. Ēh jagg miṭṭhā aglā kis ḍiṭṭhā ; ēh Panjābī a<u>kh</u>āṇ e.
19. Sons become bad sons, but parents never become bad parents. This too is a proverb.	19. Puttar kuputtar honde nē̃ par māpe kumāpe nehī̃ honde, ēh wī a<u>kh</u>āṇ e. (*See* Gram. p. 18.)
20. Love is born from love.	20. Piār piār thō̃ paidā hondā e.
21. Hence men ought to love one other.	21. Ēs karkē cāhīdā e pai bande ikk dūjje nū̃ piār karn.
22. From this we perceive the love of God that when we were sinners and enemies, Christ died for us.	22. Ēs thō̃ asī̃ <u>Kh</u>udā dī mhabbat malūm Karnēā̃ pai jad asī̃ gunāhī te wairī sā̃ Masīh sāḍḍe wāste mōeā.
23. If any one loves God, he will obey his commandments.	23. Jē kōī <u>Kh</u>udā nū̃ piār kardā e, oh ohde hukmā̃ nū̃ mannēgā.
24. Whoso hates his brother and says he loves God is a liar.	24. Jehṛā apṇē bhrā nāḷ wair rakkhe, te ākhē pai maī̃ <u>Kh</u>udā nū̃ piār karnā wā̃, ōh jhūṭhā e.
25. John, the Apostle, writes, Beloved, if God so loved us, we ought to love one another.	25. Yuhannā rasūl li<u>kh</u>dā we, Piāreo, jad <u>Kh</u>udā ajehā piār sāḍḍe nāḷ kītā, tā̃ cāhidā e pai asī̃ ikk dūjjē nū̃ piār karīyē.

Purpose, Result.

English	Panjabi
1. Mother sent him to draw water.	1. Bēbbe ohnū̃ pāṇī bharn ghalleā.
2. I went to find this thing out.	2. Maĩ ēs gall nū̃ malūm karn wāstē geā.
3. He did not come to learn Panjabi but rather to show off.	3. Ēh Panjābī sikkhaṇ nehī̃, sagõ liākat wik͟hāṇ āeā sī.
4. The women come daily to draw water.	4. Ōh rōz dihāṛī pāṇī bharn aundīā̃ nē̃.
5. The boys gave me money to buy a ball.	5. Muṇḍeā̃ menū̃ khiddō wāste paisē dittē.
6. The girls said this thing so that I should send the book.	6. Kuṛīā̃ ēs wāste ēh gall kītī pai maĩ kitāb ghall deā̃.
7. He knew it for he was there.	7. Ōsnū̃ malūm sī kyū̃jō ōh ōtthe sī.
8. I sent the girl because Mr.——told me to.	8. Maĩ kuṛī ghallī sī, kyū̃jō sāhb menū̃ ākheā sī.
9. We did this because the boy was ill.	9. Asā̃ ēs laī ēh kamm kītā pai muṇḍā bamār sī.
10. I did know it, for the boys told me.	10. Menū̃ patā hai sī, kyū̃jō muṇḍeā̃ menū̃ dasseā.
11. Why is the mare here? She's yours, that's why.	11. Ghōṛī kyū̃ ētthe we? Tuhāḍḍī jō hoī.
12. Why did you bring the box thence? Because it's yours.	12. Bakas ōtthō̃ kāhnū̃ āndā ī? Tuhāḍḍā jō hoeā.
13. Why did you put the post here? It's Mr.—'s.	13. Ḍāk ētthe kāhnū̃ dharī ā? Sāhb dī jō hoī.
14. I see, *that's* why you put it here.	14. Acchā, taddē ētthe dharī ā.
15. Though I saw it, I did not believe it.	15. Bhāwē̃ ḍiṭṭhā tā̃wī menū̃ yakīn nehī̃ sī āeā.
16. Though you saw it, you did not believe it.	16. Bhāwē̃ wēkheā, tusā̃ yakīn nehī̃ sī kītā.

17. Though he heard, he did not come.	17. **Bhāwẽ suṇeā, par nā āeā.**
18. Although she called, he did not answer.	18. **Bhāwẽ janānī wāj mārī ōs jawāb nā dittā.**
19. Though we went, she did not come.	19. **Bhāwẽ asī gae, ōh nā āī.**
20. Though you sent the money, they did not take it.	20. **Bhāwẽ tusā̃ paisā ghall-eā, ohnā̃ nā leā.**
21. Though they do know it, they'll never answer.	21. **Bhāwẽ malūm hai ī ne, ōh kadī jawāb nā dēṇgē.**
22. Though it is good, that is better.	22. **Bhāwẽ caṅgā ī e, ōh edū̃ wī caṅgā e.**
23. Though the girl is ill, the boy is worse.	23. **Bhāwẽ kuṛī bamār e, muṇḍā ōs nāḷõ wī bamār e.**
24. Though I do go, he will not go.	24. **Bhāwẽ maĩ jā̃ wī, ōh nehī̃ jāēgā.**
25. Though the horse eats his hay all right, the mare has eaten nothing since the day before yesterday.	25. **Ghōṛā te ghāh paṭṭhā caṅgī tarhā̃ khāndā e, par ghōṛī parsõ dī bilkul nehī̃ khāndī.**
26. Though we should go to their house, they will not come to us.	26. **Bhāwẽ ohnā̃ dē ghar jaīyē wī, ōh sāḍḍe kōḷ nā auṅgē.**
27. Though they come to us every day, we never go to their house.	27. **Bhāwẽ rōz sāḍḍe kōḷ aunde nẽ, asī ohnā̃ dē ghar kadī nehī̃ jāndē.**
28. I made the chair at your order but you won't take it.	28. **Maĩ te tuhāḍḍē ākkhe kursī baṇāī, tā̃ mī, tusī̃ lainde nehī̃.**
29. Although you should give more money, I will not start from here.	29. **Bhāwẽ rupae waddh deō, maĩ ētthõ nā ṭur-āgā.**
30. Though I go and tell him,	30. **Bhāwẽ calkē khabar deā̃**

he will not come.	wī, ōh kadō̃ auṇ laggā e? (*See* Gram. p. 67.)

Lesson IX.	*Nauā̃ Sabak.*
a. In the meantime his disciples came and making request said,	a. Inne wicc ohdē cēlē āe te arz karkē ākkhaṇ laggē,
b. Teacher, eat something.	b. Ustād jī, kujjh khā lao.
c. But he said, I have something to eat of which ye know not.	c. Par ōs ākhēa, mērē kōḷ khāṇ wāstē kujjh hai, jih dī tuhānū̃ k͟habar nehī.

Derived Sentences.

1. What did the disciples say to their teacher, and what did he say to them?	1. Shagirdā̃ apṇē ustād nū̃ kī ākheā te ōs ohnā̃ nū̃ kī ākheā?
2. His disciples asked him to eat, but he said, I have that to eat of which ye know not.	2. Ohdeā̃ cēleā̃ ohnū̃ khāṇ wāste ākheā, par ōs ākheā pai mērē kōḷ khāṇ wāste kujjh hai, jihdā tuhānū̃ patā nehī̃.
3. From your love shall all men know that you are my disciples.	3. Tuhāḍḍe piār thō̃ sārē bande jānaṇgē pai tusī̃ mēre shagird o.
4. He knew all men and what was in them.	4. Ōh āp sāreā̃ bandeā̃ nū̃ jāṇdā sī te jō kujjh ohnā̃ wicc sī.
5. I know my sheep and mine know me.	5. Maī apṇīā̃ bhēḍā̃ nū̃ jāṇṇā wā̃ tē ōh menū̃ jāṇdīā̃ nē.
6. If ye knew me, ye would know my Father.	6. Jē tusī̃ menū̃ jāṇdeo, tā̃ mēre Peō nū̃ wī jāṇdeo.
7. I know what and whom I	7. Jihdā maī yakīn kītā e

	English		Panjabi
	have believed.		te jihde te mãi iman rakkheā e, ohnū̃ maĩ jānnā wā̃.
8.	I know who thou art, the Holy one of God.	8.	Maĩ jānnā̃ paĩ tū̃ kauṇ ẽ, Khudā dā Kuddūs.
9.	The Lord himself knew what he would do.	9.	Khudāwand āp jāṇdā sī paĩ maĩ kī karā̃gā.
10.	I know that thou hearest me always.	10.	Maĩ jāṇṇā̃ paĩ tū̃ sadā mērī suṇṇā ẽ.
11.	We tell what we know, but you do not believe us.	11.	Jō asī̃ jaṇṇe ā̃ sō ākhne ā̃, par tusī̃ sāḍḍī gall dā yakīn nehī̃ kardē.
12.	They did not know where he was going, so they could not know the way.	12.	Ohnā̃ nū̃ patā nehī̃ sī paĩ ō kitthe jāndā e, ēs karkē rāh dā wī nehī̃ sāṇe pata.
13.	What I am doing you do not know now, but you shall know afterwards.	13.	Jō kujjh maĩ karnā wā̃ tusī̃ huṇ nehī̃ jāṇdē, par magarō̃ jāṇōgē.
14.	John wrote these things that poeple might know that Christ is the Saviour of sinners.	14.	Yuhannā ēh gallā̃ likkhīā̃ tā̃jō lōkī, jānaṇ paĩ Masīh gunāhīā̃ dā Najātdēṇwāḷā e.
15.	Then Jesus, knowing all things that were about to pass over him, went out and said, whom seek ye?	15.	Tad Yesū, sabbh kujjh jāṇkē jō ohde te bītṇā sī, nikḷeā te ohnā̃ nū̃ ākheā, tusī̃ kihnū̃ labbhde o?
16.	The world knew thee not, but I knew thee, and these too knew that thou hast sent me.	16.	Dunyā tenū̃ nā jāṇeā par maĩ tainū̃ jāṇeā te ehnā̃ wī jāṇeā paĩ tū̃ menū̃ ghalleā e.
17.	If they knew that the Lord said these things to his disciples, then why did they not believe?	17.	Jē ohnā̃ nū̃ patā sī paĩ Khudāwand ēh gallā̃ apṇe cēleā̃ nū̃ ākhīā̃ ohnā̃ phēr kyū̃ nā mannīā̃.

18. He who knows to do good but does it not, commits sin.	18. Jehṛā nēkī karnī jāṇdā e, par nehī̃ kardā, ōh pāp kardā e.
19. He who knows God hears us.	19. Jehṛā Khudā nū̃ jāṇdā e, ōh sāḍḍī suṇdā e.
20. God knows all his works from the beginning of the world.	20. Khudā dunyā de shurū thō̃ apṇe sārē kammā̃ nū̃ jāṇdā e.
21. If you do not believe my words, then believe from my works that the Father is in me.	21. Jē mēriā̃ gallā̃ dā yakīn nehī̃ karde, tā̃ mēreā̃ kammā̃ tō̃ yakīn karo paī Bāp mērē wicc e.
22. In the meantime the women came and drew the water.	22. Inne wicc buḍḍhiā̃ āṇke pāṇībhar leā.
23. He came and called the boys, saying, come here and eat what I have brought for you.	23. Ōh āeā te muṇḍeā̃ nū̃ saddke ākkhaṇ lagā, urē āo te jō kujjh maī̃ tuhāḍḍe wāste leāeā ā̃w, sō khāo.
24. He does not know what I have.	24. Ohnū̃ patā nehī̃ paī mērē kōḷ kī e.
25. He does not know what Mr.——has brought.	25. Ohnū̃ ḳhabar nehī̃ paī Sāhb kī leāndā e.
26. They do not know what we have brought for you.	26. Ohnā̃nū̃ malūm nehī̃ paī asī̃ tuhāḍḍe wāste kī kujjh leāe ā̃.
27. I know neither him nor his disciples.	27. Maī̃ tā̃ nā ōsnū̃ jāṇnā̃, nā ohde cēleā̃ nū̃.
28. I do not know who is the man who came to you yesterday.	28. Jehṛā bandā kall tuhāḍḍe kōḷ āeā sī, ohdā menū̃ patā nehī̃.
29. I am not very well acquainted with the woman to whom you gave the book the day before yesterday.	29. Jis Janānī nū̃ tusā̃ parsō̃ kitāb dittī, ohdī menū̃ cangī tarhā̃ wākafī nehī̃.

30. Did you not know that this is my boy?	30. Tusā̃ nehī̃ jātā pai ēh mērā muṇḍā e?
31. How did you know that I was in the city yesterday?	31. Tuhānū̃ kis tarhā̃ patā sī pai maī̃ kall shahr sā̃?
32. We know that this is true, but do not know who said it.	32. Asī̃ jāṇne ā̃ pai ēh sacc e, par patā nehī̃ kis ākheā.
33. Have you found out that this is true?	33. Tusā̃ malūm kītā e pai ēh gall saccī e?
34. Yes, I assured myself on that day that all these things are true.	34. Āhō, ōs dihāṛē patā kītā pai ēh sārīā̃ gallā̃ saccīā̃ nē̃.

Customary and Continuative Present.

I bring water for them daily.	Maī̃ rōz ohnā̃ laī pāṇī leaunnā wā̃.
I am taking water for them [now].	Maī̃ ohnā̃ wāste pāṇī peā lai jānnā wā̃.
I bring milk for madam [I am the milkman].	Maī̃ Mēmsāhb wāste duddh leaunnā honnā wā̃.
You bring bread daily from the city, don't you?	Tusī̃ rōz rōṭī shahrō̃ leaunde o nā?
You are taking the bread now, aren't you?	Tusī̃ huṇē rōṭī pae lai jāṇde o nā?
You are the one who brings bread from the city?	Tusī̃ ī rōṭī shahrō̃ leaunde honde o?
He sends the post twice [daily].	Ōh dō dō wārī ḍāk ghalldā e.
He is sending the post from the Post-office.	Ōh ḍāk-k͟hāneō̃ ḍāk ghalldā e peā.
He is the one who sends the post.	Ūhoī ḍāk ghalldā hondā e.
She writes to her mother every week.	Ōh aṭṭhī dī aṭṭhī dinī̃ apṇī mā̃ nū̃ ciṭṭhī lik͟hdī e.
She is writing her parents a letter.	Ōh māpeā̃ nū̃ ciṭṭhī lik͟hdī e pai.

She's the one who writes letters.	**Ōhī ciṭṭhīā̃ likhdī hondī e.**
She is always writing letters.	**Ōh ciṭṭhīā̃ likhdī raihndī e.**
We send him money for clothes every six months.	**Asī̃ cheī mahīnī ohnū̃ kapṛeā̃ wāste paise ghallne hunne ā̃.**
We are sending him money by post.	**Asī̃ ohnū̃ ḍāke rupae ghallne ā̃ pae.**
We send him money by post.	**Asī̃ ohnū̃ rupae ḍākē ghallne honne ā̃.** (*See* Gram. p. 69.)
We are always sending him money.	**Asī̃ ohnū̃ rupae ghallde raihnne ā̃.** (*See* Gram. p. 67.)
Did you bring the post?	**Tusā̃ ḍāk āndī sī?**
Yes, when you saw me, I was bringing it.	**Āhō, jad tusā̃ menū̃ wēkheā maĩ leaundā sā̃ peā.**
Did the woman bring the chairs for us?	**Ōs janānī sāḍḍe laī kursīā̃ āndīā̃?**
Yes, she was bringing them when you saw her yesterday.	**Āhō, jad tusā̃ kall ohnū̃ ḍiṭṭhā ōh leaundī sī paī.**
Did they send you the money?	**Ohnā̃ tuhānū̃ rupae ghallē?**
When you were there they were sending it.	**Jad tusī̃ ōtthe sau, ōh ghallde sāṇ pae.**

Lesson X.	*Daswā̃ Sabak.*
a. So his disciples said to one another,	*a.* **Ēs karkē cēlē āpe wicc ākkhaṇ laggē,**
b. Perhaps someone has given him something to eat [and gone away].	*b.* **Khabare, kōī ohnū̃ kujjh khāṇ wāste de geā e.**
c. He said, this is my food	*c.* **Ōs ākheā, Mērā khāṇā ēh we**
d. That I walk according to the will of my Sender and complete his work.	*d.* **paī maĩ apṇē Ghallaṇwāḷē dī marzī te callā̃ te ohdā kamm pūrā karā̃.**

Derived Sentences.

1. What answer shall we give to those who sent us?	1. **Asī̃ apṇeā̃ ghllaṇwāḷeā̃ nū̃ kī jawāb deiye?**

2.	Whoso believes on me believes on him who sent me and has eternal life.	2.	Jō mērē te imān leaundā e, mērē ghallaṇwāḷe te imān leaundā e te sadā dī zindagī ohdī e.
3.	My teaching is not mine, but his who sent me.	3.	Mērī talīm tā̃ mērī nehī̃, par mērē Ghallaṇwāḷe dī e.
4.	As the Father sent me, so I send you.	4.	Jīkū̃ Bāp menū̃ ghalle ā mammī̃ tuhānū̃ ghallnā wā̃.
5.	I will go to the Father and send the comfort-giving Holy Spirit to you.	5.	Maī Bāp kōḷ jākē Tasallī dēṇwāḷā Pāk Rūh tuhāḍḍē kōḷ ghallā̃gā.
6.	God sent his Son into the world that we should receive life through him.	6.	Khudā ēs karke apṇe Puttar nū̃ dunyā wicc ghalleā, paī asī̃ ohde sababbō̃ zindagī pāīye.
7.	I request for them also, who because of the word of these shall believe on me.	7.	Maī̃ ohnā̃ laī wī arz karnā̃, jehṛe ehnā̃ de kalām dī rāhī̃ mērē te imān leauṇgē.
8.	I seek not my own will, but the will of him who sent me.	8.	Maī̃ apṇī nehī̃ sagō̃ apṇe Ghallaṇwāḷe dī marzī cāhnnā wā̃.
9.	If anyone wills to do his will, he shall know whether this teaching is from God or from men.	9.	Jē kōī ohdī marzī mūjab karnā cāhē, ōh jāṇēgā paī ēh talīm Khudā wallō̃ e yā̃ ādmīā̃ wallō̃.
10.	Come unto me all ye that have been borne down with work, and I will give you rest.	10.	Tusī̃ jō kamm dhande hēṭh dabbe hoe o, mērē kōḷ āhō te maī̃ tuhānū̃ arām deā̃gā.
11.	Has anyone brought the chair from the city ?	11.	Kise shahrō̃ kursī āndī ? Kehṛī kursī? Ōh

	English		Panjabi
	What chair? The one that I got yesterday morning in the chief market.		jehṛī maī kall waḍḍe-weḷe sadar bazārõ leī.
12.	I beg to say, sir, that I have brought some eatables for your children.	12.	Maī arz karnā̃, janāb, paī tuhāḍḍeā̃ bacceā̃ wāste kujjh khāṇ diā̃ cīzā̃ leāeā wā̃.
13.	Has the cook gone to get eatables for his own family or for us?	13.	Khansāmā̃ apṇe ghar wāste khāṇ diā̃ cīzā̃ laiṇ geā e yā̃ sāḍḍe wāste?
14.	Do you wish to have some one water the cattle to-day?	14.	Huzūr dī marzī e paī ajj kōī ḍaṅgarā̃ nū̃ paṇī ḍāh dē?
15.	Does your master wish you to do this work in the city?	15.	Tuhāḍḍe mālik dī marzī e paī tusī̃ shahr wicc ēh kamm karō?
16.	Bring the chairs out into the verandah, so that we can sit in the sunshine.	16.	Kursīā̃ ētthe barāṇḍe wicc kaḍḍh leāo, paī dhuppe bawhīye.
17.	Early to-morrow eat your food and harness the horse quickly.	17.	Bhaḷkē waḍḍēwēḷē rōṭī khāke chētī ghōṛē nū̃ jō leī.
18.	Finish the work I gave you yesterday, and to-morrow I will bring you more.	18.	Jehṛā kamm maī tenū̃ kall dittā, mukā dē, te bhaḷkē hōr leā deāgā.
19.	Where's the waterman? He has brought the water and gone.	19.	Māshkī kitthe we? Ōh tā̃ pāṇī dē geā e.
20.	Only gave two rupees? Well, he said, just that much at first. He has fulfilled his promise exactly.	20.	Dō hī rupae ditte? Khair, paihlā̃ inne ī ākhe sāṇ, gall te apṇī pūrī kar dittī.
21.	Learn to use 1,000 or 1,500 words in a year and	21.	Warhē din wicc tusī hazār ḍēḍh hazār lafzā̃

then you will get a complete mastery of Panjabi. — dā wartṇā sikkhō, tā̃ tuhānū̃ pūrī Panjābī āwēgī.

22. It will not come at first, but gradually it will all come to you. — 22. Paund saṭṭe tā̃ nehī̃ āwēgī, par hauḷī hauḷī sabbh ā jāēgī.

23. Will you get these things to the house? I will take them there at once. — 23. Ēh cizā̃ kōṭhī pucāōde? Huṇē pucā dēnnā̃.

24. Though I did not wish it, he finished his work and went. — 24. Bhāwẽ mērī marzī nehī̃ sī, ōh kamm pūrā karke ṭur geā.

25. If you finish my work, you shall get extra money. — 25. Jēkar tusī̃ mērā kamm pūrā karō, tā̃ paise waddh lao.

INDEFINITES AND CONDITIONALS.

1. What did he say to you? — 1. Ōs tuhānū̃ kī kujjh ākheā?

2. He said nothing at all. — 2. Kujjh wī nā ākheā.

3. Did he tell my name? What else was he to tell? — 3. Ōs mērā nā̃ dasseā? Hōr kī dassṇā sī?

4. Give us something too. — 4. Sānū̃ wī kujjh deho.

5. One says one thing, another another. — 5. Kōī kujjh āhndā e, kōī kujjh.

6. Give this to no one but Mr.——. — 6. Ēh hōr kise nū̃ nā dehō, sāhb ī nū̃ deho.

7. [I ask thee] Is the boy somewhere about? He must be. [I tell you.] — 7. Muṇḍā huṇ kite hai ī? Kitale hōjēgā.

8. What is this cloth made of? Of something [or other]. — 8. Ēh kāh dā kapṛā e? Kāse dā e.

9. Where's the munshi? He's gone somewhere. — 9. Munshī kitthe we? Kite geā we.

10. When will he come? He'll come some time or other. — 10. Kadõ āwegā? Kise wēḷē āwegā.

11. Will you go in the carriage or on horse? I tell thee, I'll go some way.	11. Bagghī te jāōgē yā̃ ghōṛē te? Kise tarhā̃ jāā̃īgā.
12. If he wishes I'll do it.	12. Jēkar ōh cāhē maĩ karā̃gā.
13. If she wishes, the girl will go.	13. Jēkar ōh dī marzī hōwē, kuṛī jā̃wēgī.
14. If you wish it, I'll go at once.	14. Jē tuhāḍḍī marzī hōwē, tā̃ maĩ huṇē jāwā̃gī.
15. If they wish it, I'll pay the money at once.	15. Jēkar ohnā̃ dī marzī hōwē, maĩ rupae huṇē dē dēnnā wā̃.
16. If you want him to go, I'll send him.	16. Jē tusĩ cāhndeo paī ōh jāe, maĩ ghall deā̃gā.
17. If you come I'll go.	17. Jēkar tusĩ āō, maĩ jāā̃gī.
18. If her father sends her, she'll go.	18. Jē peō kuṛī nū̃ ghall dē, ōh jāedī.
19. If their mother calls them, the girls will come.	19. Jē mā̃ saddē, tā̃ kuṛīā̃ auṇgīā̃.
20. If they ask from us, we'll give it.	20. Jē sāthō̃ maṅgaṇ, asĩ dē chaḍḍā̃gē.
21. If I tell him, he'll do it.	21. Jēkar maĩ ākhā̃, tā̃ karēgā.
22. If you will obey me, you shall be my servant.	22. Jē tū̃ mērī marzī te callẽ, mērā naukar hō jā-ẽgā.
23. If I wish it, you'll go, won't you?	23. Jēkar mērī marzī hōwē, tā̃ tusĩ jāoge nā?
24. If I bring it, they'll take it, won't they?	24. Jē maĩ lai āwā̃, tā̃ ōh laiṇge nā?
25. If you will go and buy bread from the city, the teacher will give the money.	25. Jēkar tusĩ shahrō̃ rōṭi mull leāo, tā̃ ustād paise dēgā.

Lesson XI.	*Yāhrwā̃ Sabak.*
a. Do you not say that harvest will be in four months?	*a.* **Tusī̃ nehī̃ āhndē o pai cauhā̃ mahīneā̃ nū̃ wā̃ḍhī hōwēgī?**
b. Behold, I say unto you,	*b.* **Wēkkhō. maĩ tuhā̃nū̃ āhnnā wā̃**
c. lift up (open) your eyes and see the fields	*c.* **akkhīā̃ ughēṛkē pailīā̃ nū̃ wēkkhō**
d. that they are even now ripe for the harvest.	*d.* **pai ōh wā̃ḍhī laī huṇ wī pakkīā̃ hōīā̃ nē̃.**

Derived Sentences.

1. Ask the Lord of the harvest to [that he] send workmen into his fields.	1. **Fasl de Mālik agnē arz karo pai ōh apṇīā̃ pailīā̃ wicc kāmmē ghallē.**
2. He lifted up (opened) his eyes and looked at the crowds, then said to his disciples, Truly the harvest is great, but the reapers are few.	2. **Ōs akkhīā̃ khōlke bhīṛā̃ wall wēkkheā̃ te phēr apṇeā̃ cēleā̃ nū̃ ākheā Sacci mucci fasl bauht e, par wā̃ḍhe ghaṭṭ nē̃.**
3. The reaper gets wages and gathers fruit for eternal life.	3. **Waḍḍhaṇwā̃ḷe nū̃ mazdūrī miḷdī e te ōh sadā̃ dī zindagī laī phaḷ kaṭṭhā kardā e.**
4. In this harvest we, too, are workers.	4. **Es wā̃ḍhī wicc asī̃ wī kāmme ā̃.**
5. They bought with the wages of this sinfulness a field, and its name was called Field of Blood.	5. **Ēs gunāh dī mazdūrī nāḷ ohnā̃ ikk paiḷī mull laī, te ohdā̃ nā̃ khūn dā khēt pai geā.**
6. When the Lord said, Look at the fields, what was his meaning	6. **Jadō̃ Khudāwand ēh gall ākkhī pai, Paiḷīā̃ nū̃ wēkkhō, ohdā̃ kī mat-**

	—fields or people ?		lab sī, paiḷiā̃ yā̃ bandē ?
7.	He meant people.	7.	**Ohdā bandeā̃ dā matlab sī.**
8.	Have you wheat harvest in this country or not ?	8.	**Is mulk͟h wicc kaṇak dī fasl hondī e ke nehī̃ ?**
9.	Yes, we have, we have it two or three times a year.	9.	**Āho, hondī ē, sagõ ētthe warhe wicc dō trai wārī wī hondī e.**
10.	What different harvests do you have here ?	10.	**Kehṛī kehṛī fasl ētthe hondī e ?**
11.	Well, we have grain harvest in May and June; in September and October, maize and rice; at other times other things.	11.	**K͟hair jēṭh hāṛ wicc kaṇak dī assū kattē wicc makaī te munjī dī, te aggē picchē hōrnā̃ cīzā̃ dī.**
12.	When is the wheat harvest ?	12.	**Kaṇak dī wāḍhī kadõ hondī e ?**
13	Oh, it comes in May.	13.	**Ōh tā̃ jēṭh wicc hondī e.**
14.	When do they sow it ?	14.	**Kadõ bījde nē ?**
15.	They sow seed in October and November.	15.	**Kattē magghar wicc bījde nē.**
16.	Do they sow any thing else ?	16.	**Hōr kujjh bījde nē ?**
17.	Yes, a lot. Some ripens in a few days.	17.	**Āho bauht. Kujjh kujjh thōṛeā̃ dinā̃ wicc pakkdā e.**
18.	Some after going six or seven months ripens.	18.	**Kujjh kujjh cheī sattī mahīnī̃ jāke pakkdā e.**
19.	What month is it now ?	19.	**Huṇ kehṛā mahīnā e ?**
20.	It is now February.	20.	**Huṇ tē phaggaṇ jē.**
21.	How long is it till harvest ?	21.	**Wāḍhī wicc kinnē mahīne nē ?**
22.	Still several months.	22.	**Aje tā̃ dō cār haiṇ nē.**
23.	What kind of bread is this ? Wheaten ?	23.	**Ēh rōṭī kāh dī e ? kaṇak dī ?**

24.	**Yes, this is wheaten, but that is barley and he has maize bread.**	**24.**	**Āhō, ēh kaṇak dī e, par ōh jaũ̃ dī e te ohde kōḷ makaī dī e.**
25.	**Wheat fields colour (get pale) in March.**	**25.**	**Kaṇakā̃ cēttar wicc piḷīā̃ hondīā̃ nē̃.**

EXERCISE IN TIME.

1.	**When did you start? You have come late.**	**1.**	**Kadõ ṭur pae? Tusī kawēḷē āe o.**
2.	**I started very early, before daylight, and walking slowly got there before noon.**	**2.**	**Maĩ tā̃ bauht sawēḷē, sarghī wēḷē nāḷ, ṭur peā, te hauḷī hauḷī ṭurdeā̃ bhattēwēḷē appaṛeā. (*See* Gram. p. 31.)**
3.	**What month are you going? I am going this month.**	**3.**	**Kehṛē mahīne jāōdē? Maĩ ēs mahīnē jā̃dā.**
4.	**Is your family going too? Oh, they will go later, in September or October.**	**4.**	**Bāl baccē nāḷ jāṇgē? Ōh tā̃ picche assū katte nū̃ jāṇge.**
5.	**How long have you been ill? For a long time.**	**5.**	**Kadõk dā bamār ē̃, whaī? Cirōkṇā bamār ā̃.**
6.	**Since last year? No, since two years ago.**	**6.**	**Par dā? Parū̃ dā nehī, parār dā.**
7.	**How long do you work every day?**	**7.**	**Rōz kinnā cir kamm karde o?**
8.	**From early morning till sundown.**	**8.**	**Fajr thõ laike din ḍubdeā̃ tīkar.**
9.	**How long has the boy been absent (I ask you)? For ten days.**	**9.**	**Kadõk dā muṇḍā gair hāzar je? Dasā̃ dinā̃ dā.**
10.	**This man has been ill for eight or ten days.**	**10.**	**Ēh bandā aṭṭhā̃ nauā̃ dinā̃ dā bamār e.**
11.	**My girl has been ill since last evening.**	**11.**	**Mērī kākī shām dī bamār e.**

12. Do they come to you every day at breakfast time?	12. Ōh rōz rōṭīwēḷē tuhāḍḍē kōḷ auṇdiā̃ nē̃?
13. Sometimes at this time, sometimes at noon, and sometimes they do not come at all.	13. Kādī ēs wēḷē, kadī do-paihrī̃, kadī̃ kadāī̃ nehī wī aundiā̃.
14. Has the girl been home this year? Yes, frequently.	14. Kākī aitkī pēkē [1] gāī? Āhō, kinnī wārī gaī.
15. What time did the boys come? Oh, they came after supper last night.	15. Muṇḍe kehṛe wēḷē āe? Ōh tā̃ khāo-piye nū̃ ā gae.
16. You will go to-night, won't you?	16. Tusī̃ ajj ratī̃ jāōgē nā?
17. No, we shall start to-morrow forenoon and pass the noon hour there, then go on about two o'clock and reach home by about bedtime.	17. Nehī̃, asī̃ bhaḷkē chāh wēḷē nāl ṭurā̃gē te ōtthē bhattēwēḷā kar-ke pēshī ḍigar nū̃ agā̃h ṭur jāā̃gē te kōī sōtē nāḷ ghar jā phirā̃ge.
18. You will hurry then?	18. Phēr shitābī jāōge?
19. Yes, we'll go quickly, or we shall get there at midnight.	19. Āhō, kāhḷe kāhḷe jaā̃gē, nehī̃, tā̃ adāi rāt apparā̃gē.
20. Did the women come at dawn? No, in the evening.	20. Ōh dhammī wēlē ā gaīā̃? Nehī̃, jī, sagō̃ tar-kāḷā̃ nū̃.
21 He said he'd go at prayer time (early morning) but he started in the afternoon.	21. Ōh namāzweḷē jāṇ wāstē āhndā sī, par laudhē-wēḷē ṭureā.
22. It will take half an hour, or three quarters, to get there.	22. Kōī ghaṛī dō ghaṛī dā rāh we.

[1] Married girl's parental home.

Lesson XII.	*Bāhrwā̃ Sabak.*
a. And with this agrees the saying	*a.* Te ēs utte akhāṇ ṭhīk aundā e
b. One sows and another reaps.	*b.* Bījē kōī te waḍḍhē kōī.
c. I sent you to reap that	*c.* Maĩ tuhānū̃ ohdē waḍ-ḍhaṇ lāī ghalleā
d. of which you did no labour.	*d.* jīhdī tusā̃ mehnat nehī̃ kītī.
e. Others did the labour	*e.* Hōrnā̃ mehnat kītī,
f. and you became partners in their labour.	*f.* te tusī̃ ohnā̃ dī mehnat wicc panjhāḷ, hō gae o.

DERIVED SENTENCES.

1. Whatever a man sows that shall he reap.	1. Jō kujjh bandā bījēgā sō hī waḍḍhēgā.
2. The kingdom of heaven is like a man who sowed good seed in his field.	2. Asmān dī bādshāhī ōs bande wāṇgū̃ e jis apṇī pailī wicc caṅgā bī bījeā.
3. The field is the world. The reaping time is the end of the world, and the reapers are the angels.	3. Pailī dunyā̃ we. Wāḍhī dā wēḷā dunyā dā ākhir e te wāḍḍhē farishte nē.
4. A man found a treasure in a field and for joy sold everything he had and bought the field.	4. Ikkī bande kise pailī wicc khazānā diṭṭhā te khush hōkē apṇā sabbho kujjh wēc wācke ōs pailī nū̃ mullī leā.
5. The dead shall hear the voice of the Son of God and having heard shall live.	5. Murde Khudā dē Puttar dī āwāz suṇange te suṇke jiūṇgē.
6. A sower went out to sow, and as he sowed, some	6. Bī bījjaṇwāḷā bī bījjaṇ nikḷeā, te bījdeā̃ wēḷē

	English		Panjabi
	fell by the way.		kujjh paihe wicc ḍigg peā.
7.	The sower of the good seed is Christ, but he who sows bad seed is Satan.	7.	Caṅgā bī bījjaṇwāḷā Masīh e, par ōh jehṛā māṛā bī bījdā e, ōh Shatān e.
8.	Sir, you sowed good seed in that field, did you not?	8.	Janāb, tusā̃ caṅgā bī ōs paiḷī wicc bījeā nā?
9.	Then whence came this evil seed?	9.	Tā̃ phēr ēh māṛā bī kitthō̃ āeā.
10.	I feared thee, for I know that thou art a hard man for where thou didst not sow, there thou reapest.	10.	Maĩ tērē kōḷō̃ ḍareā, kyū̃jō maĩ jāṇṇā̃ paĩ tū̃ sak͟ht ādmī ẽ, te jitthe nehī̃ bījeā ōtthe waḍḍhnā ẽ.
11.	He who sows sparingly, shall reap sparingly.	11.	Jō sarfe nāḷ bījēgā, sō sarfe nāḷ waḍḍhēgā.
12.	He who sows bountifully, shall reap bountifully.	12.	Te jehṛā cōkhā bī pāndā e, sō cōkhā wāḍḍhēgā.
13.	He who sows for his flesh, shall reap corruption from it.	13.	Jehṛā jism wāste bījēgā, sō jism thō̃ k͟harābī waḍḍhēgā.
14.	Who sows abuse, will reap anger.	14.	Bī gāḷhā̃, phaḷ gussā.
15.	Who sows sin, will reap dishonour.	15.	Bī pāp, phaḷ be-iztī.
16.	He who sows love, shall reap kindness.	16.	Bī mhabbat, phaḷ mihrbānī.
17.	Who sows the wind, reaps the whirlwind.	17.	Wā dā bī, wāwarōḷē dā phaḷ.
18.	A nobleman went out early to set men to work on his garden (orchard).	18.	Ikk raīs waḍḍēwēḷē nikḷeā, pai mazdūr apṇe bag̲ wicc lāē.
19.	Labouring six days do all thy work, but on	19.	Chē din mehnat karke apṇā sārā kamm kar,

	the seventh day make it a habit to do no work.		par satwẽ dihāṛē kōī kār nā kareā kar.
20.	Let the thief henceforth not steal, but rather let him labour with his hands and give something [to others].	20.	Cōrī karnwāḷā aggē nũ cōrī nā karē, sagõ apṇeã hatthã nāḷ mehnat mashakkat karke kujjh dē wē.
21.	The workman has a right to his wages. Now pay him.	21.	Kāmmā apṇī kamāī dā hakkdār e, ohnũ majūrī dēh khã.
22.	If you do not become as little children, you shall not enter into the kingdom of heaven.	22.	Jē tusī nikkeã bacceã wāṅgũ nā hō jāō, tã asmān dī bādshāhī wicc nā waṛōgē.
23.	When you enter a house, then say Peace be on this house.	23.	Jad kisē ghar wicc waṛo, tad ākhō, Ēs ghar nũ salām.
24.	Enter not into the fields of the widow and orphan.	24.	Raṇḍiã te yatīmã diã paiḷiã wicc nā waṛo.

Exercises in Adverbs and comparison of Adjectives.

1.	Why do it that way, sir, do it thus.	1.	Uñ kāh nũ karnā je, aiñ karo.
2.	He is just fooling, sir. Do not mind.	2.	Aiwẽ kardā e, sāhb. Tusī nā mannō.
3.	How will you go? Just as you say.	3.	Kikũ jāoge? Jiwẽ tusī ākhō.
4.	Now, how will you do it?	4.	Huṇ kis tarhã karōgē?
5.	I'll do it somehow or other.	5.	Kiwẽ karãgā tã sahī.
6.	Don't do it so.	6.	Aiũ nā karo.
7.	Do as the teacher tells you.	7.	Jehā ustād dasse, tehā kar.
8.	Now, how will you give the money?	8.	Huṇ rupae kikar deōge?

9. I'll give it little by little, but I will most certainly give it.	9. Hauḷī hauḷī deā̃dā, par deā̃dā zarūr.
10. He treated me very badly.	10. Ōs mērē nāḷ baṛa bhaiṛ kītā.
11. Is this good cloth?	11. Ēh caṅgā kapṛā e?
12. Well, it is not bad, but this is better.	12. Khair, māṛā nehī̃ e, par ēh ōs thȭ caṅgā e.
13. I think this second is better than that other.	13. Mērē kiās wicc ēh dujjā odū̃ caṅgā e.
14. That is good, but better than all is this piece.	14. Hai te caṅgā, par sāreā nāḷȭ ēh caṅgā we.
15. That's right. This is the best.	15. Ṭhīk e, ēh sabbhnā̃ thȭ caṅgā we.
16. Are you younger or your brother?	16. Tū̃ nikkā ẽ jā̃ tērā bhrā?
17. My brother is younger than I.	17. Mērā bhrā methȭ nikkā e.
18. This cow of yours looks feeble.	18. Ēh tuhāḍḍī gā̃ māṛī jā pdī e.
19. This one I tell you is not so bad. Look at that one.	19. Ēh te ghaṭṭ māṛī je, ohnū̃ wēkho.
20. Alas! alas! She is the poorest of all.	20. Hāe hāe, ōh sabbhnā̃ thȭ māṛī e.
21. She will go more quickly than I.	21. Ōh mērē nāḷȭ jaldī jāēgī.
22. This boy runs the fastest.	22. Ēh muṇḍā sabbhnā̃ thȭ chētī bhajjdā e.
23. My mare went the quickest.	23. Mērī ghōṛī sārīā̃ nāḷȭ jaldī gaī.
24. Have you not heard how David went into the house of God and ate bread?	24. Tusā̃ suṇeā nehī̃ pai Dāūd kis tarhā̃ Khudā dē ghar waṛkē rōṭī khādhī?
25. You went not in and those who were entering you kept out.	25. Tusī̃ te nā āp waṛe te waṛanwāḷeā̃ nū̃ wī rōkeā.

26. He who will not work with his hands shall not eat, is the commandment of the Gospel.	26. Jehṛā apṇeā̃ hatthā̃ nāḷ kamm nā karē, ōh khāwē wī nā, ēh sāḍḍī Injīl dā hukm e.
27. Satan entered into Judas Iscariot and he delivered up his Lord.	27. Shatān Yahūdā Iskaryūtī wicc waṛ geā, ṭe ōs apṇe <u>Kh</u>udāwand nū̃ phaṛā dittā.
28. As you enter the city, a man carrying a water-jar will meet you, follow him.	28. Jad shahr waṛōge ikk bandā ghaṛe wāḷā tuhānū̃ miḷēgā, ohde magar hō ṭureo.
29. When we speak rapidly ourselves, we hear and understand the rapid speaking of others.	29. Jad asī̃ āpī chētī chētī bōlne ā̃, asī̃ dujjeā̃ dā chētī chētī bōlṇā suṇ te samajh bī lenne ā̃.

Lesson XIII.	*Tehrwa Sabak.*
a. God is Spirit and the time is coming	a. <u>Kh</u>udā Rūh e te ōh wēḷā aundā e.
b. when his service shall be done in spirit and in truth	b. pai jadō̃ ohdī bandagī rūh te saceāī nāḷ kītī jāēgī.
c. for such worshippers does he seek.	c. kyū̃jō ajehe bandagī karnwāḷē ōh cāhndā e.

DERIVED SENTENCES.

1. The time is coming when neither in this mountain nor in Jerusalem shall God be worshipped.	1. Ōh wēḷā aundā e pai nā ēs pahāṛ utte te nā Yarūshalēm shahr wicc <u>Kh</u>udā dī bandagī kītī jāēgī.
2. I and the boy will go and worship in that mountain.	2. Maī̃ te muṇḍā ōs pahāṛ te jākē Rabb dī bandagī karā̃ge.
3. Let all the angels of God worship him.	3. <u>Kh</u>udā de sabbh farishte ohdī bandagī karn.

4. Ye worship ye know not what.	4. Jis cīz dī tuhānū̃ k͟habar nehī̃ ōsdī bandagī karde o.
5. We worship what we know, for salvation is from the Jews.	5. Asī̃ jihnū̃ jāṇne ā̃, osē dī bandagī karne ā̃, kyū̃jō najāt Yahūdīā̃ waḷlõ e.
6. Whom ye ignorantly worship, him declare we unto you.	6. Jihdī tusī̃ jāṇeā̃ binā bandagī karde o, osē dī k͟habar asī̃ tuhānū̃ dēnne ā̃.
7. Ye shall not worship any other God, for if ye worship another god or goddess, God Almighty will cast you out of this land.	7. Tusī̃ hōr kise K͟hudā dī sēwā nā karō, kyū̃jō jēkar tusī̃ hōr dēwī deotē dī pūjā karō, K͟hudā Tālā tuhānū̃ ēs dhartī thõ kaḍḍh dēgā.
8. We are they who worship God in spirit and put no confidence in the flesh.	8. Asī̃ ōh ā̃ jehṛe K͟hudā dī bandagī rūh nāḷ karne hā̃ te apṇe jusse te āsrā nēhī̃ karde.
9. I seek that mountain in which the Jews worshipped God.	9. Maĩ ōs pahāṛ nū̃ labbhnā̃ jihde wicc Yahūdī Rabb dī bandagī karde sāṇ.
10. My worship shall be performed over all the earth.	10. Sārī dhartī utte mērī bandagī kītī jāēgī.
11. It is written, at the name of Jesus every man shall bow.	11. Likkheā e, Yesū dā nā laike sārē bandē mathā ṭekaṇgē.
12. The hour has come when true worshippers, wherever they may be, will worship the Lord.	12. Ōh wēḷā āeā e jis wicc sacce pujārī, jitthe kite hōṇ, Rabb dī bandagī karnge.
13. Is there any need that we	13. Kōī lōṛ e pai asī̃ bandagī

	should turn our face here or there, when we worship?		karde wēḷē mū̃h ēddhar yā̃ ōddhar karīye?
14.	Really there is not, it is people's custom.	14.	Asl wicc kōī lōṛ nehī̃, lōkā̃ dā dastūr e.
15.	Where is God? Is he not on all sides?	15.	<u>Kh</u>udā kitthe we? Ōh tā̃ samhnī̃ pāsī̃ nehī̃ e?
16.	Yes, he is everywhere.	16.	Āho, ōh sabbhdare we.
17.	These are the two men who were worshipping in the mosque yesterday.	17.	Ēh ōh dō bande nē̃ jehṛe kall masītī namāj paṛhdē sāṇ.
18.	Where is the mountain in which the Samaritans used to worship?	18.	Ōh pahāṛ kitthe we jihde te Sāmarī bandagī karde sāṇ?
19.	Ten has struck, and people are gathering for service.	19.	Das waj gae nē̃ te lōk bandagī wāstē kaṭṭhe honde nē̃.
20.	Lift up your eyes and see, Jerusalem is on this mountain.	20.	Akkhī̃ ughēṛke wēkhō, Yarūshalem ēs pahāṛ utte we.
21.	If you labour then perhaps other people will devour your earnings.	21.	Jēkar tusī̃ mehnat karō, tā̃ <u>kh</u>abare hōr lōk tuhāḍḍī kamāī khā laiṇgē.
22.	If you reap that which ye did not sow, then have ye entered into the labour of others.	22.	Jē tusī̃ ohdī wāḍhī karde o jihdī bajāī nehī̃ kītī, tā̃ tusī̃ dūjjeā̃ dī mehnat wicc sharīk hoe o.
23.	In this service we seek God and he is found by those who are true.	23.	Ēs bandagī wicc asī̃ <u>Kh</u>udā nū̃ labbhne ā̃, te sacceā̃ nū̃ ōh labbh bī jāndā e.
24.	Now we ought to speak English as we do Panjabi.	24.	Huṇ sānū̃ cāhīdā e pai jis tarhā̃ asī̃ Aṅgrēzī bōlne ā̃, osē tarhā̃ Panjābī wī bōlīyē.

CUSTOMARY ACTION, PRESENT, PAST.

1.	The big waterman used to draw water at that time.	1.	Ōs wēḷe waḍḍā māshkī pāṇī bhardā hundā sī.
2.	Prophets give instruction from God.	2.	Nabī Khudā wallõ sikkheā dēnde honde nẽ.
3.	This is the man who used to give false witness in the court.	3.	Ēhoī bandā kacaihri wicc jhūṭhī gawāhī dēndā hondā sī.
4.	The teacher used to teach us this.	4.	Astād sānū̃ ēhoī sikhāndā hondā sī.
5.	That is the way they used to go to Lahore.	5.	Ōse rāh Lāhaur nū̃ jānde honde sāṇ.
6.	These men used to exhibit great shows.	6.	Ēh ādmī waḍḍe tamashe wikhānde honde sāṇ.
7.	Moslems keep the feast of Baqr.	7.	Musalmān Bakr Īd karde honde nẽ.
8.	The women used to sit here and listen to the prophet.	8.	Nabī diā̃ gallā̃ ētthe baihke suṇdiā̃ hondiā̃ sāṇ.
9.	Mr.—— used to have his wood brought from this wood-yard.	9.	Sāhb ēs ṭalõ lakṛī aṇwāndā hondā sī.
10.	John baptised in the river Jordan.	10.	Yūhannā Yardan daryā wicc baptismā dēndā hondā sī.
11.	Harvest used to be at this season in our country.	11.	Sāḍḍe dēs wicc wāḍhī ēs samē hondī hondī sī.
12.	The women used to stand by and watch his work.	12.	Buḍḍhiā̃ kōḷ khlōke, ohdā kamm wēkhdiā̃ hondiā̃ sāṇ.
13.	This rogue just lives in the jail.	13.	Ēh badmāsh jēlkhāne i raihndā hondā e.
14.	I am accustomed to pay only so much for this work.	14.	Maĩ tā̃ inne i rupae ēs naukarī wāste dēnna honnā wā̃.

15. The police do not take bribes on all sides.	15. Puls sabbhnī pāsī waḍdhī nehī laindī hondī e.
16. This very shoemaker makes my shoes.	16. Īho mōcī mērī juttī baṇāndā hondā e.
17. I rest here.	17. Maĩ ētthe arām karnā honnā wā.
18. That's what people say.	18. Lōk esē tarhā̃ āhnde honde nẽ.
19. Then (at that time) I did not understand Panjabi.	19. Odō̃ Panjābī bōlī nehī samajhdā hondā sā̃.
20. The servants go to market every day.	20. Naukar rōz bazār jānde honde nẽ.
21. This servant does his work well.	21. Ēh kāmmā caṅgī tārhā̃ kamm kardā hondā e.
22. At that time my girl was reading the Third Reader.	22. Odō̃ merī kākī trījjī katāb paṛhdī hondī sī.
23. What a lot of men give abuse!	23. Kinne admī gāhḷā̃ kaḍḍhde honde nẽ!
24. It is the bad habit of big and little, of men and women.	24. Nikkeā̃ waḍḍeā̃, jaṇeā̃ janānīā̃ dī burī ādat e.

Lesson XIV.	*Cauhdwā̃ Sabak.*
a. So when the Samaritans besought him,	a.[1] Ēs karke jad Sāmarī lōkā̃ ohde agge arz kītī,
b. he stayed with them, and many more through hearing his teaching believed,	b. Ōh ohnā̃ kōḷ raih peā te hōr bathēreā̃ ohdī sikkheā suṇke mann leī,

[1] A long sentence is required to give the sequence of conjunctions, and moreover the ability to repeat long sentences gives such a consciousness of mastery over short as well as long sentences, that it delivers one from embarrassment in using the language in the presence of one's elders, a necessary preliminary to success in public speech.

c. but he remained only a little time and went on to Galilee after two days,	*c.* par ōh thōṛā hī cir raihke dūh dinā̃ picche Galīl nū̃ ṭur peā,
d. for he said himself, a prophet has no honour in his own country.	*d.* kyū̃jō ōs āp ākheā, Nabī dī apṇe dēs wicc izzat nehī̃ hondī,
e. So the works which he had done in Jerusalem at the Feast,	*e.* phēr jehṛe kamm ōs Yarūshalem wicc Īd de wēḷe kīte sāṇ,
f. seeing them the Galileans received him,	*f.* ohnā̃ nū̃ wekhke, Galīliā̃ ohnū̃ kabūleā,
g. for they too had gone to the Feast.	*g.* kyū̃jō ōh wī Īd te gae hoe sān,

DERIVED SENTENCES.

1. So men and women besought him and he stayed many more days at home.	1. Ēs karke jaṇeā̃ janāniā̃ ōs agge tarle mintā̃ kītiā̃ te ōh hōr cōkhe din ghare rehā.
2. It is reported in the city that for many years no prophet has been seen in this country.	2. Shahr wicc ākhīdā e, pai baṛeā̃ warheā̃ thī̃ ēs dēs wicc kōī nabī disseā nehī̃.
3. The woman testified that the prophet had not been honoured in his own country as he ought to have been.	3. Ōs janānī apī gawāhī dittī pai jis tarhā̃ cāhīdā sī nabī dī ādar apṇe dēs wicc nehī̃ sī hoī.
4. Leaving Jerusalem, he had to go through their land.	4. Yarūshalem nū̃ chaḍḍke ohnū̃ ohnā̃ de mulkh de wiccō̃ dī laṅghṇā̃ peā.
5. The Galileans received him gladly, for they had seen his miracles at Jerusalem.	5. Galīliā̃ khushī nāḷ ohnū̃ kabūleā, kyū̃jō ohnā̃ Yarūshalem wicc ohdiā̃ karāmtā̃ wēkkhiā̃.

6.	While he was teaching in the temple, they saw him.	6.	Jad ōh haikaḷ wicc talīm dēndā sī, ohnā̃ ohnū̃ wēkh leā.
7.	While the prophet is giving instruction, stay with us and hear him.	7.	Jicar nabī talīm dēndā e, tusī̃ sāḍḍe kōḷ rauho te ohdī suṇo.
8.	This teaching was given in the Holy City at the time of the Feast.	8.	Ēh talīm Pāk Shahr wicc Īd dē wēḷe dittī gaī.
9.	When the Lord received baptism at the hands of John, then there came a voice from heaven, This is my beloved Son in whom I am well pleased.	9.	Jad Khudāwand nū̃ Yuhannā de hatthō̃ baptismā miḷeā, tā̃ asmānō̃ ēh awāz āī, Ēh mērā piyārā Puttar e, jis te maī khush ā̃.
10.	Many saw his miracles and believed on him.	10.	Bathēreā̃ ohdīā̃ karāmātā̃ wēkhkē ōs te imān leāndā.
11.	The fuel is burnt up, so I shall have more brought from the city.	11.	Bāllaṇ mukk geā we, ēs karke maī shahrō̃ hōr aṇwāā̃gā.
12.	He stayed with us two months and went to his own country, for he said, It is near harvest now.	12.	Sāḍḍe kōḷ dō mahīne raīhke ōh apṇe dēs nū̃ ṭur geā, kyū̃jō ōs ākheā, Huṇ wāḍhī dā wēḷā nēṛe āeā e.
13.	When he was brought before the Judge, the Judge ordered his imprisonment and delivered him to the police, so they took him away and delivered him to the jailor.	13.	Jad ōh munsaf de agge hāzar kitā geā, tā̃ munsaf jēlkhāne dā hukm dēkē puls de hawāle kitā, so ohnā̃ lai jāke ohnū̃ darōge de hawāle kar chaḍḍeā.
14.	These chairs were made so that when I am tired	14.	Kursiā̃ ēs wāste baṇiā̃ paī jad maī thakk

I may sit and take my ease in them.	jāwā̃, baihke arām karā̃.
15. Whatever word is difficult, we utter it hundreds of times daily and afterwards speak it correctly.	15. Jehṛā lafs aukhā hōwe, asī̃ ōsnū̃ rōz sai sai wārī ākhke magarõ ṭhīk bōlne ā̃.
16. I do not know where to go.	16. Patā nehī̃ kitthe jā̃.
17. I did not know what to say.	17. Menū̃ patā nehī sī pai maī kī ākhā̃.
18. He does not know Arabic.	18. Ōh Arbī bōlī nehī̃ jāṇdā.
19. When I talk to them they do not understand.	19. Jad maĩ ohnā̃ nāḷ gall karnā̃ ōh samajhde nehī̃.
20. I do not see the man you are speaking of.	20. Jehṛā ādmī tusī̃ menū̃ dassde o, ōh menū̃ dissdā nehī̃.
21. Miss——does not know where your servant has gone.	21. Miss sāhb nū̃ patā nehī̃ pai Hazūr dā naukar kitthe geā we.
22. You do not believe me because you like doing wrong.	22. Tusī̃ mērī gall dā yakīn ēs karke nehī̃ karde pai bureāī tuhānū̃ piārī e.
23. Phajjū, why didn't you send the book I gave you?	23. Phajjū, jehṛī katāb maĩ tenū̃ dittī, tū̃ ghallī kyū̃ nehī̃?
24. Mary, what's the reason you are not doing your work well this week?	24. Mariā̃, ēs hafte tū̃ kamm caṇgī tarhā̃ nehī̃ kardī, kī sababb?
25. Girls, learn your lessons well.	25. Kuṛīyo, tusī̃ āpo apṇā sabak caṅgī tarhā̃ pakāo.

Root and Causal Forms.

1. Is the work done? I'll finish it to-day.	1. Kamm mukk geā e? Ajj mukā deā̃gā.

2. This water is not warm. Have it heated.	2. Ēh pāṇī garm nehī̃, garm karāo.
3. Is the boy dead? Yes, the police killed him.	3. Muṇḍā mar geā e? Āhō, puls jō māreā.
4. The Government will put them to death.	4. Sarkār ohnā̃ nū̃ marwāēgī.
5. Has Mr.——had the plants planted?	5. Sāhb buṭe luāe?
6. They are not all planted yet, the gardener is planting them now.	6. Aje sāre nehī̃ lagge, mālī lāndā e peā.
7. Have you broken the dish? Sir, it just broke accidentally.	7. Bhāṇḍā trōṛ suṭṭeā ī? Janāb, aīwẽ ṭuṭṭ geā.
8. What's the price of wheat? Did you bring it?	8. Kaṇak kis tarhā̃ āī? Tū̃ āndī sī?
9. Yes, Mr.——ordered it. Rs. 3 for 82 lbs.	9. Āhō, sāhb aṇwāī, trai rupayye maṇ pakkā.
10. Did you hear this matter? Tell it, then we'll be sure.	10. Ēh gall tusā̃ suṇī? Suṇāo, tā̃ jāṇiye.
11. Put the mare out of the field at once.	11. Ghōṛī huṇe paiḷiõ kaḍḍh, whaī.
12. She'll go out, sir. If not, I'll put her out.	12. Nikaḷ jāegī, janāb, nehī̃ te maī huṇe kaḍḍh chaḍḍā̃gā.
13. Is this my chair you are making?	13. Ēh merī kursī baṇānde o pae?
14. Yours is not made yet.	14. Aje tuhāḍḍī nehī̃ baṇī.
15. Very well, I'll get some one else to make it.	15. Caṅgā! Maī hōr kise kōḷõ baṇwāā̃gā.
16. Has the baby been fed yet? (or drunk her milk yet?) Its mother was feeding it then.	16. Bacce duddh pī leā? Mā̃ odõ ohnū̃ piāndī (or piāḷdi) sī paī.
17. Can the village be seen here? Yes, come here and see it.	17. Piṇḍ ētthõ dissdā e? Āhō, ure āṇke wēkkho.
18. I can't see it. Can't you?	18. Menū̃ nehī̃ labbhdā,

I'll show you.	halā! tuhānū̃ wikhā dēnnā wā̃.
19. Has this been known since yesterday? Yes, I found it out the day before. Come along, I'll show you.	19. Ēh kall thō̃ malūm e? Āhō, sagō̃ maī̃ parsō̃ malūm kītā sī. Calo, tuhānū̃ dass dēnnā wā̃.
20. Sold your horse? Not yet. I'll sell him to-day.	20. Ghōṛā wik geā? Aje wikeā tā̃ nehī̃. Ajj wēcā̃gā.
21. What do they call this boy?	21. Ēs muṇḍe nū̃ kī sadde nē̃?
22. His mother calls him Hassu.	22. Mā̃ ohnū̃ Hassū karke saddī e.
23. Call Saddhu, brother.	23. Saddhū nū̃ sadd, bhāī.

Lesson XV.	*Pandhrwā̃ Sabak.*
When the nobleman, whose son was sick in Capernaum, heard that Jesus had come again to Cana, where the water was made wine, he went to the Lord and besought him, saying, My son is at the point of death. Come and heal him.	Jis raīs dā puttar Kafarnahūm wicc bamār sī, jadō̃ ohnū̃ khabar hoī paī Yesū Kānā nū̃ muṛ āeā we, jitthe pāṇī mai baṇ geā sī, Khudāwand kōḷ jākē ohde tarlē kītē paī Mērā puttar marnwāḷā e, āṇke ohnū̃ wall kar.

DERIVED SENTENCES.

1. What did the nobleman do? He besought the Lord to come to Capernaum.	1. Raīs kī kītā? Ōs Khudāwand agge tarlē kīte paī Kafarnahūm nū̃ ā.
2. Why did he ask him to go to Capernaum? Because his son was sick.	2. Kafarnahūm nū̃ jāṇ wāste kyū̃ ākheā? Ohdā puttar jō bamār sī.
3. How ill was he? He was dying.	3. Kēḍḍā bamār sī? Ōh tā̃ marnwāḷā sī.

4. How did the nobleman know that Jesus could [will be able to] heal his son ?	4. Ōs raīs nū̃ kis tarhā̃ patā sī paī Yesū mēre puttar nū̃ wall kar sakēgā ?
5. Because the Lord had made the water into wine.	5. Khudāwand pāṇī nū̃ mai baṇāeā sī.
6. Did the Lord Jesus go ? He did not.	6. Khudāwand Yesū geā ke nehī̃ ? Nehī̃ geā.
7. Why didn't he go ? He did not need to, for he healed him without going.	7. Kyū̃ nehī̃ geā ? ōhnū̃ kōī lōṛ nehī̃ sī, bin geā̃ ohnū̃ wall kītā.
8. How could he do so great a work ? Because it was in his authority.	8. Ēḍḍā kamm kis tarhā̃ hōeā ? Kyū̃jō ohde wass wicc sī.
9. Did the boy get well ? Well, it was with this idea that the father went away.	9. Ōh muṇḍā tagṛā hōeā ? Khair, ēs yakīn nāḷ peō caleā geā.
10. But did he or not ? We'll see in the next lesson.	10. Par hoeā ke nā hoeā ? Agle sabak wicc wēkhā̃gē.
11. The Gospel will be proclaimed over the whole world and many people will accept it.	11. Injīl sārī dhartī te suṇāī jāēgī te bauht lōk kabūlaṇge.
12. The story of Christ will be told to every man, and before Him every one shall bow the knee.	12. Masīh dī khabar sabbh kise nū̃ dittī jāēgī, te sāre ohde agge gōḍē niwāṇgē.
13. To-morrow, by noon, said the prophet, bread shall sell cheap.	13. Nabī ākheā bhāḷke do-paihr tōṛī, rōṭī, sawallī wikēgī.
14. Some woman said, I'll get him to make a box of wood.	14. Kise ākheā, Maī ohde kōḷō lakkaṛ dā bakas baṇwāā̃gī.

15. I will beg of him that he come and heal my son.	15. Maĩ ohde agge arz karā̃gā pai āwe te mēre puttar uū̃ tagṛeā̃ karē.
16. When the teacher, whose girl was ill, heard that she was dying, he ran for a fit physician.	16. Jis ustād dī kuṛī māndī sī, jadõ suṇeā pai mērī kuṛī mārnwāḷī e, ōh kise laik hakīm kōḷ bhajj geā.
17. The physician said, she'll be well by to-morrow.	17. Hakīm ākkhaṇ laggā, Bhaḷke tōṛī rāzī hōwēgī.
18. I had this house built last year.	18. Ēh ghar maī par baṇwāeā sī.
19. I sent him to go and get some money from that sick man.	19. Maĩ ohnū̃ ghalleā pai jākē ōs mānde kōḷõ rupae maṅg leāwe.
20. Master sent the horse to the stable by the hand of the groom.	20. Sāhb sahīs dī hatthī ghōṛe nū̃ tawēle ghall dittā.
21. They told us to come down from the roof and go to the city and take that sick man to the hospital.	21. Ohnā̃ sānū̃ ākheā kōṭheõ utarke te shahr jāke ōs bamār nū̃ haspatāḷ lai jāo.
22. Why did you give us again to-day the very bread that made us so sick yesterday.	22. Jis rōṭī thõ asī̃ kall ēḍḍe bamār hoe sā̃, ōhoi sānū̃ ajj phēr kāhnū̃ khuāī ?
23. The teacher sent the boy who was ill to his father.	23. Jehṛā muṇḍā māndā sī munshī ohnū̃ peō kōḷ ghalleā.
24. I have to go to the city, for the cook's son is ill, and I am going to see him.	24. Maī shahr jāṇā e, khā̃sāmē̃ dā puttar bamār e te maī wēkkhaṇ calleā wā̃.
25. You'll have to give a rupee for that book.	25. Ōs kitāb badle ikk rupayyā dēṇā pawīgā.
26. Carpenter, I will get you	26. Mistrīā, maī tēre pāsõ

	to make me two chairs and three tables.		dō kursīā̃ tē trai mēz banwāā̃gā.
27.	When we hear with care, we also speak correctly.	27.	Jadõ asī dhiān nāḷ suṇṇe ā̃, tā̃ ṭhīk ṭhīk bōlne wī ā̃.
28.	Hence whoever wishes to speak Panjabi should listen carefully to the speech of the people.	28.	Ēs karke jehṛā Panjābī bōlṇī cāhe, ōh lōkā̃ dīā̃ gallā̃ dhiān nāḷ suṇe karē.

Exercises in miḷṇā and laggṇā.

1.	Where did you get this book?	1.	Ēh katāb tuhānū̃ kitthõ miḷī?
2.	I got it from the Sardar's shop.	2.	Sardār dī haṭṭīõ mainū̃ miḷ gaī.
3.	What did you pay for the mare	3.	Ghōṛī kinnē nū̃ leī?
4.	I got her for a hundred rupees.	4.	Ōh sau rupae tõ miḷī.
5.	Our cow won't give milk to-day.	5.	Sāḍḍī gā̃ ajj miḷdī nehī.
6.	Introduce me to the master.	6.	Mērā Sāhb nāḷ mēḷ karāo.
7.	He is not at home. Did you not meet him on the road?	7.	Sāhb ghar nehī̃. Tuhānū̃ wāṭe nehī̃ miḷē?
8.	Are the boys studying Urdu? Yes, the Government has it taught.	8.	Muṇḍe Uṛdū paṛhde nē? Āhō, sarkār pāṛhāndī ē.
9.	The teacher teaches them daily.	9.	Munshī ohnā̃ nū̃ rōz dihāṛī paṛhāndā e.
10.	You do not understand what I am saying.	10.	Tusī̃ mērī gall nehī̃ samjhde o.
11.	Please explain it to me.	11.	Zarā samjhā chaḍḍeā je (or chaḍḍīō je.)
12.	I was about to sit down there.	12.	Maĩ ōtthē baihṇ lagā sā̃.

13. The girl had just begun to bake the bread.	13. Kuṛī ōs wēḷē rōṭī pakāṇ laggī sī.
14. Have they begun to cook the meal?	14. Rōṭī aje pakāṇ lage nẽ?
15. The mother had begun to make Gujri get the supper.	15. Mā̃ Gujrī kōḷõ shām wēḷe rōṭī pakwāṇ lagī sī.
16. The boy was nearly dead.	16. Muṇḍā marn laggā sī.
17. The boys had begun to beat the dog.	17. Muṇḍe kutte nū̃ mārn lagge sāṇ.
18. The gentleman had determined to have his dog killed.	18. Sāhb apṇe kutte nū̃ marwāṇ lagge sāṇ.
19. The capatis had begun to be prepared then.	19. Ōs wēḷe rōṭīā̃ teār hōṇ laggīā̃ sāṇ.
20. The women had begun to get the meal ready then.	20. Zanānīā̃ ōs wēḷe rōṭī teār karn lagīā̃ sāṇ.
21. The mistress of the home was having the meal got ready.	21. Gharwāḷī ōs wēḷe rōṭī teār karān laggī sī.
22. The girls had begun work.	22. Kuṛīā̃ kamm karn laggīā̃ sāṇ.
23. Mother had begun to set the girls to work.	23. Bēbbe kuṛīā̃ kōḷõ kamm karāṇ lagī sī.

Lesson XVI.	*Sōhḷwā̃ Sabak.*
When the nobleman was going down his servants met him and said, Your son is living, wherefore he asked them, What hour was it when he began to get better, and when they told him the seventh hour, he knew that it was the very hour in which Jesus said to him, Thy son liveth, so he and all his house believed.	Jad raīs caleā jāndā sī, ohde naukar ohnū̃ miḷke ākkhaṇ lagge, Tuhāḍḍā puttar jiūndā e, ēs karke raīs ohnā̃ kōḷõ pucchaṇ laggā, Ōh kehṛā wēḷā sī jad ōh wall hōṇ laggā, te jadõ ohnā̃ satwī̃ ghaṛī dassī, ōs jāttā paī ōhoī ghaṛī e jihde wicc Yesū ākheā, Tērā puttar jiūndā e, sō ōh āp

te ohdā sārā ṭabbar imān leāe.

DERIVED SENTENCES.

1. Who met the nobleman? His servants.	1. Rais nū̃ kauṇ miḷ pae? Ohde naukar.
2. Where did they meet him? On the way to Capernaum.	2. Kitthe miḷ pae? Kafarnahūm de rāh wicc.
3. Why had they come to meet (escort) him?	3. Ohnū̃ aggō̃ laiṇ wāste kyū̃ āe sāṇ?
4. To give the good news that his son was well.	4. Ēh khushī dī khabar dēṇ wāste pai puttar wall e.
5. What was it he asked them?	5. Ōs ohnā̃ kōḷō kī kujjh pucchеā?
6. What time did he begin to get better?	6. Kehṛē wēḷē wall hōṇ laggā?
7. What hour did they say? The seventh.	7. Ohnā̃ kehṛī ghaṛī dassī? Satwī̃ ghaṛī.
8. What was wonderful in this?	8. Ehde wicc kī acarj gall hoī?
9. It was the seventh hour when Jesus sent him away.	9. Satwī̃ ghaṛī sī jadō̃ Yesū ohnū̃ ṭōreā.
10. What effect did this have on the nobleman?	10. Ēs gall dā rais te kī asr hoeā?
11. He knew that it was by the power of Christ that his son was healed.	11. Ōs jāṇ leā pai Masīh dī tākat nāḷ mērā puttar wall hōeā.
12. What effect did it have on the family?	12. Ṭabbar te kī asr hōeā?
13. They all believed.	13. Sāre de sāre imān leāe.
14. Should one believe on the Lord Jesus Christ?	14. Khudāwand Yesū Masīh te imān leauṇā cāhīdā e?
15. Yes, for there is no other	15. Āhō, dhartī utte hōr kōī

	name given on earth able to save.		nā nehĩ dasseā geā jihdī rāhĩ asĩ najāt pāīye.
16.	Because from his word and works it is evident that only Christ is able to do this.	16.	Ēs karke pai ohdī kalām te karāmatā̃ tō̃ malūm hondā e pai nirā Masīh ēs kamm jōgā e.
17.	Are there no other prophets sent from God ?	17.	Khudā dā ghalleā hoeā kōī hōr nabī nehĩ ?
18.	Other prophets have indeed been sent, yet it was not their work to give salvation, but rather to bear witness to the Saviour, Christ.	18.	Ghalle hoe te hōr nabī wī haiṇ nē̃, par ohnā dā kamm najāt dēṇī nehĩ sī, sagō̃ najāt dēṇwāḷe Masīh dī agwāhī dēṇī.
19.	What does Christ himself say about this ?	19.	Masīh āpī ēs gall dī bābat kī āhndā e ?
20.	That no one can come to God save by me.	20.	Pai mērē bājhō̃ kōī Khudā kōḷ jā nehĩ sakdā.
21.	Did not the prophets work miracles ?	21.	Nabīā̃ karāmatā̃ nehĩ kitīā̃ ?
22.	They often did them, and these very miracles are God's seal on them that they are true.	22.	Askar kītiā̃ sāṇ, te īhōī karāmātā̃ Khudā wallō̃ ohnā̃ lai sanad nē pai ōh sacce nē̃.
23.	Is their testimony to be found anywhere ?	23.	Ohnā̃ dī gawāhī kitale likhī hōī e ?
24.	Yes, in the Law, the Psalms, and the books of the prophets this is the testimony, that there is but one Saviour and that Christ is he.	24.	Āhō, Taurāt, Zabūr te nabīā̃ diā̃ kitābā̃ wicc gawāhī īhoī e, pai najāt dēṇwāḷā ikkoī e te ōh Masīh e.
25.	How may we get salvation ?	25.	Najāt sānū kīkū̃ miḷdī e ?
26.	People often say, If we do good works we shall get it.	26.	Lōk askar āhnde nē̃, nēk kamm kariye, tā̃ miḷēgī.

27. Can a sinful man do good works ?	27. Pāpī bandā nēk kamm kar sakdā e?
28. The Gospel says, If we believe on the beloved Son of God, whom he sent, then shall salvation be obtained.	28. Injīl āhndī e, Khudā de piāre te ghalle hoe Puttar te Imān leāwīye, tā̃ najāt miḷēgī.
29. When you meet the father, say to him, Your son is living.	29. Jadō̃ ohde peō nū̃ miḷo, tā̃ īhōī gall ākhō, Tuhāḍḍā puttar jiūndā e.
30. The father met them at sunset.	30. Din ḍubbdeā̃ peō ohnā̃ nū̃ miḷ peā.
31. When the servants knew that it was the seventh hour when Christ said, Thy son liveth, then they also realised that the boy was made well by the power of the Messiah.	31. Jadō̃ naukarā̃ nū̃ malūm hoeā pai Masīh satwī̃ ghaṛī ākheā, Tērā puttar jiūndā e, tā̃ ohnā̃ nū̃ wī patā laggā pai muṇḍā Masīh dī tafīk nāḷ wall hoeā.
32. As people hear, so they speak, hence the teacher should speak correct Panjabi and the pupil himself will hear and speak correctly.	32. Jis tarhā̃ lōk suṇde nē osē tarhā̃ bōlde wī nē, ēs karke munshī ṭhīk ṭhīk Panjābī bōlē, te shagird suṇke āpe ṭhīk bōlēgā.

Idiomatic use of auṇā, calṇā and jāṇā with laggṇa and karnā.

I was going.	Maĩ lagā jāndā sā̃.
You were coming.	Tū̃ lagā aundā saĩ.
He is going.	Ōh laga jāndā e.
She is coming.	Ōh lagī aundī e.
I (f.) am coming.	Maĩ lagī aunnī ā̃.
I was going.	Maĩ caleā jāndā sā̃.
He was going.	Ōh caleā jāndā sī.
(Habitually) come here, my boy.	Sāḍḍē wall āweā kar, puttar.

Come here, my boy.	**Mērē wall ā, puttar.**
Always draw water from this well, never from that.	**Ōs khūhō̃ nā, ēs khūhō̃ pāṇī bhareā kar.**
Draw water from this little well, waterman.	**Ēs khūhīō̃ pāṇī bhar, māshkiā.**
Never sit with them, my girl.	**Ohnā̃ nāḷ nā bawheā kar, kuṛīye.**
Sit here, my boy.	**Ētthe bauh, muṇḍeā.**
Give me that water.	**Ōh pāṇī menū̃ dēh.**
Always give us this water.	**Īhō pāṇī sānū̃ deā kar.**
Drink some milk, brother.	**Duddh piō, bhāī.**
Don't drink tea, drink milk.	**Cāh nā pīweā kar, duddh pīweā kar.**
Don't go to the city.	**Shahr nā jāh.**
Never go there.	**Ōtthe nā jāweā kar.**
Always ask me.	**Mērē kōḷō̃ puccheā kar.**
Never do that, my boy.	**Ēh kamm nā kareā kar, puttar.**
Look at me, my boy.	**Mērē wallō̃ wēkheā kar, muṇḍeā.**
Tell the truth.	**Sacc dasso.**
Always tell the truth.	**Sacc sacc dasseā karō.**
Always call him "munshiji."	**Ohnū̃ munshī jī karke saddeā karo.**
Make me a good chair, carpenter.	**Mērē wāste caṅgī kursī baṇāo, mistrī jī.**
Always make good chairs, brethren.	**Caṅgiā̃ kursiā̃ baṇāweā karo, bhāio.**

Lesson XVII.	*Satāhrwā̃ Sabak.*
When the disciples saw a man blind from birth, they asked the Lord, who did sin, this man or his parents, that he was born blind?	**Jadō̃ cēleā̃ ikk jamāndhrū ānnhe nū̃ wēkheā, ohnā̃ Khudāwand Masīh kōḷō puccheā, Ustād ji, kis pāp kītā, ēs yā ēsde māpeā̃, pai ēh annhā jammeā.**

Derived Sentences.

1. Whom did the disciples see?	1. **Cēleā̃ kih nū̃ ḍiṭṭhā.**
2. They saw a man blind from birth.	2. **Ikkī jamāndhrū annhe nū̃ ḍiṭṭho ne.** (*See* Gram. p. 105.)
3. What was he doing?	3. **Ōh kī kardā sī?**
4. He sat and begged.	4. **Ōh baihke maṅgdā hondā sī.**
5. Since when was he blind? From birth.	5. **Kadõk dā annhā sī? Jamāndhrū.**
6. What question arose in the disciples' hearts?	6. **Cēleā̃ de dil wicc kī suwāl uṭṭheā?**
7. Perhaps he sinned before birth.	7. **Khaure, ēs jammaṇ thõ paihlā̃ kōī pāp kītā.**
8. Did they believe in transmigration of souls?	8. **Ōh awāgauṇ nū̃ mannde sāṇ.**
9. No, but as it is written that Esau and Jacob strove before birth, the thought came that this man must have done something.	9. **Nehī̃, par jis tarhā̃ likkheā hoeā e pai Esāū te Yakūb, jammaṇ tõ paihlā̃, laṛde sāṇ, ēh khiāl āeā pai ēs wī kujjh kītā hōwēdā.**
10. What did the Lord say?	10. **Khudāwand ohnā̃ nū̃ kī ākheā?**
11. Neither did this man sin, nor his parents, but that the works of God may be made manifest has this happened.	11. **Nā ēs pāp kītā nā ehde mā bāp, par Khudā de kamm zāhr karn wāste ēh gall hoī e.**
12. Does sickness come from sin?	12. **Bamārī pāp thõ hundī e ke nehī̃?**
13. It is indeed the final cause, but not always our own sin.	13. **Asl gall te īhoī e, par hamēshā saḍḍē apṇe pāp thõ nehī̃.**
14. Is death from sin?	14. **Marnā wī pāp de sababbõ e?**

English	Panjabi
15. It is. It is written, The wages of sin is death.	15. Hai i. Likheā hoeā e, Gunāh dī majūrī maut e.
16. What is sin?	16. Pāp kī e?
17. To go contrary to the will of God is sin.	17. Khudā dī marzī de ulṭ calṇā pāp e.
18 Are all men sinners or not?	18. Sāre bande pāpī nẽ ke nehī̃?
19. Who is there that isn't? All are sinners and have come short of the glory of God.	19. Kauṇ khālī e? Sāre pāpī nẽ te Khudā de jalāl thõ raih gae nẽ.
20. How were God's works revealed in this blind man.	20. Ēs annhe wicc Khudā de kamm kīkũ zāhr hoe?
21. By his being healed.	21. Ohde wall hõṇ tõ.
22. Who healed him?	22. Ohnũ kis wall kītā?
23. The Lord Jesus Christ did.	23. Khudāwand Yesū Masīh.
24. Why did he?	24. Kyũ wall kītā?
25. For the praise of God.	25. Khudā dī waḍeāī wāste.
26. Did you ever see any one born blind?	26. Kade tusā̃ koī jamāndhrū annhā ḍiṭṭhā e?
27. I have seen many blind people, but few blind from birth.	27. Annhe bauht wēkhe, par jamāndhrū annhe ghaṭṭ ḍiṭṭhe nẽ.
28. Are there many boys and girls blind in the West?	28. Wilait wicc muṇḍe kuṛīā̃ bauht annhe honde nẽ?
29. Now and then there's one.	29. Ṭāwẽ, ṭāwẽ (wirlē wirlē).
30. There are lots of blind folk in the Panjab. What's the reason?	30. Panjāb wicc annhe bauht honde nẽ. Ki sababb e?
31. There is so much carelessness about diseases of the eyes.	31. Akkhīā̃ dīā̃ bamārīā̃ tõ, bē-parwāhī bauht e.
32. If you have sore eyes, what do you do in Europe?	32. Akkhīā̃ ā jāṇ, tā̃ tusī̃ Wilait wicc kī karde o?

33.	We put in medicine, keep the eyes clean, and if they are very sore, then for days or weeks we stay in a dark room. What do you do here ?	33.	Asī̃ kōī dawā dārū pānne ā̃, akkhīā̃ sāf rakkhne ā̃, te jē bauht dukkhdīā̃ hōṇ, tā̃ kaī din hanēre kamre wicc raihnne ā̃. Ētthe tusī̃ kī karde o ?
34.	We ? Oh, we don't do anything for two or three weeks, if then relief does not come, we do whatever people say. The last remedy is to bring some charm from the priests. If it is decreed, then they get well.	34.	Asī̃ ? Khair, dō cār hafte kujjh wī nehī̃ karde, māgarõ aman nā āwē tā̃ jō kujjh lōk dassde nē̃ sohī karne ā̃. Chēkaṛlā ilāj te kise paṇḍit mal wāṇe kōḷõ kōī dhāgā tawīt leaunne ā̃. Kismat hōwe tā̃ khair hō jāndī e.
35.	Would it be well to insist on cleanliness, like the foreigners or not ?	35.	Wilait de dastūr wāṅgū̃ safāī rakkhṇī caṅgī hōwēgī ke nehī̃ ?
36.	Oh, that's all right, but one can't fight with fate, is a saying of our Panjab.	36.	Khair, māṛī te nehī̃, par kismat nāḷ laṛeā nehī̃ jāndā, Ēh sāḍḍe Panjāb dā akhāṇ e.
37.	If I begin to read, there are many mistakes. What's the reason ?	37.	Jad paṛhn laggnā̃ tā̃ galtīā̃ bauht hundīā̃ nē̃. Kī sababb e ?
38.	You don't know the language and your tongue does not run smoothly. Have patience. It will run some day.	38.	Bōlī jō aje nehī̃ aundī te zabān wī nehī̃ turdī. Haūsalā rakkho, ṭur pawēgī.

Interrogatives and Past Transitives.

Who did this ?	Ēh kamm kis kītā ?
I did it, sir.	Janāb, maī kītā.

You did it ?	Tū kītā ?
Yes sir, Shana and I together did it.	Āhō, janāb, maī te Shāhṇē raḷke kītā.
Yes, you boys did it. I thought it was done by boys.	Hā̃ tusā̃ ī kītā. Maī ākheā wī sī muṇḍeā̃ ēh kamm kītā.
Who did that ? Did those boys and girls ?	Ōh kamm kinhā̃ kītā ? Ohnā̃ muṇḍeā̃ kuṛīā̃ kītā ?
No, this boy did it.	Nehī, es muṇḍe kītā.
Who gave you my book ?	Mērī kitāb tenū̃ kis dittī ?
Your boy gave it to me.	Tuhāḍḍe muṇḍe menū̃ dittī ?
Who beat my boy ?	Mērē muṇḍē nū̃ kinhā̃ māreā ?
The people of that village beat him.	Ōs piṇḍ deā̃ lōkā̃ māreā.
Who gave you the pice ?	Kis tuhānū̃ paise dittē ?
My mother gave me two pice.	Mērī mā̃ dō paise dittē.
Who gave our books to the boys.	Sāḍḍīā̃ kitābā̃ muṇḍeā̃ nū̃ kis dittīā̃. ?
The teacher did.	Munshī dittīā̃.
Who gave you both these horses ?	Ēh dōwe ghōṛe tuhānū̃ kinhā̃ dittē ?
The Government gave one, and my brother the other.	Ikk sarkār dittā, te ikk mēre bhrā dittā.

Lesson XVIII.	*Aṭhāhrwā̃ Sabak.*
While it is day, I must work the works of him that sent me, for the night cometh when no man can work. While I am in the world, I am the light of the world.	Jad tāī din e zarūr e pai maī apṇe Ghallaṇwāḷē de kamm karā̃, rāt aundī e jad kōī kamm kar nehī sakdā. Jad tikar maī jagat wicc ā̃ maī jagat dā cānnaṇ ā̃.

Derived Sentences.

1. What is the light of this world ?	1. Ēs jagat dā cānnaṇ kī e ?
2. The sun is the light of this world.	2. Ēs jagat dā cānnaṇ dīū̃b (sūraj) e.

English	Panjabi
3. What did the Lord say of himself?	3. Khudāwand apṇe hakk wicc kī ākheā?
4 I am the light of the world.	4. Ōs ākheā, maĩ Jagat dā cānnaṇ ā̃.
5. What sort of a light is he?	5. Ōh kis tarhā̃ dā cānnaṇ e.
6. The light of the hearts of men.	6. Bandeā̃ deā̃ dilā̃ dā.
7. Do all men like the light?	7. Sāre bandeā̃ nū̃ cānnaṇ caṅga laggdā e?
8. No, thieves, robbers, murderers, adulterers, all desire the darkness.	8. Nehī̃ jī, cōr, dhāṛwī, khūnī, zanāhī, sabbh hanērā cāhnde nē̃.
9. What did Christ say of such?	9. Ajeheā̃ bābat Masīh kī ākheā?
10. He said that these people prefer darkness to light.	10. Ōs ākheā, Ēh lōk hanēre nū̃ cānnaṇ nāḷō̃ waddh piār karde nē̃.
11. What is the reason of this?	11. Ēs gall da kī sababb e?
12. Because their works are evil.	12. Ohnā̃ de kamm bure jō hoe.
13. What sort of people desire the light?	13. Kehojehe lōk cānnaṇ cāhnde nē̃?
14. Those whose works are good.	14. Jihnā̃ de kamm nēk nē̃.
15. When do men work?	15. Bande kadō̃ kamm karde nē̃?
16. They work while it is day.	16. Din hondeā̃ kamm karde nē̃.
17. Does no one work at night?	17. Rātī̃ kamm kōī nehī̃ kardā?
18. Yes, but still they need light.	18. Āhō, par tad wī Ohnā̃ nū̃ cānnaṇ dī lōṛ tā̃ hai ī.
19. What do you use at night for light?	19. Tusī̃ rāt dē wēḷe cānnaṇ wāste kī wartde ho?

	English		Panjabi
20	We use lamps.	20.	**Asī̃ battiā̃ wartne ā̃.**
21.	What do they use in Europe?	21.	**Wilait wicc kī wartde nẽ?**
22.	Oil, gas and electric lights.	22.	**Tēl, gais te bijlī diā̃ battiā̃.**
23.	In the Panjab some burn mustard oil, some paraffin; gas and electricity are found only in the cities.	23.	**Panjāb wicc koī kauṛā tēl bāḷdā e, kōī miṭṭī dā tel; gais bijlī khāss shahrā̃ wicc hundī e.**
24.	Get your pens and ink and do a little dictation, boys.	24.	**Kalmā̃ duātā̃ laike thōṛī bauht ibārat likkhō, muṇḍeo.**
25.	Do not hold the pen that way, my son, you ought to hold it thus.	25.	**Ōs tarhā̃ kalam nā phaṛ, puttar, ēs tarhā̃ phaṛnī cāhīdī e.**
26.	Do not speak so slowly, speak faster.	26.	**Ēḍḍī hauḷī hauḷī nā bōleā karo, chētī chētī bōleā karo.**
27.	We work while it is day.	27.	**Jad tāī̃ diū̃h (din) e, asī̃ kamm karne ā̃.**
28.	Do your work quickly, for the night is coming and you will not be able to work.	28.	**Āpō apṇā kamm chētī karo, rāt aundī e te tusī̃ kamm nā kar sakoge.**
29.	What did Christ mean by this "night"?	29.	**Ēs rāt thō̃ Masīh dī kī murād sī?**
30.	This night means death.	30.	**Es rāt thō̃ maut murād sī.**
31.	How long does the night last?	31.	**Rāt kinnī lammī hondī e.**
32.	In summer six or seven hours, and in winter, twelve or fourteen.	32.	**Garmī wicc chē satt ghaiṇṭe, te siāḷ wicc bārā̃ caudā̃ ghaiṇṭe hondī e.**
33.	Why does the night pass away?	33.	**Rāt mukkdī kyū̃ ē?**
34.	Because the sun comes out?	34.	**Din nikaḷ aundā e.**

35. When will the night of death pass?	35. Maut dī jō rāt e, ōh kad mukkēgī?
36. When our sun, the Lord Jesus, returns.	36. Jad sāḍḍā cānnaṇ, Khudāwand Masīh muṛ āwēgā?
37. When will he come?	37. Ōh kadō̃ āwedā?
38. No one knows exactly.	38. Ēs gall dā ṭhīk patā kisē nū̃ nahī̃.

NECESSITY, ADVISABILITY, ABILITY.

I must go.	Mērā jāṇā zarūr e, or zarūr e pai maĩ jā̃.
You must come.	Tērā auṇā zarūr e, zarūr ē pai tū̃ āwē̃.
He must write.	Ohdā likkhṇā zarūr e, ōh zarūr likkhē.
The girl must go out.	Kuṛī dā nikaḷṇā zarūr e, kuṛī zarūr nikḷe.
We must send him the horses.	Ohde kōḷ ghōṛe ghallṇē zarūr [nē̃.
You must certainly tell him to come here.	Tusā̃ zarūr ohnū̃ ākhṇā pai ētthe āwē.
They must go there.	Ohnā̃ dā ōtthe jāṇā zarūr e.
You must talk Panjabi.	Panjābī bōlṇī zarūr je.
It is necessary that Panjabi be spoken.	Zarūr e pai Panjābī bolī jāe.
The munshi ought to teach well.	Cāhidā e pai munshī caṅgī tarhā̃ paṛhāe.
People ought to praise the Lord.	Cāhidā e pai lōkī Rabb dī waḍeāī karn.
The pupils must learn from the teacher.	Shagird zarūr ustād kōḷō̃ sikkhaṇ.
The boys must learn from the teacher.	Zarūr e pai muṇḍe munshī kōḷō̃ sikkhaṇ.
I can write a letter.	Maĩ ciṭṭhī likkh saknā wā̃.
Can you write Gurmukkhi.	Tū̃ Gurmukkhī likkh saknā ē̃?
No, he can write Gurmukkhi.	Nehī̃, ōh Gurmukkhī likkh sakdā we.

We can write English.	**Asī̃ Aṅgrēzī likkh sakne ā̃.**
Can you speak Panjabi?	**Tusī̃ Panjābī bōl sakde o?**
Those women can speak Panjabi.	**Ōh zanānīā̃ Panjābī bōl sakdīā̃ nẽ.**

Lesson XIX.	*Unnīhwā̃ Sabak.*
When the neighbours of the blind man asked him how his eyes were opened, he answered, The man who is called Jesus made clay and put it on my eyes and said, Go to Siloam and wash, so I went and washed and, having received my sight, returned.	**Jadõ annhe de āhṇḍ gawāhṇḍ pucchaṇ laggē paī tērīā̃ akkhīā̃ kis tarhā̃ khulīā̃, ōs jawāb dittā Jehṛā bandā Yesū sadāndā e, ōs miṭṭī guddhī te mērīā̃ akkhīā̃, te lēp karke menū̃ ākkheā, Jā te Siluām wicc nhā, ēs karke maī jāke nhā leā, te sujākhā hōke āeā.**

DERIVED SENTENCES.

1.	Where did the blind man go? To Siloam.	1.	**Annhā kitthe geā? Siluām geā.**
2.	What was Siloam? A spring of water.	2.	**Siluām kī sī? Pāṇī dā ikk cishmā.**
3.	What is the meaning of Siloam? Sent.	3.	**Siluām dā kī matlab e? Ghalleā hoeā.**
4.	What did he do there? He washed.	4.	**Ōtthe jāke ōs kī kītā? Nhā leā.**
5.	Why did he do this? He was told to.	5.	**Ēh kāhnū̃ kītā? Ohnū̃ hukm sī.**
6.	What advantage came from obedience? He received sight.	6.	**Ēs nū̃ gall mannaṇ dā kī faidā hoeā? Sujākhā ho geā.**
7.	Why did not the Lord heal him at once?	7.	**<u>Kh</u>udāwand ose wēḷe ohnū̃ wall kyū̃ nā kītā?**
8.	Because he wished to see his faith.	8.	**Ēs karke paī ōh ohdā imān wēkhṇā cāhndā sī.**

	English		Panjabi
9.	Did the blind man wish to see? That is why he went.	9.	Ōh annhā sujākhā hōṇā cāhndā sī? Taddē ī geā.
10.	How did he anoint his eyes?	10.	Kis tarhā̃ ohdiā̃ akkhiā̃ te lēp kītā.
11.	He spit on the ground and mixed spittle and clay.	11.	Jimī̃ te thukkke, miṭṭī thukk nāḷ guddhī.
12.	What day was it when he made clay?	12.	Kehṛā wār sī jadō̃ Khudāwand miṭṭī guddhī?
13.	That was the holy day of the Jews, Sabbath they call it.	13.	Ōs din Yahūdiā̃ dā pāk din sī—Sabbat ohnū̃ āhnde nē̃.
14.	Were the people pleased or sorry at the healing of the blind man?	14.	Annhe de wall hōṇ thō̃ lōkī rinj hoe yā̃ khush?
15.	The Pharisees were very much displeased.	15.	Farīsī tā̃ bauht rinj hoe.
16.	Why were they displeased?	16.	Kehṛī gallē rinj hoe?
17.	According to their tradition, healing was work, and all work was forbidden on the Sabbath.	17.	Ohnā̃ dī rawait wicc ilāj karnā kamm sī, te Sabbat nū̃ kamm karn dā hukm nehī̃ sī.
18.	But this was a matter for great rejoicing, that one born blind had received his sight.	18.	Par ēh baṛī khushī dī gall sī pai ikk jamāndhrū annhā sujākhā hoeā.
19.	It was, indeed, but to go against custom is still more vexatious to the people.	19.	Hai sī, par dastūrā̃ de ulṭ calṇā lōkā̃ nū̃ waddh burā laggdā we.
20.	Were people so bound to custom?	20.	Ēḍḍe lōk dastūrā̃ dē mannaṇwāḷe sāṇ?
21.	Were! They are still so here.	21.	Sāṇ! Ētthe aje wī haiṇ nē̃.

English	Panjabi
22. Indeed! How can you say that?	22. Halā! Ēh gall tusī kis tarhā̃, āhnde o?
23. Well, if a young man wants to become a Christian, then what do people say, and if he begins to go wrong what do they say?	23. Khair, kōī gabhrū Isāī hōṇ lagge tā̃ lōkī kī ākkhaṇge, te kōī badī karn lagge, tā̃ kī ākkhaṇge?
24. Yes, because he is giving up the customs of his forefathers.	24. Āhō, peōdādeā̃ dā dastūr jō chaḍḍaṇ laggā.
25. What is this boy's name? Phajju.	25. Ēs muṇḍe da kī nā we? Phajjū.
26. When the sun comes up, the dark night goes away.	26. Jad din nikaḷdā e tā̃ hanērī rāt calī jāndī e.
27. How was this box opened?	27. Ēh pēṭī kikū̃ khul gaī?
28. The servants opened it?	28. Naukarā̃ khōl dittī.
29. Why? Madam made them open it.	29. Kyū̃? Mēmsāhb ohnā̃ pāsō̃ khulāī sī.
30. How was that door opened?	30. Ōh būhā kis tarhā̃ laih geā?
31. I took the key and opened it.	31. Maī kunjī laike lāh chaḍḍeā.
32. Why did you open it?	32. Lāheā kāh nū̃ sāī? (*See* Gram. p. 85.)
33. Because the master made me.	33. Sāhb jō mērē pāsō̃ luhāeā sī.
34. What do you do when you get up?	34. Waḍḍe wēḷe uṭṭhke tusī kī karde honde o?
35. Wash my hands and face and put on my clothes.	35. Hatth mū̃h dhōke kapṛe pānnā wā̃. (Or pānnā hunnā wā̃.)
36. What do you do with soiled clothes?	36. Maiḷe kapṛeā̃ nū̃ tusī kī kardē honde o?
37. We get the washerman to wash them.	37. Asī̃ chīmbe pāsō̃ dhuwā lenne ā̃.

38. What do you give for washing? | 38. Dhuāī ki dēnde honde o?

39. Eight annas or a rupee for good washing. | 39. Dhēlī rupayyā caṅgī dhuāī wāste.

40. We also give something for starch, soap and soap-nuts. | 40. Kalaf, sabūn, rēṭheā̃ wāste wī thōṛā bāhḷā dēnne ā̃.

Passives and Transitives.

Open the door, my son.	Buhā lāh, puttar.
It is open, uncle (father).	Cāccā, latthā hoeā e.
Open your mouth, daughter.	Mū̃h khōl, dhīye.
Is the school opened?	Madarsā khul geā e?
The Mission will open it next year.	Mishan agle sāl khōlēgī.
You people requested its opening.	Tusā̃ lokā̃ khōlaṇ laī arjī dittī.
Whose house is being built?	Kihdā ghar baṇda e peā?
It is yours (i.e. it is mine).	Hazūr dī daulat e (or Rabbdi).
Well, when did you begin to build?	Hacchā, kadō̃ banāṇ lagge o?
I began in June—no, July.	Maī laggā baṇāṇ hāṛ—nā, sacc e, sauṇ wicc.
How did this house fall down?	Ēh kōṭhā kīkaṇ ḍhaṭṭhā?
The rain must have knocked it down.	Mī̃h nāḷ ḍhai geā hōwēgā.
Not the rain, men threw it down.	Mī̃h (or warkhē) nāḷ nehī̃—bandeā̃ ḍhā suṭṭeā.
How was your hand burnt?	Hatth kīkū̃ saṛ geā?
I was burning rags and the flame caught it.	Maī līrā̃ sāṛdā sā̃ peā, te lamb lag geī.
Has the fuel been burnt up?	Bāllaṇ baḷ geā e?
The wood is burnt up and now they are burning dried cow-dung.	Lakṛīā̃ baḷ gēīā̃ te huṇ gōhe bāḷde nē̃ pae.
Light the fire, bearer.	Agg bāḷ, baihreā.
It is burning, sir.	Baḷdī e paī, janāb.

Why is the sack here ?	Bōrī ētthe kyū̃ e ?
I put it there, my boy.	Maĩ rakkhī sī, puttar.
"Why ?" The master made me.	"Kyū̃ ?" Mālik mēre kōḷō̃ rakhāī sī.
I cannot kill the dog.	Kuttā mēre kōḷō̃ nehī̃ māridā.
I cannot go.	Methō̃ nehī̃ jāidā.
You cannot do this work.	Tuhāthō̃ ēh kamm nehī̃ hondā.

Lesson XX.	*Wīhwā̃ Sabak.*
The Jews did not believe that the blind man had received his sight, until they called his parents and asked them ; and they testified that he was their son and that he was born blind.	Yahūdiā̃ nū̃ yakīn nēhī̃ sī āeā pai Ēh annhā sujākhā hoeā, jicar ohde māpeā̃ nū̃ saddke nā pucchеā, te ohnā̃ gawāhī dittī, Ēh sāḍḍā puttar e te ōh jammaṇ hī thō̃ annhā sī.

Derived Sentences.

1. Why did the Jews not believe that the man had been born blind ?	1. Yahūdiā̃ nū̃ yakīn kyū̃ nehī̃ āeā pai ēh annhā jammeā ?
2. Because they saw that he had perfect sight.	2. Ēs karke pai ōhnā̃ ḍiṭṭhā pai ohdiā̃ akkhiā̃ bilkull ṭhīk sāṇ.
3. Did they make any investigation ?	3. Ohnā̃ kōī takīkāt kītī ?
4. Yes, they called his parents and asked them.	4. Āhō, ohde māpeā̃ nū̃ saddke pucchеā.
5. Did they believe them ?	5. Ohnā̃ nū̃ ohde mābāp dī gall dā yakīn āeā ?
6. Yes, they could not contradict them.	6. Āhō, ohnā̃ dī gall kis tarhā̃ nā mannde.
7. Why did they not wish to believe this miracle ?	7. Ēs karāmat dā yakīn karn wicc kī ohnā̃ nū̃ aukh sī ?

English	Panjabi
8. Because they were hostile to Jesus.	8. Ōh Yesū de sakht wairī sāṇ.
9. Why were they so hostile to Him?	9. Ohde sakht waiṛī kyū̃ sāṇ?
10. Because he did not keep their tradition.	10. Ēs karkē pai ōh ohnā̃ dī rawait nū̃ nehī̃ sī manndā.
11. Why did the Lord not keep their tradition?	11. Khudāwand ohnā̃ dī rawait kyū̃ nehī̃ sī manndā?
12. Because it was contrary to God's law.	12. Ēs karke pai ōh rawait Khudā dī shariat de khilāf sī.
13. Do men still put tradition above God's law?	13. Aje tikar bande rawait nū̃ Khudā dī shariat nāḷō̃ bauhtā mannde nē̃?
14. Often. Many a man gives tradition the first place and the law the second.	14. Zarūr. Bathēre bande rawait nū̃ paihlā̃ te shariat nū̃ picche sōcde nē̃.
15. Thieves say, A man must live, and so we steal, although God says Thou shalt not steal.	15. Cōr āhnde ne, Ḍhiḍḍh jō nāḷ laggā hoeā e, ēs karke cōrī karne ā̃, bhāwē̃ Khudā ākhdā e, Cōrī nā karnī.
16. Why do men believe things?	16. Bandēā̃ nū̃ gall katth dā yakīn kis tarhā̃ aundā e?
17. They hear from others and finally believe.	17. Dujjeā̃ de kōḷō̃ suṇ suṇke yakīn aundā e.
18. Do you believe things you have never seen?	18. Jehṛīā̃ gallā̃ tusā̃ kadī nehī̃ ḍiṭṭhīā̃, ohnā̃ dā yakīn aundā je?
19. Certainly. I never saw Ceylon. I believe that there is such a place.	19. Zarūr, bhāwē̃ Laṅkā kadī nehī̃ ḍiṭṭhī, ohdā yakīn hai pai Laṅkā hai we.

20. Do we believe every thing that we see ?	20. Jehṛī jehṛī gall wēkhne ā̃, ōsdā sānū̃ yakīn wī e?
21. No, not that either. Sometimes these jugglers make mangoes spring up before us and make rupees, still we do not believe that they really do so.	21. Ōh wī nehī̃. Kadī kadāī̃ eh madārī sāḍḍīā̃ akkhīā̃ agge amb ugānde nẽ, rūpayye paidā karde nẽ tā̃mī yakīn nehī̃ aundā pai es tarhā̃ hondā e.
22. Yes, that's right. If we are going to believe any one, we must know that the man is truthful and acquainted with the fact.	22. Āhō gall ṭhīk e, jis kise dā yakīn karnā hōwe zarūr e pai asī jāṇīye pai ōh saccā e te āpe gall dā wākif e.
23. So his parents knew well that this was their son and that he was born blind.	23. Te ese tarhā̃ ehde māpe khūb jāṇde sāṇ pai eh sāḍḍā puttar e te annhā jammeā.
24. Did they know how his eyes were opened ?	24. Ohnā̃ nū̃ patā hai sī pai ohdīā̃ akkhīā̃ kis tarhā̃ khullīā̃?
25. They did not know it themselves, but they believed it through hearing it from him again and again.	25. Uñ te patā nehī̃ sī, par ohde kōḷõ suṇ suṇke yakīn ā geā.
26. Did they say they knew ?	26. Ohnā̃ ākkheā, Sānū̃ patā e?
27. No, on the contrary they said, we do not know. Our son is of age. Ask him. He will tell you.	27. Nehī̃, sagõ ākkheā, Sānū̃ patā nehī̃. Puttar gabhrū e, ohde kōḷõ pucch lao, āpe jawāb dēgā.
28. Why did they say so? For fear ?	28. Ēs tarhā̃ kāhnū̃ ākkheā? Ḍar de māre?

29. Yes, they said in their hearts, We fear they will put us out.	29. Āhō, Dil wicc āhnde sāṇ, Mate sānū̃ chēk chaḍḍaṇ.
30. When the witness of the parents was heard, they bore testimony to the fact that the man with sight was their son and that he had been born blind, and no one was able to contradict them.	30. Jad māpeā̃ dī gawāhī bhugtaṇ laggī ohnā̃ ākheā, ēh sujākhā sāḍḍā puttar e te jammeā sī annhā, te kōī ehde khilāf nā ākh sakeā.
31. The teacher who wishes to teach English well will himself speak well, and the Panjabi teacher will do the same.	31. Jehṛā ustād Aṅgrēzī caṅgī tarhā̃ parhāṇī cāhe, ōh āpe caṅgī Aṅgrēzī bōlēgā te Panjābī ustād wī ese tarhā̃ karēgā.

UNTIL, UP TO, ETC.

Do this until I come.	Jicar maĩ nā āwā̃, ihoī kareā karo.
Write away, boys, till the teacher comes.	Muṇḍeo, jicar ustād nā āwe, likhde raho.
The servant sat till the post came.	Jad tōṛī ḍāk nā āī, naukar baiṭhā rehā.
As long as money keeps coming in, do not leave.	Jadō̃ tīkar rupae aunde raihṇ ētthō̃ nā ṭur jāo.
We stayed till the people came.	Jad tāī̃ lōk nā āe asī̃ ōtthe rahe sā̃.
Whenever you get news from there, send me word.	Jad kade tuhānū̃ ōtthō̃ khabar āwe, menū̃ sunehā̃ ghalleā karo.
Whenever I go, I hear this.	Jad kade jānnā ā̃, ihoī suṇnā̃.
Up till that time the boy said nothing.	Ōs wēḷe tāī̃ muṇḍe kujjh wī nā ākkheā.
The girl was there till I left.	Mēre auṇ tīkar kuṛī ōtthe sī.

They all sat by the mare till she died.	**Ghōṛī de maran tīkar, sāre de sāre kōḷ baiṭhe rahe.**
We shall stay here till you go to church.	**Tuhāḍḍe girje jāṇ tīkar asī̃ ētthe rāhā̃ge.**
He had not come yesterday.	**Kall nehī̃ sī āeā.**
The people will come by the day after tomorrow.	**Parsō̃ tāṛī lōk apparange.**
He was well up to two or three days ago.	**Parsō cauth tōṛī caṅgā bhalā sī.**
I came thus far last year.	**Agle sāl maī ētthō̃ tāī̃ āeā.**
How much will you be able to give?	**Kitthō̃ tīkar dē sakōde.**
From that day to this I watched for you.	**Ōs din thō̃ laike ajj tīkar maī̃ tuhānū̃ uḍikdā rehā.**
You will go as far as the village, won't you?	**Piṇḍ tīkar jāōge nā?**
He went to the city with me.	**Ōh shahr tīkar mēre nāḷ ṭureā.**
He died yesterday.	**Ōh kall mar geā.**
He was beaten the day before yesterday.	**Ōh parsō̃ māreā geā.**
Some one had him beaten the day before that.	**Ōh cauth marwāeā geā.**

Lesson XXI. — *Ikkīhwā̃ Sabak.*

Though his parents said these things for fear of the Jews, the son did not fear, but said, This is a wonderful thing that you do not know whence this man is, and he hath opened my eyes. We people know that God does not hear sinners, but he hears those who obey him.

Bhāwē̃ mābāp Yahūdiā̃ de ḍar deā̃ māreā̃ ēh gallā̃ ākkhiā̃, puttar nā ḍareā, sagō̃ ākkheā, Ēh tā̃ baṛī acarj gall e, pai tusā̃ lōkā̃ nū̃ patā nehī̃ pai ēh bandā kitthō̃ dā e, te ōs mēriā̃ akkhiā̃ khōl dittiā̃, Sānū̃ lōkā̃ nū̃ patā e pai Khudā pāpiā̃ dī nehī̃ suṇdā, par jehṛā ohdā mannaṇwāḷā e, Khudā ohdī suṇdā we. (*See* Gram. p. 38.)

Derived Sentences.

1. What did the parents say that showed they were afraid?	1. **Māpeā̃ kī gall ākkhī, jis tõ malūm hoeā pāī ēh ḍarde nẽ?**
2. They said, What do we know of the opening of his eyes? You ask him. He will tell you himself.	2. **Ohnā̃ ākkheā, ohdīā̃ akkhīā̃ khullaṇ dā sānū̃ kī patā e? Ohde kōḷõ tusī̃ pucch lao. Oh āpī tuhānū̃ dassēga.**
3. Why were they so afraid of the Jews?	3. **Yahūdīā̃ kōḷõ ēḍḍe kyū̃ ḍarde sāṇ?**
4. They had agreed that if any one should confess Jesus as the Messiah, he should be put out of fellowship.	4. **Ohnā̃ ēkā kītā sī pai jehṛā Yesū nū̃ Masīh karke mannē, ōh jamāt wiccõ chēkeā jāwegā.**
5. Was any one's mouth ever kept shut in the Panjab by such fear as this?	5. **Ēs tarhā̃ de ḍar nāḷ, kade Panjāb wicc kise dā mū̃h band rēhā?**
6. It is told of a teacher that his neighbours said to him, We'll shut you up in a room, if you don't give up becoming a Christian. So he never mentioned Christ's name again.	6. **Kise munshī dī gall e, pai ohde āhnḍī gawāhnḍī ohnū̃ ākkhaṇ lagge, jē tū̃ Isāī hōṇõ nā muṛẽ, tenū̃ kōṭhe wicc band karā̃ge, phēr Masīh dā nā̃ hī nā leā.**
7. What is the reason of this?	7. **Ēh dā kī sababb e?**
8. Christ himself says it is because men desire to be praised by men and not by God.	8. **Masīh āpī āhndā e pai wajhā ēh we pai bande bandeā̃ kōḷõ waḍeāī cāhnde nẽ, te Khudā pāsõ nehī̃.**
9. As the Pharisees said, If he confesses Christ before men we will cast	9. **Jis tarhā̃ Farīsīā̃ ākkheā, jē ēh lōkā̃ agge Masīh nū̃ manne asī̃ ehnū̃**

	him out, so say Hindus and Moslems.		chēk deãge, ese tarhā̃ Hindū Musalmān wī āhnde nẽ.
10.	If the parents fear the Jews, they will not say anything.	10.	Jē māpe Yahūdīā̃ kōḷō̃ ḍarde nẽ, tā̃ kujjh nā ākkhaṇge.
11.	If his parents confess Christ, they will be cast out.	11.	Jē ehde māpe Masīh nū̃ mannaṇ, tā̃ chik jāṇge.
12.	People cast him out, because he confessed that Jesus was the Messiah.	12.	Lōkā̃ ēs wāste annhe nū̃ chēkeā, paī ōs Yesū nū̃ manneā paī ōh Masīh e.
13.	If fear of the people has filled this man's heart, he will not be able to bear true witness.	13.	Jē ēs bande de dil wicc lōkā̃ dā ḍar baih geā e, ōh saccī gawāhī nehī̃ dē sakēgā.
14.	If this man had not been blind, there would not have been this miracle.	14.	Jē ēh bandā annhā nā hundā, tā̃ ēh karāmat nā hondī.
15.	Through receiving sight, the blind man recognized that Jesus was the Saviour of the world.	15.	Sujākhā hōṇ nāḷ ōs annhe jāṇ leā paī Yesū saccī muccī duṇyā dā bacāṇwāḷā e.
16.	The testimony of the soldiers about Christ is exactly right, No man ever spake like this man.	16.	Masīh dī bābat sipāhīā̃ dī gawāhī baṛī ṭhīk e, paī ehde wāṅgū̃ kadē kise gall nehī̃ kītī.
17.	It is evident that in the Panjab many persons are not able to confess Christ for fear of men.	17.	Sāf malūm e, paī Panjāb wicc lōkā̃ de ḍar nāḷ bauht bande Masīh nū̃ nehī̃ mann sakde.
18.	If this man's social privi-	18.	Jē ehdā hukkā pāṇī

	English		Panjabi
	leges were taken away he would not fear.		band hōwe tā̃ wī nehī̃ ḍardā.
19.	If he said this, he said it because the girl was afraid of her parents.	19.	Jē ōs ēḥ gall ākkhī, tā̃ ēs karke ākkhī, paī kuṛī mābāp kōḷō̃ ḍardī sī.
20.	If they said this they ought to be cast out.	20.	Jē ohnā̃ ēh gall ākkhī, tā̃ ohnā̃ nū̃ chēkṇā cāhīdā e.
21.	If you are afraid of people, know that they fear you too.	21.	Jē tusī̃ lōkā̃ kōḷō̃ ḍarde o tā̃ ēh jāṇō paī lōkī wī tuhāthō̃ ḍarde nẽ.
22.	If these people say this, then you may know that they are blind.	22.	Jē ēh lōk ēh gallā̃ āhnde nẽ, tā̃ ēh jāṇō paī ōh annhe nẽ.
23.	If sin had not come into the world, he had not been born blind.	23.	Jē pāp jagat wicc nā aundā, tā̃ ēh annhā nā jammdā.
24.	If we confess our sins, Christ will mercifully and justly forgive.	24.	Je asī̃ āpō apṇe pāpā̃, nū̃ manne ā̃, tā̃ Masīh rahm karke te niā̃ nāḷ ba<u>kh</u>shēgā.
25.	If light had not come into the world, then darkness had not been revealed.	25.	Jē lō jagat wicc nā aundī, tā̃ hanerā nā jāpdā.
26.	If we believe God's messenger, we shall not be cast out of heaven.	26.	Jē asī̃ <u>Kh</u>udā de ghalle hoe nū̃ mannīye, tā̃ bihishtō̃ nā kaḍḍhe jāā̃ge.
27.	If any thirst, said Christ, let him come to me and drink.	27.	Masīh āhnda e, jē kise nū̃ treh lagge mēre kōḷ āṇke pāṇī pīe.
28.	By using an axe, one cannot teach digging, so if one uses English or Urdu, how can one	28.	Kuhāṛā wartaṇ nāḷ kōī puṭṭaṇ dā kamm kis tarhā̃ si<u>kh</u>ā sakdā e, ese tarhā̃ jē kōī

teach the Panjabi tongue ?	Aṅgrēzī yā̃ Uṛdū bōle, Panjābi bōlṇī kīkū̃ sik͟hā sakdā e.
29. If we work hard, the language will come quickly.	29. Jē kōshat kariye, tā̃ bōlī jhabde āwēgī.

Lesson XXII.	*Bāhīwā̃ Sabak.*
So a second time they called the man who had been blind and said to him, give the glory to God, we know that this man is a sinner. He therefore answered, whether he is a sinner or not I know not, one thing I do know—I was blind and now I see.	Ohnā̃ dujjī wārī ōs jaṇe nū̃ kuāeā jeṛhā paihle annhā sī te ohnū̃ ākheā, K͟hudā dī waḍeāī kar, asī jāṇṇe ā̃ paī ēh jaṇā pāpī e. Par ōs ākhēa ēh menū̃ patā nehī̃ paī ēh papī e ke nehī̃, par ikk gall dā menū̃ patā hai we paī maī paihlā̃ annhā sā̃, te huṇ sujākhā wā̃.

Derived Sentences.

1. What one thing did the man know? That he could see.	1. Kehṛī gall dā ōs jaṇe nū̃ patā sī? Paī maī sujākhā wā̃.
2. What did the Pharisees think they knew? That Jesus was a sinner.	2. Kehṛī gall dā Farīsī āhnde sāṇ paī sānū̃ patā e? Paī Yesū pāpī e.
3. Why did they think him to be a sinner? Because he had made clay on the Sabbath.	3. Ohnū̃ pāpī kyū̃ samjhde sāṇ? Ēs karke paī ōs sabbat de dihāṛe miṭṭī gōī sī.
4. What good advice did they give? Give God the glory.	4. Ohnā̃ kehṛī caṅgī salāh dittī? K͟hudā dī waḍeāī karo.
5. Did they themselves give God the glory? No, they dishonoured Him, because they would not hear His messenger.	5. Ohnā̃ āpī wī K͟hudā dī waḍeāī kitī? Nehī̃, sagō̃ ohdī bijjtī kitī, kyū̃jō ohde ghalle hoe nū̃ nehī̃ manneā.

6. Did the man who was blind think Jesus was a sinner? No, he thought he was a prophet and worships God and walks according to His will.	6. Ōs annhe dā wī īhōī k͟hiāl sī paī Yesū pāpī e? Nehī̃, ohdā k͟hiāl sī paī ēh nabī e te K͟hudā nū̃ manndā e te ohdī marzī te caldā e.
7. How did he know this? He thought it must be so, because his eyes had been opened by him.	7. Ohnū̃ ēs gall dā kīkkaṇ patā laggā? Ohnū̃ ēs tarhā̃ yakīn āeā paī Ōs menū̃ sujākheā̃ kītā.
8. Was his conclusion correct? Yes, it seems right.	8. Ēh ohdī dalīl ṭhīk sī? Ṭhīk ī jāpdī e.
9. How can we tell that a man is a good physician? If he heals the sick, we say he is a good physician.	9. Sānū̃ kīkkaṇ yakīn āwe paī kōī jaṇā caṅgā hakīm e? Jē maḷe hoe nū̃ wall kare tā̃ asī̃ āhnne ā̃ paī ōh caṅgā siāṇā e.
10. How do you know things? Some things our teachers tell us, and others we learn by experience.	10. Tuhānū̃ uñ gallā̃ dā kis tarhā̃ patā laggdā e? Kaī te sāḍḍe ustād sānū̃ dassde nē̃, te kaiā̃ dā āpū̃ wēk͟h wēk͟hke patā lagg jāndā e.
11. How did this man know Jesus was a prophet? From the miracle which he saw he knew that Jesus had divine power.	11. Ēs jaṇe nū̃ kitthō̃ patā laggā paī Yesū nabī e? Akkhī̃ ḍiṭṭhī karāmat thō̃ jāṇdā sī paī ehḍe wicc K͟hudā dī tākat e.
12. We all ought to give glory to God, for He himself is our Creator and Preserver; He is the Al-	12. Sānū̃ sāreā̃ nū̃ cāhīdā e paī K͟hudā dī waḍeāī kariye, kyū̃jō Ōh sāḍḍā Paidā karnwāḷā te

	English		Panjabi
	mighty, Omniscient God.		Parwardigār e, sāri tākat ōse dī e te ōh sabbhō kujjh jāṇdā e.
13.	All men are sinners, therefore we are sinners and need a Saviour.	13.	Sāre jaṇe gunāh karde nẽ, ēs wāste asī̃ wī pāpī ā̃, te sāreā̃ nū̃ Bacāṇwāḷe dī lōṛ e.
14.	This man was blind, then his eyes were opened by Jesus, therefore Jesus must be from God.	14.	Ēh bandā annhā sī, te Yesū ohnū̃ sujākheā̃ kītā, sō Yesū wī Khudā wallō̃ āeā hōwēdā.
15.	I know that I was blind and that I now see, therefore I cannot believe that Jesus was, as you say, a sinner.	15.	Maī̃ jāṇṇā wā̃ pai maī̃ paihlā̃ annhā sā̃ tē huṇ sujākhā wā̃, ēs wāstē maī̃ tuhāḍḍī gall nehī̃ mann sakdā pai Yesū pāpī e.
16.	Whether this man was born blind or not I cannot tell, but he is honest and intelligent, therefore ask him himself.	16.	Ēh menū̃ patā nehī̃ pai ōh jaṇā jamāndhrū annhā sī ke nehī̃, par ōh bhalāmāṇas e te siāṇā, ōse nū̃ pucch lao.
17.	The doctor has come, so you can go and show him your tooth yourself.	17.	Ḍākdār āeā e, tusī̃ jāke apū̃ ohnū̃ haṇu wikhāō.
18.	This is the second time that I have been ill, so I want you to call a good physician.	18.	Ēh huṇ dujjī wārī maī̃ maḷ ghattā, tusī̃ kōī siāṇā hakīm saddo.
19.	When I called them they answered, they can certainly hear.	19.	Jadō̃ maī̃ ohnā̃ nū̃ kuāeā ōh bōl pae, suṇāī te ohnā̃ nū̃ dēndā e.
20.	If you can't say a word or sentence right at first,	20.	Jē tusī̃ paund saṭṭe kōī gall yā̃ fikrā ṭhīk nā

do not stop trying. but try and try again, and keep on saying it. Yes, say it 100 times a day. for a month or two and you will learn it perfectly.

ākh sako tā̃wī nā chaḍḍo, kōshīsh karde raho te āk͟hde ī raho, bhā̃wẽ mahīne dō tīkar sau sau wārī dihāṛī ākhṇā pawe. Chēkṛe tuhānū̃ pūrā ṭhik āwēdā.

21. How do children learn to talk? By first hearing and saying over a sentence hundreds and perhaps thousands of times, until they can speak fluently.

21. Añāṇe kīkarā̃ bōlṇā sik͟hde nẽ? Paihle suṇ lende nẽ, te magarõ sau sau, hazār hazār wērī āk͟hde jānde nẽ, ōṛak nū̃ ōh suāhre bōl sakde nẽ.

22. He who teaches Panjabi aright speaks Panjabi while he teaches.

22. Jehṛā Panjābī ṭhīk paṛhāe āpī paṛhāndī wārī Panjābī bōlēgā.

23. We cannot learn Panjabi by translating.

23. Tarjumā kar karke asī̃ Panjābī nehī̃ sikkh sakde.

Lesson XXIII.

Trehīwā̃ Sabak.

Since the world began it was never heard that any one opened the eyes of a man born blind. If this man were not from God he could do nothing.

Jadõ dī dunyā baṇī kade kise ēh nehī̃ suṇeā pai jamāndhrū annhe nū̃ kise sujākheā̃ kītā. Jē ēh Jaṇā K͟hudā wallõ nā hundā kujjh wi nā kar sakdā.

Derived Sentences.

1. The Pharisees did not believe that he had been blind until they had called his parents.

1. Farīsīā̃ ēh nehī̃ sī manneā pai ēh paihlā̃ annhā sī jad tīkar ohnā̃ ohde māpeā̃ nū̃ nā kuāeā.

2. They bore witness as soon as they came that he had been blind.

2. Ohnā̃ aundeā̃ sār ī agwāhī dittī pai ēh paihle annhā sī.

English	Panjabi
3. Since he washed in the pool he has been able to see.	3. Jadō̃ dā ōh hauz wicc nhātā ōh wēkh sakdā e.
4. When the man who was once blind contradicted the religious leaders and said that Jesus must be from God, they cast him out.	4. Jadōs bande jehṛā paihle annhā sī waḍḍeā̃ dī gal mōṛī te ākheā paī Yesū zarūr Khudā wallō̃ hōwēgā, ohnā̃ ohnū̃ chēk chaḍḍeā.
5. After he had been cast out Jesus told him who his Healer was—the Son of God.	5. Jad ōh chēk ghattā sī Yesū ohnū̃ dass dittā paī ōh kauṇ e jis tenū̃ wall kītā, ōh Khudā dā Puttar e.
6. How are we to know that a man is from God unless from his words and works.	6. Kise dīā̃ gallā̃ te kammā̃ de suā hōr kīkaṇ sānū̃ patā lagg sakdā e paī ēh nabī e.
7. If we begin a thing we ought to finish it, then we shall become able to do things well.	7. Jē asī̃ kōī kamm karn lagg pawīye sānū̃ cāhīdā e paī mukālye, tā̃īē sānū̃ baṇke kamm karn dī jāc āwēgī.
8. Did you hear that our house was broken open last night after we had gone to bed ?	8. Tusā̃ suṇeā e paī ajj rātī̃ suttī̃ bandī̃ sāḍḍe ghar sannh laggī sī ?
9. The rain began to fall as I was coming home.	9. Jadō̃ maī apṇe ghar lagā aundā sā̃ kaṇīā̃ laih paīā̃.
10. When we see a priest or any religious teacher teaching his followers what all other men know to be false, how can we believe him to	10. Jē asī̃ kise malwāṇe yā̃ parōhat nū̃ ajēhīā̃ gallā̃ cēleā̃ nū̃ sikhāndeā̃ wēkhīye jihnā̃ dā sāreā̃ nū̃ patā e paī jhūṭhīā̃ nē, tā̃ sānū̃

be a prophet from God ?	kīkar yakīn āwe pai ōh jaṇā **Kh**udā wallō̃ e?
11. Most religions agree on what men ought to do, (I tell thee, we can thus, distinguish between the true and the false) religion which enables men to do right ?	11. Karīb karīb sāre mazhab ēs gall wicc raḷ jānde nẽ pai bande nū̃ kī karnā cāhīdā e, jhūṭhe sacce dā te asī̃ aiñ nikhēṛā kar sakne ā̃ pai kehṛā mazhab bandeā̃ nū̃ nēk kamm karn dī tākat dēndā e.
12. When men shut their eyes that they see not truth, we then know that in them is some sin, which they do not leave, for, if a man keeps doing what he knows to be sin, he cannot find the truth. Christ said—Men love darkness rather than light because their deeds are evil.	12. Jad bande akkhīā̃ mīṭ lende nẽ pai saceāī nū̃ nā wēkkhaṇ tā̃ samjh lao pai ohnā̃ wicc kōī gunāh e jihnū̃ ōh nehī̃ chaḍḍde, kyū̃jō jē kōī bandā ajehā kamm kardā rawhe jihdā ohnū̃ patā e pai ōh gunāh e, tā̃ ōh saceāī nū̃ nehī̃ labbh sakdā. Masīh ākheā sī Bande ēs karke hanēre nū̃ cānnaṇ nāḷō̃ waddh cāhnde nẽ pai ohnā̃ de kamm bhaiṛe nẽ.
13. Whenever he calls I will come, and wherever he sends me I will go, and whatever he bids me do, so long as I live, I will do it.	13. Jad kadī ōh menū̃ kuāe maī̃ āwā̃ karā̃gā, te jitthe kite menū̃ ghalle maī̃ ōtthhe jāwā̃ karā̃gā, te jō kujjh ōh menū̃ ākhe, jicar tīkar jiūndā rāhā̃gā ūhōī kardā rāhā̃gā. (*See* Gram. p. 69.)
14. Since English-speaking	14. Jadō̃ tō̃ Aṇgrēzīdān us-

teachers have begun to teach us Panjabi, few of us have learned it well.	tād sānū̃ Panjābī sikhāṇ lagge nẽ sāḍḍe wiccõ bauht thōṛeā̃ caṅgī tarhā̃ sikhī e.
15. Why? Because they talk English so much that they learn English from us although we pay them to teach us Panjabi.	15. Kī wajhā e? Ōh sāḍḍe nāḷ innī Aṅgrēzī bōlde nẽ pai ōh sāḍḍe kōḷõ Aṅgrēzī sikh lende nẽ, te asī̃ ohnā̃ nū̃ Panjābī paṛhāṇ wāste paise dēnne ā̃.
16. If we wish to learn any language whether from the literary side or from the colloquial, we must talk it. If we are studying the literary language, the teacher should not talk the colloquial, and if we are learning the colloquial, he should not talk the literary, otherwise we shall never learn correctly.	16. Jē sānū̃ kōī bōlī sikkhaṇ dī cāh e, bhāwẽ kitābī, bhāwẽ bōl cāl dī, cāhīdā e pai asī̃ boliyē. Jē asī̃ kitābī bōlī pae sikhne ā̃, ustād bōl cāl dīā̃ gallā̃ nā kare, te jē asī̃ bōl cāl dīā̃ gallā̃ pae sikhne ā̃, ōh kitābī gallā̃ nā kare, nehī̃ te asī̃ kadī wī nehī̃ sikkhā̃ge.

Lesson XXIV. — *Cawhīwā̃ Sabak.*

Permissives and Reflexives.

From that time the Governor sought to release him, but the Jews cried out saying, If thou let this man go, thou art not Caesar's friend, for every one that maketh himself a king is an enemy of Caesar.	Ōs wakat tõ hākim ohnū̃ chaḍḍṇā cāhndā sī, par Yahūdī uccī dittī ākkhaṇ lagge pai jē tū̃ ehnū̃ chaḍḍ dẽ tū̃ Kaisar dā sajjaṇ nehī̃, jehṛā kōī apṇe āp nū̃ bādshāh baṇāndā e Kaisar dā wairī e.

Derived Sentences.

1. From that day the Gov-	1. Ōs din tõ hākim dil

	English		Panjabi
	ernor said to himself, I will let this man go, for he is not guilty.		wicc ākkhaṇ lagā maĩ ehnū̃ chaḍḍ deā̃, ohdā te kōī kasūr nehī̃.
2.	Whoever maketh himself great shall be made low.	2.	Jō kōī apṇe āp nū̃ waḍ-ḍeā̃ baṇāndā e nīwā kītā jāēgā.
3.	I am making myself a chair.	3.	Maĩ apṇe jōgī kursī peā baṇānnā wā̃.
4.	The Jews did not let him release Jesus, for they had agreed to have him put to death on the cross.	4.	Yahūdiā̃ ohnū̃ Masīh nū̃ chaḍḍaṇ nā dittā kyū̃jō ohnā̃ āpe wicc salāh kītī sī pai asī̃ ehnū̃ salīb utte caṛh-wāā̃ge.
5.	This man makes friends with everybody.	5.	Ēh jaṇā te sāreā̃ nāḷ piār pā lendā e.
6.	Know thy own heart and thus thou shalt know all men.	6.	Apṇe dil dā patā kar, te tā̃ tenū̃ sāreā̃ ban-deā̃ dā patā laggēgā.
7.	Judas Iscariot, the betrayer of his Lord, hanged himself.	7.	Yahūdā Iskariūtī jis apṇe Mālik nū̃ phaṛ-wā dittā āpū̃ phāh laike mar geā.
8.	Let it stay there, it makes no difference.	8.	Ōtthe ī raihṇ dē, kōī ḍar nehī̃.
9.	Never mind, it does not matter.	9.	Jāṇ deō kōī parwāh nehī̃.
10.	Never mind, it's of no consequence.	10.	Ōh jāṇe, gall ī kōī nehī̃.
11.	The children will not let me do my work.	11.	Ēh añāṇe menū̃ kamm nehī̃ karn dēnde.
12.	The rain will not let us go out.	12.	Kaṇiā̃ sānū̃ banne nehī̃ jāṇ dēndiā̃.
13.	Muhammadans do not allow their women to go out of the house.	13.	Musalmān janāniā̃ nū̃ gharō̃ banne nehī̃ jāṇ dēnde.

14.	Let him abuse me, what harm is it to me ?	14.	**Menū̃ bhāwē̃ ōh peā gāḷ kaḍḍhe, mērā kī wigaṛdā e?**
15.	My eyes won't let me read.	15.	**Mērīā̃ akkhīā̃ menū̃ paṛhn nehī̃ dēndīā̃.**
16.	Father did not let me go to school when I was small.	16.	**Jad maī nikkā hondā sā̃, cāccā menū̃ skūlē nehī̃ sī jāṇ dēndā hondā.**
17.	The lady will not let such a deceitful man as you be her servant.	17.	**Mēmsahb tēre jehe pharēbī ādmī nū̃ naukar nehī̃ rakkhaṇ lagge.**
18.	The noise will not let the baby sleep.	18.	**Rauḷe dā sadkā bacce nū̃ nīndar nehī̃ paindī.**
19.	I let the boys in just as he did.	19.	**Mammī ohde wāṅgar muṇḍeā̃ nū̃ andar auṇ dittā.**
20.	Sir, a man has come to see you. Well, let him in.	20.	**Hazūr, ikk bandā tuhā-nū̃ miḷṇ āeā e. Halā, auṇ dē sū.**
21.	Let him take it (come, go, give, throw, eat, drink).	21.	**Lellaiṇ dē sū (auṇ, jāṇ, dē dēṇ, saṭṭaṇ, khāṇ, pīṇ).**
22.	She would not let them sing, (speak, read, write).	22.	**Ōh ohnā̃ nū̃ gauṇ (bōllaṇ, paṛhn, likkhaṇ) nehī̃ sī dēndī.**
23.	I will get down myself.	23.	**Maī̃ āpe utar jāā̃gā.**
24.	They themselves spoke against the king.	24.	**Ōh āpī bādshāh dī nindiā karde sāṇ.**
25.	The Jews spoke against Caesar himself.	25.	**Yahūdīā̃ k͟hud Kaisar dī nindiā kītī.**
26.	He hurt himself with a knife.	26.	**Ohnū̃ apṇe kōḷō̃ cakkū lagg baiṭhā.**
27.	The house is by itself near the road.	27.	**Ghar kallā nawēkḷe thā̃ saṛak dē kaṇḍhe we.**
28.	I did not let the child go.	28.	**Maī te nehī̃ jātak nū̃ jāṇ**

	English		Panjabi
	He went to the city himself.		dittā, ōh āpe shahr ṭur geā.
29.	Let me alone. Don't bother me.	29.	Chaḍḍ wī, menū̃ nā satā.
30.	Do not give yourself so much trouble for me.	30.	Mēre wāste innī taklīf nā kar.
31.	You gave yourselves too much trouble for us.	31.	Tusā̃ sāḍḍī khātar baṛī waddh taklīf kītī.
32.	Thou saidst that God was such an one as thyself.	32.	Tū̃ ākheā pai Khudā mēre wāṇgar e.
33.	He came to his own, and they received him not.	33.	Ōh apṇeā̃ lōkā̃ kōḷ āeā, te ohnā̃ ohnū̃ nehī̃ sī kabūleā.
34.	Do to others as you wish that they should do to you.	34.	Hōrnā̃ nāḷ osē tarhā̃ warto jis tarhā̃ tusī̃ cāhnde o pai ōh tuhāḍḍe nāḷ wartaṇ.
35.	I went myself and he himself came to receive me at the door.	35.	Maĩ āpī geā sā̃, te ōh āpī būhe tāṛī menū̃ milṇ āeā.
36.	Can any one by himself learn Panjabi? Perhaps one might learn to read and translate and to speak a little, but one could not learn to understand it, and probably nobody would understand one when one spoke.	36.	Kōī āpē Panjābī sikkh sakdā e? Shait kōī paṛhnī yā maihṇe karne sikkh sake, te kujjh kujjh bōl wī sake, par ōh gallā̃ nehī̃ kōī samjhaṇ laggā, te je gallā̃ kare aglā wī nehī̃ samjhaṇ laggā.

Lesson XXV. — *Panjhīwā̃ Sabak.*

DOUBT AND CONTINUANCE.

English	Panjabi
He will have gone somewhere to hunt, as he is a god he will be asleep, and you will have to awaken him.	Ōh kitale shikār khēḍḍaṇ geā hōwēdā, deotā, jo hoeā, kite suttā peā hōwēdā, tuhānū̃ jagāṇā pawēdā.

Derived Sentences.

	English		Panjabi
1.	It must be going to rain, I think, for the salt is damp and the air, too, feels moist.	1.	Mēre bhāṇe k̲h̲aure mĩh wassaṇ wāḷā e, lūṇ te sill ghettā we, te wā wicc wī sējjaḷ jāpdī e.
2.	She must be coming home, for it is five o'clock.	2.	Huṇ ghar aundī hōwēgī, panj wajj gae nẽ.
3.	They must have been in great trouble.	3.	Ōh baṛī musibat wicc phas gae hōṇge.
4.	They must be in greater trouble to-day than yesterday.	4.	Ajj kall nāḷõ wī ohnā̃ nū̃ waddh taklīf hōwēdī.
5.	It must be true.	5.	Zarūr sacc hōwēgā.
6.	It must have been raining somewhere on the mountains, for it is cooler to-day.	6.	Pahāṛā̃ te kitale mĩh peā hōwēgā, ajj ṭhaṇḍ kujjh waddh e.
7.	They must have gone to the city yesterday.	7.	Kall shahr gae hōṇge.
8.	They must be eating dinner now.	8.	Huṇ ṭukkar pae khānde hōṇge.
9.	He must have studied hard to pass so easily.	9.	Baṛī mehnat kītī hōsūgī, tā̃i ēḍḍā caṅgā pās hoeā.
10.	He must be studying harder this year than last.	10.	Ēs sāl ōh par nāḷõ waddh mehnat kardā hōwēgā.
11.	I must have given it to him.	11.	Maĩ ohnū̃ dittā hōwēgā.
12.	I must have seen the horse, I do not remember.	12.	Maĩ ghōṛā wēk̲h̲ leā hōwēdā, thauh nehĩ rehā.
13.	The man must be dead before this.	13.	Huṇ tīkar te mar geā hōwēgā.
14.	There must be hundreds, yes thousands, dying of hunger, for the famine has been very severe this year.	14.	Kaĩ sau, sagõ kaĩ hazār, bhukkhe marde hōṇge, aitkī kāḷ burā ḍāhḍā peā e.

15. Keep on talking and you will learn to speak the language.	15. **Tusī bōlde raho, te bōlī sikkh laoge.**
16. Keep on working until I come back.	16. **Mēre part auṇ tīkar kamm karde raho.**
17. Is she eating ? Yes, she keeps on eating the whole time.	17. **Ōh khāndī e paī? Āhō, ōh te har wēḷe ī khāndī raihndī e.**
18. Is he still drinking ? He is always drinking.	18. **Ōh aje pīndā e peā? Ōh te pīnda ī raihndā e.**
19. The teacher forbade him, but he kept on singing.	19. **Ustād te ohnū̃ ṭhākeā par ōh gaundā ī rehā.**
20. Though I forbade him he goes on drinking liquor.	20. **Maī bhāwẽ ohnū̃ mōṛeā, par ōh sharāb pīndā ī raihndā e.**
21. Perhaps I shall go, I am not sure.	21. **Shait khaure jā̃gā, pakka patā nehī̃.**
22. Then he must have gone just now, I saw him here not five minutes ago.	22. **Tā̃ te huṇe geā hōwēgā, maī̃ aje ohnū̃ huṇe ētthe ḍiṭṭhā sī.**
23. Possibly it will rain to-day, one cannot say for certain.	23. **Shait ajj kaṇīā̃ paiṇgīā̃, ṭhīk nehī̃ ākheā jāndā.**
24. He will come at once if you wish.	24. **Jē cāhō jhaṭ paṭ āwēgā.**
25. It keeps on raining in some places for weeks and weeks.	25. **Bājī̃ thāī̃ kaī hafteā̃ tōṛī mī̃h wassdā raihndā e.**
26. He will never learn Panjabi, because he doesn't talk it, but keeps on reading it day after day.	26. **Ohnū̃ nehī̃ kadī Panjābī auṇ laggī, kyū̃jō gallā̃ nehī̃ kardā, bas dinī̃ rātī̃ paṛhdā ī raihndā e.**
27. She will learn Panjabi quickly for she reads only an hour or two	27. **Ōh Panjābī chētī sikkhēgī, nirē ikk dō ghaiṇṭe paṛhdī e te gallā̃**

every day and spends much time in talking.	bāhḷīā̃ kardī raihndī e.
28. Keep on, like children, reading the things you already know.	28. Bacceā̃ hār ūhōī gallā̃ paṛhde raho jehṛīā̃ agge aundīā̃ nē̃.
29. Do not expect to read readily words which you have never heard.	29. Jehṛe lafs kade suṇe nehī̃, ōh te nehī̃ nā shitābī paṛh sakōge.

Lesson XXVI.	*Chabbīhwā̃ Sabak.*

ABILITY.

As the branch can not bear fruit except it abide in the vine, so also ye, if ye separate from me, shall remain fruitless, for apart from me ye can do nothing.	Dāk͟h dī ṭāhṇī nū̃ phaḷ nehī̃ lagg sakdā je būṭe dē nāḷ nā rawhe, ese tarhā̃ tusī̃ wī apphaḷ rahōde jē methō̃ wakkh hō jāo, methō̃ wakkh tusī̃ kujjh nehī̃ kar sakde.

DERIVED SENTENCES.

1. How can these things be? How can a man be born when he is old?	1. Ēh gallā̃ kīkaṇ hō sakdīā̃ nē̃? Jad ādmī buḍḍhā hō geā̃ e ōh phēr kīkaṇ jamm sakdā e?
2. If Thou wilt, Thou canst make me whole	2. Jē tū̃ cāhē̃ tū̃ menū̃ wall kar saknā ē̃.
3. Ye shall seek me (or you will *try*) but ye shall not be able to find me.	3. Kōshish te karōge par menū̃ nehī̃ labbh sakōge.
4. Are ye able to drink of (bear) the cup that I am about to drink of (to bear)?	4. Tusī̃ ōh jhall sakōge jō kujjh maī̃ jhallaṇ laggā wā̃?
5. They cast the net and now they were not able to draw it for the multitude of fishes.	5. Jāḷ suṭṭ dittō nē, phēr bauhtīā̃ macchīā̃ dā sadkā khiccaṇ nā hoeā. (*See* Gram. p. 115.)
6. Let every man give as he is able.	6. Sāre jaṇe, jīkaṇ kise nū̃ sare, dēṇ karn.
7. Our God is able to deliver us.	7. Sāḍḍā Rabb sānū̃ chuḍā sakdā we.

8.	No man is able to pluck them out of my Father's hand.	8.	**Mēre Bāp de hatth wic-cõ kōī ohnā̃ nū̃ khōh nehī̃ sakda.**
9.	No man was able to answer him.	9.	**Ohnū̃ kōī nā jawāb dē sakeā.**
10.	I besought Thy disciples to cast out the demon but they could not.	10.	**Maī̃ tēreā̃ cēleā̃ agge tarle kīte paī palīt rūh nū̃ kaḍḍh dēṇ, par ohnā̃ kōḷõ nehī̃ kaḍḍheā geā.**
11.	I am not able to do this work, for I have been ill.	11.	**Mēre kōḷõ ēh kamm nehī̃ hondā, maī̃ maḷ-eā rehā wā̃.**
12.	Can John lift that heavy stone and put it yonder for me?	12.	**Jhaṇḍā mēre wāte ōh waḍḍā waṭṭā cukkke parhā̃ dhar sakdā e?**
13.	He was not able to go, so I did not go either.	13.	**Ohde kōḷõ jāṇ nehī̃ hoeā, maī̃ wī nehī̃ geā.**
14.	I cannot come to-morrow for I have to go to Gujranwala.	14.	**Bhaḷke mērā nehī̃ auṇ hōṇ laggā, maī̃ Kujrā̃-āḷe jāṇā e.**
15.	I cannot give each of the men an anna, for I have no change.	15.	**Jaṇeā̃ nū̃ maī̃ ānnā ānnā nehī̃ dē sakdā, mēre kōḷ bhanghaṛ nehī̃.**
16.	If each is able to do his own work, then all together will be able to do a lot of work.	16.	**Jē jaṇā jaṇā apṇā apṇā kamm kar sake, tā̃ sāre cōkhā kamm mukāṇge.**
17.	If possible get these books for eight annas each.	17.	**Jē hō sake ēh kitābā̃ dhēlī dhēlī tõ leāwī̃.**
18.	Give each of the servants a small tip.	18.	**Ikk ikk naukar nū̃ thōṛī thōṛī bakhshīsh deho.**
19.	I could not speak Panjabi when I came here, but now I can use it a little.	19.	**Jis wēḷe maī̃ ētthe āeā menū̃ Panjābī nehī̃ sī aundī, huṇ thōṛī thōṛī bōl saknā wā̃.**
20.	We can learn to speak	20.	**Jinnī tuhānū̃ Panjābī**

	English much better than you can learn to speak Panjabi. Why is it?		aundī e, odū̃ sānū̃ Aṅgrēzī waddh aundī e, kī sababb e?
21.	Because you cannot hear your own mistakes, but you hear ours.	21.	Sababb ēh we paī tusī̃ apṇīā̃ galtīā̃ nehī̃ malūm kar sakde, par saḍḍīā̃ dā patā lagg jāndā e.
22.	Do we not speak English well? Only a few of you do.	22.	Asī̃ Aṇgrēzī hacchī tarhā̃ nāḷ nehī̃ bōlde? Kōī kōī wall bōldā e.
23.	Can he inform me?	23.	Ōh menū̃ dass sakdā e.
24.	How can you know it?	24.	Tuhānū̃ kīkarā̃ patā lagg sakdā e?
25	Is it possible? No, it is impossible.	25.	Ēh hō sakdā e? Nehī̃ hō sakdā.
26.	It is not possible to do this.	26.	Ēh kamm kise kōḷō̃ nehī̃ hōṇ laggā.
27.	Can he write?	27.	Ōh likkh sakdā e?
28.	Can the child walk yet?	28.	Añāṇā aje ṭur sakdā e?
29.	Lord, evermore give us this bread.	29.	Khudāwandā, sānū̃hamēshā̃ ēh rōṭī dēh.
30.	Ye have seen Me and do not believe.	30.	Tusā̃ menū̃ wēkh leā e, te phēr wī nehī̃ mannde.

Lesson XXVII. *Satāhīwā̃ Sabak.*

PREPOSITIONS.

John testified concerning him and cried saying, This is He of whom I spake saying, He that came after me is become before me, for He was before me.	Yuhannā ohdī guāhī dittī te uccī dittī ākheā, Ēh ohī e jihdī bābat maī ākheā sī paī jehṛā mēre picchē āeā methō̃ agge hō geā e, kyū̃jō ōh methō̃ paihlā̃ sī.

DERIVED SENTENCES.

1.	Thou shalt understand after this.	1.	Edū̃ picchō̃ tū̃ samjhēgā.

2.	But all these things will they do to you for my sake.	2.	Ōh tuhāḍḍe nāḷ mēre sadkā ēh salūk (or ēh sabbho kujjh) karnge.
3.	They hated me without a cause.	3.	Ohnā̃ aiwē̃ mēre nāḷ wair rakkheā.
4.	Ye have been with me from the beginning.	4.	Tusī̃ muṇḍhō̃ mēre nāḷ raihe o.
5.	No one is righteous before God.	5.	Khudā agge kōī nēk nehī̃ e.
6.	They were with Jesus, when he went to the wedding.	6.	Ōh Yesū nāḷ sāṇ jad ōh jañe (or wīāh) geā sī.
7.	He was outside the house.	7.	Ōh gharō̃ banne sī.
8.	They believed on him.	8.	Ohnā̃ ohde te imān leāndā.
9.	"In the name of God the most merciful and compassionate" is what the Muslim says when he begins any work.	9.	Jad Musalmān kōī kamm shurū karda e ōh āhnda e "Bismillāhi rrahmāni rrahīm."
10.	In your midst is one of whom I spoke.	10.	Jih dī maĩ gall kītī sī ōh tuhāḍḍe wicce ī e.
11.	All things were made by God and without him was nothing made.	11.	Sārīā̃ cīzā̃ Khudā ī baṇāiā̃ te ohde bājhō̃ kōi cīz nehī̃ baṇī.
12.	There was a man sent from God whose name was John.	12.	Ikk Khudā dā ghalleā hoeā jaṇā sī jihdā nā̃ Yuhannā sī.
13.	He came to testify to the light, that all men might believe because of him.	13.	Ōh cānnaṇ dī guāhī dēṇ āeā sī pai sāre ohde sadkā imān leauṇ.
14.	He was the true light which lighteth every man in the world.	14.	Saccā cānnaṇ ūhōī e jehṛa dunyā de sāreā̃ jaṇeā̃ nū̃ lō dēndā e.
15.	He was in the world and the world was made by him.	15.	Ōh dunyā wicc sī te dunyā os thō̃ paidā hoī.

English	Panjabi
16 And He was made flesh and dwelt among us.	16. Ōh dēh dhārī hōke sāḍḍe wicc raihndā sī.
17. The Law was given by Moses, but grace and truth came by Jesus Christ.	17. Shariat te Mūsā wallō̃ dittī gaī sī, par fazl te saceāī Yesū Masīh dī rāhī āī.
18. What sayest thou of thyself, that we may give an answer to them that sent us ?	18. Tũ apṇī bābat kī ākhnā ẽ, paī asī̃ apṇeā̃ ghallaṇwāḷeā̃ nū̃ jawāb deiye.
19 This occurred in a city beyond Jordan, where John was baptising.	19. Ēh Yardanō̃ pār kise shahr wicc hoeā sī jitthe Yuhannā baptismā dēndā sī.
20. On the next day John saw Jesus coming towards him and said—Behold the Lamb of God that taketh away the sin of the world.	20. Dujje dihāṛe Yuhannā Yesū nū̃ apṇe kōḷ aundeā̃ ḍiṭṭhā te ākheā wēkkho Rabb dā Lēllā jehṛā dunyā dā gunāh cukkke lai jāndā e.
21. I knew Him not, but that He should be revealed to Israel, for this cause I came baptising with water.	21. Maī ehnū̃ nehī̃ sī pachātā par ēs wāte pāṇī nāḷ baptismā dēndā āeā paī Isrāīl nū̃ ōhdā patā lagge.
22. On the morrow John was again standing with two of his disciples.	22. Dujje din Yuhannā phēr apṇeā̃ cēleā̃ wiccō̃ dūh de nāḷ khlōtā hoeā sī.
23. They saw where he was staying and remained with him that day.	23. Ohnā̃ ḍiṭṭhā sī paī Ēh kitthe raihndā e te oddiṇ ohde kōḷ rahe.
24. It was about noon when he came.	24. Ōh dopaihrā̃ de nēṛe trēṛe āeā.
25. It was Andrew, brother of Peter and one of the twelve.	25. Ōh Andriās sī jehṛā Patras dā bhrā sī te bāhrā̃ wiccō̃ ikk sī.

26. He came to the city and said to his brother—Come at once.	26. Oh shahr āke apṇe bhrā nū̃ ākkhaṇ laggā pai jhaṭ paṭ ā jā.
27. He went to him and walked about with him.	27. Ohde kōḷ jāke ohde naḷ phirdā rehā.
28. He went to the door and going round the house ascended on to the roof.	28. Ōh būhe tīkar geā te ghar de duāḷe phirkē kōṭhe te caṛh geā.
29. In what direction did he go? Look, there he is standing below.	29. Kehṛī sēhd geā sī? Āh wēkh̲ā̃ thalle khlōtā hoeā e.
30. The man was like me, but he does not work like me.	30. Jaṇā te mere hār ī sī, par kamm mēre wāṅgar nehī̃ kardā.
31. We were five, counting him, and we went as far as the banyan tree and returned.	31. Ohde saṇe panj jaṇe sā̃ asī̃, bōhṛ sīdhā̃ jāke part āe.
32. He took it from below the table, put it on the table, and then threw it into the basket.	32. Mēz de hēṭhō̃ cukkke ohnū̃ utte rakkh leā sū, te phēr ṭōkrī wicc saṭṭeā sū.
33. He went all round the house, then lay down in front.	33. Kōṭhī de cār cufēre bhaū̃ke sāhmṇe lammā pai rehā.
34. Through fear she did not come in time.	34. Ḍar dī mārī wēḷe sir nehī̃ āī.
35. For joy he began to laugh at the very moment of arrival.	35. Ōh k̲h̲ushī dē māreā̃ aundeā̃ sār ī hassaṇ ḍaih peā. (*See* Gram. p. 38.)

Lesson XXVIII.	*Aṭhāhīwā̃ Sabak.*
He that entereth not by the gate but climbeth up some other way, he is a thief and robber.	Jehrā būhe rāh nā waṛe, sagō̃ kisē hōrī rāh caṛh āwe ōh cōr te ḍākū hondā e.

Derived Sentences.

1. On the second day there was a wedding in Cana and Jesus' mother was there.	1. Agle din Kānā wicc wiāh sī te Yesū dī mā̃ ōtthe sī.
2. And they invited Jesus and his disciples also to the wedding.	2. Te Yesū nū̃ te ohdeā̃ cēleā̃ nū̃ wī wiāh te saddeā sāṇe.
3. Six water jars were placed there after the custom of the Jews.	3. Yahūdiā̃ dī rīt mūjab chē maṭṭ ōtthe rakkhe hoe sāṇ.
4. Fill them with water to the brim.	4. Kaṇḍheā̃ tīkar ohnā̃ nū̃ bhar deho.
5. After this they came to the city and stayed there not many days.	5. Edū̃ picche ōh shahr āke kujjh din rahe.
6. Jesus made a scourge of cords and drove the crowd out of the temple.	6. Yesū rasseā̃ de kōṭle baṇāke lōkā̃ nū̃ haikal wiccō̃ kaḍḍh dittā.
7. Then remembered they what was written. The zeal of thy house shall eat me up.	7. Tad ohnā̃ nū̃ ēh likhī hoī gall yād āī pai tēre ghar dā menū̃, baṛā jōsh āwēdā.
8. When he was in Jerusalem at the feast many believed on his name.	8. Jad ōh 'Id wēlē Yarūshalem wicc sī cōkheā̃ ohde te imān leāndā.
9. Verily, verily I say unto thee—we tell what we know and testify what we have seen.	9. Maī tenū̃ sacc saco ākhnā wā̃ pai asī̃ ohī gall dassne ā̃ jihdī sānū̃ khabar e, te ose dī agwāhī dēnne ā̃ jehṛī akkhī ḍiṭṭhī e.
10. God sent his Son into the world that the world might be saved by him.	10. Khudā ēs wāte apṇe Puttar nū̃ dunyā wicc ghalleā pai dunyā nū̃ ohdī rāhī najāt mile.
11. No man can receive anything unless help be	11. Kōī jaṇā kise gall nū̃ nehī̃ kabūl sakdā

English	Panjabi
given him of God.	jad tōṛī Khudā wallō ohnū̃ madat nā miḷe.
12. Ye yourselves bear me witness that I said I am not the Christ but I am sent before him.	12. Tusī̃ āpū̃ guāhī dē sakde o pai maī ākheā pai maī Masīh nehī̃, sagō̃ ohde agge ghalleā hoeā wā̃.
13. Whoever believeth on the Son hath life, but he that believeth not on the Son shall not see life, but the wrath of God abideth on him.	13. Jehṛā Puttar utte imān leaundā e jiū̃ndā e, par jehṛā Puttar te imān nā leāwe ōh zindagī nū̃ wēkhēgā wī nehī̃, sagō̃ ohde te Khudā dā kahr rawhēgā.
14. The Jews said to him that was cured, it is not lawful for thee to carry thy bed to-day.	14. Yahūdīā̃ ohnū̃ ākheā jehṛā wall kītā geā sī pai ajj manjī khaṛan dā hukm nehī̃.
15. For this cause the Jews sought the more to kill him, because he not only broke the Sabbath but also said that God was his Father, making himself equal with God.	15. Ēs karke Yahūdīā̃ hōr wī ohnū̃ mār suṭṭaṇ dī kōsht kītī pai Ōs Sabbat nū̃ wī nehī̃ manneā, te Apṇe Āp nū̃ Khudā dā Puttar ākhke Khudā de barōbar baṇ baiṭhā̃.
16. The sheep hear his voice and he calleth his sheep by name, and goeth before them and they follow him, for they know his voice.	16. Bhēḍā̃ ohdī wāz suṇdīā̃ nē te ōh apṇīā̃ bhēḍā̃ nū̃ nā̃ laike kuāndā e, te ohnā̃ de agge ṭurdā e, te ōh ohde magar magar ṭurdīā̃ nē, kyū̃jō ohdī wāz nū̃ pachāṇdīā̃ nē.
17. What do you say about yourself?	17. Tū̃ apṇī bābat kī āhnnā ē?

English	Panjabi
18. They filled twelve baskets with the fragments which remained over after eating.	18. Ohnā̃ ṭukkarā̃ nāḷ jehṛē khāṇe tõ bac rahe sāṇ bārā̃ ṭokrīā̃ bhar dittīā̃.
19. She seeth the stone taken away from the grave.	19. Ōs patthar nū̃ kabrõ haṭeā hoēā ḍiṭṭhā.
20. If any one knocketh the door shall be opened.	20. Jē kōī kharkāe būhā lāheā jāēgā.
21. Never man spake like this man.	21. Ēs jaṇe hār kade kise gall nehī̃ kītī.
22. Whoever first went down into the water was healed of whatever disease he had.	22. Jehṛā pāṇī wicc paihlā̃ waṛdā sī ōh apṇī bamārī tõ wall hō jāndā sī bhā̃wẽ kehṛī bamārī hondī sī.
23. There was a man there who had been ill for 38 years. Jesus saw him lying and knew that he had been ill for a long time.	23. Otthe ikk jaṇā sī jehṛā aṭhattīā̃ warheā̃ tõ bamār sī, Yesū ohnū̃ peā hoeā̃ wēkhke jāṇ leā pai ēh cōkhe cir dā māndā peā e.
24. I have no one to put me into the pool when the water is moved, but while I am coming another enters in before me.	24. Mēro kōl kōī nehī̃ jehṛā menū̃ hauz wicc wāṛe jadpāṇī halāeā jāe. pār jyōn jyōṇ aunnā wā̃ (or mere āuṇdeā̃ āuṇdeā̃) kōī hōr methõ paihlā̃ waṛ jāndā e.
25. He went to the field by way of the well.	25. Ōh khūh de uttõ dī paiḷī wicc geā.
26. He has been here since 3 o'clock.	26. Ōh trai waje dā otthe we.
27. The Lord performed many miracles on the sick.	27. Khudāwand bamārā̃ laī baṛīā̃ karāmātā̃ kītīā̃
28. This is without a cause.	28. Ēh bilkull be wajah e.
29. He told me about you yesterday when we were among the trees.	29. Ōs mēro nāḷ kall tuhāḍḍī gall kītī si jad asī rukkhā̃ wicc sāṇ.

30. The well is near the city.	30. Khūh shahr de nēṛe we.

Lesson XXIX.	*Unattīhwā̃ Sabak.*
They slipped out one by one beginning with the oldest even unto the youngest.	Ōh waḍḍe tō̃ laike nikke tīkar ikk ikk karke khisk gae.

Derived Sentences.

1. Do not go without me.	1. Menū̃ chaḍḍke nā jā.
2. In your very midst is a thief and a robber.	2. Tuhaḍḍe wicce ī ikk cōr te ḍākū we.
3. That is under the table near you.	3. Ōh tuhāḍḍe kōḷ mēz de thalle we.
4. We came for his sake.	4. Asī̃ ohdī k͟hātar āē.
5. Great trouble came upon him.	5. Ohde utte baṛī baḷā āī.
6. The well is before the large gate.	6. Khūh waḍḍe phāṭak de sāhmṇe we.
7. Behind the gate, near the Mosque, is a little house.	7. Phāṭak de picche masīt de kōḷ ikk nikkā kōṭhā e.
8. I will go up to the gate with you, but not beyond that.	8. Maĩ būhe sīdhā tērē nāḷ jāā̃gā par parhā̃ nehī̃ jāā̃gā.
9. Besides these three girls I have two boys also.	9. Ehnā̃ triū̃h kuṛia de suā mēre dō muṇḍe wī nē̃.
10. Some time after dinner I shall come for him and play behind the house with him.	10. Maĩ rōṭī khāke kise wēḷe ohnū̃ laiṇ āwā̃gā te ohde nāḷ ghar de picche khēḍ-ḍā̃gā.
11. Instead of this chair, bring me another.	11. Ēs kursī de thā̃ menū̃ ikk hōr leā de.
12. He was downstairs, sitting on the floor.	12. Ōh hēṭhā̃ bhuñe baiṭhā hoeā sī.
13. He looks like a donkey and fights like a lion.	13. Khōte wargā jāpdā e par shēr wāṅgar laṛdā e.

14. I wrote this book with a reed pen.
14. Ēh kitāb maĩ dēsī kalam nāḷ likhī sī.

15. He struck him with his sword.
15. Ōs talwār nāḷ ohnū̃ māreā.

16. He came in the morning twilight and said to him peace to you.
16. Ōs jhusmusṛe āke ohnū̃ salām alaikum ākkhī.

17. He said, said he, I shall come on such a day of such a month.
17. Ōs ākheā sī akhe maĩ fulāṇe mahīne dī fulāṇī tarīk āwā̃gā.

18. A clever boy is better than an ignorant old man.
18. Siyāṇā muṇḍā jaihl buḍhṛe nāḷō̃ caṅgā e.

19. I did all I could to stop him.
19. Maĩ te apṇe wallō̃ ohnū̃ ḍakkaṇ (moṛan) wāte sabbhō kujjh kītā.

20. He went away from home with money in his pocket.
20. Ōh rupae bōjhe pāke gharō̃ ṭur peā.

21. Five times three are fifteen.
21. Panjū̃ trīye pandrā̃.

22. I have not seen him this month.
22. Ēs mahīne maĩ ohnū̃ nēhī̃ ḍiṭṭhā.

23. I did not see him until to-day.
23. Maĩ ajj tō̃ paihle ohnū̃ nehī̃ wēkheā.

24. He threw a stone against the house.
24. Ōs ghar nū̃ waṭṭā māreā.

25. There is a tree in the city street which is larger than this one.
25. Shahr dī gaḷī wicc ikk būṭā we jehṛā edū̃ waḍḍā e.

26. According to your wish I will go with him to the wedding.
26. Tērī marzī mūjab maĩ ohde nāḷ jañe jā̃ā̃gā.

27. Why does he rise before me and stand in front of me, when I ought to be before him for I am
27. Ōh kyū̃ methō̃ paihle uṭṭhke mērē agge khlōndā ē, jad menū̃ ohde agge hoṇā cāhī-

	above him in rank.		dā e, mērā darjā jō ohde nā̤lō waddh e.
28.	This chair is made of wood, that one of iron.	28.	Ēh lakkaṛ dī kursī e te ōh lohe dī e.
29	In his hands he held a small bird.	29.	Hatthā̃ wicc ōs nikkā jehā janaur phaṛeā hōeā sī.
30.	Within the house an old man sat weeping, while outside the house the children were walking and running and playing.	30.	Ghar wicc buḍḍhā rōndā baiṭhā hoeā sī, te banne ā̃ā̃ṇe ṭurde phirde te bhajjde khēḍde sāṇ.
31.	There was a division among the Muhammadans on his account.	31.	Ohde sadkā Musalmā̃nā̃ wicc phuṭṭ pai geī sī. (*See* Gram. p. 303.)
32.	What do men say about me? There was a great crowd round him.	32.	Mērī bābat kī āhnde nē̃? Ōh de duā̤le baṛā mulkh sī.
33.	He is at home.	33.	Ōh ghare we.
34.	He was at the post-office yesterday.	34.	Kall ōh ḍāk-k͟hāne sī.
35.	Do not be angry with me.	35.	Mēre nā̤l rinj nā hōwī̃.
36.	Judge not according to appearance, but judge righteous judgment.	36.	Wik͟hāwe picche faislā nā karī̃, saccā insāf karī̃.

Lesson XXX.	*Trīhwā̃ Sabak.*
From that time many of his disciples turned back and walked no more with him. He said to the twelve, Have not I chosen you twelve and one of you is a devil.	Odū̃ agge ohdeā̃ cēleā̃ wiccō̃ bāhḷe pishā̃ muṛ gae te ohde nā̤l jāṇā chaḍḍ dittā. Ōs bāhrā̃ nū̃ ākheā paī Maī̃ tuhānū̃ bāhrā̃ nū̃ nēhī̃ cuṇeā? te tuhāḍḍe wiccō̃ ikk shatān e.

Derived Sentences.

1.	For God's sake have mercy on poor me, and	1.	Rabb de wāste mēre ājaz te rahm karo te maī̃

English	Panjabi
without his help, I will provide money suitable to thy rank.	ohdī madatō̃ binā tuhānū̃ ōnne rupayye dēā̃gā jinne tuhaḍḍe jehe darjewāḷe nū̃ cāhīdē nē̃.
2. I put the purse in your charge. Where is it ?	2. Maĩ baṭūā tēre hawāle kītā sī, kitthe we?
3. For fear of the storm he ran quickly home.	3. Hanērī de ḍar de māreā̃ ōh chētī ghar nass geā.
4. In spite of his promise he went by way of the river.	4. Ōh daryā de rāh geā sī, bhāwẽ ōs rāh nā jāṇ dā karār kītā sāsū.
5. I heard this from Mr. Smith.	5. Ēh gall maĩ Smit sāhb kōḷō suṇī sī.
6. I looked into her face and said, There *is* a God.	6. Maĩ sāf ōh de mū̃h te ākheā si Khudā te zarūr hai we.
7. Let us run up and down the bank as fast as we can.	7. Asī̃ jinnī jaldī hō sake kanḍhe kanḍhe urhā̃ parhā̃ bhajjīye.
8. He alone came secretly. The rest came openly.	8. Ūhoī luk lukke āeā sī, hōr sāre khule khule āe sāṇ.
9. My brothers alone sent them money.	9. Nire mēre bhrāwā̃ ohnū̃ rupayye ghalle.
10. He lifted up his eyes toward heaven and said Father, I thank thee that thou heardest me.	10. Asmān wall wēkhke ākheā sū pai Hē Bāp maĩ tērā shukr karnā wā̃ pai tū̃ mērī gall suṇī sī.
11. He spoke Panjabi like a Panjabi.	11. Ōh Panjābīā̃ wāṅgar Panjābī bōldā sī.
12. Then said some of the people of Jerusalem, Lo, he speaketh openly.	12. Phēr Yarūshalēm de raihṇwāḷeā̃ wiccō̃ kise kise ākheā pai ōh khulī gall kardā e.

13.	They do nothing to him. Can it be that the rulers also know that this is the Christ?	13.	Ohnā̃ kujjh nehī̃ karde. Eh ho sakdā e, pāī Sardārā̃ nū̃ wī patā lagg geā e, pai Ēh Masīh we?
14.	I am with you for a little while yet, then I go to him who sent me.	14.	Maī aje thōṛā cir tuhāḍḍe nāḷ ā̃, te phēr maī apṇe Ghallaṇwāḷe kōḷ jāṇnā wā̃.
15.	On the last day the great day of the feast, Jesus stood and cried saying, If any one thirst, let him come unto me and drink.	15.	Īd de chēkaṛle dihāṛe, jehṛā waḍḍā din sī, Yesū khlōke uccī uccī ākheā sī paī je kise nū̃ trēh lagge ōh mēre kōḷõ āke pāṇī pīe.
16.	The Book says that Christ will come of the family of David and will be from Bethlehem, the village of David.	16.	Katāb wicc li<u>kh</u>eā hoeā e pai Masīh Dāūd de <u>kh</u>āndān dā hōwēgā te Baitlahm piṇḍ dā jehṛā Dāūd dā piṇḍ sī.
17.	When they came without him, they said to them, why have ye not brought him?	17.	Jad oh ohnū̃ chaḍḍke āe ohnā̃ nū̃ ākheo ne pai nāḷ kyū̃ nehī̃ leāndā je? (*See* Gram. p. 372.)
18.	Then the disciples looked on one another, doubting of whom he spake.	18.	Phēr cēle ikk dujje wallõ wēkkhaṇ lagge pai kihdī gall kardā e peā.
19.	One by one they went across the river by the bridge road about 12 o'clock.	19.	Ikk ikk karke kōī dopaihr nū̃ ōh puḷ wāḷe rāh daryāõ pār gae.
20.	According to their promise they fought against the enemy alongside of me.	20.	Jikkaṇ ohnā̃ karār kītā sī ōh mēre saṅg wairīā̃ nāḷ laṛe.

21. He went along with me round the city as far as the north gate.	21. Ōh mēre nāḷ shahr de duāḷe pahāṛ wāḷe phāṭak tīkar geā.
22. Beside the stream, behind and below the hill, is the tomb of a renowned saint.	22. Nāḷī de kōḷ ṭibbe de muṇḍh pishle pāse ikk baṛe mashāhūr pīr dī k͟hāngāh sī.
23. You ask me to decide between you concerning the cow, and I feel that for the sake of your parents I must draw lots.	23. Tusī menū̃ āk͟hde o paī sāḍḍe wicc gā̃ dā faislā karo, te mērā k͟hiāl e paī tuhāḍḍe māpeā̃ dī k͟hātar maī guṇe pāā̃gā̃.
24. In spite of my former liking for this place, as I again look on both sides of the question, I am persuaded that I ought to leave, and to move up to the hill and live at the top.	24. Mērā jī ēs thā̃ laggdā te haisī, par huṇ maī sārī gallī sōc leī e te menū̃ pakkā k͟hiāl aundā e paī ētthō̃ nikaḷke menū̃ ṭibbē de utte jāke raihṇā cāhīdā e.
25. The children were in charge of their aunt, but, in place of guiding them, she let them do as they pleased.	25. Bacce te apṇī phupphī kōḷ chaḍḍe hoe sāṇ, par ōh ohnā̃ nū̃ matt nēhī̃ sī kōī dēndī, aīwē̃ chaḍḍ dēndī sī paī jō marzī e karn.
26. Over the bridge, opposite the palace and outside the city walls, they ran, and within a half hour, as they ran, they ran right into a body of the enemy.	26. Ōh mahall de sāhmṇe puḷ de uttō̃ dī shahrō̃ banne bhajj gae, te addhe . ghaiṇṭe de andar ī andar nassde nassde wairiā̃ dī ikkī ṭōlī wicc jā phase.
27. By means of the boat, they went round the	27. Ōh bēṛī wicc shahr de cufēre phire, caṛhdēō̃

city, from the east side by way of the south and west to the north fort.

laggke paihle dakkhaṇ dakkhaṇ, phēr laihnd e laihnde, chēkṛe pahāṛ pāse de kile wicc jā waṛē.

28. Within and without the house, up and down the hill, all the boys, except John, chased each other during the half hour's recess.

28. Addhe ghaiṇṭe dī chuṭṭī wicc sāre muṇḍe, kade ghar wicc, kade gharō̃ banne, kade ṭibbe utte kade phēr hēṭhā̃, ikk dujje de picche nassde phirde rahe.

29. He fell on his face before the king and said, Forgive me.

29. Ōs bādshāh de sāhmṇe mū̃h parne ḍiggke tarle kīte sāṇ paī Menū̃ muāf karo.

Lesson XXXI.

Ikattīhwā̃ Sabak.

On the morrow the multitude which stood on the other side of the sea saw that there was none other boat there but one, and that Jesus entered not into the boat with his disciples, but that they went away alone. (Howbeit there came boats from Tiberias to the place where the Lord blessed the bread and they ate.) So when they could not find him they got into these other boats and came to Capernaum seeking him.

Dujje bhaḷak sāreā̃ lōkā̃ jehṛe daryā de parle daṇḍe khlōte hoe sāṇ wēkh lēa paī ikkoī bēṛī e te Yesū ohde wicc cēleā̃ nāḷ nehī̃ geā, sagō̃ ōh kalle ṭur gae nē̃. Hā̃ kujjh hōr bēṛīā̃ Tibriāsō̃ ōs thā̃ āīā̃ sāṇ jitthe Khudāwand rōṭī te barkat maṅgī sī te ohnā̃ khādhī sī. Bas jad ōh ōhnū̃ nā labbh sake ōh ehnā̃ bēṛīā̃ wicc baihke Kafarnahūm tīkar ohnū̃ labbhde labbhde āe.

DERIVED SENTENCES.

1. After that Jesus met him in the temple and said

1. Odū̃ picche Yesū ohnū̃ haīkal wicc miḷeā te

to him—Sin no more lest a worse thing come unto thee.	oknū̃ ākheā pai phēr gunāh nā karī̃ cētā tenū̃ edū̃ burī balā nā cambṛe.
2. My Father worketh until now and I work.	2. Mērā Bāp hū̃ṇ tīkar kamm kardā e te Mammī̃ kamm karnā wā̃.
3. For whatsoever he doeth the Son doeth also in like manner.	3. Kyū̃jō jō kujjh ōh kardā e Puttar wī ū̃hōī kardā ē.
4. The Father loveth the Son and showeth him all things that he himself doeth, and greater works than these will he show him that ye may all marvel.	4. Bāp Puttar nāḷ mahabbat kardā e te ohnū̃ sabbhō kujjh wikhāndā e jō kujjh Āpī kardā e, te ehnā̃ tō̃ wī waḍḍe kamm wikhāēgā paī tusī̃ sāre acarj hōwo.
5. As the Father raiseth the dead, so the Son also maketh alive whom he will.	5. Jīkaṇ Bāp murdeā̃ nū̃ jiwāḷdā e ose tarhā̃ Puttar wī jihnū̃ cāhndā e jiwāḷdā e.
6. The Father judgeth no man but hath given all judgment unto the Son that all should honour the Son as they honour the Father.	6. Bāp kise dī adālat nehī̃ kardā sagō̃ adālat dā kamm ōs Puttar de pēṭe pā dittā e pai sāre lōk Bēṭe dī ose tarhā̃ izzat karn jīkarā̃ Bāp dī karde nē̃.
7. Whosoever doth not honour the Son doth not honour the Father who sent him.	7. Jēhṛā kōī Puttar dī ādar nā kare ōh ohde Ghallaṇwāḷe dī wī ādar nehī̃ kardā.
8. When ye sent to John he bore witness to the	8. Jadō̃ tusā̃ Yuhannā kōḷō̃ pucch ghalleā ōs

	English		Panjabi
	truth, but I receive not witness from man, howbeit I say this that ye may be saved.		hakk dī guāhī dittī, par maĩ insān dī guāhī nehĩ laindā ēh gallā̃ maĩ ēs wāste ākhnā wā̃ pai tuhānū̃ najāt miḷe.
9.	He was a burning and shining light, and ye were willing for a season to rejoice in his light, but I have witness greater than John's, because the works which the Father gave me to fulfil—these works themselves bear witness that God hath sent me.	9.	Ōh te baḷdā camakdā dīwā sī te tusĩ kujjh cir tīkar ōh dī lō wicc raihṇ nū̃ khush sau, par Mēre kōḷ Yuhannā dī agwāhī nāḷō caṅgī agwāhī e kyū̃jō jehṛe kamm Bāp Menū̃ karn wāste dasse sāṇ ūhōī kamm agwāhī dēnde nẽ pai Khudā Menū̃ ghalleā e.
10.	Ye have neither heard his voice nor seen his form, for no man hath seen God at any time.	10.	Tusā̃ nā te ohdī wāz suṇi e te nā ohdī shakl ḍiṭṭhī, Khudā nū̃ kise nehĩ kade diṭṭhā.
11.	His word abideth not in you, for ye do not believe him whom he sent.	11.	Ohdī kalām tuhāḍḍe wicc nehĩ raihndī, kyū̃jō tusĩ ohnū̃ nehĩ mannde jihnū̃ ōs ghalleā e.
12.	Ye search the Scriptures because ye think that in them ye have eternal life, but ye will not come to me that ye may have eternal life.	12.	Tusĩ Pāk Katāb nū̃ ēs laī sōc sōcke paṛhde ō pai tuhāḍḍā khiāl e pai ehde wiccō̃ sānū̃ hamēshā dī zindagī miḷdī e, par tā̃mī tusĩ Mēre kōḷ hamēshā dī zindagī laiṇ nehĩ aunde.

13 Man, whoever thou art, thou hast no excuse, for the word of God is nigh thee.	13. Jaṇeā, tū̃ bhāwẽ kauṇ hōwẽ, kōī bahāna nehī̃ kar saknā ẽ, Khudā dī kalām tēre nēṛe we.
14. If thou wilt believe with thine heart and confess with thy mouth that God raised the Lord Jesus from the dead thou shalt be saved.	14. Jē tū̃ dil nāḷ yakīn karẽ te mū̃hõ mann wī laẽ pai Khudā Yesū nū̃ murdeā̃ wiccõ jiwāḷeā tenū̃ najāt miḷēdī.
15. Murmur not among yourselves.	15. Āpe wicc buṛbuṛ nā karo.
16. Show thyself to the world.	16. Apṇā āp dunyā nū̃ wikhā.
17. What can I say about myself?	17. Maī apṇī bābat kī ākh saknā wā̃?
18. What sayest thou about thyself?	18. Tū̃ apṇī bābat kī āhnnā ẽ?
19. What does he say about himself.	19. Ōh apṇī bābat kī ākhdā e?
20. What do we say about ourselves.	20. Asī̃ apṇī bābat kī ākhne ā̃?
21. What do you say about yourselves.	21. Tusī̃ apṇī bābat kī ākhde o?
22. What do they say about themselves.	22. Ōh apṇī bābat kī ākhde nẽ?

Lesson XXXII.

Battīhwā̃ Sabak.

Nevertheless even of the rulers many believed on him, but because of the Pharisees they did not confess it, lest they should be put out of the synagogue, for they regarded men more than God.

Tā̃mī sardārā̃ wiccõ bauht sāreā̃ ohde te imān leāndā sī, par Farīsīā̃ dā sadkā lōkā̃ agge mannde nehī̃ sāṇ, mate ibādatkhāneā̃ wiccõ chēke nā jaṇ, kyū̃jō ōh Khudā nāḷõ bandeā̃ dī waddh parwāh karde sāṇ.

Derived Sentences.

1. Show us a miracle we shall be satisfied.	1. Sānū̃ kōi karāmāt wikhā te asī̃ rāzi hōwā̃ge.
2. What sign doest thou that we may see and believe on thee ?	2. Tū̃ kehṛi karāmāt karnā ẽ, pai asī̃ wēkhke Tēre te imān leā-wīye ?
3. As the living Father sent me and I live by the Father, so whoever believeth on me, he shall live by me.	3. Jis tarhā̃ Bāp menū̃ ghalleā e te Maĩ ohdī rāhī̃ jiūnnā wā̃, ose tarhā̃ jehṛā Menū̃ manne mēri rāhī̃ jīwēgā.
4. When his brothers had gone up to the feast, then he also went up, not openly but as it were in secret.	4. Jad ohde bhrā īd te ṭur gae saṇ, tā̃ ōh wī geā, par khullam khullā nehī̃, sagõ lōkā̃ kōḷõ lukke.
5. And many of the people believed on him and said, When the Messiah cometh, will He do more signs than these ? Where is he going to so that we cannot find him ?	5. Te lōkā̃ wiccõ bāhḷē ohnū̃ mannaṇ lage te ākkhaṇ lage pai Jad Masīh āwēdā Ōh ehde nāḷō waddh karāmātā̃ karēga, Ēh - whalā kitthe jāēgā pai asī̃ ehnū̃ nehī̃ labbh sakā̃ge ?
6. Although he had done so many signs before them, yet did they not believe.	6. Bhāwẽ ohnā̃ agge inniā̃ karāmātā̃ kītiā̃ sāsū tad wī ōh nehī̃ sāṇ mannde.
7. If I then who am your Lord and Teacher have washed your feet, ye also ought to wash one another's feet.	7. Je Maĩ jehṛā tuhāḍḍā Khudāwand te Ustād wā̃ tuhāḍḍe pair dhōte nẽ, tuhānū̃ cāhīdā e pai ikk dujje de pair dhōhwo.
8. I tell you now before it comes to pass so that	8. Maĩ ōs gall de hōṇ tõ paihle tuhānū̃ dass

	English		Panjabi
	when it comes to pass ye may believe.		chaḍḍnā wā̃ paī jad ho jāe tusī̃ manno.
9.	If ye had believed Moses ye would have believed me for he wrote of me.	9.	Tusī̃ Mūsā nū̃ manno ā te Menū̃ wī manno ā kyū̃jō ōs Mērī bābat likheā sī. (*See* Gram. p. 319.)
10.	If ye believed not Moses how can ye believe my word.	10.	Mūsā nū̃ jō nehī̃ manneā je, mērī gall dā tuhānū̃ kīkkaṇ yakīn āwe.
11.	If ye had known me ye should have known my Father also.	11.	Menū̃ kade jāṇdeo tā̃ Mēre Bāp nū̃ wī jāṇdeo.
12.	Ye shall lament, but your lamenting shall be turned to joy.	12.	Tusī̃ rōwōge par tuhāḍḍā rōṇā khushī hō jāegā.
13.	He did not need any one to tell him what was in man for he knew himself.	13.	Ohnū̃ lōṛ nehī̃ sī paī kōī Ohnū̃ dasse paī insān wicc kī e, Ōh āpe jō jāṇdā sī.
14.	He said to thee, "Thou shall not see me" and now thou hast not seen him for a long time.	14.	Ōs tenū̃ ākheā sī paī tū̃ menū̃ nehī̃ wēkhẽgā te huṇ tū̃ cōkhe cir tõ ohnū̃ nehī̃ wēkheā.
15.	It is a long time since he came here.	15.	Ohnū̃ ētthe āeā̃ cōkhā cir hō gēā e.
16.	John and James, also Peter and Andrew, were brothers.	16.	Yuhannā te Yakūb bhrā sāṇ, te Patras te Andriās wī.
17.	Tell him as you come to bring his book.	17.	Aundī wārī ohnū̃ ākhī̃ paī katāb lendā āwī̃.
18.	Pīrā was older than Barkat, I think.	18.	Mērī jāc wicc Pīrā Barkat nāḷõ waḍḍā sī.
19.	Was Mīrū as old as Nawab? No, not so old.	19.	Mīrū Nawāb dā hāṇī sī? Nehī̃ ohde nāḷõ nikkā sī.

20. This box is heavier than that.	20. **Ēh sandūk ohde nāḷõ bhārā we.**
21. Let Pira or Nawab or Dula come to-day.	21. **Yā̃ Pīrā yā̃ Nawāb yā̃ Dūlā ajj āwe.**
22. Whether he comes or goes it makes no difference to me.	22. **Bhā̃wẽ āwe bhā̃wẽ nā āwe Menū̃ kī?**
23. Though he offered them gifts none of them would accept them.	23. **Bhā̃wẽ ōh ohnā̃ nū̃ aṇām dēndā sī, kōī nehī̃ sī lendā.**
24. Nawab is bigger than Rahmat.	24. **Nawāb Rahmat nāḷõ waḍḍā e.**
25. The congregation is greater than that of yesterday.	25. **Ēh jamāt kall wālī nāḷõ waḍḍī e.**
26. If the king had not been on our side we should never have been saved.	26. **Bādshāh sāḍḍe wall nā hondā tā̃ asā̃ kadī nehī̃ sī bacṇā.**
27. Wherever the master goes the servant goes with him.	27. **Jitthe mālik jāe naukar wī nāḷ jāndā e.**
28. These are wicked men, some one else will have to save them, they cannot save themselves.	28. **Ēh jaṇe sharīr nẽ, hōr kōī ohnā̃ nū̃ bacāe, āpe nehī̃ bac sakde.**
29. Tell me whether he has come or not.	29. **Menū̃ dassī̃ pai ōh āeā ke nehī̃.**
30. Whether he comes or goes you must stay.	30. **Ōh bhā̃wẽ āwe bhā̃wẽ nā āwe, raīhṇā pawīgā.**
31. He started before I could start.	31. **Maī aje teār nehī̃ sā̃ te ōh ṭur pēā.**
32. He went back the way he came.	32. **Jehṛe rāh āeā ose rāh parteā.**
33. I tell you I did not know whether I was awake or dreaming.	33. **Menū̃ shakk sāje pai maī khaure jāgnā wā̃ ke suttā.**

34. Though you told him he did not obey.	34. Bhāwẽ ohnū̃ ākheā sāī, manneā nehī̃ sāsū.
35. It is my will to give these last as much as I gave to the first.	35. Mērī marzī e paī ehnā̃ chēkaṛleā̃ nū̃ ōnnā ī deā̃ jinnā maī paihlēā̃ nū̃ dittā e.
36. Would that I had never seen this man! (Had I never seen this man, what a nice thing it would have been!)	36. Maī kade ēs jaṇe nū̃ wēhndā ī nā, te kehī sōhṇī gall sī.
37. Would that all men had kept God's commandments!	37. Kade sāre bande Khudā de hukm mannde baṛī caṅgī gall hondī.
38. He said he would come some day or other.	38. Ākheā sāsū paī kise din āwā̃gā.
39. Unless you agree you will be punished.	39. Je mannẽ nā, tenū̃ sazā miḷēgī.
40. Then he severely rebuked the girls because they would not leave off.	40. Phēr ōs kuṛīā̃ nū̃ baṛī jhāṛ kītī, paī ōh muṛdīā̃ nehī̃ sāṇ.

Lesson XXXIII. — *Tēhlīwā̃ Sabak.*

When they went out to see what had happened they found the man in his right mind, clothed and sitting at Jesus' feet.	Jadõ ōh wēkkhaṇ gae sāṇ paī kī hoeā e ohnā̃ jaṇe nū̃ purī hōsh wicc, kapṛe pāe hoe te Yesū de pairā̃ kōḷe baiṭhā hoeā ḍiṭṭhā.

DERIVED SENTENCES.

1. Hīrā saw him coming.	1. Hīre ohnū̃ aundeā̃ wēkheā.
2. He saw them coming.	2. Ōs ohnā̃ nū̃ aundeā̃ wēkheā. [sāje?
3. Did you see me coming?	3. Menū̃ aundeā̃ ḍiṭṭhā
4. I see the heaven opened and the angels of God ascending and descending.	4. Menū̃ asmān khulā dissdā e, te Khudā de firishte caṛhde te uttarde.

English	Panjabi
5. This was done that the written word might be fulfilled.	5. Ēh ēs wāste hoeā sī pai likkhī hoī kalām pūri howe.
6. It is written in the word of God.	6. Ēh Khudā dī kalām wico likhea hoeā e.
7. The world could not hold the books.	7. Ōnnīā̃ katābā̃ duniā wico nehī̃ ā sakdīā̃.
8. I am sent to find out when the letter was sent.	8. Mai patā karn wāste ghalleā geā sā̃ pai ōh ciṭṭhī kadō̃ likkhī gei sī.
9. There were sixteen beds placed there.	9. Ōtthe sōḷā̃ manjīā̃ ḍaṭ-ṭhīā̃ hoiā̃ sāṇ.
10. What is born of man is man.	10. Jō kujih insān thō̃ jammdā e insān e.
11. They saw him walking on the bank and drawing nigh the mosque.	11. Ohnā̃ ohnū̃ dande te ṭurdeā̃ te masīt de nēṛe appaṛdeā̃ ḍiṭṭhā.
12. This is my much loved boy.	12. Ēh mērā baṛā piārā puttar e.
13. I gave you a written request but you gave me no answer.	13. Mai tuhānū̃ likhke arzī dittī sī par tusā̃ koī parwāh nā kītī.
14. Here is your rejected petition.	14. Āh wēkhā̃ tuhāḍḍī nā manzūr arzī e.
15 Everything that the Father hath given me, it shall come to me, and whoever cometh to me I will in no wise cast out.	15. Jō kujih Bāp menū̃ dittā e mēre kōḷ āwēgā, te jō kōī mēre kōḷ āwē Mai ohnū̃ kaḍī nā kaḍḍhāgā.
16. It is written in the prophets—They shall all be taught of God.	16. Nabīā̃ dīā̃ katābā wico likkheā hoeā e pai ohnā̃ sāreā̃ nū̃ Khudā kōlō̃ talim miḷēgī.
17. The servant is not greater than his Lord nor the messenger greater than the sender.	17. Naukar apṇe mālik tō̃ waḍḍā nehī̃ hondā, te nā ghalleā hoeā ghallaṇwāḷe tō̃.

18.	You can get ready-made boots and clothing in this shop.	Baṇīā̃ battrīā̃ juttīā̃ te kapṛe es haṭṭī tõ miḷ sakde nẽ.
19.	There is water (mixed) in this milk.	Ēs duddh wicc pāṇī raḷeā hoeā e.
20.	If you can get ready-cooked food it will be best.	Je pakkīā̃ pakāīā̃ rōṭīā̃ miḷ sakaṇ tā̃ acchā hōwēdā.
21.	I am watching my mother bake bread.	Maĩ apnī bēbbe nū̃ rōṭīā̃ pakāndeā̃ wēhnnā wā̃ peā.
22.	The dog came barking toward me.	Kuttā bhauṅkdā hoeā mēre wall āeā.
23.	Did you see him dead ?	Ohnū̃ moeā hoeā ḍiṭṭhā sāī ?
24.	He kept me seated by him from 11 o' clock till 4.	Ōs menū̃ apṇe kōḷ yārā̃ waje tõ laike trai waje tīkar naṭṭī bahā rakkheā.
25.	They came as it was getting light.	Lō laggdeā̃ āe sāṇ.
26.	They came while it was yet light.	Lō hondeā̃ āe sāṇ.
27.	He is coming with a kettle of boiled water in his hand.	Kaṛhe hoe pāṇī dī kētlī hatth wicc laike lagā aundā e.
28.	They were standing with heads thrust out of the window.	Sir bārī wiccõ kaḍḍhke khlōte hoe sāṇ.
29.	Why did you take it without asking ?	Bin puccheā̃ kyū̃ leā sāī?
30.	Why ? They gave it to me unasked.	Menū̃ maṅgeā̃ binā dittā sāṇē.
31.	Bring my book as you come.	Kitāb nāḷ lendā āwī̃.
32.	Go on doing the work of your master.	Apṇe mālik dā kamm karde jāho.

33. How long have you been in the Panjab?	33. **Panjāb wicc āeā̃ kinnā cir hoeā̃ je?**
34. Give my torn trousers to the tailor to be mended.	34. **Mērī pāṭī hoī patlūn darzī nū̃ marammat wāste deho.**
35. Having eaten he went away.	35. **Ōh khāke ṭur geā.**
36. He will go eating.	36. **Ōh khandā jāēgā.**
37. Having eaten he begins his work.	37. **Ōh khāke kamm shurū kardā e.**
38. Rising with difficulty he went his way.	38. **Masā̃ masā̃ uṭṭheā te ṭur geā.**
39. Go on giving the medicine.	39. **Duāī dēnde jāo.**
40. The stick broke on the boy being struck.	40. **Muṇḍe nū̃ laggdeā̃ sōṭī bhajj geī.**
41. The horse fell on arriving.	41. **Ghōṛā appaṛdeā̃ ī ḍigg peā.**
42. We want a swift running mare.	42. **Sānū̃ ikk trikkhī ṭurnwāḷī ghōṛī cāhīdī e.**
43. He took bread and giving thanks broke it.	43. **Ōs rōṭī laike te shukr karke trōṛī.**
44. This mortal body shall live again.	44. **Ēh marnwāḷā jussā phēr jiū̃ pawēgā.**

Lesson XXXIV. — *Cautīhwā̃ Sabak.*

RELATIVES AND INDEFINITES.

My Father gave you the true bread from heaven, for the bread of God is that which cometh down from heaven and giveth life to the world.	**Mēre Bāp tuhānū̃ saccī rōṭī asmānō̃ dittī, Khudā dī rōṭī ōh we jehṛī asmānō̃ aundī e te dunyā nū̃ zindagī dēndī e.**

DERIVED SENTENCES.

1. Immediately they were at the shore to which they were going.	1. **Ōh jhaṭ paṭ ōs dande lagg gae jitthe jāṇā sāṇe.**

2. The man whom you saw yesterday at the city gate is a servant of the old prophet.	2. Ōh jaṇā jihnū̃ tusā̃ kall shahr de phāṭak utte ḍiṭṭhā buḍḍhe nabī dā naukar e.
3. The mare that you saw in the market to-day is an Arab.	3. Ōh ghōṛī jihnū̃ tū̃ ajj bazār wicc wēkheā sī Arb dī e.
4. This is the will of him that sent me that every one who seeth the Son and believeth on him should have eternal life, and I should raise him up at the last day.	4. Mēre Ghallaṇwāḷe dī ēh marzī e pai jō kōī Puttar nū̃ wēkkhe te ohde te imān leāwe ohnū̃ hamēshā dī zindagī miḷe te maĩ ohnū̃ ōṛak de dihāṛe jiwāḷā̃.
5. Is not this Jesus, the son of Joseph the carpenter, whose father and mother we know?	5. Ēh Yesū nehī̃ e, Yūsaf tarkhāṇ dā puttar, jihde māpeā̃ nū̃ asī̃ jāṇne ā̃?
6. And the bread which I give is my flesh which I shall give for the people of the world.	6. Te jēhṛī rōṭī maĩ dēnnā wā mērā mās e jō maĩ dunyā de lōkā̃ wāste deā̃gā.
7. The man to whom you gave the money is my son-in-law.	7. Jihnū̃ tusā̃ rupayye ditte mērā juāī e.
8. I have not come of myself, he who sent me is true whom ye know not.	8. Maĩ āpū̃ nehī̃ āeā, par jis menū̃ ghalleā saccā e, jihnū̃ tusī̃ nehī̃ jāṇde.
9. Some of the common people hearing this thing said, This is truly that prophet. Others said, This is the Christ, but some of them wished to	9. Ām lōkā̃ wiccō̃ kaiā̃ ēh gall suṇke ākheā pai saccī muccī ēh ōh nabī e. Hōrnā̃ ākheā pai ēh Masīh e, te kaī ohnū̃ phaṛnā̃ cāhnde sāṇ,

	take him. However no one laid hands on him.		tad wī kise ohnū̃ hatth nā lāeā.
10.	He that receiveth whomsoever I send receiveth me, and he that receiveth me receiveth him that sent me.	10.	Jehṛā ohnū̃ kabūle jis kise nū̃ Maĩ ghallā̃ ōh menū̃ kabūldā e, te jehṛā menū̃ kabūldā e mēre Ghallaṇwālē nū̃ kabūldā e.
11.	Ask him who it is that he is speaking about.	11.	Ohnū̃ pucchī̃ paī kihdī gall kardā e peā.
12.	Whoever would be my disciple let him take up his cross daily and follow me.	12.	Jehṛā mērā cēlā baṇnā cāhndā e rōz apṇī salīb cukkke mēre magar magar āwe.
13.	They hated him more and more.	13.	Ohnā̃ dā jehṛā ohde nāḷ wair sī waddhdā geā.
14.	Let us go to the place where Martha met him.	14.	Asī̃ ōs thā̃ calīye jitthe Marthā ohnū̃ miḷī.
15.	When the spirit of truth cometh whom I will send, he will testify of me.	15.	Jad saceāī dā Rūh āwēgā jihnū̃ maĩ ghallā̃gā ōh mērī guāhī dēgā.
16.	Whatsoever he saith to you, do it.	16.	Jō kujjh ōh tuhānū̃ ākkhe tusī̃ karo.
17.	He will remind you of everything that I told you.	17.	Jinnīā̃ gallā̃ maĩ tuhānū̃ ākhīā̃ nē ōh tuhānū̃ yād duāēgā.
18.	We want to see Jesus.	18.	Asī̃ Yesū nū̃ wēkẖṇā cāhnne ā̃.
19.	They came that day to hear him.	19.	Ōh oddiṇ ohdīā̃ gallā̃ suṇan wāste āe.
20.	We want to see you, to show you a new book.	20.	Asī̃ ikk nawī̃ kitāb wikẖāṇ laī tuhānū̃ miḷnā cāhnne ā̃.
21.	He did these things that they might understand	21.	Ōs ēh kamm ēs karke kītā paī ōh samjh laiṇ

English	Panjabi
that he truly loved them.	pai ēh saccī muccī sānū̃ piār kardā e.
22. This came to pass that the word written in their law might be fulfilled, they hated me without a cause.	22. Ēh ēs wāste hoeā̃ pai jehṛī gall ohnā dī shariat wicc likkhī hoī e pūrī howe pai ohnā̃ dhigāṇe mēre nāḷ wair rakkheā.
23. While you have light believe on the light that you may become sons of light.	23. Jicar tīkar tuhāḍḍe kōḷ cānnaṇ hai we cānnaṇ utte imān leāo, tā̃jō tusī̃ cānnaṇ de puttar baṇo.
24. The high priest of that year said to them, you know nothing at all, and do not consider that it is well that one man die for the people that the whole nation perish not.	24. Ōs sāl de sardār kaihṇ ohnā̃ nū̃ ākheā tusī̃ kakkh wī nehī̃ jāṇde te khiāl nehī̃ karde pai ikk jaṇe dā sārī kaum wāste marnā caṅgā e, sārī kaum nā na mare.
25. He got tit for tat.	25. Jehā kītā tehā pāeā.
26. Take as much as you need.	26. Jinnā lōṛīdā ī lellai.
27. Stay as long as you like.	27. Jinnā cir cāho raho.
28. He is as tall as I am.	28. Ōh mere jeḍḍā lammā e.
29. She is as black as a griddle.	29. Ōh tawe jehī kāḷī e.
30. I did as he did.	30. Jikaṇ ōs kītā ose tarhā̃ mammī̃ kītā.
31. As far as possible I will care for it.	31. Jitthõ tōṛī hō sake maī̃ ohnū̃ sāhmbā̃gā.
32. As many as believed on him to them gave he the right to become sons of God.	32. Jinneā̃ ohde te imān leāndā ōnneā̃ nū̃ ōs Khudā de puttar baṇan dā hakk dittā.
33. As the Father hath loved	33. Jis tarhā̃ Bāp mēre nāḷ

	me, even so have I loved you.		mahabbat kītī ōse tarhā̃ maĩ tuhāḍḍe nāḷ mahabbat kītī.
34.	The more he loved them the more they hated him.	34.	Jinnī waddh ōs ohnā̃ nāḷ mahabbat kītī ōnnā ī waddh ohnā̃ ohde nāḷ wair kītā.
35.	At most there will be a maund.	35.	Waddh tõ waddh ikk maṇ hōwēdā.
36.	There will be at least eighty men there.	36.	Ghaṭṭ tõ ghaṭṭ ōtthe cār wīhā̃ jaṇā hōwēgā.

Lesson XXXV. — *Paĩhtīwā̃ Sabak.*

Relatives and Indefinites.

God so loved the world that he gave his only begotten son, that whosoever believeth on him should not perish but have eternal life.	Khudā dunyā nāḷ ajehī mahabbat rakkhī paī ōs apṇā kalauta puttar bakhsheā paī jō kōī ohde te imān leāwe, ohdā nās nā hōwe sagõ ohnū̃ hamēshā dī zindagī miḷe.

Derived Sentences.

1.	The man who first brought his brother to Christ was Andrew	1.	Ōh jaṇā jis paihle apṇā bhrā Masīh kōḷ leāndā ohdā nā̃ Andriās sī.
2.	The man who betrayed his master was Judas Iscariot.	2.	Jis jaṇe apṇe Ustād nū̃ phaṛāeā sī Yahūdā Iskariūtī sī.
3.	The woman who anointed the feet of the Lord was Mary.	3.	Jis zanānī Khudāwand de pairā̃ te atr maḷeā Mariam sī.
4.	What is the meaning of the word that you used just now.	4.	Ōs lafaz dā kī matlab e jehṛā huṇ ākheā je ?
5.	Whoever came went away rich.	5.	Jō kōī āeā bakhtāwar hōke ṭur geā.

6. Whatever is your honour's will is acceptable to me.	6. Jō kujjh janāb dī marzī e menū̃ manzūr e.
7. He will tell you the things from which you and your household may get salvation.	7. Ōh tuhānū̃ ōh gallā̃ dassēgā jihnā̃ tō̃ tuhānū̃ te tuhāḍḍe ṭabbar nū̃ najāt miḷe.
8. The boys who beat my boy are the bad boys of the street.	8. Jihnā̃ muṇḍeā̃ mēre muṇḍe nū̃ māreā bajār de sharīr muṇḍe nē̃.
9. I beat that boy most thoroughly, who was blackguarding you yesterday.	9. Maĩ caṅgī tarhā̃ ōs muṇḍe nū̃ phaṇḍeā jehṛā kall tuhānū̃ nakhiddhdā sī.
10. Write down what every one owes or is owed, and whatever is owing any of them will be given him.	10. Ēh likkh lai paī har ikk kī laiṇā yā̃ dēṇā e, te jō kujjh kise nū̃ aundā e ohnū̃ miḷ jāēgā.
11. To whoever you gave it, he will give it back.	11. Jis kise nū̃ dittā̃ sāī ōh partā dēdā.
12. What is this chair made of? Which chair do you want?	12. Ēh kursī kāh dī baṇī hoī e? Kehṛī kursī cāhnde o?
13. What cloth do you want? What men are you asking for?	13. Kehṛe kapṛe dī lōṛ je? Kehṛeā bandeā̃ nū̃ labbhde o pae?
14. Of what use is this? This is quite useless, but that is very useful.	14. Ēh kis kamm dā e? Ēh te kise kamm dā nehī̃, par ōh baṛā kamm aundā e.
15. Whoever believes on him shall not be condemned.	15. Jehṛā ohnū̃ manne, ohde te sazā dā hukm nehī̃ hōwēgā.
16. Whoever does not believe on him, he is already	16. Jehṛā nā manne, ohde te hukm hō geā e, kyū̃jō

condemned, because he does not believe on God's only begotten Son.	ōh Khudā de iklaute Puttar de utte imān nehī̃ leaundā.
17. What is sin? And how can sinful man come before a holy God? These are questions which should be answered.	17. Gunāh kī e, te pāpī bandā kīkarā̃ Pāk Khudā de agge khlō sakdā e? Ēh ajehe suāl nẽ jihnā̃ dā jawāb dēṇā cāhīdā e.
18. Can God be both merciful and just or are not these two attributes irreconcilable?	18. Khudā rahm te insāf dōwe kar sakdā ē, ke ēh dō siftā̃ ikk dujjī dā ulṭ nẽ te raḷ nehī̃ sakdīā̃?
19. Christians claim that the justice and mercy of God are both shown in the death of Christ. Since Christ died by his own choice, there was no compulsion on God's part.	19. Masīhī āhnde nẽ pai Khudā dā rahm te insāf dōwe Masīh dī maut wicc dissde nẽ. Masīh jō apṇī marzī nāḷ moeā Khudā kōī jabr nehī̃ kītā.
20. He willingly paid our debt, and so it is written, God reckoned our trespasses not to us but to him.	20. Ōs apṇī khushī nāḷ sāḍḍā karz lāh dittā, te jīkaṇ likheā hoeā e, Khudā sāḍḍe gunāh sāḍḍe lēkhe wicc nehī̃ sagõ ohde lēkhe wicc pāe.

PRINCIPAL SUBJECTS ILLUSTRATED IN PART III.

Panjabi Grammar.

PARTS OF SPEECH.

There are eight parts of speech, *viz.*, noun, adjective, pronoun, verb, adverb, conjunction, preposition and interjection. There is no article. The indefinite article in English, if emphatic, is sometimes expressed by ikk (a one, certain) or kōī (some), and the definite article, if emphatic, by the demonstrative pronoun ēh (this) or ōh (that), but usually the English article is not expressed in Panjābī.

Noun.

There are two genders, masculine and feminine; and two numbers, singular and plural.

Gender.

A few words are both masculine and feminine as—

kiās	opinion.	manshā	intention.
*awāz, wāz, wāj	voice.	kalām	speech, word.
taih	fold.	Panjab	the Panjab.
mehma	praise.	chatt	roof.
sair	walk.	parhez	restraint.
fikr	case.	ghāh	grass.
salām	salutation.	dard	pain.
thā̃	place.	dahī̃	curdled milk.
k͟hāb	dream.	wēhl	leisure.
rūh	spirit.	gaū	need, profit.
akl	intelligence.	wāhz, wāhd	sermon.
rūl	pencil, ruler.	yār	friend, paramour.
sharm	shame.	jāṇū	acquaintance.
pūshal	tail.	carcā	talking about.
lām	war.	kadr	value.

As a general rule, words which signify males are masculine and those which signify females are feminine, *e.g.*, ghōṛā (horse),

* awāz, wāz (voice, sound) is fem., except in the expression "wāz bhārā hōṇā"—to become hoarse.

is masculine, and **ghōṛī** (mare) feminine; but note **ṭabbar**, m., wife, family; **aulād**, f., descendants. The only rules that can be given to determine the gender of nouns which signify inanimate objects are these:—

(1) Words ending in **-ā** or **-ā̃** and words of more than one syllable having the letter **a** in the last syllable are usually masculine, *e.g.*, **āṭā** (flour), **jaṅgal** (forest), **bāllaṇ** (firewood), **cikkaṛ** (mud), **haḷak** (rabies). But there are many exceptions as **saukaṇ** (co-wife), **ākaṛ** (pride), **haīkaḷ** (necklace).

(2) Words ending in **-ī** are usually feminine, *e.g.*, **battī** (lamp, etc.), **kannī** (border). There are some exceptions—**jī** (wish, individual), **pāṇī** (water), **mōtī** (pearl), and many words in **-ī** denoting males. (See examples on pages 268, 269.)

(3) Words common to Urdu and Panjabi generally have the same gender in both languages. The following are exceptions. Their Panjabi gender is given, **rāh**, m., way; **mēz, mēc**, m., table; **hōsh**, f., sense; **akhbār**, f., newspaper; **tār**, f., telegram, wire; **mazāj**, f., pride; **sharab**, m., spirits; **fasl**, m., harvest; **Urdu**, m., Urdu; **gār**, f., cave; **jang**, m., war; **lām**, generally masc., war; **gūnd**, f., gum; **takrār**, m., fuss, quarrel; **'marz**, f., disease; **gēnd**, m., ball. See also the double-gender words given above. Educated people tend to copy the Urdu gender; in pure village Panjabi the other is more used. The word **fikr**, thought, anxiety, is usually masc.

Words nearly the same in form as Urdu words, but different in gender are **nakk**, m., nose; **cikkaṛ**, m., mud.

Formation of Feminine.

The very large class of masculine nouns and adjectives ending in **-ā**, and past participles in **-eā** or **-ā** form the feminine by changing that termination into **-ī**.

Note.—If the thing signified be an inanimate object, the masculine form generally means a large specimen of the class and the feminine a small one.

Masculine.		Feminine.	
ghōṛā	horse.	**ghōṛī**	mare.
lēllā	he-lamb.	**lēllī**	she-lamb.

Masculine.		Feminine.	
wacchā	male-calf.	**wacchī**	female-calf.
caṅgā	good.	**caṅgī**	
kāḷā	black.	**kāḷī**	
māreā	struck.	**mārī**	
būṭā	large plant.	**būṭī**	small plant.

Note.—Dissyllables in **-eā** change this in the feminine into **eī** or **aī**, *e.g.*—

Masculine.		Feminine.
geā	gone.	**geī.**
peā	fallen.	**paī.**
leā	taken.	**leī.**

2. Where the masculine ends in a consonant, the feminine is sometimes formed by adding **ī, ṛī, ṇī,** or if the final consonant be **r**, by adding **nī** to the masculine—

Masculine.		Feminine.	
lohār	blacksmith.	**lohārī**	female of the lohār class.
jaṭṭ	peasant.	**jaṭṭī**	female peasant.
karāṛ	shop-keeper.	**karāṛī**	
tarkhāṇ	carpenter.	**tarkhāṇī**	
kumhiār	potter.	**kumhiārī**	
Awāṇ	an Awāṇ	**Awāṇī**	
harn	ravine-deer.	**harnī**	
tittar	partridge.	**tittrī**	
bāl	boy.	**bālṛī**	girl.
jātak	boy.	**jātakṛī**	girl.
naṭṭ	acrobat.	**naṭṭṇī**	
ḍūm	musician.	**ḍūmṇī**	
fakīr	beggar.	**fakīrnī**	
zimīndār	peasant.	**zimīndārnī**	

4. A noun or adjective (when used as a noun) ending in **-ī** forms its feminine sometimes by changing the **-ī** into **aṇ** changing to **m** after **r**. If the masculine ends in **āī** or **āī̃**, the feminine generally changes this termination into **aiṇ**—

Masculine.		Feminine.
Panjābī	Panjabi.	**Panjābaṇ.**
Kashmīrī	Kasmiri.	**Kashmīran.**
mirāsī	bard, musician.	**mirāsaṇ.**

	Masculine.	Feminine.	
tēlī	oil-presser.	**tēlaṇ.**	
Musallī	sweeper (Muhammadan).	**Musallaṇ.**	
Kurēshī	Kureshi.	**Kurēshaṇ.**	
mushkī	black.	**mushkaṇ.**	
azārī	ill.	**azāran.**	
wairī	enemy.	**wairan.**	
dōdhī	cowherd.	**dōdhaṇ.**	
mōcī	cobbler.	**mōcaṇ.**	
waṅgālī	glass bangle-maker.	**waṅgālaṇ.**	
māchī	baker, waterman.	**māchaṇ.**	
darjī	tailor.	**darjaṇ.**	
bhāī	brother.	**bhaiṇ**	sister
kasāī	butcher.	**kasaiṇ.**	
arāī	market gardener.	**araiṇ.**	
pirhāī	drummer.	**pirhaiṇ.**	
sāī	holy man.	**saiṇ** (rare) wife of **sāī.**	
ṇāī	barber.	**naiṇ.**	

Peculiar forms of caste feminines are—

	Masculine.	Feminine.
khattrī	shop-keeper (or caste).	**khatrāṇī**
Malak	name of caste (Malik).	**Malakāṇī**
Isāī or Asāī or Shāī	Christian.	**Asaiṇ or Shaiṇ**

In **Shāī** and **Shaiṇ**, the **s** and **h** are kept separate, the pronunciation being nearly **s'āī, s'aiṇ.**

5. **Many common words have the feminine formed from an entirely different root or in an irregular manner—**

	Masculine.		Feminine.
peō	father.	**bebbē, mā̃**	mother
puttar	son.	**dhī**	daughter.
bhrā	brother.	**bhaiṇ**	sister.
sauhrā	father-in-law.	**sass**	mother-in-law.
mīā̃	holy man, etc.	**bīwī**	female of the **mīā̃** class.
Sayyad	holy caste (Sayyid)	**Sayyadzādī**	female of the Sayyid [caste.
jawāī	son-in-law.	**nūh**	daughter-in-law.
muṇḍā	boy.	**kuṛī**	girl.
sāhn	bull.	**gā̃**	cow.

Masculine.		Feminine.	
ūṭh	he-camel.	ḍācī	she-camel (or ūṭhṇī.)
saṇḍhā	buffalo-bull.	majjh	buffalo-cow. saṇḍh means barren.
chatrā	ram.	bhēḍ	ewe.
ṭaṭṭū	pony-horse.	ṭair	pony-mare.
ūndhā	boar.	bhūhn	sow.

Number.

Masculine Nouns.

1. Masculines ending in a consonant or in any vowel except unaccented -ā or ā̃ generally make no change in the absolute plural, *e.g.*, ghar (house), piṇḍ (village), kā̃ (crow), nāī (barber), peō (father), ṭaṭṭū (pony).

2. Masculines ending in unaccented -ā and participles ending in -eā or -ā change these endings to -ē for the nominative plural. Unaccented -ā̃ becomes -ē̃.

Singular.		Plural.
ghōṛā	horse.	ghōṛē.
kuttā	dog.	kuttē.
caṅgā	good.	caṅgē.
māreā	struck.	mārē.
Exceptions—		
bhrā	brother.	bhrā.
geā	gone.	gaiē.
peā	fallen.	paiē.
leā	taken.	laiē.
rehā	remained.	raihe.
ḍehā	engaged in.	ḍaihe.

Monosyllables ending in -ā or -ā̃ and nouns of more than one syllable ending in ā or ā̃ with the accent on the last syllable do not change for the absolute plural. Thus bhrā brother; ghumā̃ measure of land, (about an acre), do not change.

Feminine Nouns.

3. Feminines usually form the absolute plural by adding ā̃ to the singular; if the singular ends in -ā, or -ā̃ they generally add -wā̃ :—

Singular.		Plural.
bhēḍ	ewe.	**bhēḍā̃.**
bhaiṇ	sister.	**bhaiṇā̃.**
gall	word.	**gallā̃.**
billī	she-cat.	**billiā̃.**
dhī	daughter.	**dhīā̃.**
caṅgī	good.	**caṅgiā̃.**
mā̃	mother.	**mā̃wā̃.**

4. Some feminine nouns, especially those ending in **-a, -ā̃** and **-āh** frequently form the nominative plural by adding **-ī̃** instead of **-ā̃** to the singular :—

Singular.		Plural.
salāh	advice.	**salāhī̃.**
tanḵẖāh	pay.	**tanḵẖāhī̃.**
balā	calamity.	**balāī̃.**
sazā	punishment.	**sazāī̃.**
zāt	caste.	**zātī̃.**
gā̃	cow.	**gā̃ī̃.**
rāt	night.	**rātī̃.**
kanāḷ	a land-measure.	**kanāḷī̃.**
ḵẖāngāh	saint's tomb.	**ḵẖāngāhī̃.**
duā	prayer.	**duāī̃.**

gā̃, cow, very frequently has plural **gāīā̃.**

Most such words take the regular plural also.

5. A few feminine nouns form the absolute plural by adding **-ū̃** to the singular—

Singular.		Plural.
hanj	tear.	**hanjū̃.**
khumb	mushroom.	**khumbū̃.**
pīhl	fruit of **waṇ** tree.	**pīhlū̃.**
wast	thing.	**wastū̃.**
atthar	tear.	**atthrū̃** (the a being dropped).
chill	rupee (slang).	**chillū̃.**

Most of these words have the regular plural also.

CASE.

Nominative or Absolute Singular.

The absolute form of a noun or adjective is used when the word is in the nominative ; it may also be used as an accusative, *e.g.*, **ēh mērā ghōṛā we** (this is my horse), or **mērā ghōṛā laiā** (bring my horse).

In all other cases (except in the vocative and locative cases of certain nouns) the absolute form of the noun or adjective is apt to change into what may be called the prepositional form, regarding which the following rules may be given.

Oblique or Prepositional Singular.

(1) Feminines, whatever be their termination, and masculines ending in a consonant, or in any vowel except unaccented -ā or -ā̃, usually undergo no change in the prepositional singular, *e.g.*, **bhaiṇ** (sister), **cūcī** *f.* (chicken), **piṇḍ** *m.* (village), **nāī** *m.* (barber), **ṭaṭṭū** *m.* (pony), **sarā̃**, *f.* (sarāē).

Masculine monosyllables ending in -ā or -ā̃ and masculine nouns of more than one syllable ending in -ā or -ā̃ with the accent on the last syllable do not change for the prepositional singular.

(2) The rest of the large class of masculine words ending in ā change it into ē in the oblique singular, thus making it the same as the absolute plural. Unaccented -ā̃ becomes -ē̃.

Absolute Singular.		Oblique Singular.
ghōṛā	horse	**ghōṛē.**
kuttā	dog.	**kuttē.**
caṅgā	good.	**caṅgē.**
mīā̃	holy man.	**mīē̃.**

Prepositional Plural.

The plural is formed by adding ā̃ to the absolute plural ; but in masculine nouns if the absolute plural ends in ā or ā̃, a 'w' is inserted, and in feminine nouns the ending -ā̃ of the absolute plural does not change for the prepositional plural.

Absolute Plural.		Prepositional Plural.
mā̃wā̃	mothers.	**mā̃wā̃.**
gāīā̃	cows.	**gāīā̃.**
gallā̃	words.	**gallā̃.**
caṅgē *m.*	good.	**caṅgeā̃.**
caṅgīā̃ *f.*	good.	**caṅgīā̃.**
ghar	houses.	**gharā̃.**
kuttē	dogs.	**kutteā̃.**
ghōṛē	horses.	**ghōṛeā̃.**
bhrā	brothers.	**bhrāwā̃.**
nā̃	names.	**nā̃wā̃.**

Plurals in **-ī̃** or **-ū̃** usually have the alternative form in **-ā̃** and in the prepositional tend to revert to the **-ā̃** form, though **-ī̃** and **-ū̃** are not unknown, thus **atthrū̃**, tears, prep. **atthrā̃**, or **atthrū̃**, **k͟hāngāhī̃**, saints' tombs, prep., **k͟hāngāhī̃** or **k͟hāngāhā̃**.

The Agent Case.

The agent case, used for the subject when the verb is a transitive verb in a tense expressed by the past participle and its compounds, is the prepositional form of the noun without any termination. Occasionally **nē** is used as a kind of preposition, after the oblique form of the noun, but not in villages.

peō kītā	the father did it.	**kutte kītā**	the dog did it.
puttar kītā	the son did it.	**kutteā̃ kītā**	the dogs did it.

kuṛī nē kītā, the girl did it.

The Genitive Case.

The genitive case is formed by adding to the prepositional form the preposition **dā**, which resembles the *'s* in English, but converts the noun into a sort of adjective declined like an adjective in **ā**, so as to agree with the following or governing noun in gender, number and case :—

Genitive Preposition.		*Number and Case of following noun.*
Masculine.	Feminine.	
dā	**dī**	singular absolute.
dē	**dī**	,, prepositional, agent locative.

Masculine.	Feminine.		
deā	dīē	singular	vocative.
dē	dīā̃	plural	absolute.
deā̃	dīā̃	,,	prepositional, agent.
dī	dī	,,	locative.
deō	dīō	..	vocative.

Examples.

jaṇē dā ghōṛā	the man's horse.	**jaṇē dē ghōṛē**	the man's horses.
jaṇē dē ghōṛē dā.	of the man's horse.	**jaṇē deā̃ ghōṛeā̃ dā.**	of the man's horses.
jaṇē dī ghōṛī	the man's mare	**jaṇē dīā̃ ghōṛīā̃**	the man's mares.
jaṇē dī ghōṛī dā.	of the man's mare.	**jaṇē dīā̃ ghōṛīā̃ dā.**	of the man's mares.
jaṇe dī hatthī	with the man's hands.	**piṇḍ dīō kuṛīō**	O girls of the village.

THE DATIVE CASE.

The dative case, which may also be used as an accusative, is formed by adding the preposition **nū̃** to the prepositional form:—

Examples.

ghōṛē nū̃	to the horse.	**ghōṛeā̃ nū̃**	to the horses.
ghōṛī nū̃	to the mare.	**ghōṛīā̃ nū̃**	to the mares.

THE LOCATIVE CASE.

The locative case means *to*, *at*, or *in*, a place, time or thing, *by* or *with* an instrument, *for* a price, etc. It is formed as follows:—

(1) A masculine in ā changes the ā into ē, *e.g.*, **Kujrā̃āḷē**, at **Gujrā̃wāla, Jaṇḍeāḷē**, at **Jaṇḍeāḷa; rōṭī wēḷē**, at breakfast-time.

(2) A masculine noun in the singular ending in a consonant either remains unchanged, or adds ē to the root:—

Examples.

gharē hai	he is at home.	**skūlē chalīyē**	let us go to school.

ghar gēā	he has gone home.	**Sambṛeāḷe raihndā e.**	he lives at **Sambṛeāḷ.**
Wazīrābād geā e	he has gone to Wazīrābād.		
Siāḷkōṭ kamm kardā e	he works in Siāḷkōṭ.		

(3) In the plural masculine nouns take **-ī** as the locative termination, plural names of towns and villages ending in **-ē** take **-ī**, except those ending in **-kē** which take **-kī**.

ōh dī hatthī	by his hands.	**Nattī**	in or to **Natt.**
apṇī gharī	in their own houses.	**Wairōkī**	in or to **Wairōkē.**
Kulārī	in or to **Kulār.**	**Aujḷī**	in or to **Aujḷē.**
Ḍhabbī	in or to **Ḍhabb.**	**aṭṭhī dinī**	every eighth day or in eight days.

hatthī baddhī gulām, devoted slave (slave with hands joined in supplication).

Most place names which end in a consonant and are singular have no special locative form. Exceptions are **Panjāb, f. or m. Hindustān, m., Gujrāt, f., Ambarsar, m.** (Amritsar), **Sambṛeaḷ, m., Wilait** (Europe, America) which may add **-ē.**

In the case of names of villages whose form does not at once decide whether they are singular or plural, no rule can be given. Each one must be ascertained separately. A large number of such are plural, and of these it will probably be found that nearly all are names of castes (Musalmān or Hindu) and conversely that most names of villages which are also names of castes are plural.

(4) Feminines take **-ī** or **-ē** as the sing. loc. termination, but those in **-ī** remain unchanged. Some words denoting time take **-ī.**

rātī	at night.	**masītī**	in the mosque (also **masīt**).
shāmī	in the evening.		
dopaihrī	at midday.	**bhaṭṭhī**	at the oven.
tasīlē	at the tahsīl.	**haṭṭī**	at the shop.
Gujrāte	in Gujrāt.	**dhuppē**	in the sun.
fajrī	in the morning.	**ḍigarī**	in the afternoon.

The feminine plural locative ending is **-ī**, as **Bāgṛī**, in **Bāgṛīā.**

In some districts fem. plurals in **īā** change **īā** to **īē** for the locative, as **Bāgṛīẽ** and adjectives in agreement which would have ended in **ī** also change to **īẽ**. In numerals too we hear **cāhlīẽ** for **cāhḷī**, **wīhẽ** for **wīh**, etc.

(5) The locative case is frequently used in connection with prices, **sattī paisī** for seven pice, **pañī rupaī**, for five rupees.

(6) The locative is often formed by means of prepositions, as **wicc** or **icc**, in : **nū̃**, to, **utte** or **tē**, upon ; **tō̃**, from.

The Vocative Case.

Most nouns in the singular, especially those ending in a consonant, may keep the nominative form for the vocative. But very frequently they have a special form according to the following rules :—

(1) A masculine in the singular makes the vocative by adding **ā** to the prepositional form, *e.g.*, **hē sacceā Rabbā**, O true God ; **puttarā**, O son ; **sūrā**, you pig ; **O Jahān K͟hānā**, O Jahān K͟hān ; an exception is **bāpū**, (rare), O father.

Some nouns in **-ā** indicating persons do not take a special vocative form, such are **cāccā**, uncle, father ; **bābbā**, grandfather, uncle, old man ; **māmmā**, maternal uncle ; **dādā**, professional singer ; **dāddā**, paternal grandfather ; **nānnā**, maternal grandfather.

bhrā, brother has **bhrāwā** ; plur., **bhrāwō**.

(2) A feminine in the singular generally makes the vocative by adding **-e**. Many do not change at all. **nī mērīē dhīē**, O my daughter, **nī sāwīē**, O grey mare ; **nī Tābaṇē**, O Tāban ; **Karam Bībīē**, O Karam Bībī ; **bhaiṇā**, O sister ; (also **bhaiṇē**) **bēbbē**, O mother.

(3) The plural, whether masculine or feminine, makes the vocative by adding **ō** to the singular oblique form ; *e.g.*, **puttarō**, O sons ; **dhīō**, O daughters.

Prepositions.

All prepositions require the word they govern to have the prepositional form. See under the heading Prepositions, page 300.

Examples.

Examples may now be given of the declension of nouns of various classes. In every case the agent, genitive and dative are simply the prepositional with or without the addition of prepositions.

(1) **Masculine nouns ending in ā unaccented.**

ghōṛā, horse.

Case.	Singular.		Plural.	
Nominative ..	**ghōṛā**	a horse.	**ghōṛē**	horses.
Agent ..	**ghōṛē**	a horse.	**ghōṛeā̃**	horses.
Genitive ..	**ghōṛē dā**	of a horse.	**ghōṛeā̃ dā**	of horses.
Dative, Accusative ..	**ghōṛē nū̃**	to a horse.	**ghōṛeā̃ nū̃**	to horses.
Vocative ..	**ghōṛeā**	O horse.	**ghōṛeō**	O horses.

(2) **Ordinary masculine nouns not ending in -ā unaccented.**

ghar, house.

Case.	Singular.		Plural.	
Nominative ..	**ghar**	a house.	**ghar**	houses.
Agent	**ghar**	a house.	**gharā̃**	houses.
Genitive	**ghar dā**	of a house.	**gharā̃ dā**	of houses.
Dative, Accusative ..	**ghar nū̃**	to a house.	**gharā̃ nū̃**	to houses.
Locative ..	**ghar or gharē**	at a house.	**gharī̃**	in houses.
Vocative ..	**gharā**	O house.	**gharō**	O houses.

bhrā, brother.

Case.	Singular.		Plural.
Nominative ..	**bhrā**	brother	**bhrā.**
Agent ..	**bhrā**		**bhrāwā̃.**
Genitive ..	**bhrā dā**		**bhrāwā̃ dā.**
Dative, Accusative ..	**bhrā nū̃**		**bhrāwā̃ nū̃.**
Vocative ..	**bhrāwā**		**bhrāwō.**

mōcī, shoemaker.

Case.	Singular.		Plural.
Nominative ..	**mōcī**	shoemaker	**mōcī.**
Agent, Prepositional ..	**mōcī**		**mōcīā̃.**
Vocative ..	**mōcīā**		**mōcīō.**

(3) Feminine nouns ending in a consonant

bhaiṇ, sister.

Case.	Singular.		Plural.	
Nominative ..	**bhaiṇ**	a sister.	**bhaiṇā̃**	sisters.
Agent ..	**bhaiṇ**	a sister.	**bhaiṇā̃**	sisters.
Genitive ..	**bhaiṇ dā**	of a sister.	**bhaiṇā̃ dā**	of sisters.
Dative, Accusative ..	**bhaiṇ nū̃**	to a sister.	**bhaiṇā̃ nū̃**	to sisters.
Vocative ..	**bhaiṇ -ā, -ē**	O sister.	**bhaiṇō** / **bhāiṇā̃**	O sisters.

(4) Feminine nouns in ī—

ghōṛī, mare.

Case.	Singular.		Plural.	
Nominative ..	**ghōṛī**	a mare.	**ghōṛīā̃**	mares.
Agent ..	**ghōṛī**	a mare.	**ghōṛīā̃**	mares.
Genitive ..	**ghōṛī dā**	of a mare.	**ghōṛīā̃ dā**	of mares.
Dative, Accusative ..	**ghōṛī nū̃**	to a mare.	**ghōṛīā̃ nū̃**	to mares.
Vocative ..	**ghōṛīē**	O mare.	**ghōṛīō**	O mares.

To express direction from **ō̃** is added to the prepositional singular; **ō̃** is not added to plurals, but plural names of villages add **-īō̃**, or if ending in **-ē** change **-ē** to **-īō̃**—

kuṛhō̃	from the cow house.	**Kulārīō̃**	from Kulār.
haṭṭīō̃	from the shop.	**Kujrā̃āḷeō̃**	from Gujrā̃wāla
Nattīō̃	from Natt.	**Wāirōkīō̃**	from Wairōkē.

Maṛdēkīō̃ from Mardēkē.

Direction from may also be expressed by the use of the preposition **tō̃, thō̃, thī̃**—

haṭṭī tō̃. **Wairōkeā̃ tō̃.**
Kulārā̃ thī̃ **Nattā̃ tō̃.**

Diminutives.

Diminutives are often formed, in the case of inanimate objects, by changing a masculine into a feminine—

Examples.

cappā	a large oar.	**cappī**	a small oar.
būṭā	a large plant.	**būṭī**	a small plant.
sōṭā	a stick.	**sōṭī**	a small stick.
bhaṛōhlā	large mud receptacle for corn.	**bhaṛōhlī**	small do.
khūh	well.	**khūhī**	small well.
ghaṛā	large earthen vessel.	**ghaṛī**	small ghaṛā.
sūā	big needle.	**sūī**	small needle.

Irregular diminutives are—

billā	a cat	**bilūṅgā**	a kitten.
paṭṭhā	a kid.	**paṭhōrā**	a small kid.
kuttā	a dog.	**katūrā**	a puppy.
bakrā	a goat.	**bagrōṭā**	a kid.
ḍhōl	drum.	**ḍhōlkī**	a little drum.
saṇḍhā	buffalo.	**jhōṭā, kaṭṭā**	small buffalo.
majjh	buffalo-cow.	**jhoṭi, kaṭṭi**	small buffalo-cow.
ūṭh	camel.	**bōttā, ṭōḍḍā**	young camel.
kukkaṛ	cock.	**cūcā**	chicken.
ḍhaggā	bull.	**waihṛā,**	calf.
		wacchā.	calf.
ghōṛā	horse.	**wachērā**	foal (washera).
ciṛī	small bird.	**bōṭ**	young of small bird.

COLLECTIVE NOUNS.

kaṭṭh, *m.*	assembly.
triñjaṇ, *f.*, or **bhōhrā,** *m*	a spinning-bee of girls or women.
ijjaṛ, *m.*	flock of goats and sheep.
wagg, *m.*	herd of cattle.
ḍār, taraṇḍā	flock of birds.

CONTRACTIONS.

Names are often contracted *e.g.*—

Mhammā, **Mhandā**	for **Muhammad**—.	**Fajjā, Fajjū**, **Phaillā, Phallā**	for **Faal**—.
Bakkū	„ **Barkat**—.	**Jāmū**	„ **Nizām**—
Jānnā	„ **Ramzān**—.		

Similarly with girls' names.

Tābā, Tābō, Tābaṇ for Mahtāb—.		Phaillā (or Phajjlā) for Fazl—.
Barkatē (Bakke)	,, Barkat—.	Ishrū for Ishwar—.
Phattō	,, Fateh—.	Kammō for Karm—.

The second part of the name is left blank above, for it is immaterial. Thus Phaillā stands equally for Fazl Dīn, Fazl Dād and Fazl Ahmad.

Doublets.

Nouns and other words are sometimes extended by an addition or repetition; the effect is that of familiar reference to something well known and sometimes of emphasis. See p. 339.

dāṇā phakkā	grain of sorts.
kall mukallā chaṛā chāṇḍ or chaṛā muṛā	quite alone.
lakkaṛ shakkaṛ	wood of sorts.
ukkā mukkā	at all or altogether.
autrā nikhattrā	childless.
ḍaṅgar caukhar	cattle of sorts.
kitāb shitāb	a book of sorts.
ghōṛā shōṛā	a horse of a sort.
cauṛ capaṭṭ	utterly useless.
ḍiṅg phaṛiṅgā	crooked.
caṅgā bhalā	all right, quite well.
gōḷ mōḷ	ambiguous.
fulāṇī . . . ḍhīṅgṛī	one thing or another.

This repetition is used with verbs also as—

baṇā ū kē = baṇākē	having made.
puccheā giccheā	asked.

Adjectives.

Adjectives ending in -ā agree with their nouns in gender, number and case, and generally precede them. The great majority of adjectives end in the termination ā for the masculine, which is changed to ī for the feminine, and are declined like nouns in ā and ī. Other adjectives make no change. Even with those ending in -ā one often finds -ē before a noun for all cases, singular and plural, except the nominative singular and locative plural. These adjectives sometimes, and pronominal adjectives generally, take -ī for -ī̃ in the loc. plur.

Masculine.

Singular.

caṅgā ghōṛā	a good horse.
caṅgē ghōṛē dā	of a good horse.

Plural.

caṅgē ghōṛē	good horses.
caṅgeā̃ ghōṛeā̃ dā	of good horses.

Feminine.

Singular.

caṅgī ghōṛī	a good mare.
caṅgī ghōṛī dā	of a good mare.

Plural.

caṅgīā̃ ghōṛīā̃	good mares.
caṅgīā̃ ghōṛīā̃ dā	of good mares.

Note.—The declension of **sabbh** (all) is peculiar. In the singular it does not alter for either gender or case ; in the plural it is **sabbh** (emphatic **sabbhē**) in the absolute case for both masculine and feminine, and **sabbhnā̃** in the prepositional case (locative plural **sabbhnī̃**).

Common adjectives are—

waḍḍā	big.	**nikkā**	little.
buḍḍhā, budhṛā	old.	**nikkā**	young.
lammā	long.	**chōṭā** or **nikkā**	short.
uccā	high.	**nīwā̃**	low.
cauṛā	broad.	**sauṛā** or **bhīṛā**	narrow.
mōkḷā	roomy.	**sauṛā**	non-roomy, cramped.
caṅgā	good.	**bhaiṛā**	bad.
wall	fair, good.	**māṛā**	poor, feeble.
sajjā	right.	**khabbā**	left.
bhārā	heavy.	**hauḷā**	light.
nāwā̃	new.	**purāṇā**	old
sajhrī	fresh.	**bahī**	stale.
suāhrā	level.	**kuāhrā**	rough.

àyāṇa	childish.	**siyāṇa**	wise.
saukhī	easy.	**aukhī**	hard.
mōṭā	thick.	**patlā**	thin.
ākrā	stiff (paste, etc.).	**ḍhillā**	loose.
ḍūṅghā	deep.	**thōṛā**	shallow, little.
siddhā	straight.	**ḍiṅgā**	crooked.
		puṭṭhā	upside down.
kāḷā	black.	**ciṭṭā** or **baggā**	white.
rattā	red.	**nīlā**	blue.
pīḷā	yellow.	**sāwā**	green, grey.
bhūsḷā	brown.	**hōr**	other.
tagṛā	strong.	**māṛā** or **lissa**	weak.
wadhīk	excessive.	**kassā**	deficient.
gillā	wet.	**sukkā**	dry.
silla	damp.		
kharā	genuine, good.	**khōṭā**	counterfeit, false.

Formation of Adjectives.

Some adjectives are formed from nouns by the addition of **ā**, with or without an alteration in the root, but many are formed irregularly.

Noun.		Adjective.	
aukh	difficulty.	**aukkhā**	difficult.
bhukkh	hunger.	**bhukkhā**	hungry.
bhār	weight.	**bhārā**	heavy.
cir	a long time.	**cirōkṇā**	of a long time ago.
		cirkā, cirākā	late.
majjh	a buffalo.	**mājhā**	of a buffalo.
gā̃	cow.	**gōkā**	of a cow.
bakrā	goat.	**bākrā**	of a goat.

The affix **-kā** is used with proper names to form adjectives signifying belonging to or connected with. It is added to the prepositional case of the singular. These adjectives are declined like other adjectives in **-a**. **Būṭekeā wicc ajj laṛāī e**, there is a quarrel to-day among Buta's people, *i.e.*, his family.

Būṭēkā piṇḍ, Buta's village.

This resembles in form, but not in usage, the Urdu preposition kā.

The prefix su- means good, and ka- or ku- means bad; puttar kuputtar hundē nē, māpē kumāpē kadī nehī̃ hundē, sons are bad, parents never are bad; kucajjā, unsuitable, improper, sucajjā, proper, suitable.

Comparison.

There are no comparative or superlative forms. To express comparison the prepositions nāḷō̃, than, and tō̃ or thō̃, from, are used governing in the prepositional case the name of the thing with which comparison is made, the adjective remaining in the positive form. ōh methō̃ tagṛā e, he is stronger than I; mērī kuṛi nāḷō̃ tērī waḍḍī e, your daughter is bigger than mine; shikrē nāḷō̃ lāllī māṛī e, a maina is weaker than a shikra.

The words waddh, more and ghaṭṭ, less are sometimes used, as ēh waddh tagṛā e, oh ghaṭṭ tagṛā e, this is stronger, that is less strong.

Sometimes the final ā is changed into ērā to signify 'rather, like the English ending -ish, but this termination frequently makes no change in the meaning. When the adjective ends in -ṛā, the ṛ becomes r, and the -ērā then becomes -ēṛā.

Examples.

Positive.		Comparative.	
mōkḷā	roomy.	mokḷērā	rather roomy.
caṅgā	good.	caṅgērā	rather good.
waḍḍā	large.	waḍērā	rather large.
patlā	thin.	patlērā	rather thin.
kassā	deficient.	kasērā	a little less.
bhārā	heavy.	bharērā	rather heavy.
māṛā	feeble, weak.	marēṛā	rather feeble.
nikkā	small.	nikērā	smallish.
mōṭā	fat.	muṭērā	fattish.
sauṛā	narrow.	surēṛā	rather narow.
cauṛā	broad.	curēṛā	broadish.
lammā	long.	lamērā	longish.
uccā	high.	ucērā	rather high.

	Positive.		Comparative.
haulā	light, not heavy.	**hulērā**	lightish.
tagṛā	strong.	**tagrēṛā**	rather strong.

Superlative.

The superlative is expressed by making a comparison with the word "all" **ēh sabbhnā̃ tō̃ nikkā e**, this is smaller than all, *i.e.*, the smallest. **ōh sāreā̃ nāḷō̃ māṛā e**, he is the weakest of all.

For **nāḷō̃** or **tō̃** we might have **wiccō̃**, out of, he is small or weak out of all, *i.e.*, he is the smallest or weakest.

Numerals.

The numerals are as follows:—

1.	ikk.	24.	çawī, cawwī.
2.	dō.	25.	panjhī.
3.	trai.	26.	chabbī.
4.	cār.	27.	satāī.
5.	panj.	28.	aṭhāī.
6.	chē.	29.	unattī, unattrī.
7.	satt.	30.	trīh, tīh.
8.	aṭṭh.	31.	ikattī, ikattri.
9.	naũ.	32.	battī, battrī.
10.	das.	33.	tē̆tī or tēttī, tētrī.
11.	yārā̃.	34.	cauttī or caũtī, cautrī.
12.	bārā̃.	35.	paĩtī, paĩtrī.
13.	tērā̃.	36.	chattī, chattrī.
14.	caudā̃.	37.	saĩtī, saĩtrī.
15.	pandrā̃.	38.	aṭhattī, aṭhattrī.
16.	sōḷā̃.	39.	untāḷī.
17.	satārā̃.	40.	cāḷī.
18.	aṭhārā̃.	41.	iktāḷī.
19.	unnī̃.	42.	batāḷī, bĕtāḷī.
20.	wīh.	43.	tartāḷī.
21.	ikkī.	44.	cutāḷī.
22.	bāī.	45.	paĩtāḷī panjtāḷī.
23.	trēī.	46.	chatāḷī.

47. saitāḷī, (santāḷī).
48. aṭhtāḷī.
49. unanjā, unwanjā or uṇwanjā.
50. panjāh.
51. ikwanjā.
52. bawanjā.
53. tarwanjā.
54. curinjā.
55. pacwanjā, pachwanjā.
56. chiwanjā, chawinjā.
57. satwanjā.
58. aṭhwanjā.
59. unāhṭh.
60. saṭṭh.
61. ikāhṭh.
62. bāhṭh.
63. trēhṭh.
64. cauhṭh.
65. paiṅhṭh.
66. cheāhṭh.
67. satāhṭh.
68. aṭhāhṭh.
69. unhattar.
70. sattar, shattar.*
71. ikhattar.*
72. bahattar.
73. tihattar, tirhattar.
74. cuhattar, curhattar.
75. panjhattar.
76. chehattar.
77. satattar, sathattar.*
78. aṭhattar, aṭhhattar.*
79. unāsī.
80. assī.
81. ikāsī.
82. beāsī.
83. tirāsī.
84. curāsī.
85. panjāsī.
86. cheāsī.
87. satāsī.
88. aṭhāsī.
89. unānawe.
90. nabbe, nawwe.
91. ikānawe.
92. bānawe.
93. tirānawē.
94. curānawē.
95. pacānawe, panjānawe.
96. cheānawe.
97. satānawe.
98. aṭhānawe.
99. naṛinawe.
100. sāu, sai.
200. dō sau.
300. trai sau.
400. cār sau.
1000. hazār or hajār.
100,000. lakkh.
10,000,000. karōṛ.

* In these words the h of the syllable hat is to be pronounced in the deep way described under Pronunciation. The words resemble s'attar, sat'attar, aṭh'attar, where ' stands for the Arabic ' ain.

DECLENSION OF NUMERALS.

Cardinal numbers have two oblique forms, prepositional and locative, which are used before plural nouns in these cases. The others take the following forms:

ikk, one.....ikk, ikkī both prepositional and locative.
dō, two.....dūh .. .. ..
trai, three...trūh, treūh .. .. ..
cār, four....caūh .. .. ..

The rest add-ā̃ for the prepositional; those already ending in -ā̃ (11–18) add nothing, those ending in -ā (49, 51–58) change -ā to -ā̃. For the locative -ī̃ is added, those ending in -ā̃, -ā, -ē, -ī change these to -ī̃, while unnī remains unaltered. chē takes both chī̃ and cheī̃, wīh and trīh become wī̃h and trī̃h. sau and sai declined only when several hundreds are spoken of.

Nominative.	Prepositional.	Locative.	Meaning.
satt.	sattā̃	sattī̃	7.
pandrā̃.	pandrā̃	pandrī̃	15.
wīh.	wīhā̃	wī̃h	20.
panjhī.	panjhīā̃	panjhī̃	25.
panjāh.	panjāhā̃	panjāhī̃	50.
satwanjā.	satwanjā̃	satwanjī̃	57.
bāhṭh.	bāhṭhā̃	bāhṭhī̃	62.
nabbe.	nabbeā̃	nabbī̃	90.
sau, sai.	sauā̃, saiā̃	saiī̃	100.

panjhī̃ rupaī̃ miḷeā, it cost 25 rupees; panjā̃ ghumawā̃ dī paiḷī, a field of five ghumaos (acres).

Above 100 the numbers are joined without the copulative, ikk sau ikk 101, do sau panjhī, 225, cār sau unānawe, 489.

The first few numerals have emphatic forms. For the sake of emphasis -ē is added to the cardinal. Beyond das, ten, this is rare except perhaps for saṭṭhē, from saṭṭh, sixty. dō, two, trai, three, chē, six, insert w making dōwē, traiwē, chēwē. ikk, one, becomes ikkō. The first four are declined.

Ordinary.	Intensive.	Prepositional.	Meaning.
ikk.	ikkō.	ikksē.	one.
dō.	dōwē.	dōhā̃.	two.

Ordinary.	Intensive.	Prepositional.	Meaning.
trai.	traiwē.	triũhā̃.	three.
cār.	cārē.	cauhā̃.	four
das.	dasē.	(none.)	ten.
chē.	chēwē.	(none.)	six.

Peasants generally count by scores, though sau, hundred, hajār, thousand, and lakkh, 100,000 are common.

panjā̃ utte satt wīhā̃ = 145 (seven score on five).
caudā̃ utte sau = 114 (a hundred on fourteen).
chēā̃ utte chē wīhā̃ = 126 (six score on six).
chēā̃ ghaṭṭ chē wīhā̃ = 114 (six score less six).

ORDINALS.

Ordinal numbers, after the first four, are formed by adding wā̃ to the cardinal. All ordinal numbers from 11th to 99th, except those from 69th to 78th, are pronounced with an h which raises the tone, whether such an h is found in the cardinal or not.

paihlā	first	panjāhwā̃	fiftieth.
dujjā, dūsrā	second	trīhwā̃	thirtieth.
trījjā, tījjā, tīsrā	third	nawwhēwā̃	ninetieth.
cauthā	fourth	sauwhā̃	hundredth.

Ninth is often nāwā̃ or nauā̃ being thus distinguished from nawā̃, new.

These are all adjectives declinable like adjectives in ā and ā̃.

Ordinal numbers are not very much used after the first ten or twelve. The accent is on the syllable which is accented in the cardinals. For reckoning the days of the Ramzan fast and for the days of Muhammadan months generally a different form is usually given to the following numbers. In more northerly districts they are common for all purposes. It is to be noted that in all *these* the accent is changed from the first syllable to the second.

19th	unīhwā̃	25th	panjihwā̃.
21st	ikīhwā̃	26th	chabīhwā̃.
22nd	bawīhwā̃	27th	satīhwā̃.
23rd	tarwīhwā̃	28th	aṭhīhwā̃.
24th	cawīhwā̃		

In panjihwā̃ the first h of panjhī is dropped.

Tonic 'h' is omitted in 60 and 80.

MULTIPLES.

The first few numbers have forms ending in -ṇā, which are declinable adjectives. Comparison in size, cost, etc., may be made by the use of the word **hissa**, part. For the idea of frequency of occurrence, three times, four times, etc. **wārī** or **wērī**, time, is employed.

dūṇā	double.	**chē hissē**	six times (parts).
trīṇā	treble.	**das hissē**	ten times.
cauṇā	four-fold.	**trai wārī**	three times.
panjauṇā	five-fold.	**car wērī**	four times.

mērā ḍhaggā tērē waihṛe nāḷõ dūṇā e, my bull is twice the size of your calf. **ēh ōh dē nāḷõ dūṇā nīwā̃ sī**, this was twice as low as that. **ēh paiṇḍā ōh dē nāḷō cār hisse waddh e**, this distance is four times as great as that. **malwāṇā trai wērī āeā**, the priest (Muhammadan) came three times.

FRACTIONAL NUMBERS.

addhā	half.	**pauṇā**	a quarter less than
munnā	three quarters.	**ḍēḍh**	one and a half.
sawā	a quarter more than.	**ḍhāī**	two and a half.
sāḍhē	half more than.		

ḍēḍh and **ḍhāī** are used by themselves or with **sau**, **hazār**, **wīhā̃ lakkh**, **karōṛ** :—**ḍhāī lakkh** 250,000, **ḍēḍh sau** 150.

pauṇā is used with the numerals 1 to 99 and **sāḍhē** with 3 to 99 :—**pauṇē trai** 2¾, **pauṇē trai sau** 275, **sāḍhē panjāh** 50½, **pauṇa ikk sau** 75.

pauṇā and **sāḍhē** agree with their nouns in number and gender, **pauṇīā̃ dō waṭṭīā̃**, 1¾ wattis (**waṭṭī** is two ser).

sawā is used with all numbers:—**sawā cār**, four and a quarter, **sawā sau** 125. **ḍēḍh**, and **sawā** are unchangeable.

Fractions less than a half are expressed by means of the word **hissa**, part. **daswā̃ hissa**, a tenth part, **sattwā̃ hissa** a seventh part. **pā**, quarter is employed chiefly for divisions of a ser (two pounds). Thus **ikk pā**, quarter ser, **ḍēḍh pā**, three-eighths of a ser, **addh pā**, one-eighth.

DISTRIBUTIVE NUMBERS.

The idea of so many each is expressed by repeating the number. Hundreds, thousands, etc., not followed by lower numbers, repeat only the number qualifying, others above a hundred repeat the last number.

dō dō, two each, **dō dō sau**, two hundred each, **dō sau cāḷī cāḷī**, two hundred and forty each, **ḍēḍh ḍēḍh hazār**, 1500 each.

PRONOUNS.

The personal pronouns are as follows :—

	First person.	*Second person.*	*Third person.*	
	I.	Thou.	He. she. it.	
Case.	Singular.	Singular.	This.	That.
Absolute ..	**maĩ**	**tū̃**	**ēh, āh**	**ōh, aūh.**
Agent ..	**maĩ**	**tū̃**	**ēs**	**ōs.**
Genitive ..	**mērā**	**tērā**	**ēsdā, ehdā**	**ōsdā, ohdā.**
Dative ..	**mĕnū̃**	**tĕnū̃**	**ēsnū̃, ehnū̃**	**ōsnū̃, ohnū̃.**
	Plural.	Plural.	Plural.	Plural.
Absolute ..	**asī̃**	**tusī̃**	**ēh**	**ōh.**
Agent ..	**asā̃**	**tusā̃**	**ehnā̃**	**ohnā̃.**
Genitive ..	**sāḍḍā**	**tuhāḍḍā**	**ehnā̃dā**	**ohnā̃dā.**
Dative ..	**sānū̃**	**tuhānū̃**	**ehnā̃nū̃**	**ohnā̃nū̃.**

Note.—In the third person, **ēh** or **ōh** is used for 'he,' 'she' or 'it,' according as the person or object spoken of is near the person speaking or at some distance off.

For the agent of the third person **ēsnē, ehnē, ōsnē, ohnē**, in the singular and **ehnā̃ nē, ohnā̃ nē** in the plural are rarely found.

The accent of **tuhāḍḍā** and **tuhānū̃** is on the second syllable, that of all other personal pronouns on the first. Rarely, however, one hears the following for the genitive and dative of the 3rd person plural with the accent on the second, **enhā̃dā, enhā̃nū̃, onhā̃dā, onhā̃nū̃.**

When the preposition **tō̃**, from, etc., is compounded with the singular **ēh, ōh**, the regular forms are **estō̃, ōstō̃**, but **edū̃, odū̃** are extremely common, in fact are the usual forms when the reference is to something without life, and especially in comparison and in reckoning of time :—

oddū aggē, hence forward, from this on, **oddū aggē**, from then on, **ēh oddū nirs e**, this is inferior to that.

With the first and second pronouns the forms are **methō̃**, **tethō̃**, **sāthō̃**, **tuhāthō̃**.

For emphasis **ī** or **hī** is added to the pronouns; if a preposition is used, it precedes ī or hī. If the previous syllable contains a nasal the particle of emphasis become **ī̃** or **hī̃**.

The following additional forms are found for emphasis: **maīhyē**, for **maīhī**, **tūē̃** for **tūhī**. For the third personal pronoun singular **ese**, **ose**, are common. **ese**, **ose**, precede a preposition, as **ese dā**, **ose nū̃**. It is the usual form for the agent, **ose ḍiṭṭhā**, he saw.

In the nominative we get **ēhwāī**, **ihō**, **ēhōī** and **ūhō**, **ūhā**, **ōhwāī**. In some districts **ēk͟hā**, **ēk͟hāī**, **ōk͟hā**, **ōk͟hāī** are used. These too are emphatic.

wī also is added to the pronouns, giving rise in the case of **maī** and **tū** to the contractions **mawī̃**, **mammī̃**, **tuwī̃**, **tumī̃**, while **maī wī** and **tū wī** are sometimes heard.

Interrogative Pronouns.

Interrogative pronouns are as follows :—**kauṇ**, who, **kī**, what.

	Singular.	Plural.	Only singular.
Nominative ..	**kauṇ.**	**kauṇ.**	**kī.**
Agent ..	**kis or kin.**	**kinhā̃.**	none.
Genitive ..	**kihdā kisdā,** etc.	**kinhā̃ dā,** etc.	**kāhdā, kāsdā,** etc.

The following table gives the most common pronominal forms :—

Class of Pronoun.		Absolute.	Oblique.	Quantity.	Size.	Likeness.	Share.
Near demonstrative		ēh (this)	ēs, eh	innā (thus much).	ēḍḍā (thus big).	ajēhā, ēhōjēhā. (like this).	innwā̂ (such).
Far demonstrative		ōh (that)	ōs, oh	unnā, ōnnā (so much).	ōḍḍā (so big).	uhōjēhā (like that).	ōnnwā̂ (such).
Interrogative.	*m f.*	kauṇ (who ?)	kis				
	n.	kī (what ?)	kāh	kinnā (how much ?)	kēḍḍā (how big ?)	kēhā *m.* kēhī *f.* (like what ?)	kinnwā̂ (what share ?)
	adjective	kehṛā (which ?)	..				
Relative	..	jehṛa (who)	jis ..	jinnā (as much).	jēḍḍā (as big).	jēhā *m.* jēhī *f.* (like which).	jinnwā̂ (as much).
Indefinite	*m. sing.*	kōī someone anyone	kisē *sing.*				
	m. pl.	kōī some	kāsē (*very* indefinite).				
	n.	kujjh something.					

OTHER PRONOMINAL FORMS.

kōī and **jō** are declined as follows :—

	Singular.	Plural.	
Nominative	**kōī**	**kōī**	some one, anyone.
Oblique	**kisē**	not	found.
Nominative	**jō**	**jō.**	
Oblique	**jis**	**jinhā̃.**	

In addition to the forms here given for the oblique singular of **kauṇ** and **jō** the following are found—**kih, jih.** Thus we get not only **kisdā, kisnū̃, jisdā, jisnū̃** but also **kihdā, kihnū̃, jihdā, jihnū̃**. The agent is **kis, kisnē** or **kihnē, jis, jisnē, jihnē,** but not **kih** or **jih** alone.

ēhō jēhā	*m.*	the same as this.
ēhō jēhī	*f.*	
uhō jēhā	*m.*	the same as that.
uhō jēhī	*f.*	
ajēhā kajēhā	*m.*	so so (i.e. inferior).
ajēhī kajēhī	*f.*	

hōr, has **hōr** or **hori** in sing. oblique; in the plural it has nominative **hōr,** agent and prepositional **hōrnā̃,** locative **hōrnī̃.**

The word **horī** (*obl.* **horā̃**) is used in the plural in a curious way as a sign of respect for a third person, somewhat like **sāhb** or **jī.**—nominative **hōrī,** agent and prepositional **horā̃.**

mērē bhrā horī āē nē̃	my brother has come.
Natthū horā̃ ākheā	**Natthū** said.

horī, horā̃, can never take the accent, so **bhrā horī** is pronounced almost like **bhrāorī,** with raised tone.

jēhā (*fem.* **jēhī**) is used after an adjective to mean 'a little,' 'rather,' *e.g.*—

ciṭṭā jēhā waṭṭā, a whitish stone.

sārā is used with a slightly emphatic sense after some adjectives signifying big or much. **waḍḍā sārā,** decidedly big; **ēḍḍā sārā,** so big.

āpē, āpī, āpū̃, āpō̃, āpēī, self, both in absolute and agent, *e.g.*—

maī̃ āpē gēā	I went myself.
ōs āpē kītā	he did it himself.

The genitive is **apṇā**, own, and the locative plural is **āpē wicc, āpō wicc**, among themselves. The distributive of **apṇā** is **apṇā apṇā, āpō dhāpṇā, āpō apṇā** :—**āpō dhāpṇī marzī** or **apṇi apṇi marzī**, each one's wish.

hamātaṛ means people like us, **tumhātaṛ**, people like you, as, **tumhātaṛā̃ wāstē saukhā e, hamātaṛā wāstē aukhā e**, it is easy for people like you, difficult for people like us.

The following pronominal adjectives should be noted. **sabbh** all, emphatic **sabbhe, sabbhō**, all of them, prep. **sabbhnā̃**, loc. **sabbhnī**.

Nominative plural.	Prepositional.	Meaning.
kaī	**kaiā̃**	some.
bāzē	**bāzeā̃**	some.
bauht, bauhtē	**bauhteā̃**	many.
bāhḷē	**bāhḷeā̃**	many.
cōkhē	**cōkheā̃**	many.
baṛē	**baṛeā̃**	many.
ghaṭṭ	**ghaṭṭā̃**	few.

ikknā̃, used in the prepositional plural, but not found in the nominative, means some.

Of the above it will be seen that bāhḷē, **cōkhē, baṛē** are simply the plural of the adjectives **bāhḷā, cōkhā, baṛā.**

ghaṭṭ waddh, few more, more or less, is generally used to mean few, or, as an adverb, very little.

Compound pronouns are jō **kōī, jehṛā kōī**, whoever, declined regularly, but always in the singular.

kōī kōī, few; always singular.

kōī na kōī, some one or other, **kōī . . kōī, (singular) some . .** others. **har kōī, jehṛā kōī,** every one **(har is not declined) ; kōī nehī̃,** no one.

kujjh na kujjh, something or other, **kujjh nehī̃**, nothing.

kujjh kujjh, a little.

hōr is often used with the sense of 'else,' as **hōr kōī**, some one else, **hōr kī**, what else, **hōr kauṇ**, who else. **hōr kī is frequently** contracted to **hōr**, thus **te hōr?** what else ? *i.e.*, what else could it be ? what else would you expect ?

ADVERBS.

What may be called the pronominal adverbs are shown in the following table in continuation of the similar table of pronouns. The forms **ēttal, ēddhar**, etc., sometimes, but rarely, express 'rest.'

Class.	Manner.	Time.	Place (rest).	Place (motion).	Condition.	Cause.
Near demonstrative.	**aiñ, iñ** (thus) **es tarhā̃.**	**huṇ** (now) ..	**ētthē, ēttal** (here)	**ētthē, ēttal, ēddhar** (hither).	..	..
Far demonstrative.	....	**odō̃** **tadō̃** (then). **(tad)**	**ōtthē, ōttal** (there).	**ōtthē, ōttal, ōddhar** (thither).	**tā̃** (then)	**tā̃, taddē.**
Interrogative.	**kikaṇ, kikaṇā̃, kikū̃, kikar, kikarā̃, kiñ, kis tarhā̃.** (how)?	**kadō̃** (when ?) **(kad).**	**kitthē, kittal** (where ?)	**kitthē, kittal, kiddhar** (whither ?)	..	**kiū̃** (why ?) **kāhnū̃, kāh de laī, kāh de jōgā̃.**
Relative ..	**jikaṇ** or **jikar, jis tarhā̃, jiwō̃.** (as) ..	**jadō̃** (when) .. **(jad).**	**jitthē, jittal** (where)	**jitthē, jittal, jiddhar** (whither).	**jē** or **jēkar** (If).	**kiū̃jō** (because). **kiū̃ paī.**
Indefinite. .	**kiwē̃** (somehow).	**kadē** or **kadī̃ kadāī̃** (sometime or sometimes).	**kitale** (somewhere).	**kitale, kidhare, kite** (somewhither).	..	..

Other common adverbs are—

ADVERBS OF PLACE.

urē, urā̃	hither.
parē, parhā̃	farther off, beyond.
nēṛē	near.
dūr	far.
aggē or agāhā̃	ahead.
picchē or pishā̃	behind.
sāhmṇē	in front.
uttē, utā̃	above.
bhuñē̃, bhūē̃	on the ground.
urār	on this side.
pār	on the further side.
agērē	ahead.
pichērē or pishērē	behind.
kōḷ, kōḷe	close by.
hēṭh, hēṭhā̃, thallē	below.
nāḷ	near, with.
bannē	outside.

ADVERBS OF TIME.

jadō̃, tadō̃	when, then.
odō̃	then.
aje	as yet.
ajj	to-day.
ajjēī	this very day.
kall	yesterday.
bhaḷkē, kall	to-morrow.
parsō̃	the day before yesterday. / the day after to-morrow.
cauth	the fourth day (forward or back.)
panjauth	the fifth day (forward or back.)
chĕauth	the sixth day (forward or back.)
paund saṭṭē, paihlū̃, paihlā̃, paihlē	at first, at once.

phēr, muṛ	again.
ōṛak, chēkṛē, chēkaṛ	at last.
hālī	at present.
jhaṭ, jhaṭ paṭ	at once.
dine, diṇe	by day.
rātī̃	by night.
shāmī̃	in the evening.
ais wārī or wērī, ais phērē, ait wārī or wērī	this time.
aitkī̃, aitkā̃ or aitkī	this time, this year.
ais sāl	this year.
par or parū̃	last year.
parār	the year before last.
aundē sāl	next year.
aggē nū̃	in future.
nitt, hamēshā, sadā	always.
sawēlē, sawaktē	early.
kuwele	late, at the wrong time.
dhammī	at dawn.
jhalāṅghē	at sunrise.
fajrī̃	in the morning.
dō paihrī̃	at noon.
weḷe sir, wakat sir	in time, at the proper time.
innē wicc	in the meantime.

The following names are common for different daily times. The time given in each case is only approximate; in some cases it varies according to the season of the year:—

sarghī wēḷā	an hour and a half before dawn.
namāz wēḷā	forty-five minutes before dawn.
dhammī wēḷā	dawn.
muhânjḷā, jhusmusṛā	time of morning twilight.
fajr	morning, especially early morning.

waḍḍēwēḷā	morning, especially early morning.
chāh wēḷā (lassī weḷa)	8 or 9 A.M.
rōṭī wēḷā	about 10 or 11 A.M.
kūḷā bhattē wēḷā	10 A.M.
bhattē wēḷā	about 11 or later.
dopaihr	midday.
kaccī pēshī	about 1 P.M.
pēshī	about 2 P.M.
nikki ḍīgar	3 P.M.
ḍīgar	4 or 5 P.M.
lauḍhē wēḷā	about 5 P.M.
shām	about sunset.
tarkāḷā̃	about half an hour after sunset.
ḍūṅghi shām	when full darkness sets in.
khau pīyā	about 8 P.M.
sōtā	about 9 or 10 P.M.
rāt	night.

Other Adverbs.

kīkaṇ, kīkar, kikū̃, kīkaṇā̃, kīkarā̃	how ?
jīkaṇ, jikar, jiwē̃	as.
kiwē̃	somehow, with difficulty
aíwē̃	anyhow.
āhō, akhō, āh, hā̃, ā, hāhō	yes.
na, nehī̃	not, no.
āhā̃	no.
ukkā	quite, thoroughly.
ukkā, bilkull, aslō̃	altogether.
zarūr, jarūr or lā jarūr	certainly.
waddh	more.
wakkhō wakkh	separately.

hāĩ māĩ	easily.
jhaw jhabdẽ jabdē	quickly, recently.
shitābī jaldī chētī	quickly.
te	then, particle of emphasis and reasoning.
jũ	when, for a long time.
shaid, shait	perhaps, 'I do not know.'
karīb	nearly.
maslan	for instance.
yānī	that is.
ī, hī	adverb of emphasis.
<u>kh</u>ā̃	then, particle of reasoning (used only with imperat.).
nāḷē	moreover.
taddē tā̃, tāī̃, tàiẽ	for that reason, then, in that case.
whalā̃	particle of argument, all right then.
ukkā na, attē na	not at all.
bī, wī	also, too.
hōr	more, otherwise, what else ?
ghaṭṭ	less.
ghaṛī muṛī jhaṭē bindē, jhaṭē jhaṭē bhaũ jhaũ ghaṛī ghaṛī	repeatedly.
masā̃	hardly.
hauḷī	slowly, softly.
yōrō yōrī or zōrō zōrī or badō badī.	by force.
nishaṅg or beshakk	of course, without doubt.
wārō waṭṭī, wārī wārī	by turns.
mū̃h drūī āhmṇe sāhmṇe	face to face.

uṅ	anyhow, after all, without special reason.
sahj nāḷ, **sahjē sahjē** **sahē sahē**	} quietly.
malkṛī	quietly, suddenly.
accaṇcēt **acāṇcak** **cāṇcakke**	} suddenly.
muṇḍhō̃	from the beginning.
palleō̃	at one's own expense.
(mērē) pēṭē	in (my) responsibility.
hōr dare	somewhere else.
dhigāṇē	uselessly, to no purpose.

Some of these adverbs are the locative case of substantives or adjectives, and others are locatives of nouns signifying time or place similarly used, *e.g.*,—

rātī at night. **waḍḍē wēḷē** in the morning.
fajrī in the morning.

There is a difference in usage between **baṛā** and **waḍḍā**. The latter means big in size, *great* in age or dignity, and is not frequent in connection with abstract ideas. **baṛā** is used with abstract nouns also in the adverbial sense of very and in the sense of many or much.

waḍḍē jaṇē sāṇ	they were big men.
baṛē jaṇē sāṇ	there were many men.
ōh **baṛē waḍḍē**jaṇē sāṇ	they were very big men.
baṛā jhallpuṇā	great folly.
ōh **baṛā ṭurdā** e	he walks much or fast.

Most adjectives *can* be used adverbially, agreeing with their noun or pronoun, and some are used in no other way. Thus we have **nirā,** only, **ucēcā,** especially, **ḍāhḍā,** lit. severe, hard, **baṛā,** great, **sōhṇā,** beautiful. Adjectives which do not change their form for agreement with nouns do not change when used as adverbs.

ḍāhḍī caṅgī gā	an exceedingly good cow.
ōh ucēcī geī	she went specially.

nirā ēh kamm nehī	not only this work.
ghōṛī baṛī sōhṇī ṭurdī e	the mare goes very well or prettily.

Comparison.

Adverbs are compared in the same way as adjectives. It will suffice to give examples.

sāreā̃ wiccõ ōh trikkhā ṭurdā e, he walks fastest of all.

kutūrē nāḷõ bilūṇgā bauhtā bhajjdā e, a kitten runs more or faster than a puppy.

The absolute superlative, *i.e.*, the idea of very, exceedingly, is formed by means of such adjectives, used as adverbs, as **baṛā, ḍāhḍā,** bauhtā, **bāhḷā,** all of which agree with the noun qualified, and bauht which is not declined.

ōh bāhḷā ṭurdā e, he walks a lot.

ōh bauht jhallā we, he is very mad.

See also the examples given above. It cannot be too clearly remembered that the idea of intensity is never obtained by repeating a word. Repetition gives a distributive sense. See p. 338.

Prepositions.

Some of the commonest prepositions have been given along with the nouns. They are repeated here with some others. They are nearly always placed after the noun they govern, as in the English forms " henceforth," " therewith," " hereby," " homeward," " seawards," and the noun is always put in the prepositional form. Some of them are the locative case of nouns and govern the preceding noun with the help of the preposition **dē,** of (feminine **dī**), *e.g.*, **piṇḍ dē nēṛē,** close to the village. Some are used both with and without **dē,** *e.g.*, **ōs wal** or **ōh dē wal,** towards him. The only prepositions that are declinable are those of the genitive, **dā, dē, deā̃, dī, dīā̃** (of), and **wargā,** like, which agree with the governing noun in gender, number and case like adjectives. **wargā** is really an adjective. See **jōgā, gōcrā,** p. 303.

ōh mērē wargī e she is like me.

Prepositions.

nē	by (for the agent).	**bābat** (*f.*) **bārē wicc**	about.

nū̃	to, for.
thō̃, thī̃, tē, tō̃, -ō̃	from.
wicc	in.
tē	on. at, to (a place).
uttē	above, upon.
kōḷ, kōḷe	with, in possession of.
nāḷ	along with.
binā, bin, bājhō̃, bijn	without. except.
sawā, wall, wallō̃, pāsē, sēhd (*f.*)	towards.
wishkār, wickār.	between.
hēṭh, thallē	below.
aggē	before.
andar	inside.
āḷē duāḷē	on all sides of.
wāstē, wātē, laī, khātar (*f.*)	for the sake of.

tāī̃, tōṛī, tīkar, tākar, sīdhā	up to. as far as.
tīkar, tōṛī, tāṛī, tāī̃	till.
nērē	near.
mūjab	according to.
zabānī (*f.*)	by word of, mouth of.
urē, urār	on this side.
parē	beyond.
saṇē	together with.
sāhmṇē	in front of.
wāṅgū̃, wāṅgar, wāṅgur, wāṅgaṇ, wargā, hār	like.
picchē, magar	behind.
bāhr	outside.
duāḷē, cufērē, cārcufērē, cufēr	round about.
rāhī̃ (*m. pl.*)	by means of.

The above prepositions, with the exception of nē, nū̃, thō̃, thī̃, tē, (when it means 'from') and -ō̃, are added to the genitive of the first and second pers. pronouns.

For mārā and sadkā see below. Sir, sār, see p. 358.

The following do not take the preposition **dē or dī :—nē, nū̃,-õ, tāī̃, tōṛī, tākar, hār.**

Of those which take the preposition **sēhd, k͟hātar, rāhī̃, bābat zabānī** are feminine and take **dī** for **dē**. They are marked (*f.*) above.

Most of those which are used with **dē or dī** can also be used without it, but the following nearly always have it :—**pāsē, sēhd, wishkār, thallē, bārē, wicc, āḷē duāḷē** (though not necessarily the simple **duāḷē**), **k͟hātar, bāhar, cār cufērē, cufērē, cufēr, rāhī̃, urār, mūjab** ; the following rarely have **dē :—thõ, thī̃, tõ, tē** (from), **tīkar.**

Sometimes the prepositional affix **-õ** is employed instead of **dē**, thus **piṇḍõ parē**, beyond the village.

Similarly this **õ** may be added to all prepositions whose meaning admits the addition of the idea of " from," thus **ghar wiccõ āeā**, he came from within the house, so **bāhrõ**, from outside, **picchõ**, from behind, **kōḷõ**, from beside.

This form of the preposition (with **-õ**) when followed by **dī** gives the sense of " by the way of," thus **wiccõ dī** means by way of inside, *i.e.*, through. It is not clear what word, if any, is understood. Probably it is the locative form, **rāhī̃**, as we have **mērī rāhī̃**, by means of me, where **mērī** is loc. pl. in agreement with **rāhī̃.**

mērē kōḷõ dī laṅgheā	he passed close to me.
kuṛh dē picchõ dī geā	he went by way of behind the cowhouse.
nēṛeõ dī na jāh	do not pass by near.

In the case of a few of these still another form is found with the same sense, **-dū̃** taking the place of **-õ dī.** This is heard only with **kōḷ, nāḷ, wicc, hēṭh, nēṛē.**

kōḷdū̃, nāḷdū̃, wiccdū̃, heṭhdū̃, nēṛēdū̃ have the same meaning as **kōḷõ, dī, nāḷõ dī, wiccõ dī, hēṭhõ dī, nēṛeõ dī.**

haḷkā kuttā ōh diā̃ lattā̃ dē hēṭhdū̃ geā the mad dog went by under his legs.

mārā and (**dā**) **sadkā** have a peculiar construction. **mārā**, on account of, is used in reference to mental conditions, and agrees with the subject, although the preposition **dā** intervenes.

ḍar dā mārā nehī̃ āeā, through fear he did not come.

sharm dīā̃ mārīā̃ kuṛīā̃ kūndīā̃ nehī̃, through shyness the girls do not speak. **dē mārēā̃** (indeclinable) may also be used in all cases.

(**dā**) **sadkā** also means on account of, but with a much wider range. When a noun is governed by **dā sadkā**, **dā** does not change, with a pronoun **dā** changes to **dē**.

peō dā sadkā	on account of the father.
bēbbē dā sadkā	on account of the mother.

mērē sadkā, on my account. **kih dē sadkā**, on whose account. Occasionally with a noun, too, **dā** is changed to **dē**.

Some nouns preceded by **dē** are used as prepositions, as **sababb**, reason, **thā̃** place; as **ōhdē sababb**, on account of him.

tū̃ kih dē thā̃ kamm karnā ē̃, in whose place, instead of whom are you working?

The adjective **jōgā** is used as a preposition, and agrees with the following noun. It means fit for, suitable to, and so simply 'for,' **guzārē jōgā**, sufficient for sustenance; **mērē jōgī rōṭī leā**, bring bread for me. Similar is **gōcrā**, as **tuhāḍḍe gōcrā kamm e**, there is work for you (to do).

CONJUNCTIONS.

Common conjunctions are as follows:—

te **hōr**	and.
jēkar **jē**	if.
bhā̃wē̃	although.
bhā̃wē̃ .. bhā̃wē̃ **cāhē cāhē**	whether....or.
sagō̃, sagō̃	on the contrary, not only so but.
nehī̃ tē	otherwise.
kyū̃jō, kyū̃pai	because.
pai **bhai**	that.
yā̃, jā̃	or.

yā̃ . . . . yā̃ **jā̃ . . . jā̃**	either . . or.
na . . . na	neither . . nor.
par	but.
matē, cētā	lest, that not, so that if.
kĕ	or, that.

Interjections.

In calling to a person, the translation of the interjection O varies according to the sex of the person addressing or addressed. These forms of address imply that each person is addressed as tū̃, thou.

ō, ōē	man calling to man.	wē	woman calling to man.
ē	man calling to woman.	nī	woman calling to woman.

Husband and wife avoid calling each other by name, but if possible bring in a son's name, usually the eldest son's and less frequently a daughter's if she be the eldest :—

Karm Bashk dā cāccā.	Karm Bakhsh's father.	**Jhaṇḍū dī bēbbē.**	Jhandu's mother.

hē is used in sorrow, joy, or wonder, *e.g.*—

hē sacceā Rabbā	O true God.
hē pāk Parwardigārā	O pure Cherisher.

Other interjections or exclamations are :—

jīwē̃ tū̃	mayest thou live.
Khudā jāṇē	God knows.
kī nā̃ lēīdā e	what d'ye call it ?
majāl e	impossible ! never !
dhann	bravo ! blessings on !
phiṭṭ	curse on !
hāē hāē	alas !
hōē hōē	for shame, alas !
halā	very well, yes, indeed ! (surprise).
haī, āhē̃	expressive of displeasure.
hāl ōē	expressive of pain.
lai	expressive of protest.
durē	get away ! (to a dog).
" **jhā** "	" peekaboo," (to a baby).

ũ, hũ	don't! don't!
chir chir or chirē.	get away! (to a cat).
jhaw, chētī, etc.	quick.
khlō jā	wait a bit.
jam jam	by all means.
jam jam ā	welcome.
ãwī, ãwē	welcome.
sadkē, ballē ashkē, shābāsē, shābā.	bravo.
ballē, ballē, bāī, bāī,	astonishment.
ma<u>kh</u>ē	said I.
a<u>kh</u>ē	said he, they say.
ōh jāṇē	it does not matter.
<u>kh</u>abrē, <u>kh</u>aurē	I don't know.
hēkkhā̃, wēkkhā̃	expressive of incredulity.
jī sadkē sir matthe te	by all means, with pleasure.
caṅgā	very well, good
shukr e	thanks be (to God).
<u>kh</u>air mehr e or Khairi mihre	all is well, it's all right.
bismillāh	in God's name.
radd balāī dūr balāī	may misfortunes be far from thee, used as a welcome by women.
bhaṭṭh	curse on, *lit.* to the oven with.

hēkkhā, wēkkhā̃, are probably contracted from wēkh, look and <u>kh</u>ā̃.

Modes of Address.

The following are frequently heard :—

To a friend ..	yār gall suṇ.
To a stranger ..	ōē bhāīā, bhaleā lōkā, sāī lōkā, mīā̃.
To an old man	bābbā or buḍḍheā, O old man!
To a father ..	cāccā, mīā̃ (by Musalmāns), lāllā (Hindūs).
To a grandfather	bābbā.
To a woman ..	bhaiṇ, sister; māī, mother.
To a old woman	bēbbē (mother); mātā, ammā.
To a grandmother or old woman.	mā̃, māī.

20

THE VERB.

Transitive and Intransitive.

Verbs may be divided into intransitive and transitive Verbs. In a great many cases an intransitive root has a corresponding transitive root, usually formed by strengthening the vowel of the root; and this again can often be turned into a double-transitive or causal verb by a further change in the root.

Formation of Transitive Verbs.

A transitive or double-transitive verb is formed by adding to the root -ā or -wā, the vowel of the original root being shortened, generally from ā to a, from ē or ī to i, from ō or ū to u, sometimes otherwise.

The root thus formed becomes a new verb, subject to the usual inflections.

Infinitive.	Meaning.	Transitive or Double-Transitive.	Meaning.
mārnā	strike.	**marwāṇā**	cause to be struck.
bhajjṇā	run.	**bhajāṇā**	cause to run.
pīṇā	drink.	**piāṇā**	cause to drink.
bhaũṇā	turn.	**bhũāṇā**	cause to turn.
cukkṇā	raise.	**cukāṇā**	cause to raise.
appaṛnā	reach.	**apṛāṇā**	cause to reach.
pāṇā	put.	**puāṇā**	cause to put.
dēṇā	give.	**duāṇā**	cause to give.

Most of the common roots, however, form their transitive irregularly, the vowel being generally strengthened, and sometimes the consonants changed.

Intransitive.		*Transitive.*	
Infinitive.	Meaning.	Infinitive.	Meaning.
bhajjṇā	break.	**bhannṇā**	break.
ṭuṭṭṇā	break.	**trōṛnā, tōṛnā**	break.
paiṇā	lie.	**pāṇā**	put.
gaihṇā	be threshed.	**gāhṇā**	thresh.

Infinitive.	Meaning.	Infinitive.	Meaning.
ḍhaiṇā	fall down.	ḍhāṇā	knock down.
laihṇā	come down.	lāhṇā	take down.
laggṇā	be applied.	lāṇā	apply.
chuṭṭnā	escape.	chaḍḍṇā	set free.
wikṇā	be sold.	wēcṇā	sell.
nikalṇā	go out.	kaḍḍhṇā	put out.
waṛnā	go into.	wāṛnā	put into.
ḍubbṇā	be drowned.	ḍōbṇā	drown.
ṭurnā	move, walk.	ṭōrnā	make to move, walk.
caṛhnā	mount, go up.	cāṛhnā	put up, cause to mount.
nikkhaṛnā	separate.	nakhēṛnā	separate.
phissṇā	be squeezed.	phēhṇā	squeeze.
dissṇā	be seen.	{ wēkhṇā	see.
		dassṇā	point out.
pāṭṇā	be torn.	pāṛnā	tear.
riṛhnā	roll.	rēṛhnā	roll.
ruṛhnā	be swept away.	rōṛhnā	sweep away.
saṛnā	burn.	sāṛnā	burn.
ḍhukkṇā	arrive.	ḍhōṇā	carry.
auṇā	come.	aṇwāṇā	cause to be brought.
tapṇā	be hot.	tāṇā	heat.
khussṇā	be seized.	khōhṇā	seize.
rijjhṇā	be cooked.	rinnhṇā	cook.
ḍiggṇā	fall.	ḍēgṇā	cause to fall.
guācṇā	be lost.	guāṇā	lose.
khaṛācṇā	be lost.	khaṛāṇā	lose.
dhuccṇā or dhuppṇā	be washed.	dhōṇā	wash.
cubbhṇā	pierce (needle, thorn).	cōbhṇā	cause to pierce.
khubbhṇā	stick (in mud, etc.).	khōbhṇā	cause to stick.

Infinitive.	Meaning.	Infinitive.	Meaning.
uggharṇā	open (intr.).	ughēṛṇā	open (trans.), especially of eyes, mouth, fist, awaking.
phasṇa	be entangled.	phasāṇa	entangle.
wijjhṇā	be pierced.	winnhṇā	pierce.
chiṛnā	go to pasture.	chēṛnā	take to pasture.
bhijjṇā	be moistened.	bheōṇā	moisten.
waggṇā	be ploughed.	wāhṇā	plough.
juṛnā	be joined.	jōṛnā	join.
muṛnā	go back.	mōṛnā	turn back.
pīsṇā	be ground.	pīhṇā	grind.
gujjhṇā	be kneaded.	gunnhṇā	knead.
traihṇā	be startled.	trāhṇā	startle.
ḍaihṇā	be placed (bed, etc.).	ḍāhṇā	place.
bajjhṇā	be fastened.	bannhṇā	fasten.
raihṇā	stay.	rakkhṇā	place.
jammṇā	be born.	jammṇā	bring forth young.
cōṇā	trickle through.	cōṇā	milk.

ākhṇā, say, has a causative **akhwāṇā** with two meanings, (*i*) cause to say, (*ii*) be called or named ; **bōlṇā** has **bulāṇā**, call or cause to say.

Formation of Causal Verbs.

Some difficulties are removed if one observes the following vowel changes which frequently occur in forming causal or transitive verbs. A double consonant becomes single.

a and **ai** become **ā** : **balṇā**, burn, **bāḷṇā** ; **traihṇā**, be startled, **trāhṇā** ; so also **saṛnā**, be burnt ; **caṛhnā**, ascend ; **marnā**, die ; **waṛnā**, enter ; **ḍhalṇā**, be poured in mould ; **uddhalṇā**, elope ; **ubbalṇā**, boil ; **paiṇā**, fall ; **ḍhaiṇā**, fall ; **laihṇā**, descend ; **gaihṇā**, be threshed ; **ḍaihṇā**, be placed (bed, etc).

a in second unaccented syllable of root sometimes becomes **ē** : **ukhaṛnā**, be loosened **ukhēṛṇā** ; so also **nikkhaṛnā**, be separated, **nikhērṇā**; **uggharṇā**, open (eyes, etc.), **ughērṇā**; **uddharṇā**, be ripped, **udhērṇā**; **nibbarṇā**, be settled, **nabērṇā**; the double consonant of course becomes single.

i becomes ē: **riṛhnā**, roll, **rēṛhnā**; so also **chiṛnā**, go to pasture; **giṛnā**, be turned (wheel, etc.); **ḍiggṇā**, fall, **ḍegṇā**; note too **wikṇā**, be sold, **wēcṇā**.

u becomes o: **ghuḷṇā**, melt, **ghōḷṇā**; so also **ḍubbṇā**, sink, **ḍōbṇā**; **muṛnā**, turn; **ruṛhnā**, flow away; **cubbhṇā**, pierce; **khubbhṇā**, sink (in mud, etc.); **juṛnā**, be joined; **khurnā**, melt; note also with change of consonant **ṭuṭṭṇā**, break, **tōṛnā**, **trōṛnā**; **ḍhukkṇā**, draw near, **ḍhoṇā**; **khussṇā**, be seized, **khohṇā**; **dhuccṇā** or **dhuppṇā**, be washed, **dhōṇā**; **juppṇā**, be yoked, **joṇā** (sometimes **juttṇā**, be yoked, **jōtṇā**).

The Infinitive or Verbal Noun.

The infinitive is formed by adding **-ṇā** to the root. If the root ends in r, ṛ, rh or ṛh, ḷ, ṇ, the termination is **-nā**.

Examples.

Root.	Meaning.	Verbal Noun.	Meaning.
jā	go.	**jāṇā**	going, to go, etc.
bhajj	run.	**bhajjṇā**	running.
lai	take.	**laiṇa**	taking.
wēkh	see.	**wēkhṇā**	seeing.
wāh	plough.	**wāhṇā**	ploughing.
kar	do.	**karnā**	doing.
nikaḷ	go out.	**nikaḷṇā**	going out.
khlō	stand.	**khlōṇā**	standing.
khā	eat.	**khāṇā**	eating.
pī	drink.	**pīṇā**	drinking
dē	give.	**dēṇā**	giving.
māreā jā	be struck.	**māreā jāṇā**	being struck.
bhaũ	turn.	**bhaũṇā**	turning.

Irregular.

ā	come.	**auṇā**	coming.
nahā	wash.	**nahauṇā**	washing.

The infinitive may be used as gerund, and as a gerundive, though these names as applied to Panjābī are only approximately correct, and it is difficult sometimes to decide under which head to class a particular use of the infinitive.

The gerund is declined by adding ṇ to the root if the root ends in a vowel or a vowel followed by h, n if the root ends in r, ṛ, rh or ṛh, ḷ, ṇ and -aṇ if it ends in any other consonant. It is frequently used to express will or necessity, and when so used takes the subject in the agent or dative case. See further details under Syntax, p. 368.

The Verbal Agent.

(1) The verbal agent is formed by adding wāḷā or āḷā to the oblique form of the verbal noun or infinitive. This is declinable like nouns in -ā, taking -ī in the feminine.

Examples.

Root.	Meaning.	Verbal Agent.	Meaning.
kar	do.	karanwāḷā	a doer.
bhajj	run.	bhajjaṇāḷā	a runner.
pī	drink.	pīṇwāḷā	a drinker.
ā	come.	auṇwāḷā	a comer.
dē	give.	dēṇwāḷā	a giver.

This verbal agent often expresses the idea that something ought to be, also that something is about to be. When it has the sense of "ought" it is noticeable that the active voice is often used for the passive.

ōh auṇwāḷā we	he is about to come.
ēh marammat karnwāḷā e	this requires mending.
ōh bhāṇḍē sāf karnwāḷē or hoṇwāḷē nē	those vessels should be cleaned.
ēh kapṛē dhōṇwāḷē nē	those clothes need washing.

See p. 373.

(2) Many, but not all verbs, have a second verbal agent, formed by adding -ū to the root. It expresses the idea of one who habitually does a thing.

ḍarnā, fear, ḍarū; chaḍḍṇā, leave, chaḍḍū: tū baṛā ḍarū

ādmi ē, your are a very timid man, ōh chaḍḍū nehī̃ jē, he is not one who will leave or drop the matter.

There is no rule for deciding what verbs may have this form of agent. When speaking jokingly one may use this form with verbs which do not usually employ it.

The Present Participle.

The present participle of all verbs ends in -dā, and is declinable like an adjective in -ā.

All verbs, the root of which ends in a consonant, simply add -dā to the root. Those verbs whose root ends in a vowel or a vowel followed by -h take -ndā. With the 1st and 2nd personal pronoun singular and with the 1st personal pronoun plural -dā is replaced by -nā, and -nē respectively in the Present Indicative. For the feminine -nā and -nē become -nī and -nīā̃.

Examples.

Root.	Meaning.	Present Participle.	Meaning.
mar	die.	mardā	dying.
ṭur	move.	ṭurdā	moving.
wik	be sold.	wikdā	being sold.
nikaḷ	come out.	nikaḷdā	coming out.
pī	drink.	pīndā	drinking.
jiū	live.	jiūndā	living.
laih	descend.	laihndā	descending.
khlō	stand.	khlōndā	standing.
pai	lie.	paindā	lying.
saū	sleep.	saundā	sleeping.
bhaū	turn.	bhaundā	turning.
piā	make to drink.	piāndā	making to drink.
bhajā	make to run.	bhajāndā	making to run.
apṛā	cause to reach.	apṛāndā	causing to reach.
kar	do.	kardā	doing.
mār	strike.	mārdā	striking.
ṭōr	make to move.	ṭōrdā	making to move.
dē	give.	dēndā	giving.
lai	take.	laindā	taking.
chaḍḍ	let go.	chaḍḍdā	letting go.

Root.	Meaning.	Present Participle.	Meaning.
wēc	sell.	**wēcdā**	selling.
kaḍḍh	put out.	**kaḍḍhdā**	putting out.
sāṛ	burn.	**sāṛdā**	burning.
mōṛ	turn.	**mōṛdā**	turning.
bheõ	moisten.	**bheōndā**	moistening.
khā	eat.	**khāndā**	eating.

Irregular.

wēkh	see.	**wēhndā** or **wēkhdā**	seeing.
ākh	say.	**āhndā** or **ākhdā**	saying.
ā	come.	**aundā**	coming.
nahā	wash.	**nahaundā**	washing.

The present participle is used with **hōeā,** the past participle of **hōṇā, to denote a state.**

nakhēṛdā hōeā in the state of separating.

The Past Participle.

Past Participle in -eā or -ā.

Past participles end in -eā or -ā, and occasionally in both. It is not possible to give such rules as will enable students to decide in every case which form to use, but the following will perhaps be of some use. (The presence or absence of h makes no difference to the rules.)

(1) Irregular past participles, whether transitive or intransitive, end in -ā, not -eā : **traihṇā, be startled, traṭṭhā : sihāṇṇā,** recognise, **sihāttā** (but note **sihāṇeā** in -eā, a regular past part.).

Exceptions : **marnā,** die, **moeā : jāṇā, go. geā.**

Slight vowel changes are not here considered irregularities.

(2) The following intransitive verbs whose roots end in a consonant have past parts. in -ā:—

bujjhṇā be extinguished (but note the transitive bujjhṇā, guess, solve, **bujjheā**): **ḍiggṇā, fall : ḍubbṇā,** sink : juttṇā, be yoked, harnessed : **labbhṇā, be found (cf. below labbhṇā, find)**: laggṇā, be applied, beg... : **pāṭṇā, be torn : ṭuṭṭṇā,** break : bhajjṇā, break (cf. below **bhajjṇā, run**) : **ḍhukkṇā,** draw near.

The following intrans. verbs have either -ā or -eā :—

bhajjṇā, run : **bhijjṇā**, get wet : **bajjhṇā**, be fastened : **dhuccṇā**, be washed : **gijjhṇā**, become accustomed : rijjhṇā, be cooked : **rujjhṇā**, be busy : **wajjṇā**, strike : **wijjhṇā**, be pierced : **chuṭṭṇā**, escape : **khubbhṇā**, stick (in mud, etc.) : **gijjhṇā** and **rujjhṇā** have also irreg. past. parts. which of course end in -ā, **giddhā**, **ruddhā** : with **bhijjṇā** -eā is rare.

(3) All regular verbs with roots ending in a vowel, and all regular transitive verbs (whether the roots end in a vowel or not) have past parts. in -eā, not -ā : **khṛāṇā**, lose, **khṛāeā** : dhrūhṇā, drag, **dhrūheā**.

Exceptions : **cubbhṇā**, pierce, **cubbhā**, and **cubbheā** : **labbhṇā**, find, **labbhā** and **labbheā**.

Verbal Roots ending in g, kh.

Confusion is sometimes caused by the change of g into g̲, and kh into k̲h̲. The following general rules will be a guide :—

(1) Verbs with roots ending in a single g or kh change g to g̲ and kh to k̲h̲ in the simple imperative sing. (not in the -ī form), and when d, k and n (but not ṇ) follow : thus—

wēkhṇā, **wēkhaṇ**, **wekhãgā**, **wekheā**, but **wēk̲h̲**, **wēk̲h̲dā** **wek̲h̲ke**, **wek̲h̲nā**.

wagṇā, **wagaṇ**, **wagegā**, **wagi**, but **wag̲ jā**, **wag̲dā**, **wag̲ke**, **wag̲nā**.

So also **ākhṇā**, say.

Some people use g̲ throughout in **wag̲ṇā** : others say **wagke**, not **wag̲ke**.

(2) Verbs with double g or kkh tend to keep gg or kkh throughout : so **ḍiggṇā**, fall ; **rakkhṇā**, place ; **sikkhṇā**, learn. It is, however, not uncommon to say **rak̲h̲dā**, **rak̲h̲**, **sik̲h̲dā**, **laggṇā**, begin, gener'lly has past part. **lag̲ā**. **lik̲h̲ṇā**, write, **bhak̲h̲ṇā**, blaze, do not come under either rule. They have k̲h̲ in every part.

(3) The causal forms have g̲ and k̲h̲ : **wak̲h̲āṇā**, show ; **ak̲h̲wāṇā**, be called, cause to be said ; **sik̲h̲āṇā**, teach ; **rak̲h̲āṇā** have placed ; **wag̲āṇā**, cause to flow.

Exception : **ḍegṇā**, make fall.

The causal of laggṇā drops the g altogether, lāṇā, attach. These rules are not strictly adhered to.

(1) The regular mode of forming the past participle is by adding -eā to the root.

Examples.

Root.	Meaning.	Past Participle.	Meaning.
mār	strike.	māreā	struck.
ā	come.	āeā	come.
saṭṭ	throw.	saṭṭeā	thrown.
ṭur	move, go.	ṭureā	moved, gone.
wēc	sell.	wēceā	sold.
hō	become.	hōeā	become.

(2) Some verbs add only -ā to the root.

Examples.

Root.	Meaning.	Past Participle.	Meaning.
labbh	be obtained.	labbhā and labbheā	obtained.
bhajj	be broken.	bhajjā	broken.
bhajj	run.	bhajjā, bhajjeā	run.

(3) Many verbs, however, form their past participle irregularly. Most of them will be found in the following list:—

Examples.

Infinitive.	Meaning.	Past Participle.	Meaning.
laihṇā	descend.	latthā latthea	come down.
dēṇā	give.	dittā	given.
wēkhṇā	see.	ḍiṭṭhā or wēkheā	seen.
bannhṇā	bind.	baddhā	bound.
nassṇā	flee.	naṭṭhā or nasseā	fled.
khaṛācṇā	be lost.	khaṛāceā or khaṛātā	lost.
khlōṇā	stand.	khlōtā	stood.
ḍhaiṇā	fall.	ḍhaṭṭhā	fallen.
sanjhāṇṇā	recognise.	sanjhātā	recognised.
sihāṇṇā	recognise.	sihātā, sihāṇeā	recognised.

Infinitive.	Meaning.	Past Participle.	Meaning.
laiṇā	take.	leā	taken.
khāṇā	eat.	khādhā	eaten.
ḍaihṇā	be placed.	ḍaṭṭhā	placed.
ḍaihṇā	be engaged in.	ḍehā	engaged in.
traihṇā	be startled.	traṭṭhā	startled.
kūṇā	speak.	kōeā	spoken.
guācṇā	be lost.	guāceā, guātā	lost.
phasṇā	be entangled.	phāthā, phaseā.	entangled.
rinnhṇā	cook.	riddhā	cooked.
rujjhṇā	be occupied.	ruddhā, rujjheā.	occupied.
winnhṇā	pierce.	winnheā, widdhā	pierced.
pīṇā	drink.	pītā	drunk.
baihṇā	sit.	baiṭhā	sat.
jāṇṇā	know.	jātā or jāṇeā	known.
jāṇā	go.	geā	gone.
paiṇā	lie.	peā	lain.
pīhṇā	grind.	pīṭhā	ground.
saũṇā	sleep.	suttā	slept.
gunnhṇā	knead.	guddhā (gunnhea)	kneaded.
nahāuṇā	bathe.	nahātā	bathed.
karnā	do.	kītā	done.
marnā	die.	mōeā	dead.
kōhṇā	butcher.	kuṭṭhā or kōheā	butchered.
āṇṇā	(not used) bring.	āndā	brought.
siũṇā	sew.	sītā	sewed.
raihṇā	stay.	rehā	stayed.
gijjhṇā	become accustomed.	giddhā, gijjheā	accustomed.

The past participle is used with hōeā, the past participle of hoṇa, become, to denote a state. With transitive verbs this is passive.

ḍiṭṭhā hōeā	seen.	**phaṇḍeā hōeā**	beaten.
geā hōeā	gone.		

Any past participle may be used as an adjective by adding **hōeā** to it, *e.g.*, **ujṛeā hōeā thā̃**, a deserted place; **khādhī hōī rōṭī**, bread that has been eaten.

In the Sialkot district instead of the form with **hōeā** we find a single word made by adding **-dā** to the past participle, thus:— **phaṇḍeādā** for **phaṇḍeā hōeā**. This has fem. **phaṇḍīḍī**, plur. **phaṇḍēdē**, fem. **phaṇḍīdīā̃**.

Conjunctive Participle.

The conjunctive participle is formed by adding **-kē** to the root.

Examples.

Part.	Meaning.
bhajjkē	having run, or running.
wēkhkē	having seen.

When this participle is repeated to express continuance or repetition **-kē** is omitted the first time, **labbh labbhkē** having kept on searching for it.

The Imperative.

(1) The ordinary imperative in the 2nd person singular consists simply of the root of the verb without any termination, and in the plural is formed by adding **-ō** to the root.

Examples.

Root.	Meaning.	*Imperative.* Second person singular.	Second person plural.
ā	come.	**ā**	**āō.**
kar	do.	**kar**	**karō.**
dē	give.	**dē (also dēh)**	**dēō (dehō).**
ṭur	start.	**ṭur**	**ṭurō.**
jā	go.	**jā (also jāh)**	**jāō (jāhō).**

Exceptions.

Root.	Meaning.	*Imperative.* Second person singular.	Second person plural.
raih	remain.	rauh	rauhō.
laih	descend.	lauh	lauhō.
pai	lie.	pau	pauō.
lai	take.	lai	lauō.

(2) The polite imperative is formed by adding to the root of the verb in the singular **-ī̃**, and in the plural **-eō** or **-iō**. If the root ends in a vowel, the terminations are sometimes **-wī̃** and **weō** or **-wīō**. It should be noted that the plural is always more polite than the singular, thus this form in order of politeness will be **takkeō, takkō, takkī̃, takk,** look.

Examples.

Root.	Meaning.	*Polite Imperative.* Singular.	Plural.	Meaning.
takk	see.	takkī̃	takkeō (-īō)	be pleased to look.
uṭṭh	get up.	uṭṭhī̃	uṭṭheō (-īō)	be pleased to get up.
ā̃	come.	ā̃wī̃	ā̃weō (-īō)	be pleased to come.

The plural polite imperative is often used with jē as uṭṭheō jē, takkeā jē.

AUXILIARY VERB OR VERB SUBSTANTIVE.

As this is used in the conjugation of ordinary verbs it is now given in its simple form contracted, the other forms being reserved for fuller treatment.

Present.

Singular.		Plural.	
maī ā̃	I am.	asī̃ ā̃	we are.
tū̃ ē̃ (aī)	thou art.	tusī̃ ō	you are.
ōh e (ai)	he, she, it is.	ōh nē̃	they are.

Past.

maī sā̃	I was.	asī̃ sā̃	we were.
tū̃ saī	thou wert.	tusī̃ sau	you were.
ōh sī	he, she, it was.	ōh sāṉ	they were.

It will be seen that it does not vary for gender.

The Present Conditional.

This tense is formed in the singular and second plural by adding the parts of the present auxiliary verb to the root. If the root ends in a vowel a w is often inserted. It is generally used in a sort of suggestive, potential or conditional sense, but in proverbs and poetry it often has the meaning of a present tense.

The third plural is formed by adding -ṇ to the root if the root ends in a vowel or a vowel followed by h, n if the root ends in ṛ, r, rh, ṛh, ḷ, ṇ and -āṇ if it ends in any other consonant.

Present Conditional Active.

Person.	Singular.	Meaning.	Plural.	Meaning.
First	**karā̃**	I may do.	**karīyē**	we may do.
Second	**karē̃**	thou mayest do.	**karō**	you may do.
Third	**karē**	he may do.	**karn**	they may do.

Exceptions.

Root.	Meaning.	Third Person Singular.
pai	lie.	**pawē.**
lai	take.	**lawē, laē.**
saũ	sleep.	**sā̃wē.**
bhaũ	turn.	**bhā̃wē.**

Examples.

maĩ kī karā̃ ?	what am I to do ?
maĩ matē mārea jā̃wā̃	lest I be beaten.
jē ōsnū̃ ākheā jāē	if it be said to him.

THE PAST CONDITIONAL TENSE.

The past conditional tense is formed (1) by using the present participle with inflection for number and gender but not for person, or (2) by the use of the present conditional with the addition of ā. This latter construction is very rare in the first singular or third plural. In the case of (1) the second sing. fem. ends in -īē̃. See Syntax, pp. 377–380.

maĩ kardā	I should have done, (if) I had done.
tū̃ kardīẽ or **kardī**	thou (*fem.*) wouldst have done, (if) thou hadst done.
asī̃ kardē	we should have done, (if) we had done.

For the second singular and the second plural the forms **kardõ** (*fem.* **kardīõ**) and **kardeõ** (*fem.* **kardīõ**) are extremely common.

Second Form.

First	..	rare	**karīyē ā.**
Second	..	**karẽ ā**	**karō ā.**
Third	..	**karē ā**	rare.

The first singular and third plural are heard.

Examples.

jē tū̃ aundīõ maĩ tainū̃ dēndā.

If thou (*f.*) hadst come I would have given thee.

tusī̃ na mandeō tā̃ gall ṭhik sī.

If you had not agreed it would have been all right.

je tusī̃ bhajjō ā tā̃ mār na khāō ā.

If you had run you would not have been beaten.

The Future Tense.

The future is formed by adding to the present conditional the termination **gā** or **dā**. In the first plural the termination is added to the first singular of the present conditional. **gā** or **dā** varies for number and gender like an adjective in **-ā**.

Future Tense **kar** (do).

maĩ karā̃ -gā or **-dā**	I shall do.
tū̃ karẽ -gī or **-dī**	thou (*fem.*) wilt do.

Examples of other Futures.

Root.	Meaning.	Third Person Singular Future.
mar	die.	**marēgā.**
jā	go.	**jāēgā** or **jāwēgā.**

Root.	Meaning.	Third Person Singular Future.
pai	lie.	**paēgā or pawēgā.**
bhaũ	turn.	**bhãwēgā.**

They may also end in **-dā**.

The Present Tense.

The present imperfect tense is formed as in the English "I am doing" by combining the present participle (declined for gender and number) with the present tense of the auxiliary verb "to be." The termination **-dā** is changed to **-nā** for the first and second singular and **-nē** for the first plural.

maĩ karnā hã (or ã or wã)	I am doing.
ōh kardā e	he is doing.

Past Imperfect Tense.

The past imperfect tense is formed from the present participle by adding the past tense of the verb 'to be.'

Examples.

maĩ kardā sā	I was doing.
tū̃ kardā saĩ	thou wert doing.

The Indefinite Past Tense.

The indefinite past tense is formed by using the past participle without any auxiliary verb.

(1) In the case of intransitive verbs the noun which forms the subject of the verb is put in the nominative case, and the verb agrees with it in gender and number.

Examples.

Indefinite Past Tense.	Meaning.
maĩ geā	I went.
ōh mōeā	he died.

The second often takes. **-õ**, fem. **-īõ**, plur. **-ō**, fem. **-īō**. instead of **-ā**, etc.: as, **jē tū̃ āeõ maĩ tainū̃ mārā̃gā**, if you come, I will beat you; jō ṭur chalīõ, if you (fem.) are going. See Syntax, pp. 378–380.

(2) In the case of transitive verbs the noun which forms the subject of the verb is put in the agent case, and the noun which forms the object of the verb may be either in the absolute form or in the prepositional form with the dative preposition nū̃. If the object is in the absolute form, the verb agrees with it in gender and number; if in the prepositional form with nū̃, the verb maintains unchanged its ending in -ā. The rule applies to all tenses of transitive verbs formed from the past participle. The addition of nū̃ usually makes the noun more definite.

Examples.

ōs ghōṛā ḍiṭṭhā	he saw the horse or a horse.
ōs ghōṛī ḍiṭṭhī	he saw the mare or a mare.
ōs ghōṛīā̃ ḍiṭṭhīā̃	he saw mares or the mares.
ōs ghōṛīā̃ nū̃ ḍiṭṭhā	he saw the mares (or, less often, he saw mares).

For the forms ending in -ō, fem. -īō, plur. -eō, fem. -īō, see Syntax, pp. 378–380.

The Perfect Tense.

The perfect tense is formed from the past participle with the present tense of the auxiliary verb "to be." In the perfect and pluperfect tenses if the verb is intransitive, the auxiliary agrees with the nominative, if it is transitive it agrees with the object, except when the preposition nū̃ is employed after the object, in which case the auxiliary is in the third singular.

Examples.

	Meaning.
maĩ āeā wā̃	I have come.
tusĩ āē ō	you have come.
ōs kamm kītā e	he has done the work

For "I have come" āeū̃, contracted from āeā ū̃ is often used, but only in addressing those who may be spoken to as tū̃.

THE PLUPERFECT TENSE.

The pluperfect tense is similarly formed from the past participle with the past tense of the auxiliary verb "to be." It should be noted that in practice this tense almost always has the meaning of a simple past. To express the idea of a pluperfect, if it requires clear expression, some adverb of time or other such word is usually inserted.

Examples.

	Meaning.
maĩ geā sā̃	I had gone, I went.
tusī̃ gaiē sau	you had gone, you went.
ōh kamm kītā sī	he had done the work, he did the work.

COMPOUND TENSES.

Compound tenses are formed from the present and past participles combined with the auxiliary verb **hōṇā** (to become).

Examples.

	Meaning.
ōh kamm kardā howēgā or **hōwēdā.**	he will be doing the work.
ōs kamm kītā hōwēgā or **hōwēdā.**	he will have done the work.
kardē hōṇgē	(they will be doing) perhaps they do, *or* no doubt they do

AUXILIARY VERB, SUBSTANTIVE.

Present Tense (I am, etc.).

Singular.

Person.	Contracted form.	Full form.	Emphatic form.	Meaning
First	.. **ā̃**	**hā̃**	**hā̃ wā̃, hai wā̃**	I am.
Second	.. **ẽ (aĩ)**	**haĩ**	**haĩ wẽ**	thou art.
Third	.. **e (ai)**	**hai**	**hai wē**	he is.

Plural.

Person.	Contracted form.	Full form.	Emphatic form.	Meaning.
First ..	**ã̄**	**hã̄**	**hã̄ wã̄, hai wã̄**	we are.
Second ..	**ō**	**hō**	**hai ō**	you are.
Third ..	**nẽ̄**	**haiṇ**	**haiṇ nẽ̄**	they are.

Note (2).—The singular has another form **wã̄, wẽ̄, wē**, with emphatic form as above **hã̄wã̄, haīwẽ̄, haiwē. wã̄** and **wẽ̄** are used chiefly after the vowel **ā**, as **maĩ kīṛā wã̄**, I am a worm, **tũ̄ mērā bhrā wẽ̄**, you are my brother.

Note (3).—Another, a specially emphatic form, is really a duplication :—

	Singular.	Plural.
First	**hã̄ ī ã̄**	**hã̄ ī ã̄, hai ī ã̄.**
Second	**haī ī ẽ̄**	**hai ī ō.**
Third	**hai ī e**	**haiṇ ī ẽ̄.**

Past Tense (*I was*).

Singular.

		Meaning.
First	**sã̄ or haisã̄**	I was.
Second	**saī or haisaī**	thou wast.
Third	**sī or haisī**	he or she was.

Plural.

First	**sã̄ or haisã̄**	we were.
Second	**sau or haisau**	you were.
Third	**sāṇ or haisāṇ**	they were.

The masculine and feminine are the same throughout.

Passive Voice.

(1) The regular passive is formed by using the past participle in **-ā** with the necessary tenses of **jāṇā**, go, the past participle agreeing in gender and number with the nominative, *e.g.*, **ōh mārеā gеā**, he was beaten or killed; **kaṇakã̄ waḍḍhiã̄ geiã̄**, the wheat was cut.

(2) A very common way of forming the passive is to use the root of the verb with the required parts of **ghattṇā**. Thus to express he was killed, he will be killed, he may be killed, one puts the verb **ghattṇa** in the past, future, and present subjunctive tense, respectively, and prefixes the root **mār** of the verb **mārnā**, kill, thus **mār ghatteā, mār ghattēgā, mār ghattē.** This method is used chiefly with those transitive verbs which have not a special intransitive form. But cases are found even with verbs having such forms, as **paiḷīā̃ wāh ghattīā̃** or **wagg geīā̃**, the fields have been ploughed.

Examples.

Active.		*Passive.*	
Infinitive.	Meaning.	Past Tense.	Meaning.
mārnā	strike, kill.	**mār ghatteā** or **māreā gēā.**	was killed.
waḍḍhṇā	cut.	**waḍḍh ghatteā** or **waḍḍheā gēā.**	was cut.
bījṇā	sow.	**bīj ghatteā** or **bījeā gēā.**	was sown.
gunnhṇā	knead.	**gunnh ghatteā** or **guddhā gēā.**	was kneaded.
saddṇā	call.	**saddeā gēā**	was called.
likkhṇā	write.	**likkh ghatteā** or **likkheā gēā.**	was written.
phaṛnā	seize.	**phaṛ ghatteā** or **phaṛeā gēā.**	was seized.
paṛhnā	read.	**paṛh ghatteā** or **paṛheā gēā.**	was read.

Very occasionally one hears **ghattṇa** used in the following peculiar ways; (*i*) with an intransitive verb, as, **nahā ghatteā** = **nahātā,** he washed himself. (*ii*) in an active sense, as, **je ōh rupayya dē ghattē,** if he gives the rupee. This latter seems to occur only with the verb **dēṇā,** give. See also under (4).

(3) Many transitive verbs, however, as will be explained, have a corresponding intransitive verb, which has a passive signification. Some of these are given here for convenience.

Transitive.		*Intransitive or Passive.*	
Infinitive.	Meaning.	Infinitive.	Meaning.
wāhṇā	plough.	**waggṇā**	be ploughed.
bheōṇā	moisten.	**bhijjṇā**	be moistened.
khōhṇā	seize.	**khussṇā**	be seized.
tānā	heat.	**tapṇā**	be heated.
phēhṇā	squeeze.	**phissṇā**	be squeezed.
sāṛnā	burn.	**saṛnā**	be burned.
pīhṇā	grind.	**pīsṇā**	be ground.
gunnhṇā	knead.	**gujjhṇā**	be kneaded.

Indeed almost every intransitive verb which has a corresponding transitive root may be said to be a passive voice of the latter.

(4) For tenses in which the present participle is used there is still another method of forming the passive; this is the employment of a passive present participle, the only relic in these districts of the organic passive in **-ī**. The present participle passive is formed by insertiug **-ī** between the root of the verb and the termination **-dā**. If the root ends in **-ō** or **-ā** the letter **w** is frequently inserted before the **-ī**. The use of the present participle passive is confined to the third person singular and plural. This participle is employed for the most part to express general truths.

Examples.

mērē kōḷō nehī̃ jāīdā e	I cannot go.
aiñ nehī̃ karīdā e	it is not done so, one ought not to do so.
paiḷīā̃ wāhīdīā̃ nē̃	fields are ploughed.
ākhīdā hundā sī	it used to be said.
dūh hatthā̃ nāḷ chukkīdā hōwēgā	it is probably (as a rule) lifted with two hands.
but **chukkeā jāwēgā**	it will be lifted with two hands.

Occasionally also **ghattṇā** itself receives a passive form as in—
likkh ghattīdā e = **likkīdā e** it is written or one writes.

See p. xviii last 8 lines; p. xix lines 3 to 10 from foot; and Grammar, p. 332, 1 to 6.

CONJUGATION OF TRANSITIVE VERB.

Root **dass**, show, tell.

Infinitive **dassṇā**, show, showing.

agent **dassaṇwāḷā**, **dassū** (not used in this particular verb).

present participle **dassdā**, showing.

past participle **dasseā**, shown.

progressive **dassdā hōeā**, in the act of showing.

passive participle **dasseā hōeā**, shown (or **dasseāda** in **Sialkote, and Jammū**).

conjunctive **dasskē**, having shown.

adverbial participle **dassdeā**, or **dassdeāī**, while or on showing.

TENSES FORMED FROM THE ROOT.

Imperative.

Singular.	Plural.
tū dass, show.	**tusī dassō**, show.
(politer) **dassī**.	**dasseō**, or **dasseō jē**.
	dassīō, or **dassīō jē**.

Present Conditional.

I may show, I show, shall I show, etc.

maĩ dassā̃.	**asī dassīyē.**
tū dassē̃.	**tusī dassō.**
ōh dassē.	**ōh dassaṇ.**

Future.

I shall show.

maĩ dassā̃gā or **dassā̃dā**.	**asī dassā̃gē** or **dassā̃dē**.
tū dassē̃gā or **dassē̃dā**.	**tusī dassōgē** or **dassōdē**.
ōh dassēgā or **dassēdā**.	**ōh dassaṇgē** or **dassaṇdē**.

TENSES FORMED FROM THE PRESENT PARTICIPLE.

(1) *Past Conditional.*

(If) I had shown, I should or would have shown.

maĩ dassdā.	**asī dassdē.**
tū dassdā or **dassdō**.	**tusī dassdē** or **dassdeō**.
ōh dassdā.	**ōh dassdē.**

(2) *Present.*

I am showing or I show.

maĩ dassnā wā̃, dassnā̃, dassnāeā̃ or dassnā ā̃.	**asĩ dassne ā̃.**
tū̃ dassnā ē̃.	**tusĩ dassde ō.**
ōh dassdā e.	**ōh dassdē nē̃.**

(3) *Imperfect.*

I was showing.

maĩ dassdā sā̃.	**asĩ dassde sā̃.**
tū̃ dassdā saĩ.	**tusĩ dassde sau.**
ōh dassdā sī.	**ōh dassde sāṉ.**

TENSES FORMED FROM THE PAST PARTICIPLE.

(1) *Past Indefinite.*

I showed.

maĩ dasseā.	**asā̃ dasseā.**
tū̃ dasseā.	**tusā̃ dasseā.**
ōs dasseā.	**ōhnā̃ dasseā.**

(2) *Present Perfect.*

I have shown.

maĩ dasseā e.	**asā̃ dasseā e.**
tū̃ dasseā e.	**tusā̃ dasseā e.**
ōs dasseā e.	**ōhnā̃ dassea e.**

(3) *Pluperfect.*

I had shown, I showed.

maĩ dasseā sī.	**asā̃ dasseā sī.**
tū̃ dasseā sī.	**tusā̃ dasseā sī.**
ōs dasseā sī.	**ōhnā dassea sī.**

(4) *Future Perfect.*

I shall have shown or may have shown.

maĩ dasseā hōwēgā or hōwēdā.	**asā̃ dasseā hōwēgā or hōwēda.**
tū̃ dasseā hōwēgā ,, ,,	**tusā̃ dasseā hōwēgā** ,, ,,
ōs dasseā hōwēgā ,, ,,	**ōhnā̃ dasseā hōwēgā** ,, ,,

See other compound tenses below.

Roots ending in a Vowel.

If the root ends in a vowel there will be slight changes or alternative forms. Thus with **aprāṇā, cause to arrive,** we have agent **apṛāṇwāḷā,** past participle **apṛāeā,** present participle **apṛāndā.**

Imperative polite	**apṛāī or apṛāwī.**	**apṛāeō, apṛāweō, apṛāīō or apṛwāīō.**
Present cond.	**apṛāā̃ or apṛāwā̃.**	**apṛāīyē or apṛāwīyē.**
	apṛāē̃ or apṛāwē̃.	**apṛāō or apṛāwō.**
	apṛāē or apṛāwē.	**apṛāṇ.**
Future ..	**apṛāā̃gā or apṛāwā̃gā.**	**apṛāā̃gē or apṛāwā̃gē.**
	apṛāē̃gā or apṛāwē̃gā.	**apṛāōgē or apṛāwōgē.**
	apṛāēgā or apṛāwēgā.	**apṛāṇge.**
Present ..	**apṛānnā wā̃.**	**apṛānne ā̃.**
	apṛānnā ē̃.	**apṛānde ō.**
	apṛāndā e.	**apṛānde nē̃.**

Intransitive verbs differ from transitive only in the past tenses.

ṭurnā, walk.

Past Indefinite.

maī ṭureā.	**asī̃ ṭurē.**
tū̃ ṭureā or ṭureō.	**tusī̃ ṭurē or ṭureō.**
ōh ṭureā.	**ōh ṭurē.**

Present Perfect.

maī ṭureā wā̃.	**asī̃ ṭurē ā̃.**
tū̃ ṭureā ē̃.	**tusī̃ ṭurē ō.**
ōh ṭureā e.	**ōh ṭurē nē̃.**

Pluperfect.

maī ṭureā sā̃.	**asī̃ ṭurē sā̃.**
tū̃ ṭureā saī.	**tusī̃ ṭurē sau.**
ōh ṭureā sī.	**ōh ṭurē sāṇ.**

Future Perfect.

maĩ ṭureā hōwā̃gā or **hōwā̃dā.**	**asĩ ṭurē hōwā̃gē** or hōwā̃dē.
tū̃ ṭureā hōwẽgā ,, ,,	**tusĩ ṭurē hōwōgē** ,, hōwōdē.
ōh ṭureā hōwēgā ,, ,,	**ōh ṭurē hōṇgē** ,, hōṇdē.

hōṇā, be or become, used also as auxiliary.

Imperative	.. **hō**	**hō, hōwō.**
	hōwĩ.	**hōweō, hōwīō.**

Agent **hōṇwāḷā,** Pres. Part. **hundā hondā,** Past Participle hōeā.

Present Conditional.	. **hōwā̃.**	**hōwīyē.**
	hōwẽ.	**hōwō.**
	hōwē.	**hōṇ.**
Future	.. **hōwā̃gā** or **hōwā̃dā.**	**hōwā̃gē** or **hōwā̃dē.**
	hōwẽgā or **hōwẽdā.**	**hōwōgē** or **hōwōdē.**
	hōwēgā or **hōwēdā.**	**hōṇgē** or **hōṇdē.**

Other tenses are regular, thus **maĩ hundā, hunnā wā̃, hundā sā̃, hōeā, hōeā wā̃, hōeā sā̃, hōeā hōwā̃gā.**

With the tenses of **hōṇā** compound tenses may be formed.

maĩ dassdā hōwā̃gā	I shall be showing or may be showing.
maĩ dassdā hōwā̃	I may be showing.
maĩ dasseā hōwē	I may have shown.
maĩ dasseā hōwēgā	I shall have shown or may have shown.
maĩ dasseā hundā	I might have shown, (if) I had shown.

With intransitive verbs these last three tenses would be as follows :—

maĩ ṭureā hōwā̃, maĩ ṭureā hōwā̃gā, maĩ ṭureā hundā.

They are all regular.

The following will show the chief changes for the feminine :—

Future .. **maĩ dassā̃gī** or **dassā̃dī, tū̃ dassẽgī** or **dassẽdī, ōh dassēgī** or **dassēdī.**
asĩ dassā̃gīā̃ or **dassā̃dīā̃, tusĩ dassōgīā̃** or **dassōdīā̃, ōh dassaṇgīā̃** or **dassaṇdīā̃.**

Past Conditional.. **maĩ dassdī, tū̃ dassdī** or **dassdīō̃, ōh dassdī, asĩ dassdīā̃, tusĩ dassdīā̃,** or **dassdīō, ōh dassdīā̃.**

Present .. **maĩ dassnī ā̃, tū̃ dassnī ē̃, ōh dassdī e.**
asī̃ dassniā̃ ā̃, tusī̃ dassdiā̃ ō, ōh dassdiā̃ nē̃.

Imperfect **dassdā** changes to **dassdī** and **dassdē** to **dassdiā̃.**

Past. In the past tenses **dasseā** changes in agreement with the object to **dassē** for the masculine plural and **dassī, dassiā̃** for the feminine singular and plural.

In intransitive verbs similar changes are made in agreement with the nominative, thus **ṭureā,** went, becomes **ṭurē, ṭurī, ṭuriā̃.**

It will not be necessary to give the passive voice in full. It is perfectly regular. The past tense of **jāṇā** is irregular, but when that is known the rest offers no difficulty, **jāṇā** makes its past **geā,** plural **gaiē,** feminine **geī, geiā̃.**

phaṛeā jāṇā, be seized.

Present Participle	**phaṛeā jāndā, phaṛīdā.**
Past Participle	**phaṛeā geā.**
Conjunctive Participle	**phaṛeā jākē.**
Imperative	**phaṛeā jāh, jāī̃, jāwī̃, phaṛē jāhō, jāwō, jāweō, jāīō, jāwīō.**
Present Conditional	**phaṛeā jā̃ or jāwā̃ or jāā̃.**
Future	**phaṛeā jāā̃gā or jāwā̃gā.**
Past Conditional	**phaṛeā jāndā.**
Present Indicative	**phaṛeā jānnā̃ or jānnā wā̃.**
Imperfect	**phaṛeā jāndā sā̃.**
Past Indefinite	**phaṛeā geā.**
Present Perfect	**phaṛeā geā wā̃.**
Pluperfect	**phaṛeā geā sā̃.**

Compound tenses may also be formed, as **maī phaṛeā geā howā̃gā,** I may have seen seized.

The second form of the passive, that with **ghattṇā,** is quite regular. **ghattṇā** is used with the root of the verb.

maĩ phaṛ ghattā̃gā	I shall be seized.
maĩ phaṛ ghattā̃	I may be seized.
maĩ phaṛ ghatteā	I was seized; and so on.

Irregular Verbs.

Among the more common irregular verbs are the following :—

Root.	Meaning.	Infinitive.	Present participle.	Past participle.	Imperative.	Third singular pres. cond.	Third singular future.
pai ..	lie ..	paiṇā ..	paindā ..	peā ..	pau ..	pawē, paiē ..	pawē -gā or -dā.
bhaũ ..	turn ..	bhaũṇā ..	bhaũndā ..	bhā̃weā ..	bhaũ ..	bhā̃wē ..	bhā̃wē -gā or -dā.
jā ..	go ..	jāṇā ..	jāndā ..	geā ..	jāh ..	jāwē ..	jāwē -gā or -dā.
saũ ..	sleep ..	saũṇā ..	saundā ..	suttā ..	saũ ..	sā̃wē ..	sā̃wē -gā or -dā.
lai ..	take ..	laiṇā ..	laindā ..	leā ..	lai ..	lawē, laē ..	lawē -gā or -dā.
laih ..	descend	laihṇā ..	laihndā ..	latthā ..	laih, lauh ..	laihē, lawhē	laihē -gā or -dā. lawhe -gā or -dā.
baih ..	sit ..	baihṇā ..	baihndā ..	baiṭhā ..	bauh ..	bawhē, baihē	bawhē -gā or -dā. baihē -gā or -dā.
raih ..	remain	raihṇā ..	raihndā ..	rehā ..	rauh ..	rawhē, raihē	raihē -gā or -dā. rawhē -gā or -dā.

The organic passive participle in **idā** is a relic of a complete passive inflection. The full passive still exists in some dialects, thus we might have **ghalīṇā**, to be sent, regularly conjugated. In ordinary Panjabi, however, the organic passive form is found only in the present participle passive and tenses which employ the present participle.

COMPOUND VERBS.

Compound verbs are of many different kinds and are very common. The following are the most frequently employed. They are here divided according as they are formed, with the root, the infinitive and the present participle. The expression of habit does not fall under any of these headings.

Verbs formed with the root (see also under 5).

(1) *Emphasis* or *thoroughness* or *completeness*. Sometimes the meaning of a verb is intensified by adding to it the root of another verb. In such a case the second root only is subject to inflection. The important verb, that which gives the real meaning, is kept unchanged in the root; the other verb, which adds the emphasis, is conjugated. Very often no emphasis is apparent.

Infinitive.	Literal meaning.	Acquired meaning.
mār chaḍḍṇā	strike-leave.	kill.
mār saṭṭṇā	strike-throw.	kill.
lellaiṇā	take-take.	take altogether.
kar chaḍḍṇā	do-leave.	finish.
leā dēṇā	take-come-give.	bring.
ṭur paiṇā	go-lie.	start.
baih jāṇā	sit-go.	sit down.
saṭṭ dēṇā	throw-give.	throw away.
ā jāṇā	come-go.	come.

The root **cā** or **cukk** (lift) is often prefixed to another root to imply the suddenness or unreasonableness of the action, e.g. **ōs cā ākheā**, he up and said, **gāḷ cukk kaḍḍhī**, he up and abused me.

(2) *Completion*, to express the idea of having finished doing something. These are constructed as in (1). There are four verbs used, **baihṇā**, sit, **cukṇā**, finish, **raihṇā**, remain, **haṭṇā**, move away.

huṇ pī baiṭhē ō?	have you finished drinking?
maĩ te ākh cukeā wā̃	I have finished saying.
jad ōh khā raihṇgē	when they will have finished eating.
ōh kar haṭeā	he finished doing.

The use of **cukṇā** is copied from Urdu, and is therefore less common in villages. **cukṇā** cannot be used alone. **raihṇā** is not very common in this sense. **haṭṇā** is still less so.

(3) *Ability* expressed by prefixing the root to **sakṇā**, be able. The construction is as in (1) and (2). **sakṇā** cannot be used by itself.

tū̃ haḷ wāh sakṇā ẽ	can you plough?

Ability is also simply expressed by the passive participle.

tērē kōḷō̃ innā bhār nehī̃ cukkīdā, you cannot lift such a weight.

See also the next heading.

Verbs formed with the Infinitive.

These may be divided into two classes: (*a*) those formed with the infinitive in its prepositional form, (*b*) those which inflect the infinitive in agreement with the object.

(3*a*) *Ability*. Prepositional infinitive with the verb **hōṇā**. **huṇ te mērē kōḷō̃ khlōṇ wī nehī̃ hundā**, now I cannot even stand. **ajj nehī̃ mērā jāṇ hundā**, I cannot go to-day.

(4) *Permission*. Prepositional infinitive with **dēṇā**, give. **tenū̃ puṭṭaṇ dēgā**, he will let you dig. **kaṇakā̃ nehī̃ waḍḍhaṇ dittiā̃**, he did not allow the corn to be cut.

(5) *Commencement*. Prepositional infinitive with **laggṇā**. **laggṇā** has other senses and frequently it seems to be meaningless.

ōh kamm karn laggā we	he has begun to work.

With **ākhṇā**, say, it has practically no meaning. **ōh ākkhaṇ laggā**, he said.

laggṇā sometimes has a future sense in negative sentences or interrogatives implying a negative. It then expresses an emphatic negative.

ōh kadō̃ dhēlī waṭāṇ laggā, when will he change (i.e., he will never change) the eight-anna bit?

ōh mannaṇ nehī̃ laggā, he will not agree.

By prefixing the root of a verb to **calṇā** we get the idea of an action commencing or about to commence. The roots of **ṭurnā** and **calṇā** when prefixed to **paiṇā** suggest a similar idea.

gaḍḍī ṭur callī	the train is about to leave.
gaḍḍī ṭur paī	the train is leaving, i.e., has begun to move.
gaḍḍī ṭur geī	the train has gone.
mērā bhrā mar calleā sī	my brother was about to die, nearly died.
mar geā	he died.

See also **ḍaihṇā** under (9).

(*b*) infinitive agreeing with object.

(6) *Wish, desire.*

maī dhār kaḍḍhṇī nehī̃ cāhndā	I do not wish to milk (the cow, etc.).
dō hallā̃ baṇāṇīā̃ cāhnnā wā̃	I wish to make two ploughs.

(7) *Advisability, duty.* The passive participle of **cāhṇā,** wish, is used with the inflected infinitive.

ēh gallā̃ nehī̃ ākhṇīā̃ cāhīdīā̃ nē̃	one should not say such things.
menū̃ naukar cāhīdā e	I want a servant.

(8) *Necessity.* Infinitive with **paiṇā** or **hōṇā.**

jāṇā pawēgā	it will be necessary to go.
dāṇē leauṇē hōṇgē	it will be necessary to bring grain.

Verbs formed with the Present Participle.

(9) *Progression,* to express that an act is actually in progress. The tenses, chiefly of the present participle (but not the past conditional) are employed with the past participle of **paiṇā.**

battīā̃ peīā̃ baḷdīā̃ nē̃	lamps are burning.
ṭukkar paē khānde hōṇgē	they will be having their food.

With tenses other than those of the present participle the idea rather changes to that of continuance.

maĩ peā khāā̃gā, tū̃ gallī̃ peā kar, I shall keep on eating, you go on speaking, **peā hassē,** let him keep on laughing (what do I care ?).

ḍaihṇā with the prepositional infinitive gives the sense of being engaged in and actually doing something.

rōṛ puṭṭaṇ ḍehā hōeā e, he is digging kankar.

ajj ōh kamm nehī̃ kardē ? ā wekhā̃ ḍaihē hōē nē̃, are they not working to-day ? Look, they are at work.

(10) *Continuance,* present participle with **raihṇā,** see also under (9).

ōh māl cārdā rehā	he continued to graze cattle.
jē tū̃ ṭurdā rawhē̃	if you keep on walking.

Instead of **raihṇā** we may employ **jāṇā** or less often **calṇā.** These have a shade of meaning different from that of **raihṇā.** They, especially **jāṇā,** suggest a parallel course of action. Thus **maĩ cōkhā cir paṛhdā rehā,** means simply I read for a long time, whereas **paṛhdā geā** would imply that I kept on reading, while so-and-so was doing something else (working, etc.), **maĩ suṇāndā jāā̃gā, tū̃ likhdā cal,** I shall keep on relating, you keep on writing down.

Continuance is expressed also by prefixing the root (with -ī added) to the various parts of **jāṇā** and **calṇā.**

suṇāī cal, keep on telling (fire away !): **kamm karī cal,** work away.

ākhī jāh, keep on saying : **ōh wagī jāndā e,** he is keeping on hurrying away.

Habit or Repetition.

This idea is expressed in different ways according to the tense. The second verb is always **karnā** for the infinitive, imperative, present conditional and future, and **hōṇā** for the tenses of the present participle.

(i) **Karna.** Infinitive, imperative and present conditional and future. Both verbs are put in the same tense, i.e., both are infinitive or both imperative, and so on. For the simple imperative singular see below.

jhaṭē bindē nehī̃ auṇā karnā cāhīdā e, one should not make a practice of coming repeatedly.

tū̃ rinnhẽ karẽ tā̃ caṅgī gall e, if you make a habit of doing the cooking it will be a good thing.

ētthē na hassī̃ karī̃, do not make a habit of laughing here.

The imperative has a second construction—the past participle with the imperative **karnā.** This is always used in the case of the simple imperative singular (i.e., the root). **mērē kōḷ bawheā karō,** make a practice of sitting beside me.

In the future the terminations **-gā,** etc., of the first verb are omitted. **maī̃ ghallā̃ karā̃gā,** I shall make a habit of sending.

(ii) **Hona.** Tenses formed from the present participle. Both verbs in the same tense. Verb substantive never occurring more than once.

maī̃ masītī paṛhdā hundā sā̃	I used to read in the mosque.
ōh mucchā̃ nehī̃ munāndē hundē	they do not get their moustache shaved.
jē ōh kadī ghuḷdā hundā maī̃ wehnnā honnā mā.	if he had ever been in the habit of wrestling.

In connection with the second imperative construction under habit and repetition above it should be noted—

(*a*) that the past participle is indeclinable, thus in **bawheā karō, bawheā** remains unchanged,

(*b*) that the past participle is for this purpose always formed directly in a regular manner from the root even though no such past participle is in ordinary use in the verb, thus we have—

rinnheā kar	make a habit of cooking,
khlōweā kar	make a habit of standing,
nahāweā kar	make a habit of washing,

where the ordinary past participles are **riddhā, khlōtā, nahātā**

jāṇā, go.

A note on jāṇā will perhaps be useful. It has three uses in connection with other verbs.

(1) To form the passive, as ōh **phaṇḍeā geā,** he was beaten. (See under passive voice.)

(2) When joined to the root of many *intransitive verbs* to express completeness, it does not add the idea of going—but that may be inherent in the root itself.

Sometimes it is almost meaningless. **mukk jāṇā,** be finished off, **bhull jāṇā,** forget, **ṭuṭṭ jāṇā,** break. The idea of "going" is absent, save in *transitive verbs,* where it is found.

(3) Joined to the contracted conjunctive participle of verbs of action it *retains* its meaning of going or moving away. As the contracted conj. part. is the same in form as the root, this use must be carefully distinguished from (2). In the case of (3) the verbs are all verbs of action, i.e., they indicate a definite action, and may be either trans. or intrans. In the case of (2) they are not verbs of action. To this statement there are three exceptions. The verbs **baihṇā,** sit, **auṇā,** come, though indicating action fall under (2) and **pīṇā,** drink, comes under both (2) and (3).

ākh jāṇā, tell and go: **wēkh jāṇā,** look and go: **haṭ jāṇā,** go to one side. **nass jāṇā,** run away: **suṇ jāṇā,** hear and go. See also Syntax under Conj. Part., p. 375.

In **bhull jāṇā,** forget, and **ā jāṇā,** come, there is no idea of "going." **pī jāṇā,** has two senses either with (2) **drink up,** or with (3) **drink and go.** Contrast **mukk geā, it is finished,** and **mukā geā, he has finished it and gone. mar geā, he is dead,** and **mār geā e, he has beaten him and gone.**

(4) For phrases like **dassī jāh, ākhdā jāh,** see Compound Verbs above, p. 335.

SYNTAX.

ORDER OF WORDS.

The normal order of words in Panjabi is, (1) attribute of nominative, (2) nominative, (3) attribute of object, (4) object, (5) adverbs, **(6) verb, thus, tērā jōṛīdār ōhnā aṇāṇeā nū̃ kāh dē**

jōgā ṭhākdā sī? why was your partner forbidding those children?

The flexibility of conversational Panjabi is, however, extraordinary, and there is hardly any order in which the words of a sentence are not found. The order changes according to the emphasis.

Thus for **ōh jaṇē kī paiē kardē sāṇ?** what were those men doing? we may hear **kardē kī sāṇ ōh jaṇē paiē?**

Similarly **Dīnā te Gāmmā lagē aundē nẽ,** Dīnā and Gāmmā are coming along, may appear as **aundē nẽ Dīnā wī lagā te Gāmmā wī lagā.**

sārē rupaē lagg gaiē sāṇ, all the rupees were spent. may become **gaiē sāṇ rupaē sārē lagg.**

jē ōs ōhnū̃ wēkh lēā e te bin puccheā̃ kaḍḍh dittā e, if he has seen him and without inquiring turned him out, may be changed to **jē ōs ōhnū̃ leā e wēkh te bin puccheā̃ dittā e kaḍḍh.**

The difficulty lies in knowing how and when to vary the order of a sentence, and only practice and experience can solve the problem.

The Repetition of Words.

The repetition of words never gives an intensive or emphatic sense. It indicates distribution over time or space, or over a number of objects, or the English word 'nice'——"nice and clean," etc., "**Ṭhanḍa ṭhanḍa pani**'——nice cold water **sajrī sajrī malāi**—nice fresh cream.

bauht sārē tagṛē tagṛē khiḍārū, many strong (good) players.

chētī chētī paṭṭhē kutarī, quickly cut up the fodder.

ōh kāhḷā kāhḷā ṭurdā e, he walks fast.

gōḍē gōḍē (paṭṭ paṭṭ, lakk lakk) pāṇī sī, there was water up to the knees (thighs, waist).

rāh masā̃ cappā cappā jā̃ giṭṭh giṭṭh cauṛā sī, the road was scarcely a hand breadth or a span broad.

trai trai sagõ cār cār	three each, nay rather four each.
jaṇē jaṇē dī marzī	each man's wish.
jī jī dā jīkaṇ jī karē	as each person's desire may be.

In each of these examples it will be seen that the idea of the repeated word is, as it were, spread out over a number of objects or over a period of time.

The conjunctive participle is repeated to express repetition or continuance. Thus **phaṇḍ phaṇḍkē**, having kept on beating: **suṇā suṇākē**, having kept on relating: **ākh ākhkē**, having repeatedly said.

DOUBLETS.

When words are repeated in a more or less altered form one of two ideas seems to be present to the mind. (1) a more or less jocular reference to something familiar, and (2) a spreading out of the sense for the sake of emphasis. The first case occurs when the second word is very slightly altered from the first and is a mere jingling repetition of it, the other when the second is a totally different word. Of course these two senses merge into one another and it would be a mistake to draw any hard and fast distinctions.

gall katth	word, matter.	**jhūṭhī mūṭhī**	falsely.
kūndā saihndā	speaking.	**kuṛī mucī**	falsely.
dē duākē	having given.	**jaṇē shaṇē**	men.
kar katarkē	having done.	**jaṇā khaṇā**	Tom, Dick and Harry.
baṇeā battreā	made.		
ākh wēkhkē	having said.	**inām shinām**	reward.
saccī muccī	truly.	**inām ūm**	reward.

The second word in all these cases is interesting. Sometimes it is an ordinary Panjabi word; if so it usually gives up its own meaning and merely emphasises the meaning of the first. Thus above **saihndā**, means enduring; **duākē**, having caused to give; **katarkē**, having cut; **wēkhkē**, having seen; **katth** is a Kashmiri word not otherwise used in Panjabi, and means the same as **gall**. For the 'familiar reference' it is usual to change the first consonant to **sh** or prefix **sh** to an initial vowel. Otherwise the first accented vowel may be a changed to **ū** and this is generally done if the word already begins with **sh**.

THE AGREEMENT OF SUBJECT AND PREDICATE.

As a rule the verb agrees with its nominative in number and, where the form of the verb permits, in gender.

In the case of two or more nominatives of different gender the rule is (*a*) for living things or material objects the verb is masculine plural, (*b*) for abstract nouns in the case of two or more singular nouns, the verb is singular and agrees with the word nearest to it.

õh dē dhīā̃ puttar ṭur gaiē	his sons and daughters went away.
pāgalpuṇa tē bēwukūfī baṛī kītī	he committed great madness and folly.

tusī̃ addressed to a single person may have a plural masculine verb, whether the person be a man or a woman.

A word denoting a woman, if used for politeness' sake with a plural verb, always has that verb masculine, and in this case the attribute of politeness, "**horī**," is almost invariably added. The words **miss sāhb** and **mēm sāhb** may omit **horī**. An adjective preceding one of these words is kept feminine.

miss sāhb or mēm sāhb āhndē nẽ	the lady says.
bēbbē horī rū̃ piñjdē nẽ	mother is carding cotton.
sāḍḍī bhaiṇ horī bauhkar phērn laggē nẽ	our sister has begun to sweep.

Two nouns are frequently used together without a conjunction, so that they are considered one and take a singular verb, thus—

õh dā kōī dhī puttar nehī̃	he has no son or daughter.

mēz kursī daṭṭhī hoī e, or **mēz te kursī daṭṭhē hoē nẽ**, the table and chair have been placed.

Similarly we have **rōṭī ṭukkar**, food, **khaṇḍ caul**, sugar and rice; **dāḷ caul**, dal and rice, **hāl hakīkat**, condition or state. Such compounds usually take the gender of the second component. **ṭukkar** is masculine, **caul** is masculine plural, **hakīkat** is feminine, but some make the compound **hāl hakīkat** masculine.

Pairs.

Most articles which we think of in English as in pairs are referred to in Panjabi in the singular unless several pairs are meant. The following come under this rule. The gender of each word is indicated.

tambī (f.), **sutthaṇ** (f.), **salwār** (f.), **paejāma** (m.), **ghuṭannā** (m.), **patlūn** (f.) are used for various kinds of trousers worn by men, **patlūn** being reserved for English trousers. **sutthaṇ** is used also for the baggy trousers worn by Panjabi women. Other examples are **jutti**, shoe or pair of shoes, **caplī**, sandal; **kaincī**, scissors; **uccā**, tongs, pincers; thus **muṇḍē tambī pāī, juttī lāhī**, the boy put on his trousers and took off his shoes. Words for socks are exceptions, they are generally used in the plural. Socks are **julāb** (f., more often **jarēb** or **jalēb**), **massī** f., **mauzā** m. Other exceptions are **dastānā** (m.) glove; **paūā** (m.) and **khṛā̃**, (f.) wooden shoe used by Hindus.

The Agent Case.

When a transitive verb is used in one of the tenses formed from the past participle the subject of the sentence is put in the agent case and the participle agrees with the object unless the word **nū̃** intervenes and governs it. This construction is really passive, thus **maī̃ ikk turumtī mārī**, I killed a turumtī (merlin), is properly "by me a turumtī was killed."

ōs kitābā̃ paṛhīā̃ hoṇgīā̃	he will have read the books.
mērē bhatrīyē mērē te arzī pāī	my nephew brought a case against me.
tērī majjh nū̃ kise ḍiṭṭhā ?	has any one seen your buffalo ?

kūṇā, speak, **bōlṇā**, speak, and **laggṇā**, begin, **bhullṇā**, forget, **ḍarnā**, fear, etc., do not of course take this transitive construction.

> **kehṛā kōeā**, who spoke ?
>
> **huṇ wāhṇ laggā e**, now he has begun to plough.

Compound verbs in which the second verb is intransitive do not take the agent construction. **ōh kih dī manjī lai ṭureā**, whose bed has he taken away. **ōh gā̃ dē geā**, he has given the cow and gone.

The word **leauṇā** or **laiauṇā** has two past participles, **leāndā** or **laiāndā**, which takes the agent construction, and **leāeā** or **laiāeā**, which does not.

Forms like **phaṛāī dēṇī**, let oneself be caught, **wikhāḷī dēṇī**, appear, let oneself be seen, take the agent construction, thus their usage differs from that of corresponding words in Urdu.

saṇḍhē pharāī nehī̃ dittī, sagō̃ wikhāḷī wī nehī̃ dittī, the buffalo did not let himself be caught, he did not even show himself.

If **nū̃** comes after the object the verb ceases to agree with it and is put in the masculine singular.

ōhnā̃ kuṛīā̃ nū̃ maī̃ dhīā̃ baṇāeā sī, I made those girls my daughters.

The infinitival construction with the agent, whereby intention or necessity is expressed, is employed equally with transitive and intransitive verbs; **ōs chētī ṭurnā e,** he has to walk fast

tū̃ bhaḷkē jāṇā we? are you going to-morrow?

THE GENITIVE CASE.

The uses of the genitive (formed by means of the preposition **dā**) are very similar to those found in English. The following typical phrases which are somewhat different in idiom from English should be noted. They indicate the common usage.

ōh dī baṛī cāh	great desire for it.
ōh dī mhabbat	love for him, or, his love.
baṛī afsōs dī gall	a matter for regret, a regrettable affair.
kufr dī gall	blasphemy.
mērā ōhdā wair e	there is enmity between him and me.
"happy" dā lafs	the word "happy."
caū̃ warheā̃ dā	four years old.

THE DATIVE CASE.

The preposition **nū̃** generally indicates the dative case. It has the sense of to, for, for the sake of.

ōh nū̃ dēh	give it to him.
kuṛī duddh nū̃ geī	the girl has gone for milk.
maī̃ tĕnū̃ teār kar dēnnā wā̃	I will get it ready for you.
maī̃ tĕnū̃ teār karnā wā̃	I will make you ready.

nũ is used with verbs of necessity or advisability **tĕnũ lōṛīdā e**, you need.

ōh nũ paṇḍ cukkṇī pawēgī, he will have to lift the weight. **milṇā**, be obtained, meet, and **auṇā**, come, in many senses take **nũ**.

wāṭē ōhnũ bāhrlā miḷeā	on the way he met a pig.
tĕnũ kinnā aundā e?	how much is your share?

The idea of possession, expressed in English by "have" is often rendered by the auxiliary verb or **auṇā**, come, with **nũ**, especially if an abstract thing is referred to.

mērē panjhāḷ nũ baṛā gussā āeā	my partner got very angry.
ōhnũ kujjh hōsh nehī̃	he has no sense or consciousness.
menũ patā nehī̃ laggā	I got no trace.

nũ is used in expressions of time, the time at which anything happened. **rāt nũ**, by night, **caũh dinā̃ nũ**, in four days, **aṭhwẽ din nũ**, on the eighth day, in a week.

THE ACCUSATIVE CASE.

This case is formed with or without **nũ**. Nothing but long practice will fully show when to insert and when to omit **nũ**. It may, however, be said that **nũ** is always employed with proper nouns; with other nouns it has the effect of making more definite or of indicating something already referred to or previously known. Frequently no meaning can be attached to it.

Jhanḍū nũ kōḷ khalhārkē ill mārī, he put Jhandu standing beside him and killed a kite.

ill nũ te mār chaḍḍeā	as for the kite he killed it.

Compound verbs, having for the second part an intransitive verb, the whole being transitive in sense, take or omit **nũ** according to the same rules as other verbs. Such verbs are **leauṇā, lai jāṇā, lai ṭurnā, dē jāṇā, pī jāṇā**, etc.

In the case of cognate accusatives in which the verb and noun express the same thought, and of combinations of a noun and a verb in which the two words express a single idea, the noun does not take **nū**. Such phrases are the following:—

hūrē mārnē or **gubbhā̃ mārniā̃**, to strike blows with the fist, **laṛāī laṛnī**, fight a fight, **gāḷhā̃ kaḍḍhṇiā̃**, give abuse, **mār khāṇī**, receive a beating, **jhūṭh mārnā**, tell a lie.

Many verbs take two accusatives, such as causative verbs, verbs meaning to consider, call, believe, name, teach. Generally one noun takes **nū** and the other omits it, occasionally both omit it.

muṇḍē nū Arbī paṛhā — teach the boy Arabic.
tū ōhnū hāfaj mannā ē — you believe him to be a Hafiz (one who knows the Quran by heart).
maĩ tērī beiztī apṇī beiztī samjhnā wā̃. — I consider your dishonour mine.

If in place of the second noun we have an adjective, it is put in the nominative singular masculine; if it ends in **-ā** it is put in the nominative singular masculine or takes the ending **-eā̃**.

ḍāgdār kuṛī nū tagreā̃ kītā. — the doctor made the girl well.
kōṭhī nū baṛā sōhṇā baṇāeā — made the house very beautiful.

Of course if a noun is understood with the adjective, the adjective may take the number and gender of that noun, thus **maĩ ōh dīā̃ dhīā̃ nū apṇiā̃ samjhnā wā̃**, I consider his daughters mine.

Locative Case.

The locative case may be expressed with or without a preposition. The presence of an organic locative (without a preposition) is a phenomenon of considerable interest. The organic locative is used as follows:—

(i) with words indicating villages, countries, towns or other places, to express to, at or in, **Panjābe**, in the Panjab, **masītī**, in the mosque, **Nattī**, to or in Natt, **skūlē**, at school, **Wilaitē**, in Wilāyat (Europe, America). Not all such names have an organic locative form.

(ii) with ordinary nouns to indicate with or in, often to indicate the means or instrumentality and seems confined to those parts of the body found in pairs, **dūh hatthī**, with two hands, **kehṛī gallē**, for what reason or matter? **sāḍḍī nazrī nehī peā**, he did not come within our sight (sights). **asī gallī lagg paie**, we got into matters, we got talking, **hatthī baddhī**, with hands joined (in supplication).

(iii) with words expressive of time and other words, to indicate time at or during or after which an event occurs. **wajjī būhī**, with doors shut, when doors are shut, **latthī buhī**, when doors are open. These two phrases are generally used in connection with earthquakes. **suttī bandī**, when people are asleep. **dinē**, by day, **rātī**, by night, **do paihrī**, at noon. **panjhī warhī**, in 25 years, **kehṛē wēḷē**, at what time? **kuwēḷē**, at a wrong time, late, **chī dinī**, in six days. There is a peculiar phrase **warhī dinī**, meaning in a year or every year.

(iv) with words expressing sums of money, to indicate price **caūh ānnī waṭṭī**, at the rate of a watti (two ser) for four annas. **pāuṇī dasī rupaī**, for nine and three quarter rupees.

Vocative Case.

The special vocative endings are often omitted, the nominative forms being used instead of the vocative. The vocative forms generally imply a certain degree of familiarity and are not much used in polite speech. The vocative ending generally implies that the person is addressed as **tū**, in the second singular. Thus we may address a servant or school-boy as **Karm Dīnā**, but to one requiring a little more ceremony, we should say (if we employ the name) "**Karm Dīn.**" For this reason we do not usually find the vocative form used with titles of respect. We hear **Māsṭar Aziz Ahmad**, not **Māsṭar Azīz Ahmadā**, **Sardār Hākim Siṅh**, not **Sardār Hākim Siṅhā**. If an adjective agreeing with a noun is given the vocative ending the noun must have it also, but the noun may have it while the adjective has the ordinary prepositional termination. Thus we may have **mēreō bhrāwō, mērē bhrāwō,** but not **mēreō brā.**

A descriptive noun or adjective is sometimes put in the plural for the sake of ceremony even when only one person is addressed. Thus **bādshāhō, zōrāwarō,** O kings, despotic ones, meaning simply 'you who in comparison with me are a king, you who are so insistent.'

The ending -eā̃.

In certain cases where in Urdu we should have the oblique singular in **-ē** or the absolute form in **-ā** we find in Panjabi a form ending in **-eā̃.** It is confined to participles and adjectives ending in **-ā.** The chief cases are the following:—

(1) when the participle or adjective is complementary to a subject in the agent case, as—

tū̃ te lageā̃ jāṇā sī	you were to go on.
maĩ ṭurdeā̃ ṭurdeā̃ ōhnū ḍiṭṭhā	I saw him while I was walking.

(2) when in logical agreement with an infinitive, or with some subject not expressed in the impersonal construction of the infinitive or passive participle.

ḍiggdeā̃ ī sawār hōwīdā e	one becomes a rider by falling.
mērē kōḷō siddheā̃ nehī̃ khlōṇ hundā	I cannot stand straight.
nī̃weā̃ hōkē jāṇā sī	one should have gone stooping.
siddheā̃ nehī̃ khlōtā jāndā or **siddheā̃ nehī̃ khlōwīdā e**	it is not possible to stand straight.

(3) in logical agreement with an object which has **nū̃** after it. (See also under past participle.)

ōhnū̃ tagreā̃ karnā	to make him well.
maĩ ōhnū̃ ṭurdeā̃ ḍiṭṭhā	I saw him walking. Cf. (1) above.
mĕnū̃ ētthē āeā̃ cār warhē hōē nē	it is four years since I came here.

(4) in agreement with a nominative this construction is sometimes found to indicate a state. Generally, however, the participle is nominative.

maĩ paṛhāndeã paṛhāndeã āeā — I came here immediately after teaching him. (lit. I came while teaching him.)

hassdeã hassdeã lagā jāndā sī — he was going along laughing.

(5) with the preposition **bin, bijn, binā, bājhõ,** without.

bin khādheã — without eating.

pīteã binā āi — she came without drinking.

PERSONAL PRONOUNS.

Order. Pronouns of the first person usually precede those of the second and third persons, those of the second usually precede those of the third, similarly first and second personal pronouns usually precede nouns.

maĩ tū̃ lagē jāā̃gē — you and I will go.

maĩ te mērī wauhṭī gaiē — my wife and I went.

In the dative and accusative personal pronouns always take the preposition **nū̃** except in the case of the third personal pronouns which may omit it if the thing referred to is not a person.

maĩ ōh mallā̃gā — I shall take possession of that.

The **ī** or **hī** (or -ē) of emphasis, when used with personal pronouns, always follows the preposition **nū̃** except in the case of the third singular.

mēnū̃ ī ākheā — he said it to *me*.

osē nū̃ māreā — he struck *him*.

In the case of other prepositions the particle of emphasis precedes the preposition.

For the use of the pronouns with **jehā jēḍḍhā** see under adjectives.

ATTRIBUTIVE NOUNS AND ADJECTIVES.

When an attributive noun or adjective is used with a personal pronoun the pronouns retain their ordinary case forms except in the first and second pronoun, and if there is a preposition, the attributive adjective comes between the pronoun and the preposition.

ōs bhalēmāṇas sārā ī ragaṛleā	he, worthy man, disposed of (used up, etc.) all.

First and second persons. In the singular the genitive is used except in the agent case where the ordinary agent form is found: thus—

maī garīb kī ākhṇā sī	what could I, poor man, say?
mērē garīb dā	of me poor man.

In the dative and accusative singular we find the two forms. **mēnū̃ garīb nū̃, tōnū̃ garīb nū̃,** and **mērē garīb nū̃, tērē garīb nū̃,** to me poor man, to you poor man; that is, the ordinary genitive form may precede the adjective.

In the plural either the genitive form or the form used for the agent precedes the adjective, thus—

sāḍḍeā̃ sateā̃ hōeā̃ nū̃	to us worried persons.
tusā̃ bādshāhā̃ nū̃	to you kings (great men).

The forms **sāthō̃** and **tuhāthō̃** become **asā̃ thō̃** and **tusā̃ thō̃, sāḍḍeā̃ . . thō̃, tuhāḍḍeā̃ . . thō̃**; as **tusā̃ jaṇeā thō̃**, from you men. In this case the **thō̃** may be replaced by **thī̃** and **tō̃**, which are not common with the simple words **sāthō̃** and **tuhāthō̃**; **methō̃** and **tethō̃** become **mērē . . thō̃** and **tērē . . thō̃**, **thō̃** being replaceable by **thī̃** and **tō̃**.

Use of tū̃ and tusī̃.

There is sometimes a little difficulty in the use of **tū̃** and **tusī̃** in addressing single individuals. The following rules may be of some assistance; all servants, all ordinary school-boys and school-girls, all ordinary villagers, and all persons more or less corresponding in rank to these, such as common policemen, small shopkeepers, should be addressed as **tū̃**. Persons of higher rank such as village officials (zaildārs, paṭwārīs), clerks in offices, teachers in schools (except sometimes the lower teachers), city officials, bigger shopkeepers and all others of corresponding rank should be addressed as **tusī̃**.

When there is a doubt it is better to err on the side of extra ceremony, but the practice among some of speaking to servants and school-boys and school-girls as **tusī** is to be deprecated. However usage varies here.

The word **horī**, see p. 292, is always masculine plural even when referring to women : thus—

tuhāḍḍī bhaiṇ horī āē nē, your sister has come, where **tuhāḍḍī** is feminine in agreement with **bhaiṇ** and yet **horī** attracts the verb into the masculine. Without **horī** the sentence would be **tuhāḍḍī bhaiṇ āī e**. For polite reference to a woman it is generally necessary to insert **horī**.

Sometimes **horī** has the effect suggesting someone's family instead of merely the person himself. This is especially the case if the word is used with a junior member of the family. Thus **Kutbē horā̃ dī jhōṭī** may mean, and if Qutba is a junior member of the family, probably will mean, not Qutba's buffalo calf, but one belonging to Qutba's family.

PRONOMINAL SUFFIXES.

Very frequent use is made of pronominal suffixes which are sometimes added at the end of a word, with or without change in the ending of the word, and are sometimes used independently; in the future tense they are often infixes, being inserted in the middle of the word. They indicate personal pronouns. The characteristic letters are as follows :—

Person.	Singular.	Plural.
Second	-ū̃, -ī, -ā, ī,	jē
Third	s-, -sū	nē, ṇē

There are no suffixes for the first person. It should be noted that the suffixes must be used instead of, not along with, the pronoun or noun to which they refer. Thus one may say **maī mārū̃gā** I will beat thee, or **maī tēnū̃ mārāgā**, but not **maī tēnū̃ mārū̃gā**, for in that case the **-ū̃** in **mārū̃gā** and the **tēnū̃** would both mean 'thee' and there would be redundancy. They are never used reflexively.

Suffixes are employed :

(i) to indicate the object, direct or indirect,

(ii) to indicate possession or connection,
(iii) with the past tenses of transitive verbs to indicate the agent or subject of the verb,
(iv) for the second person, singular and plural, to indicate the person addressed.

It is usually quite easy to know which of these meanings is intended ; thus in **dē sū dhēlī**, give him eight annas, **sū** means to him, in **mār sū**, beat him, **sū** is him, in **dō bhrā sū** indicates possession, two brothers are to him.

The second plural suffix is always jē, that of the third singular sū, the u being sometimes pronounced so short that the suffix becomes **-s**, the third plural suffix is **ṇē**, or **nē**. It is **nē** when it is a separate word or when **r, ṛ, rh, ṛh** precede it. This becomes ṇẽ or **nẽ** in the infixes for the future. See below.

The suffix for the second singular varies as follows :—

The second singular suffix for the agent is—ī if the verb is singular, -ĩ if the verb is plural. When it is not the agent it varies according to the number and person of the nominative of the sentence. If the nominative is first person, singular or plural, the suffix is -ũ, if the nominative is third person singular, it is -ī if plural -ĩ. Finally -ī is always changed to **-ā**, if the preceding vowel is itself ī, thus instead of **kī ī**, we have **kī ā**, what is it, etc.

Infixes are found only in the future. The following cases are common—

maĩ kaḍḍhũgā	I shall expel thee.
ōh kaḍḍhīgā	he will expel thee.
maĩ mārjēgā	I shall beat you.
ōh mārjēgā	he will beat you.
ōh kaḍḍhsūgā	he will expel him.
ōh kaḍḍhṇẽgā	he will expel them.
asĩ kaḍḍhũgē	we shall expel thee.
ōh kaḍḍhṇīgē	they will expel thee.
asĩ mārjēgē	we shall beat you.
ōh mārjēgē	they will beat you.
ōh kaḍḍhsūgē	they will expel him.
ōh kaḍḍhṇẽgē	they will expel them.

Similarly for other verbs; some of these are commoner than others, and generally speaking the beginner would do well to watch for these suffixes or infixes and use those which he hears.

In the present conditional there are only two cases common, a first singular nominative with a second singular suffix and a third singular nominative with a second singular suffix. Thus **maĩ ki karũ**, what shall I do in thy affair? **pīṛ pawī**, pain be to thee (abuse). **sũ** and **nē**, the suffixes for the third singular and plural, and **jē** the suffix for the second plural, may in addition to the above examples, be used as separate words following the different parts of the future and present conditional.

The auxiliary verb shows the following changes. The present tense is omitted altogether in favour of the suffix, except when the verb is emphatic in which case the word hai is used for all persons and numbers followed by the suffix. In the past tense suffixes are added only to **sī** and **sā̃**, which both become **sā** before the suffix, and to **sāṇ** which can take two suffixes, the second singular, becoming **sāṇī**, and the third plural, becoming **sāṇē**.

In a clause containing a transitive verb in any of the tenses formed with the past participle, the suffix indicates the agent and not the object, etc. Thus we may say **mai mārā̃gā sū**, I shall beat him, but not as a rule **mai mārea sū**, I beat him. This should be **maĩ ōsnũ mārea**. The violations of this rule are infrequent and it does seem safe to consider them as regular usage.

Exception: the 1st sing. or plur. agent with 2nd sing. or plur. pronominal suffix, is fairly common in the pluperfect and infin., and is sometimes heard in the past indef. and pres. perf.

SECOND SINGULAR SUFFIX.

(i) with the nominative of the verb in the first person singular or plural.

maĩ mārũ kuṭṭū̃gā	I shall beat and belabour thee.
asī khlōtē hōē ũ	(I tell thee) we are standing.
āeā ũ	(I tell thee) I am coming (lit. have come).
sārē jhallē ũ	we are all mad (I tell thee); but **sārē jhallē nī** *they* are all mad (see under iii).

asī jhallē te hai ū	mad we certainly are.

(ii) with the nominative in the third singular.

beṛā ruṛhī = tērā bēṛā ruṛhē	may thy boat be carried away, perdition take thee.
gōḷī laggī = tenū gōḷī laggē	a bullet strike thee, perdition take thee.
ōh mārīgā = ōh tenū mārēgā	he will strike thee.
bhrā āwīgā	thy brother will come.
lambaṛdār āwī jāwī karīgā	the village headman will come and go (to and from thy house).
rōṭī hai ī	hast thou got bread?
kī ā, peō āeā ī?	what is it (I ask thee), or what is the matter with thee, has thy father come?

(iii) with third plural nominative.

paisē labbh gaie nī	didst thou get the pice?
paisē labbh gaie sāṇī	hadst thou got the pice?
sārē jhallē nī	(I tell thee) they are all mad.
na jāī, mārnīgē	do not go, they will beat thee.

(iv) as agent.

rōṭī khādhī ā	hast thou eaten bread (i.e., thy food)?
kī ākheā ī, pīṇḍ jāṇā ī	what didst thou say, has thou to go to the village?
kī ākheā sāī, kuṛī nāḷ khaṛnī sāī	what didst thou say, hadst thou to take the girl with thee?

Second plural suffix—always jē.

ōtthē dō jē	(I say to you) there are two there.
maī āeā jē	(I say to you) I have come, am coming.
ōh aujēgā te mārjēgā	he will come to you and beat you (aujēgā for ājēgā).
kī jē, ṭakkreā nehī jē	what is it, did he not meet you?
ākhṇā kī sājē	what had you to say or what ought you to have said?
ṭurnā jē	are you going to walk?

Third singular, sū or s.

lai ā sū, dē sū pauḷī	bring him, give him a four-anna bit.
ikk kuṛī sū te dō puttar sū	he has one daughter and two sons.
ghar geī hōsūgī	she will have gone to his house.
ausūgā te mārsūgā.	he will come to him and beat him.
maĩ nehī̃ sū geā piṇḍ.	I did not go to him to the village.
jad wēkhẽgā sū tā̃ ākhī̃ sū	when thou seest him say to him.
bhrā geā sū mar te bēbbē hōgeī sū bamār	his brother has died and his mother has got ill.
dō kuṛīā̃ sā sū ikk mar geī sā sū	he had two girls, one died.
kī akheā sū or kī ākheōs	what did he say?
kitthõ auṇā sū	where has he to come from, where is he coming from?

Third plural nē or ṇē (as a separate word always nē).

kas caṛhī nē, dehō nē dāwāī	they have got fever, give them medicine.
māmmā mar geā nē	their mother's brother has died.
āwēdā te mārnẽdā	if he comes he will beat them.
hup jāṇā nē kĕ paihlē jāṇā sāṇē	have they to go now or had they to go before.
ākheā sāṇē? ākheā ī hōṇēga	did they say so? (yes, doubtless) they will have said so.

The following differences should be noted:—aunnā ẽ, thou art coming: auṇā ī, hast thou to come? aundā ī, I ask thee is he coming: kitthõ āeā ẽ, whence hast thou come? kitthõ āeā ī, whence has he come (I ask thee): kitthõ āī ẽ, whence hast thou (feminine) come? kitthõ āī ā, I ask thee whence has she come.

PRONOMINAL SUFFIXES, pp. 348–351.

To avoid confusion it should be remembered that, while these suffixes never indicate the nominative case, they do indicate the agent case, which Europeans often think of as the nominative. As the use of the suffixes is always found difficult

it will be well to give the conjugation of the whole verb with the suffixes attached. Some parts do not usually take a suffix, but usage on this point is not invariable.

WITH AUXILIARY VERB OR VERB SUBSTANTIVE.

Examples.

maĩ sajjaṇ ũ?	I ask thee, am I a friend?
maĩ sajjaṇ sũ,	I am his friend.
tũ naṇān sũ?	art thou her sister-in-law?
asĩ jhalle ũ,	I tell thee we are mad.

Present Tense.

Person.	Possible suffixes. Singular.	Possible suffixes. Plural.
First ..	**(maĩ) ũ, je, sũ, ne,**	**(asĩ) ũ, je, sũ, ne.**
Second ..	**(tũ) sũ, ne,**	**(tusĩ) sũ, ne.**
Third ..	**(oh) ī, (or ā), je, sũ, ne,**	**(oh) nĩ, je, sũ, ne.**

Emphatic.

First ..	**hai ũ, je,**	**hai ũ, je.**
Second ..	**none,**	**none.**
Third ..	**hai ī, je, sũ, ne,**	**haiṇ nĩ, je, sũ, ne.**

Past Tense.

First ..	**(maĩ) sāje, sāsũ, sāṇe,**	**(asĩ) sāje, sāsũ, sāṇe.**
Second ..	**tũ, none,**	**tusĩ, none.**
Third ..	**(oh) sāī, sāje, sāsũ, sāṇe.**	**(oh) sāṇĩ, sāje, sāsũ, sāṇe.**

WITH TRANSITIVE VERBS.

Suffixes with **dassṇā**, show.

Imperative.

tũ dass or dassĩ sũ, ne,	**tusĩ dasso or dasseo sũ, ne.**

Present Conditional, I may show, etc.

maĩ dassũ, dassā̃ je, sũ, ne,	**asĩ dassiye je, sũ, ne (not ũ).**
tũ dassẽ sũ, ne,	**tusĩ dasso sũ, ne.**
oh dassī, dasse je, sũ, ne,	**oh dassaṇ ĩ, je, sũ, ne.**

Future, I shall show.

maĩ dassâ -gā (fem. **-gī**) **je, sū, ne** : also **dassū̃ -gā** (fem. **-gī**), **dassjegā** (f. **-gī**).

tū̃ dassẽ-gā (f. **-gī**) **sū, ne.**

oh dasse-gā (f. **-gī**) **je, sū, ne** : **dassigā, dassjegā, dassūgā, dassṇẽ-gā** (f. **-gī**).

asĩ dassãge je, su, ne (f. **-gīã**) : **dassūge, dassjege** (f. **-gīã**).

tusĩ dassoge sū, ne (f. **-gīã**).

oh dassaṇge je, sū, ne (f. **-gīã**) : **dassṇĩge, dassjege, dassūge, dassṇẽge** (f. **-gīã**).

The future may also end in **-dā, -dī, -de, -dīã.**

Past Conditional. I should show, if I showed, etc

Suffixes are used only with the **-o** forms : see *Grammar*, pp. 378–381.

maĩ dass-do (f. **-dīo**) **ī, je, sū, ne.**

tū̃ dass-dõ (f. **-dīõ**) **sū, ne.**

oh dass-do (f. **-dīo**) **ī, je, sū, ne.**

asĩ, none.

tusĩ dass-deo (f. **dīo**) **sū, ne.**

oh dass-dẽo (f. **-dīõ**) **nĩ, je, sū, ne.**

Present Indicative, I am showing, I show.

maĩ dass-nā ū̃, dass-dā je, sū, ne : f. **-nī ū̃, -dī je, sū, ne.**

tū̃ dass-dā sū, ne : f. **-dī sū, ne.**

oh dass-dā ī, je, sū, ne : f. **-dī ā, je, sū, ne.**

Imperfect.

maĩ dass-dā (f. **-dī**) **sāje, sāsū, sāṇe.**

tū̃ dassdā sāsū : f. **dassdī sāsū.**

oh dass-dā (f. **-dī**) **sāī, sāje, sāsū, sāṇe.**

asĩ dass-de (f. **-dīã**) **sāje, sāsū, sāṇe.**

tusĩ dass-de (f. **-dīã**) **sāsū, sāṇe.**

oh dass-de (f. **-dīã**) **sāṇĩ, sāje, sāsū, sāṇe.**

In the past indefinite, present perfect, pluperfect and future perfect of transitive verbs, tenses in which the passive participle is used, agreement is with the logical object (except, of course, where agreement is blocked by **nū**), and the use of pronom. suff. is generally confined to the 3rd sing. and plur. suffixes to indicate the agent. Occasionally the 2nd sing. and plur. suffixes are used when the logical nominative is **maĩ** or **asā̃** to express the idea "I am (or we are) speaking to thee" or "you."

Note.—To express the simple past with a suffix we must use the **-o** form or the pluperfect. The ordinary past if followed by a suffix, has the force of a present perfect.

Present Perfect.

The following cases therefore arise:—

maĩ **ṭukkar khādhā ī (je),**	I tell thee (you) that I have eaten my food.
maĩ **roṭī khādhī ā (je),**	I tell thee (you) I have eaten bread.
maĩ dō paraunṭhe khādhe nĩ (je),	. . . . two chapatis (masc.).
maĩ dō roṭīā̃ khādhīā̃ nĩ (je),	. . . . two chapatis (fem.).

Instead of **maĩ** we may have **asā̃**, we.

ṭukkar khādhā sū (ne),	he has (they have) eaten food.
roṭī khādhī sū (ne),	. . . . bread.
dō paunṭhe khādhe sū (ne),	. . . . two chapatis (masc.).
dō roṭīā̃ khādhīā̃ sū (ne),	. . . . two chapatis (fem.).

For the simple past use **-o** forms or pluperfect, **ṭukkar khādho sū (ne),** he (they) ate food: **roṭī khādhīo sū (ne),** he (they) ate bread.

Pluperfect (also means simple past).

The above sentences will become—

maĩ or asā̃ khādhā sāī (sāje),	I etc. ate or had eaten.	
maĩ or asā̃ khādhī sāī (sāje),	do.	do.
maĩ or asā̃ khādhe sāṇĩ (sāje),	do.	do.
maĩ or asā̃ khādhīā̃ sāṇĩ (sāje),	do.	do.
khādhā (fem. khādhī) sāsū or sāṇe,	he (they) ate or had eaten.	
khādhe (f. khādhīā̃) sāsū or sāṇe,	do.	do.

Future Perfect.

maĩ khādhā howīgā (hojegā),	I tell thee (you) that I shall have eaten.
maĩ khādhī howīgī (hojegī),	do. with fem. sing. object.
maĩ khādhe hoṇĩge (hojege),	do. with masc. plur. object.
maĩ khādhīā̃ hoṇīgīā̃ (hojegīā̃),	do. with fem. plur. object.

So also with **asā̃**, we.

khādhā hosūgā (hoṇegā),	he (they) will have eaten.
khādhī hosūgī (hoṇegī),	do. fem. sing. object.
khādhe hosūge (hoṇẽge),	do. masc. plur. object
khādhīā̃ hosūgīā̃ (hoṇẽgīā̃),	do. fem. plur. object.

If the future in **-dā** is used the forms will be **howīdā, howīdī, hosūdā, hoṇẽdīā̃**, etc., with **d** substituted for **g**.

The suffixes may also follow the verb as mentioned above.

Infinitive.

maĩ ṭukkar khāṇā ī (je),	I tell thee (you) I have to eat food.
maĩ roṭī khāṇī ā (je),	do. fem. sing. object.
maĩ khāṇe nĩ (je),	do. masc. plur. object.
maĩ khāṇīā̃ nĩ (je),	do. fem. plur. object.

and so on. The infinitive may be used all through the present, past and future exactly in the same way as **khādhā** except that **khāṇā, khāṇī, khāṇe, khāṇīā̃** occur instead of **khādhā, khādhī, khādhe, khādhīā̃** : thus—

asā̃ roṭīā̃ khāṇīā̃ sāje,	we tell you that we had to eat chapatis.
parauṇṭhe khāṇe sāṇe,	they had to eat chapatis (masc. plur.).
maĩ caul khāṇe hoṇĩge,	I tell thee I shall have to eat rice.
roṭīā̃ khāṇīā̃ hosūdīā̃,	he will have to eat chapatis.

WITH INTRANSITIVE VERBS.

The only difference is in the past tenses where with intransitive verbs the agent case is not used. It must be observed that even in intr. verbs the agent case is regularly found with the agent -infinitive, thus—

kikaṇ ṭurnā sāsū? how was he to walk?

roṭiā̃ laike jāṇiā̃ ne, they have to take the chapatis and go.

Here we should have expected **jāṇā ne,** but the infin, is attracted into the form of the noun which is the object of **laike**: see Grammar. p. 372.

Present Perfect

Examples:—

maĩ geā ũ, I tell thee I have gone.

maĩ geā sū ghar, I have gone to his house.

We get the following forms (using **geā,** went)—

maĩ geā ũ, je, sū, ne,	**asī̃ gae ũ, je, sū, ne.**
tū̃ geā, sū, ne,	**tūsī̃ gae sū, ne.**
oh geā ī, je, sū, ne,	**oh gae nī̃, je, sū, ne.**

Fem. change **geā** to **geī** and **geā** to **geiā̃** otherwise exactly the same except that 3rd sing. is **geī ā,** not **geī ī.**

Simple past: use -o forms:—

jaṇā geo sū ghar, the man went to his house.

janānī geio sū ghar, the woman went to his house.

Pluperfect (also means simple past).

maĩ geā (f. geī) sāje, sāsū, sāṇe,	**asī̃ gae (f. geiā̃) sāje, sāsū, sāṇe.**
tū̃ geā (f. geī) sāsū, sāṇe,	**tusī̃ gae (f. geiā̃) sāsū, sāṇe.**
oh geā (geī) sāī, sāje, sāsū, sāṇe,	**oh gae (f. geiā̃) sāṇī̃, sāje, sāsū, sāṇe.**

Future.

In addition to the following forms we may have **maĩ geā howā̃gā ī, oh geā howegā je,** etc., with the pronom. suffixes after the verb.

maĩ geā hoũgā, hojegā: fem. **geī hoũgī, hojegī.**

tū, none.

oh geā howigā, hojegā, hosūgā, hoṇegā: fem. **geī howigī,** etc.

asī gae hoũge, hojege: fem. **geiā̃ hoũgiā, hojegiā.**
tusī, none.
oh gae honīge, hojego, hosũge, hoṇẽge: fem. **geiā̃ honīgiā,** etc.

Pronominal Suffixes in Negative Sentences.

With the negative **nā**: (for the interrogative **nā, and nehī nā** see lower down). The rule is the same as for affirmative sentences. **nā** comes before the verb as a rule, occasionally after the suffix, in which case it is strongly accented.

je nā mārdo sū,	if he had not struck him.
diṭṭhā sū nā.	he has *not* seen him.
ākhī sū nā,	do *not* say it to him.

The second and third sentences, if **nā** is unaccented, will mean "he has seen him, hasn't he?" and "just say it to him, won't you?"

With the negative **nehī**. Two cases arise—

(1) Tenses not containing the past auxiliary **sā̃, sāẽ, sī,** etc.

(i) *First rule*.—The suffix follows **nehī** (almost always).

nehī je bhanneā?	did you not break it?
nehī sū hikkaṇ lage,	they will not drive it out.

(ii) *Second rule*.—The 2nd sing. suffix is always **õ**, no matter what it was in the affirmative sentence.

labbhā ī? hast thou found it?	**labbhī ā?** (fem. object).
nehī õ labbhā (labbhī)?	hast thou not found it?
labbhe nī (fem. labbhiā̃)?	hast thou found them?
nehī õ labbhe (labbhiā̃)?	hast thou not found them?
maī dassnā ū,	I am telling thee.
maī nehī õ dassdā,	I will not tell thee.

(2) Tenses with past auxiliary.

Rule.—The suffix is attached to **sā̃, sī,** etc., which become, as in affirmative sentences, **sāī, sāṇī, sāje, sāsū, sāṇo.** These words are preceded by **nehī.**

nehī sāī murnā?	wert thou not going to stop?

Unaccented interrogative **nā.**

Rule.—The **nā** follows the suffix.

huṇe chāṅgṇā ī, nā?	you're going to prune now, aren't you?

Interrogative **nehī̃ nā.**

Rule.—The suffix generally comes between **nehī̃** and **nā**; **nehī̃ ō nā ḍiggā?** I am asking thee, it has not fallen, has it? Cf. **nehī̃ ẽ nā ḍiggā**, thou hast not fallen, hast thou?

Interrogative Pronouns.

Interrogative pronouns are often used in place of a negative:

maī ehnū̃ kī karā̃	what shall I do with it, i.e. it is of no use to me.
ōh dā kitthē innā akl e	he has not got so much sense (**akl** also feminine).
ōh kadō̃ wāhṇ laggā	he will never plough.

kī, unlike the Urdu **kyā**, is never used merely to indicate a question, nor is **kī** employed in the sense of whether..or, Urdu **kyā..kyā**. For that Panjabi uses **bhāwẽ..bhāwẽ.**

kyā is sometimes used along with adjectives in interjections with the sense how, this—

kyā sōhṇī gall or **kehī sohṇī gall**, what a good thing!

Indefinite Pronouns.

The indefinite pronouns are **kōī**, some one, any one, and **kujjh** something, anything. The following examples illustrate p. 293.

kōī kōī āeā (sing. verb), some people, very few people came.

kujjh kujjh e, there is a little.

kōī nehī̃ āeā, no one came; **kujjh nehī̃ miḷeā**, nothing was obtained.

kōī .. kōī (both singular) some .. others, thus **kōī manndā we, kōī nehī̃ manndā**, some agree, others do not.

kōī na kōī hōwēgā, there will be someone or other; **kujjh na kujjh miḷēgā**, you will get something or other.

kōī is sometimes used with the sense of 'about' in connection with numbers or measures of any kind, such as time, quantity, etc. In this sense it is never declined. It is often contracted to **ku, ko.**

kōī ghaiṇṭē nū̃	in about an hour.
ēh ko caūh waṭṭīā̃ dā bhār hōwēgā	this is about four wattis (eight ser) in weight.

A word **ku,** whether this or another, with the same meaning, often follows numbers, and the words **kinnā, innā, kēḍḍā, ēḍḍā.**

kinnā ku hōwēgā? trai ku sēr hōwēgā.	How much will there be? About three ser.

kōī nehī̃ is sometimes used with the sense of not at all, as—

chīmbā te kōī nehī̃ āeā	the washerman has not come at all.
Gangū te kōī nehī̃ āeā	Gangu has not come at all.

Reflexive Pronoun.

In the nominative this is merely emphatic, giving the sense of myself, yourself, himself, themselves, etc. In the oblique cases it is really reflexive. The nominative is **āpē, āpī, āpū̃, āpō̃** or **āp.** In the prepositional case **apṇā** is used, except in the accusative or dative where **apṇē āp nū̃** is the form found.

The oblique cases of the reflexive pronoun are used whenever the reference is to the nominative of the sentence. The ordinary pronouns **mērā, tuhāḍḍā, ōhnā̃ dā,** etc., must not be used in a reflexive sense.

Pīrā ōhdī panjāḷī apṇī samjhdā e	Pira considers his (the other man's) yoke his own.
tusā̃ mērī lēllī nū̃ apṇā karkē rakkhea	you have kept my lamb, considering it your own.

ōh āpē jākē apṇā bandobast karangē, apṇe āp nū̃ te jhallēā̃ nehī̃ na samjhdē, they will go themselves and make their own arrangement, they do not consider themselves idiots.

When the reflexive pronoun is in apposition with a noun or pronoun it is often kept in the nominative even though the other word is in the prepositional, thus—

sānū̃ āpū̃ Panjābī nehī̃ aundī, we ourselves do not know Panjabi.

If the preposition takes the genitive of a noun or pronoun the genitive **apṇā** is generally employed, as **sāḍḍē apṇē kōḷ kujjh nehī̃ e,** we ourselves have nothing.

This pronoun often has the sense of without assistance, by itself, etc., **āpē wall hō jāēdā,** it will get well by itself.

apṇā is often used for one's own where one might expect **sāḍḍā** or **mērā or tuhāḍḍā,** thus—

ēh te apṇā e, this is our own. Or a servant will say **ēh apṇā mēc e,** meaning this is our table. i.e., it belongs to the house.

PREPOSITIONS.

nē, by, is used only as the sign of the agent. Some Panjabis never use it at all. It should not be used with pronouns although speakers under the influence of Urdu do so use it.

-õ is added to the singular of nouns (never to the plural except names of villages), and words used as nouns, such as adjectives, infinitives, etc., to adverbs and to other prepositions. It has the sense of 'from' in time and place, and sometimes is practically meaningless.

For the plural of nouns a detached preposition is employed thus **gharõ** from the house; **gharā̃ thõ,** from the houses.

The changes produced in nouns by the addition of **-õ** have been explained under the heading of declension of nouns, p. 278.

The adverbs of place **ētthē, ōtthē, jitthē, kitthē. kitale, kite, kidhare, uttē, aggē, picchē,** drop the final **e** before **-õ.** When one of these words is used with the preposition **dā,** it commonly though not invariably takes the suffix **-õ** before the **dā,** thus—

ōtthõ dā jaṇā, a man from there, **ētthõ dī gall,** a matter belonging to here. We also have **ōtthē dā jaṇā, ētthē dī gall.**

Other examples with adverbs are :—

sāhmṇeõ	from in front.	**nēṛeõ**	from near.
uttõ	from above.	**aggõ**	from before.
banneõ	from outside.	**pareõ**	from beyond.

In the following **-õ** seems to have no meaning :—

edõ then, **jadõ** when, **tadõ** then,

also wallō in the phrase mērē wallō wēkhdā e, he is looking at me.

-ō and the detached prepositions thō, tō, thī, te, have in addition to the meaning of from in time and place, the meanings of 'from' in free from, get well (from sickness), prevent (from), be evident (from), escape (from), deny (from), refuse (from), refrain (from), fear (from), ask (from), source (from in time or place).

-ō, however, has not the sense which these others have of 'than' in comparison, 'to' in superiority or inferiority to, or the sense of 'for' in prices (for so much) or exchange. -ō may be used along with nāḷ in comparison, mērē nāḷō, than I. kōḷō may frequently be used for these prepositions.

auṇō inkār kītā, auṇ tō inkār kītā	he refused to come.
pañjā paiseā tō miḷeā	it was obtained for five pice.
tuhāthō waḍḍā e	bigger than you.
bimārīō wall hōeā	he has got well *from* his sickness.

jānō māreā geā, he was beaten from his life, i.e. killed.

methō or mērē kōḷō kasūr hōeā, I have committed a fault.

waihṛē tō wachērā waṭāeā	exchanged a foal for a calf.

tē, uttē, on, upon, is sometimes used where we should expect another preposition, thus—

khūh tē, at the well. talā tē, at the tank, haṭṭī uttē, at the shop.

mērē tē arzī pāi	he brought a case against me.
apṇī gall te wī khlōweā kar	stick to your position or word.
hukm uttē calṇā	to keep an order.
ōh dē tē karz caṛh geā	he got into debt.

kisē te āshik hoṇā, be in love with someone. āshik has the oriental sense of love.

nāḷ is used for 'with' of contiguity, also for 'with' or other prepositions compounded with verbs, e.g., fight with, work with, deal with (treat well or ill), speak to (with), feel disgust at (with), be pleased or displeased with, tie to, unite with, love, come into contact with.

waihṛā rukkh nāḷ bannhī	tie the calf to a tree.
puttar nāḷ baṛī mhabbat kītī	loved his son much.

ōh dī sutthaṇ nāḷ mērā pair lagg geā.	my foot touched his trousers.
caliyē nāḷō nāḷ	let us go together.

Abstract nouns compounded with **nāḷ** give the sense of adverbs, as—

chētī nāḷ	quickly.
sababb nāḷ	by accident, by chance.
ṭill nāḷ	by force or with effort.

kōḷõ is frequently employed for 'by' of agency

ōh dē kōḷõ nehĩ cukkidā	he cannot lift it.
ōh dē kōḷõ cukkāṇ nehĩ hundā	he cannot lift it.
ōhnū̃ ustād kōḷõ paṛhāū̃gā	I will have him taught by a teacher.

nāḷõ is employed for the purposes of comparison, meaning 'than.' (See under **-õ**).

bin, binā, bijn, bājhõ are used with the inflected past participle to express our 'without' with the gerund.

bin khādheā̃ ṭur geā	he went away without eating.
bin saddeā̃ āeā	he came without being called.

This is also expressed by the two prepositions **thõ(thĩ, etc.)**, and **binā**, as **ākkhaṇ tõ binā**, without saying. In this case the inflected infinitive is used.

wallõ often means on behalf of, from—

mērē wallõ ōh dē aggē hatth jōṛnā or bannhṇā.	beseech him from me (put your hands together).
mērē wallõ ōhnū̃ ākhṇā	say to him from me.

The ordinary meaning is from the direction of, **sāḍḍē wallõ**, from our party, from us.

hēṭh, below, said of rupees has the sense of "*temporarily* kept back."

ōs dō rupae hēṭh rakkhē	he kept back two rupees.
chē din hēṭh rakkhē	he kept back the wages of six days.

aggē has often the meaning of in comparison with, or in the opinion of, thus—

ōh dē aggē ōh kujjh nehī̃ e, means, according to context, compared with him this is worthless, and in his opinion this is worthless.

sir is used with **wēḷā, wakat,** time, and **thã̂,** place, to mean 'in,' **wēḷē sir,** or **wakat sir,** in time, at the right time; **thã̂ sir,** in the right place.

sār in conjunction with the form in **eã̂** of present participles means just at the time of, **aundeã̂ sār,** on arrival; **ākhdeã̂ sār,** while speaking; **waṛdeã̂ sār mar geā,** he died on entering.

ADJECTIVES.

The relative adjectives **jehā,** as, **jinnā,** as much as, **jēḍḍā,** as large as, have almost a prepositional force, being used with the prepositional of nouns and pronouns, while themselves agreeing with the noun, or pronoun to which they refer.

ōh kaṭṭī mērē wachērē jeḍḍī e	that young buffalo is as large as my foal.
tuhāḍḍē jēhā te kōī ghulāṭīā nehī̃	there is no wrestler like you.
Gujrāt jinnī kisē duāḷē dē piṇḍ dī abādī nehī̃	no village round about has as much population as Gujrat.

In these sentences **jēḍḍī, jehā, jinnī** agree with **kaṭṭī, ghulāṭīā, abādī,** respectively, while **wachērē, tuhāḍḍē, Gujrāt** are in the prepositional case.

This use of **jehā** is not to be confounded with that mentioned in the earlier part of the grammar, p. 292, where the meaning is rather, -ish, and where **jehā** is used not with the prepositional case of the noun, but in simple agreement with it, as in the following:—

gōrī jehī gã̂	a reddish cow.
māṛā jehā ḍhaggā	a rather weak bull.

Instead of the plural prepositional form adjectives frequently employ the form in -**ē** when in agreement with masculine nouns, thus—for **sāḍḍeã̂ kutūreã̂ dā,** of our puppies, **sāḍḍē kutūreã̂ dā** is quite common.

In the vocative the adjective usually follows the usage of the noun, if the noun takes the vocative form the adjective generally, does so also. Sometimes the noun has it, while the adjective retains the ordinary oblique form, singular or plural, but the adjective never takes the vocative form unless the noun has it, thus—

mērē mālik, mēreā mālikā or **mērē mālikā,** but not **mēreā mālik,** my master.

For the agreement after the prepositional **nū̃** and for a similar rule applying to a complementary attributive when the noun is in the agent case, and also when there is an impersonal sense with no nominative expressed, see under accusative case.

All adjectives singular and plural may be used as nouns, as, **ikk garīb,** a poor man, **kōī māṛā jehā,** some feeble man, **buḍḍhīā̃** married women.

NUMERAL ADJECTIVES.

Numeral adjectives, after the first, generally take their noun in the plural. The word **rupayyā,** rupee is not infrequently used in the singular. The numbers **sau,** hundred, **hazār,** thousand, **lakh,** 100,000, frequently take their noun in the singular if it is masculine.

dō sau ghōṛā	two hundred horses.
ḍhāī hazār bandā	two thousand five hundred men.

When a number is counted by scores the word **wīhā̃** often has its noun in the singular.

cār wīhā̃ jaṇā	four score men.

If the noun is expressed the word **wīhā̃** does not affect the gender or number of the verb, but if the noun is omitted **wīhā̃** takes its verb in the feminine plural.

trai wīhā̃ rupeā miḷeā sī	he got sixty rupees.
traī wīhā̃ miḷīā̃ sāṇ	he got sixty.

When the noun qualified by a numeral is governed by a preposition, the numeral is nearly always inflected, thus—

pañjā̃ jaṇeā̃ dī mazdūrī	five men's wages.
saṭṭhā̃ rupayyā̃ tō̃ āeā	it costs sixty rupees.
dasī̃ paisī̃	for ten pice.

If, however, the noun is in the singular the adjective is not inflected.

Thus cār rupae tõ miḷeā, it was obtained for four rupees.

Agreement of Adjectives.

Panjabi frequently uses adjectives where we should have adverbs, as in phrases like "he plays well," "he writes well." The question of their agreement causes some difficulty. The rules are—

(i) Intrans. verbs with no object. The adjective agrees with the nominative.

oh caṅgī khẽḍdī e, she plays well.

(ii) Trans. verbs with no object. The objective is masc. governed by the verb.

oh baṛā caṅgā likhdī e, she writes very well.

(iii) Trans. verbs with an object or intrans. verbs with a cognate object. The adjective agrees with the object.

oh kāpī caṅgī likhdā e, he does his copy well.

oh kirkaṭ caṅgā khẽḍdī e, she plays cricket well.

Adverbs.

There is some difference between āhō and hā̃. āhō, āh and, less frequently, hā̃, are used in giving an affirmative answer to a question. āhō, but not āh, often means "well, go on, I am listening." hā̃ is used to reply to one's name, while hā̃ te means "yes, indeed, what else would you expect? The following questions and answers between A and B will exemplify the usage.

A. ṭur caleā ẽ? B. āhō (or āh). A. are you off? B. yes.

A. wāḷ karṛ barṛē hō gaē nī? B. kī? A. wāḷ. B. āhō? A. karṛ barṛē hō gaē nī? B. hō gaē nẽ kujjh kujjh. A. has your hair got grey? B. what? A. your hair. B. well? A. has it got grey? B. somewhat.

A. ōē Būṭeā! B. hā̃! A. Būṭā! B. yes.

A. mukkar geā e ukkā mukkā? B. hā̃ tē. A. has he refused altogether? B. yes, I should rather think he has.

A long-drawn-out hā̃ on two or three notes may mean "Oh, I see now. Is *that* the way of it?" In this case āhō would not be used.

THE VERB.

The Infinitive.

The uses of the infinitive are complicated. Its flexibility is one of the characteristic features of Panjabi.

(i) As a noun. When so used it may be nominative to a verb, governed by a verb, or governed by a preposition. Whether it is nominative or objective it may itself govern an object. In this case it generally agrees in gender and number with its object, and if it is nominative the verb to which it is nominative also agrees in gender and number. If the object is governed by the preposition nū̃, the infinitive does not agree with it, but remains in the nominative singular. When the infinitive has no object it retains the form of the nominative singular.

The prepositional form of the infinitive is found by adding ṇ to the root if it ends in a vowel (or a vowel followed by h), n if it ends in r, ṛ, rh, ṛh, and -aṇ if it ends in any other consonant.

(*a*) simple nominative or objective, infinitive in agreement with its object.

nahauṇā cangā we	it is good to wash oneself.
ēs rāh auṇā jāṇā baṛā hundā e	there is much coming and going on this road.
laiṇā dēṇā	dealings.
maĩ apṇā laiṇā lellea e	I have taken what I had to take.
huṇ ōs muṇḍē paṛhnā chaḍḍ dittā e	now that boy has given up reading.
cōrī karnī māṛī e	it is wrong to steal.
gā̃ cōṇī bhull geā	he forgot to milk the cow.
kaṇakā̃ gāhṇīā̃ raih geīā̃	it remains to thresh the wheat.

(*b*) governed by preposition. Sometimes the preposition is understood. This is specially the case with prepositions expressing cause or reason, such as nū̃, wāstē, lai.

ōh mērē auṇ tō̃ paihlū̃ mōeā	he died before I came.
gaḍḍā jāṇ nū̃ teār ai	the cart is ready to go.
puchhaṇ gicchaṇ dī lōṛ nehī̃	there is no need to enquire.
asī̃ khlōṇ jōgē nehī̃	we are not able to stand (live, etc.).
maī̃ kamm karn geā	I went to work.
bhrā ḍhaggā wēccaṇ geā	my brother went to sell a bullock.
ōh wēkkhaṇ āeā	he came to look.
ōh mārn geā, sagō̃ mār khāṇ laggā	he went to beat but began to be beaten.
maī̃ pucchaṇ pucchaṇ kardā sā̃	I was on the point of asking, I wished to ask.

It will be noticed that the above uses correspond in great measure to the Latin gerund and gerundive.

The infinitive in agreement often expresses purpose. It may be in tense.

maī̃ gāīā̃ cugṇīā̃ chaḍḍ dittīā̃ sāṇ	I left the cows to graze.
sunyārē apṇī dhī paṛhnī pāī	the goldsmith has sent his girl to read.
phatūhīā̃ dhōṇīā̃ dittīā̃ sū	he gave the waistcoats to be washed.
manjī uṇṇī or uṇāṇī dittī nē	they gave the bed to be woven.
patlūn sukkṇī pāī	he put out the trousers to dry.

There is a usage with the verb pāṇā which does not appear to come under the rule, it differs from that of the last examples.

chīmbē kamīzā̃ sūkṇē pāīā̃	the washerman put out the shirts to dry.
jhiggā sukṇē pāeā sājē ?	did you put out the shirt (native) to dry ?

Here it will be seen that the form sukṇē does not vary. It is peculiar inasmuch as a form in -nē does not occur in the singular in the normal inflection of the infinitive.

The verb **laggṇā** governs the infinitive in the prepositional.

ōh kadō̃ partāṇ laggā	when will he ever give or take it back ?
kuṛī rōṇ laggī	the girl began to cry.

(*c*) with some word signifying advisable, necessary, etc. This is merely a variation of (a). **cāhīdā e** (the organic passive of **cāhṇā**, wish) is used with the sense of it is advisable or desirable or one ought; **paiṇā**, to lie, with the infinitive means, have to, it will be necessary to; and **hōṇā**, be, become, with an infinitive has practically the same sense. These verbs agree in number and gender with the infinitive which is nominative to them, that in turn being attracted into the number and gender of the noun, if any, which is governed by it, unless the word **nū̃** governs the noun, in which case the infinitive remains in the nominative singular masculine, this being the form which it assumes also when there is no noun.

kitābā̃ paṛhnīā̃ cāhīdīā̃ nē̃	one ought to read books.
ēhnā̃ kitābā̃ nū̃ paṛhnā cāhīdā e.	one ought to read these books.
bagghī jōṇī pawēdī	you will have to harness the trap.
khāṇā paiē gā	it will be necessary to eat.
maḷāī lāhṇī wē	the cream has to be taken off.
bhaḷkē pīhāī dēṇī hōwēdī	to-morrow one will have to give the price of grinding.

(*d*) with prepositional inflection to indicate ability. The infinitive is used in the prepositional case, even when nominative, to indicate ability. This use is common only in negative sentences. When found in affirmative sentences the affirmation is generally in close connection with a negation. This infinitive may govern an object, and in that case it will, though remaining unchanged itself, attract the verb to which it is nominative, into the number and gender of its object except, of course, when nū interposes, and breaks the concord.

mērē kōḷō khlōṇ nehī̃ hundā I cannot stand.

ṭurn te hundā e par ēḍḍī panḍ nehī̃ cukkaṇ hundī, I can *walk*, but I cannot lift so heavy a load. (This probably in reply to a question "can't you walk?")

bhaḷkē miṭṭī nehī̃ puṭṭaṇ hōwēdī, to-morrow one will not be able to dig earth (but **puṭṭṇī hōwēdī** would mean will not *have* to dig earth).

ēḍḍīā̃ aukhīā̃ kitābā̃ munḍē kōḷō nehī̃ paṛhn hōṇ laggīā̃, the boy will not be able to read such difficult books.

dḕh rāt caukīdārī nehī̃ karn hundī, one cannot watch day and night.

(*e*) The infinitive is often used as an imperative. When so used it agrees with its object if there is any.

aiñ nehī̃ karnā	do not act thus.
rōṭī mērī lai auṇī	bring my food.
gāīā̃ ētthō̃ kaḍḍhṇīā̃	turn out the cows from here.

(*f*) The infinitive is used with the agent case of nouns and pronouns to express the idea of to have to, to intend to. In this case the rule for the agreement of the infinitive is exactly the same as the rule for the agreement of the past participle in the agent construction of transitive verbs. This use of the infinitive is extended to all verbs, transitive and intransitive, the latter, however, not being able to take an object.

kitthē jāṇā nē? ōhnā̃ shaihr jāṇā e	where have they to go? they have to go to the city.
ōs nehī̃ paṛhnā	he will not read.
tū̃ muṛnā nehī̃?	will you not desist?
pishā̃ te sārēā̃ partṇā e	all have to turn back.
maī̃ ōsdē rupayyē dēṇē nē̃	I have to give him money.
rōṭī ajē khāṇī jē?	have you still to have your food?
ḍhaggē kitthē laijāṇē nī̃?	where have you to take away the bullocks?

ciṭṭhīā̃ khōlṇīā̃ sāṇē they had to open the letters.
maĩ ōhnā̃ dōhā̃ nū̃ waḷkē partā leauṇā sī I had to turn them both and bring them back.

(*g*) When the nominative is a purely involuntary agent, and no intention is attributed to it, the construction (*f*) is often changed for one in which the infinitive and finite verb agree with the nominative. This construction is found only with intransitive verbs

gāīā̃ wall te hōṇīā̃ ī nehī̃ the cows will not get well.
es tarhā̃ bamār hōṇē nē̃ in this way they will get ill.
ōh ghōṛīā̃ wigaṛ zarūr jāṇīā̃ nē̃. those mares are sure to be spoiled.
ṭōē te kharāb hōṇē ī hoē the holes are bound to be bad.

The difference between the two usages may be seen in the following:—

caūh jaṇeā̃ sauṇā e, four men intend to or are going to sleep.
cār jaṇē sauṇē nē̃ four men will be sleeping here (a calculation as to how many men can be got into the space).

mērī manjī wī jāṇī e my bed too is to go. [etc.
mērīā̃ bhaiṇā̃ wī jāṇā e my sisters are to go, intend to go,
ēhnā̃ cūhīā̃ muṛnā nehī̃ these mice *will* not desist.
ēh cūhīā̃ suddharnīā̃ nehī̃, these mice will not become good.

(Here the mice are treated as acting without volition.)

With the verbs auṇā, come, and jāṇā, go, the infinitive is often attracted into agreement with some noun which is object to a conjunctive participle and has therefore no connection with the infinitive which it attracts.

tū̃ kaṛchīā̃ chaḍḍkē auṇīā̃ come after leaving the spoons.
maĩ ṭiṇḍā̃ cukākē jāṇīā̃ nē̃ I have to go after having helped someone to lift the earthen pots.

In the first sentence we should expect **auṇā**, and in the second **jāṇā**.

-wāḷā.

This is perhaps a convenient place for a note on **-wāḷā. wāḷā** may be added to any noun with the meaning of "connected with", "possessing" or "belonging to"; thus we have **majjhā̃wāḷā**, buffalo man, **ghōṛē wāḷā**, man with a horse, **billī akkh wāḷā**, man with a cat-like eye. The noun with **wāḷā** is put in the prepositional case.

Unlike Urdu, Panjabi makes a clear distinction between singular and plural in the words to which **-wāḷā** is attached. Thus **trēṛā̃ wāḷī kandh**, a wall with cracks: **trēṛ wāḷī kandh**, a wall with a crack: **ciṭṭeā̃ challeā̃ wāḷā**, someone with white rings: **ciṭṭē challē wāḷā**, someone with a white ring.

The word **rōṭī wāḷā**, bread-man, is a word imported from Urdu for the benefit of Europeans. It ought really to be **rōṭīā̃ wāḷā.**

-wāḷā may be added to the genitive of pronouns and the prep. case of nouns to mean "having connection with" as distinguished from "belonging to." Thus **mērī wadhrī**, my thong, but **mērē-wāḷī wadhrī**, the thong which I had in my hand or which was formerly mine (but now perhaps is yours). **camraṅg dā saṇḍhā**, the buffalo of the tanner, but **camraṅg wāḷā saṇḍhā**, the buffalo which has some connection with the tanner; perhaps was his and was sold by him. See Appendix.

Exceptions.—Pronouns in the third sing. may, and in the third plur. must, take the prep. case before **wāḷā**. See Appendix.

Care must be taken never to use **-wāḷā** for the English 'one' after an adjective. The red one or the white one must be represented simply by **sūhā** or **baggā** and not by the use of **-wāḷā.**

When **wāḷā** is used with an adjective a noun is understood. Thus if one were speaking of two boys wearing shirts one might say: **ikkī dā kāḷā jhiggā sī te ikk dā ciṭṭā; ciṭṭē wāḷā ṭur geā, te kāḷē wāḷā ajē ētthē ī e**, one had a black shirt and one a white, the one with the white (shirt) has gone away, the one with the black shirt is still here. **ciṭṭē wāḷā** could never mean the white one. Similarly in speaking of girls and boys with buffaloes, **būrī wāḷā** would mean the boy with the grey buffalo, **būrī wāḷī** the girl with the grey buffalo.

-wāḷā never takes the accent. The accent of **ghōṛeā̃ wāḷā** is on ō, of **nakhēṛanwāḷā**, one who separates, on ē, of **wēkkhaṇwāḷīā̃**, women who are looking, on ē: in no case does it fall on any part of **wāḷā**.

Past Participle.

As explained in the Accidence, when **hoeā**, the past participle of **hōṇā**, is added to the past participle of a verb a state is indicated, and if the verb is transitive the state is passive.

riddhē hoē caul	cooked rice.
tusā̃ Khushāb ḍiṭṭhā hoeā e	have you seen Khushab? (is Khushab in the state of having been seen by you?)

The **hoeā** is sometimes omitted as **baiṭhā baiṭhā saũ rehā**, while seated he fell asleep.

The past participle may be used as a noun :—

phāthā sabbh kujjh kardā e, one entangled will do anything.

An exception to the passive use is found in the phrases **paṛheā hoeā** and **sikkheā hoeā** which may mean both having studied or learned and having been studied or learned.

ōh Fārsī paṛheā hoeā e	he is one who has studied Persian.
ōs Fārsī paṛhī hoī e	he has studied Persian.

When the past participle is used in apposition to an object it agrees with the object unless when **nū̃** intervenes, in which case it remains masculine, singular, or, rarely, takes the ending **-eā̃**. (See also note on **-eā̃** at the end of the noun cases.)

maĩ ikk muṇḍā moeā hoeā ḍiṭṭhā	I saw a boy dead.
ōh nū̃ peā hoeā chaḍḍeā	he left him lying.

baihṇā, sit. **khlōṇā**, stand, sometimes take the ending in **-eā̃**, but with other verbs it is rare in this connection.

jē tū̃ kuṛī nū̃ baiṭheā̃ jā̃ khlōteā̃ wēkhẽ	if you see the girl sitting or standing.

Conjunctive Participle.

This generally has the meaning of having done something, but it often has a present signification and very frequently is used as an adverb.

kard phaṛākē jā	having handed the knife go.

bhajjkē jā, nāḷē sōc samajhkē gall karī̃	go running, moreover speak thoughtfully and understandingly.
wāzā̃ (awāzā̃) mār mārkē gaḷ pāṭgeā	my throat has burst through calling out.
bhaṅgākē wēhndā e	he looks squintingly.

jāṇkē, knowingly: **hōsh karkē**, carefully: **bacākē**, carefully (savingly).

This participle generally refers to the nominative of a sentence, but other uses are found, as—

mēnū̃ wēkhkē gussā āeā	I got angry on seeing it (anger came to me).
jīwī̃ māṛī karkē paī hoī e	the land, being considered bad, is lying idle.

When a verb is repeated to indicate continuance or when two verbs having a single idea are used together, the ending **-kē** is attached only to the second : see **mār mārkē** above.

khā pīkē having eaten and drunk.

For phrases like **maī kitābā̃ chaḍḍkē jāṇiā̃ nē̃** or **auṇiā̃ nē̃**, see under Infinitive, p. 372.

When the conjunctive participle of a verb is joined to a verb of motion or one meaning to send, it is common to omit the ending **-kē** or with the simple imperat. sing. of **auṇā**, come, to substitute **-e** for **-kē**. The two verbs thus connected express practically a single idea which is very often somewhat different from the idea which would be expressed if the ending **-kē** were retained :—**dass jāṇa**, tell and go: **dē jāṇā**, give and go ; **uṭṭh khlōṇā**, get up and stand ; **uṭṭh nassṇā**, get up and run away ; **uṭṭhe ā**, get up and come ; **wēkhe ā**, look and come ; **dē auṇā**, give and come. In all these there is a special nuance of meaning not found in the fuller form, but very difficult to put into words. Thus **ōh uṭṭh naṭṭhā**, is 'he was up and off' : **uṭṭhkē naṭṭhā (or nass geā)** he got up and ran away. Sometimes the meaning is considerably changed.

maī pauḷī dē ṭōrī, I sent four annas (by someone) ; **pauḷī dēkē**

ṭōrnā, to give four annas to someone and send him. **ā**k**h**g**hallṇā**, to send a message, **ākhkē ghallṇā**, tell someone and send him.

This use must be clearly distinguished from that of intensive compound verbs (see compound verbs in the Accidence, p. 332). In the latter case the second verb entirely gives up its own meaning and serves merely to emphasise the meaning of the first verb.

Present Conditional Tense.

This tense is used much more than in English. It is often found instead of the present tense in the case of proverbs or sayings of a proverbial nature, also in statements of two parallel occurrences, e.g.—

Rabb diā̃ Rabb jāṇē God (alone) knows God's affairs, i.e., God alone knows.

Baṛī mauj hōī, maī peā puṭṭā̃, te ōh kōḷō peā ḍakkē. There was a great joke. I was digging and he was hindering me.

When one verb is contingent on another in the way of advisability, duty, desire, necessity, command, condition, result, the contingent verb is generally put in the present conditional, e.g.—

mērā rūh nehī̃ kardā sī pai adhwāṭē khlō jā̃, my spirit did not desire (I did not wish) that I should stand still half way.

tū̃ khlō jā maĩ bhajjkē wēkh **āwā̃**	you stand here, I will run and see.
bēbbē āhndī e pai ṭur jāē	mother says he is to go away.
nishaṅg lagā jā, jē jāṇ dē tē	by all means go if he lets you.

Similarly questions about a course of action to be pursued, action advisable or the reverse, necessary or permitted, dependent on the will of another or doubtful, naturally have their verbs in this tense.

maĩ jā̃, shall I go? **ōh jāē**, may he or shall he go? **asī̃ ki karīyē**, what shall we do?

This tense is also used for blessings and curses, e.g., **marẽ** mayest thou die, **pīṛ pawī** mayest thou have pain.

Rabb tērā bhalā karē	God bless you.
waḍḍā din mubārak hōwē	a happy Christmas.

For conditional clauses see under Past Conditional, p. 377.

PRESENT TENSE.

The auxiliary is never omitted in this tense except in negative sentences, though it is frequently uttered very rapidly. In the first person singular the auxiliary is often merely a nasalising of the vowel, e.g., **maĩ āhnnā̃** or **āhnnā wā̃**, I say, **asī̃ āhnneā̃**, we say.

In negative sentences there are two forms: (i) the ordinary form with the negative particle prefixed, in which case the auxiliary is always inserted. (ii) the present participle without the auxiliary. This latter form is more usual, e.g.—

maĩ nehī̃ karnā wā̃, but more commonly **maĩ nehī̃ kardā**, I do not or will not do it.

The present tense is sometimes used for greater vividness in relating past events, though this is not very common. It is also, and very commonly, used for the future to indicate immediate action; e.g., in past narrative, **mai ēddharõ lagā̃ aunnā wā̃, te ōh ōddharõ bhajjā lagā̃ jāndā e**, I was coming from this direction and he was running along in that direction.

We also have **āh wēkhā̃, huṇē ōh nū̃ kaḍḍh dēnnā wā̃**, look, I will turn him out at once. This tense sometimes expresses will or intention, as **tusī̃ ēh tarjumā nehī̃ wēkhdē?** will you not look at this translation?

IMPERFECT.

This tense indicates continuance or sometimes habit in the past. The auxiliary must never be omitted even in negative clauses. In negative clauses the auxiliary may precede the present participle, e.g., **ōh nehī̃ puṭṭdā sī** or **ōh nehī̃ sī puṭṭdā**, he was not digging.

PAST CONDITIONAL.

This tense is used in the protasis and apodosis of conditional sentences, i.e., in the clause containing the word "if" or some similar word and also in that containing result. It implies that the condition stated has not been fulfilled.

CONDITIONAL SENTENCES.

The following sentences will explain the method of expressing conditions with different tenses.

(1) jē ōh **kamm mukāē maĩ dihāṛī dēāgā,** if he finishes the work I will give him a day's wages.

For vividness we may have ōs **mukāeā,** instead of ōh **mukāē** past indefinite.

(2) jē ōh **kamm mukāndā** e **maĩ dihāṛī dēāgā,** if he is finishing the work I shall give him, etc.

(3) je **ōh mukāndā maĩ ōhnū̃ dēndā,** if he had finished I should have given him. **jē ōhdī bēbbē wēhndī tā̃ rinj hundī,** if his mother saw him she would be displeased.

It will be seen that the past conditional is used for two different tenses in English, corresponding to saw and had seen. The correct meaning is gathered from the context. The compound tense, pluperfect conditional, is rarely used especially in the apodosis. We do not generally hear such phrases as **jē ōh geā** hundā, if he had gone ; **maĩ zarūr nāḷ geā hundā,** I should certainly have gone with him. would not be heard in the apodosis. This should be **maĩ zarūr** jāndā. The compound tense, if used, should be confined to the protasis.

The other form of the past conditional may be employed.

jē ōh **āwēā caṅgī gall hōwē ā**	if he had come it would have been a good thing.
(4) jē ōh **kardā sī tā̃ mukā wī laēgā**	if he was doing it he will finish it.
(5) jē **kadē rassī waṭṭdē hōwō menū̃ dasseō**	if you should ever be plaiting a rope tell me.

Sometimes the condition is only implied, e.g., **kadē wēhndeō,** if you would only some time look, **āhō, geā te tā̃,** yes, if he goes, then—(then you may talk, or then we shall see, etc.). See also pp 380, 1.

-ō *forms in the Past Conditional and Indicative.*

The following paradigms will indicate these forms. In the past conditional **-ā is changed to -ō for the 2nd person mas. sing., -īō for fem. sing.,** -eō for masc. pl. **and -īō for fem. pl.** In the **past indicative of transitive verbs the ending -eā is changed to -eō, īō, eō, -īō respectively, the sing. being the same as the pl.,** but with different pronominal affixes. If the past indic. ends in -ā (but not -eā) the endings become -ō̃, -īō, -eō, īō̃. In intransitive verbs -eā changes to -eō̃, -īō̃, -eō, -īō; and -ā (not eā) to -ō̃, -īō̃, -eō, īō. If in any of the above cases the ending -eā has the accent on -ē it is treated like the ending -ā, not -eā.

Past Conditional cukkṇā, lift.

Person.	Singular.	Plural.
Second ..	cukkdō̃, fem. cukkdīō.	cukkdeō, fem. cukkdīō.
Third ..	cukkdō (ī, jē, sū, nē), fem. cukkdīō (ī, etc.).	cukkdeō (nī̃, jē, sū, nē), fem. cukkdīō̃ (nī̃, etc.).

Past Indicative, transitive verb.

Here number and gender apply to agreement with the object.

cukkṇā, lift : karnā, do.

Person.	Singular object.	Plural object.
Second ..	cukkeō ī, jē : fem., cukkīō ī, jē.	cukkeō nī̃, jē : fem., cukkīō̃ nī̃, jē.
Third ..	cukkeō sū, nē : fem., cukkīō sū, nē.	cukkeō sū, nē : fem., cukkīō̃ sū, nē.
Second ..	kītō ī, jē : fem., kītīō ī, jē.	kīteō nī, je : fem., kītīō̃ nī̃, jē.
Third ..	kītō sū, nē : fem., kītīō sū, nē.	kīteō sū, nē : fem., kītīō̃ sū, nē.

(Intransitive Verb.)

Second ..	geō̃, fem. geīō̃.	geō, fem. geīō.
Third ..	geō (ī, jē, sū, nē), fem. geīō (ī, etc.).	geō (nī̃, jē, sū, nē), fem. geīō̃ (nī̃, etc.).
Second ..	ṭureō̃, fem. ṭurīō̃.	ṭureō, fem. ṭurīō.
Third ..	ṭureō (ī, jē, sū, nē), fem. ṭurīō (ī, etc.).	ṭureō (nī̃, jē, sū, nē), fem. ṭurīō̃ (nī̃, etc.).

On these forms a few notes are necessary. They are essentially conditional. In the past cond. they emphasise the conditional nature of the sentence, and in the past indicative they usually import the idea of a strong condition. Hence these forms are specially suited to threats. The condition expressed by this past indic. is always future. In the past cond. of all verbs and the past indic. of intrans. verbs the pronouns which are nominative to the verb may be expressed. In the past of the trans. verbs it is incorrect to express them; they are always expressed by means of pronominal affixes. In the 3rd sing. of the past cond. the form in -ō always has a pronominal suffix as object, and may not be used without it.

jē patā laggdō ī, te dā nā khāndīō̃, if you had known, you (fem.) would not have been tricked.

jē bēbbē ṭhākdīō sū, te nā russdā, if his mother had stopped him, he would not have taken a huff.

jē khiskeō̃, makkū ṭhappū̃gā, if you run away, I'll jump on you (slang).

jē dātrī bhannīō ī, if thou breakest the sickle: **jē dātrīā̃ bhannīō̃ nī̃**, if thou breakest the sickles: by changing the last word in both sentences to **je**, we get if '*you*' break, etc.

Sometimes we find this ending in the past indic. when no condition is implied. In this case the verbs denote past time. This is most common in 3rd person transitive and 2nd person intransitive.

kī bhāṛā dittōs, what fare did he give?

muṛ cōkhā bāllaṇ sāṛeō nē, afterwards they burned a lot of firewood.

As these constructions are difficult it will perhaps be well to give an example of each possible case.

PAST CONDITIONAL.

jē tū̃ waṭṭā cukkdō̃	if thou hadst lifted the stone.
jē tū̃ waṭṭā cukkdīō̃	if thou (fem.) hadst lifted the stone.
jē jaṇā ghalldō ī (or **jē**)	if the man had sent thee (or you).
jē jaṇā ghalldō sū	if the man had sent him or her.
jē jaṇā ghalldō jē	if the man had sent you.
jē jaṇā ghalldō nē	if the man had sent them.
jē kuṛī ghalldīō ī (jē, sū, nē)	if the girl had sent thee (you, him or her, them).

jē jaṇē ghalldeō nī̃ (jē, sū, nē)	if the men had sent thee (you, him or her, them).
jē kuṛīā̃ ghalldīō̃ nī̃, etc.	if the girls had sent thee, etc.

PAST INDICATIVE.

Kyūn geō̃	why didst thou go ?
jē waṭṭā cukkeō ī	if thou liftest the stone.
jē waṭṭā cukkeō jē	if you lift the stone.
jē waṭṭē cukkeō nī̃	if thou liftest the stones.
jē waṭṭē cukkeō jē	if you lift the stones.
jē kuṛī cukkīō ī (or jē)	if thou liftest (or you lift) the girl.
jē kuṛīā̃ cukkīō̃ nī̃ (jē)	if thou liftest the girl (you lift).
jē waṭṭā cukkeō sū	if he (or she) lifts the stone.
jē waṭṭā cukkeō nē	if they lift the stone.
jē waṭṭē cukkeō sū (nē)	if he (she) lifts the stones (they lift).
jē kuṛī cukkīō sū or nē	if he (she) lifts or they lift the girl.
jē kuṛīā̃ cukkīō̃ sū or nē	if he (she) lifts or they lift the girls.
jē geō̃, jē geō	if thou goest, if you go.
jē geīō̃, je geīō	if thou (fem.) goest, if you (f.) go.
jē nāḷ ṭureō ī or sū	if he goes with thee or him (her).
jē nāḷ ṭureō jē or nē	if he goes with you or them.
jē nāḷ ṭurīō ī or sū	if she goes with thee or him (her).
jē nāḷ ṭurīō jē or nē	if she goes with you or them.
jē nāḷ ṭureō nī̃ or jē	if they go with thee or you.
jē nāḷ ṭurēō sū or nē	if they go with him (her) or them.
jē nāḷ ṭurīō̃ nī̃ or jē	if they (fem.) go with thee or you.
jē nāḷ ṭurīō̃ sū or nē	if they (fem.) go with him (her) or them.
bhrā geō i ?	did thy brother go ?
kī kītō i ?	what didst thou do ?
gal ẽ hoīo je.	I tell you, the matter happened thus.

PAST, PERFECT AND PLUPERFECT TENSES.

These do not call for much comment.

The past is often used for the sake of vividness in conditional clauses and may have a future sense.

jē ōs wēkh leā, te maĩ bajjh geā.	if he saw, I shall be imprisoned.
jē te ā geā, maĩ bac geā	if he really comes, I shall be saved.

The pluperfect is usually used without special differentiation between it and the simple past. It is very commonly used for the past.

maĩ kujjh nehĩ ākheā sī	I said nothing.

A distinction is however not at all rare, e.g.—

kitthē geā	where has he gone?
kitthē geā sī	where did he go?

Some verbs are used in the past tense when we might expect the present. Such are **baihṇā,** sit; **khlōṇā,** stand; **saũṇā,** sleep. The fact is these words really mean seat oneself, rise up, go to sleep. Therefore we have: **baiṭhā e,** he is sitting, i.e., seated; **baihndā e,** is in the act of seating himself; **khlōtā,** standing; **khlōndā,** in the act of rising; **suttā,** sleeping, i.e., asleep; **saundā,** going to sleep.

Similarly care must be exercised with **laggṇa.** Thus **pāḷā laggdā e** means that in certain circumstances one feel cold, or one is now beginning to feel cold, but **pāḷā laggā e,** I feel cold (now). So **bhukkh or treh laggdī e** means 'in the circumstances indicated one feels hunger or thirst,' whereas **bhukkh laggī e** is 'I am hungry,' and so on.

IMPERATIVE.

The imperative is used to express commands, requests, blessings and curses.

The infinitive is often used instead of the imperative to express commands and requests.

khush rauh	mayest thou be happy.
jiũndā rauh	live long.

aiñ nā ḍāhṇā	do not place it thus (i.e., place the bed chair, etc.).

CAUSATIVE VERBS.

It is worth noticing that the causative form of a verb has often a meaning which differs considerably from that of a mere causative. Thus **suṇāṇā**, cause to hear, means simply to relate; **phaṛāṇā**, cause to seize, means to hand something to someone; **paṛhāṇā**, cause to read, means to teach, **bulāṇā** means both to cause to say and to call, and **akhwāṇā** to be called and also to cause to say. See further below.

ōh nū̃ bulā	call him.
ōhdē kōḷō̃ ṛ bulā	get him to say the letter ṛ.
ōh Kammō akhwāndī ē	she is called Kammo.
Kammō kōḷō̃ ēh gall akhwā	get Kammo to say this.

Sometimes a causative verb has the meaning of *help* to do so-and-so.

mĕnū̃, bhrā, manjī kaḍhā, brother, help me out with the bed

bhaiṇ, mĕnū̃ ēh carkhā dharā, sister, help me to put this spinning wheel there.

Frequently, if the contrary is not expressed, a causative verb implies that the nominative of the sentence is the object direct or indirect of the action of the verb, thus **beiztī karnī**, insult; **beiztī karāṇī**, permit oneself to be insulted: **luṭṭṇā**, rob: **luṭāṇā**, let oneself be robbed, i.e. distribute alms, etc.

Sometimes when we should expect the causative of a verb to be used, we find that some other verb is used instead, either an ordinary transitive verb or the causative of some other verb. Thus **sāh laiṇā** means to take breath, but to give an animal or burdened man a rest by letting him stop for a bit is **sāh duāṇā** (the causative of **dēṇā**, give), and if one carries a man's load for a time, the verb used is **sāh kaḍhāṇā**, to let him get a breath.

Again **dā khāṇā** is be tricked, but to trick another is **dā lāṇā**: **dhōkhā khāṇā** is to be deceived and **dhōkhā dēṇā**, to deceive.

With reference to the meaning of causal verbs it is worth noting that while the causal of an intrans. verb means to cause to perform the action indicated by the simple verb, that of a trans. verb means to cause the action to *be* performed. Thus we have **bhajjṇā**, run, **bhajāṇā**, cause to run : **ṭurnā**, walk, **ṭōrnā**, cause to walk : **khēḍṇā**, play, **khiḍāṇā**, cause to play ; and on the other hand **cukkṇā**, lift, **cukāṇā**, cause to be lifted : **dēṇā**, give, **duāṇā**, cause to be given : **chaḍḍṇā**, leave, **chuḍāṇā**, cause to be left. It follows that a double causal, i.e., the causal of a causal, always has the second signification, for the causal of which it is a causal is transitive. Another result is that while we can express in Panjabi "make a man run or walk or sit or stand," we cannot directly say "make him give or throw or cut." For "I will *make* him give four annas" we have to say **ōh de kōlō̃ pauḷī duāā̃gā**, I will cause it to be given by him. "I will force him to look" is **maĩ ōhnū̃ majbūr karā̃gā paĩ wēkhē**, i.e., I will force him that he may see. **ōhnū̃ wikhāā̃gā** would be merely "I will show him." But "I will compel him to enter" may be directly expressed **ōhnū̃ zōrī wāṛā̃gā**. A few verbs are either exceptions to this rule or have both significations :—

saddṇā, call,	**sadāṇā**, be named.
ākhṇā, say.	**akhwāṇā**, be named or cause to be said.
bōlṇā, speak or ring (of coin).	**bulāṇā**, call, cause to be said, cause to ring.
kūṇā, speak.	**kuāṇā**, call.
paṛhnā, read.	**paṛhāṇā**, cause to read or to be read.
sikkhṇā, learn.	**sikhāṇā**, cause to learn or to be learned.

cubbhṇā, pierce (thorn, etc.), **cōbhṇā**, **cubhāṇā**, cause to pierce.

The meanings given on p. 306 'cause to raise,' 'drink,' 'give,' 'put,' are correct for ordinary purposes, but as has been explained above, the meanings should, strictly speaking, be 'cause to be raised,' 'to be drunk,' 'to be given,' 'to be put.'

Compound Verbs.

Completeness or Intensity.

Europeans employ compounds to excess. They are uncommon in interrogative sentences, and rare in negative ones. If used in interrogative sentences it definitely implies *completion*.

To express completeness or intensity five verbs are used, joined to the roots of other verbs. **chaḍḍṇā**, leave : **dēṇā, give** : **laiṇā, take** : **suṭṭṇā**, throw : **jāṇā**, go. The first four are almost invariably used with transitive and the last with intransitive verbs. (See note on **jāṇā** at end of Accidence, p. 337.) **Suṭṭṇā** is the least used of the five. Sometimes one hears one of the first four with an intrans. verb, as **bōl chaḍḍeā, bōl dittā**, spoke : **raih leā**, remained. In such cases the verb is considered trans. **ōs raih leā**, he or she remained.

With the word **chaḍḍṇā** in composition (often pronounced **chaṛna, sarna, sharnā**) there is just a soupçon of carelessness or casualness. For this reason in solemn speech, in prayer or in reference to things usually spoken of with reverence, it is often better to use another verb. Thus **maĩ Kurān paṛh chaḍḍeā**, I have read the Qur'ān, is slightly more casual than **paṛh leā**. In addressing God, to translate 'Thou hast told us (in Thy Word)' by **ākh chaḍḍeā**, would suggest flippancy.

When, in speaking of doing something *for* someone, the verb **dēṇā** is used in composition with another, the idea of 'for' is generally rendered by **nū̃**, as with the direct object, e.g., **maĩ tènū̃ huṇē pakā dēnnā̃**, I will cook it for you at once. **pakā chaḍḍnā̃** would require **tērē wāstē**. **ōh mēnū̃ baṇā dēgā**, he will make it for me.

laiṇā has two uses—

(i) With the simple idea of completion or intensity as above it is used with many transitive and one or two intransitive verbs. In this sense there is a contrast with **dēṇā**. **Laiṇā**, meaning take, rather suggests that the action has a special connection with, or is for the benefit of, the agent; **dēṇā**, meaning give, rather passes on the action to someone else. It is therefore natural to say **wēkh lai**, look : **kuā lai sū̃**, call him : **mall lai**, take possession of : and on the other hand **chaḍḍ dē**, leave off : **ghall dē**, send : **piā dē**, give to drink. Intransitive verbs used in this way are **nahā laiṇā**, wash oneself : **khēḍ laiṇā**, play. This distinction must not be pressed too far.

(ii) To express the idea of getting something over in order to do something else. When laiṇā has this meaning almost any verb, transitive or intransitive, may be compounded with it. With intransitive verbs, however, it is not very commonly used in the past indic. and pluperfect tenses.

ōh nū̃ auṇ dē, let him come: **ōh nū̃ ā laiṇ dē,** first let him come (and then we shall do so-and-so).

ōh mar laiē, let him die first (and then we shall see).

mukkaṇ dē is simply "let it finish," but **mukk laiṇ dē,** let it finish first (and then do so-and-so).

The verbs auṇā, come, and **ṭurnā, go, have a peculiar construction with cāhṇā to express the idea that someone or something is just about to come or go. The participle of auṇā or ṭurnā is used with the required tense of cāhṇā and agrees with its nominative in number and gender. This construction is found with only those tenses of cāhṇā which are formed from the present participle.**

gaḍḍi ṭurī cāhndī e, the train is just about to start.

huṇ āē cāhndē hōṇgē, now they will be about to come, they must be coming now.

karnā with a repeated infinitive in the prepositional case, gives the idea of wishing to do something and yet hesitating about it.

maĩ ciroknā pucchaṇ pucchaṇ kardā rehā, for a long time I have wished to ask.

Uses of calṇā.

(i) Accompany:	**mērenāḷcal,**	accompany me.
(ii) Start ..	**cal, āeā ũ,**	start off, I am coming.
	cal pher,	start off then.
	kadõ cale sao,	when did you start?

(iii) With roots of verbs to express "almost" or "about to," see Grammar, p. 334.

mukk caleā e,	it is almost finished.
mērā hatth lagg caleā si,	my hand was just about to touch it.

(iv) In negative sentences to express ability. Grammar, p. 386.

mēre kolō̃ nehī̃ puṭṭeā caleā,	I shall not be able to dig it.

(v) Like the English go or work (intrans.). go on, do its work. perform its functions, etc.

kamm caldā e,	the work is going on (well).
mashīn caldī e (nehī̃ caldī),	the machine is working (won't work).
dārū nehī̃ caldā,	the powder or medicine is not working. i.e., is not efficacious.
rupayyā caldā e,	the rupee passes or circulates (i.e. is not bad).
ohdā mukadmā nehī̃ lagā calaṇ,	his case will not go on, he has no case.
paṭāke or goḷe nehī̃ calde,	the fire-works (special kinds) will not go off.

(vi) **Cal, cal whai, calo,** or **calo jī** often means "that's all right now," "there that's settled," etc.

Uses of **paiṇā** (see also G. 397. 408. 409).

It expresses—

(1) The idea of actually doing a thing at the moment spoken of. G. 334, 335 : **oh gōḍdā e peā, oh peā gōḍdā e (never gōḍdā peā e),** he is hoeing.

(2) Indifference (with the pres. subj.) : **peī uḍīke, let her wait** (I do not mind). (1) and (2) only with past part. **peā.**

(3) Beginning or suddenness **bhakh paiṇā,** blaze up : **akk paiṇā,** get tired of : **ḍigg paiṇā,** fall : **phull paiṇā,** blossom : **miḷ. paiṇā,** meet : **raḷ paiṇā,** join oneself to, and many more.

(4) Necessity. to have to, must. G. 334 : **otthe aṭaknā pawidā,** you will have to wait there.

(5) Fall, in a wide sense of the word : **raḷā paiṇā,** be adulterated : **peā hoeā,** fallen, lying (of ground) fallow : **lammā paiṇā,** lie down : **suttā peā,** asleep : hence also with words for rain, drops of water. etc., dew, shadow, reflection (in water.

etc.), night, darkness, cold, famine: also of blows, abuse, and of instrument with which blows are administered, as stick, cane, shoe.

(6) Worry, annoy, attack: **mārn paiṇā, ṭuṭṭke paiṇā, hatthī paiṇā**, all mean rush at or attack: **kuttā paindā e**, the dog attacks: **magar or picche paiṇā**, follow annoyingly, not to cease following: **gal paiṇā**, harass, etc.

It expresses mental or physical feelings or conditions.

(7) Mental feelings: words for habit as **hiltar gējh** or **ādat paiṇī**: **saur** or **āhl paiṇī**, be in a hurry: hence also with **sāṛā**, envy; **jhass** or **caskā**, taste; **rohb**, influence: of a person, **bhaiṛā paiṇā**, become ashamed: **sauṛā, kāhlā p.**, impatient, etc.

(8) Physical conditions: with words like **challā**, blister: **bakhōṛ**, cramp: **trāṭ, waṭṭ, pīṛ**, all meaning pain or kinds of pain: **phollā, ciṭṭā**, white ulcer in eye: **pāṇī**, water (in eyes): **laūs, lās**, weal: **jhurṛī**, wrinkle: **pāk**, pus (in wound, etc.): **khurk**, itch: of person, **pīḷā paiṇā**, become pale.

(9) Happen, occur, with words for love, friendship, discord, noise, disturbance, loss, also hole, hollow, indentation, turn.

(10) Happen, occur, become, and meanings difficult to classify: **waḷā paiṇā**, long way round: **pherā paiṇā**, have to pay visit: **phal** or **phull paiṇe**, fruit or flowers be formed: **dalīlī paiṇā**, argue, hesitate: **bhann paiṇī**, become creased: **piṛ palle nā paiṇā**, not understand: **kurāhe paiṇā**, go astray: **warhā paiṇā**, get respite for year: **jādū paiṇā**, be bewitched: **peṭe paiṇā**, be responsible for: **wāh paiṇā**, have to do with: **kamm paiṇā**, work turn up: **tarīk paiṇī**, date be appointed: **nazrī paiṇā**, become visible: **pīṅgh paiṇī**, rainbow be formed: **āgat paiṇā**, name be struck off list of debtors: **kāṇō paiṇī**, get warped: **wagāṛ (phuṭṭ) paiṇā (-ī)**, discord, dispute occur: **moche paiṇe**, short logs be cut up: **wagyār paiṇī**, forced labour.

Ability and Inability.

The idea of ability (or inability) can be expressed in five ways, thus for "I cannot thresh" we may have **maĩ nehī gāh sakdā**: **mērē kōḷō nehī gāheā jāndā**: **mērē kōḷō nehī**

gāhīdā : mērē kōḷō nehī̃ gāhṇ hundā : mērē kōḷō nehī̃ gāheā calleā.

Of these constructions only the first, with **sakṇā,** is common in affirmative sentences. The other four are generally employed in negative sentences or in interrogative sentences which are practically negative. Of the five the first and fourth are mentioned under compound verbs in the accidence. The second is the ordinary passive construction, the third is the organic passive construction (**-īdā**). The fifth is peculiar in that it is confined to the past tense. Its meaning, however, is future. The above sentence in the fifth case means "I'm not going to be able to thresh."

Parts of Verbs with Unusual Forms or Meanings.

In the case of a few verbs only one part is found, or a particular meaning is found in only one part. Thus we have—

leā (pl. **leāo**), imperat. of **leauṇā,** bring, means hand it to me. No other part has this meaning.

bhannā, is found, as well as **bhajjā** (past part. of **bhajjṇā**), with the verbs **auṇā,** come, and **jāṇā,** go, as **ōh bhannī lagī jāndī sī,** she was running along.

āndā (āndī, ānde, āndīā̃), brought, is a past part.; the rest of the verb is not found. In some dialects a verb **āṇṇā,** bring, is heard and Panjabi has **aṇwāṇā,** cause to be brought.

lagā with **auṇā** and **jāṇā** indicates that the action is actually taking place, as **janānīā̃ lagīā̃ jāndīā̃ sāṇ,** the women were going along. It may be a past part of **laggṇā,** but no other part of **laggṇā** has this sense.

See **āhndā** and **wēhndā** in Appendix.

Direct and Indirect Speech.

In Panjabi direct speech, oratio recta, is employed much more than in English. Indirect speech is little used.

I asked him why he would not obey, **maĩ ōhnū̃ puccheā paĩ tū̃ ākkhē kyū̃ nehī̃ laggdā.**

Direct speech is often found, when the idea of saying or thinking is only implied.

They were afraid of his taunting one of them, **ōhnā̃ nū̃ ḍar sī paī cētā sānū̃ kisē nū̃ mehṇā nā dē.**

It should be noted that the English word 'if' in 'asked if,' 'wondered if,' 'know if' must not be translated by the ordinary word for 'if': the word for 'that' must be used, **paī** or **ke**. Often, of course, the whole phrase must be changed.

Ask him if he will be able to come, **ōhnū̃ pucchō paī tū̃ ā sakẽdā.**

I wonder if he will return, **k͟haure (k͟habre) partẽdā ke nehī̃.**

Euphemisms.

A few interesting euphemisms are in common use.

duddh saur geā, the milk has turned sour (lit. has become good).

dīwā waḍḍā kar, put out the lamp (lit. make it big).

pagg or **kapṛe wadhā,** take off your pagri or clothes (lit. increase).

ōh pūrā hō geā e, he has died (lit. he has become complete).

dāṇe waddh gae, the grain is finished (lit. increased).

bāhrla, bāhr dī shai, pig, boar (lit. outside thing).

The Days of the Week.

Sunday, **aitwār.**

Monday, **suār, somwār.**

Tuesday, **maṅgaḷ, maṅgaḷwār.**

Wednesday, **buddh buddhwār**

Thursday, **jumerāt.**

Friday, **jumā.**

Saturday, **haftā, abbaḷ haftā.**

(Sabbath, **sabbat**).

Hindus use the following special words never used by Musalmans:—

Thursday, **wīr, wīrwār.**

Friday, **sukkar, shukkar, sukkarwār, shukkarwār.**

Saturday, **saniccar, saniccarwār, chanicchar, chaniccharwār, chiṇchiṇwār.**

The Months.

The English names, somewhat altered, are most commonly used, but villagers very often use the Hindu names.

English Months.

janwarī, farwarī, mārc (mārac), aprail, mai, jūn, julāī (jaulāī); agast, sitambar, aktūbar, nawambar, dasambar.

Here, as in the case of all words taken directly from English, people who know English attempt to approximate their pronunciation more closely to the English pronunciation.

Hindu Names.

wasākh	April—May.
jēṭh	May—June.
hāṛ	June—July.
sauṇ	July—August.
bhādrõ	August—September.
assū̃	September—October.
kattẽ	October—November.
magghar	November—December.
pōh	December—January.
māh	January—February.
phaggaṇ	February—March.
cēttar	March—April.

The Hindu month usually begins about the 14th of the English month.

RELATIONSHIPS.

peō, cāccā, bāp	father.
bēbbe, mā̃	mother.
dāddā	father's father.
dāddī	father's mother.
paṛdāddā	father of dāddā.
paṛdāddī	mother of dāddā.
nānnā	mother's father.
nānnī	mother's mother.
paṛnānnā	father of nānnā.
paṛnānnī	mother of nānnā.
bābbā	father's elder brother. father's father.
tāeā	father's elder brother.

tāī	wife of **tāeā**.
cāccā	father's younger brother.
cāccī	wife of ditto.
phupphī	father's sister.
phupphaṛ	husband of **phupphī**.
māmmā	mother's brother.
māmmī	wife of **māmmā**.
māsī	mother's sister.
māsaṛ	husband of **māsī**.
dōhtrā	daughter's son.
dōhtrī	daughter's daughter.
paṛpōtrā	son of **pōtrā**.
paṛpōtrī	daughter of **pōtrā**.
bhatrīyā	brother's son.
bhatrī	brother's daughter.
sauhrā	father-in-law.
sass	mother-in-law.
patiauhrā, patrauhrā	father-in-law's brother.
patēhas	wife of **patiauhrā**.
dadiauhrā	father-in-law's father.
dadēhas	wife of **dadiauhrā**.
maliauhrā	mother-in-law's brother.
malēhas	wife of **maliauhrā**.
naniauhrā	mother-in-law's father.
nanēhas	wife of **naniauhrā**.
kuṛm	father of son (or daughter)-in-law.
kuṛmnī	mother of son (or daughter)-in-law.
bhrā	brother.
bhaiṇ	sister.
sāḷā	wife's brother.
sāḷihār, sālihāj	wife of **sāḷā**.
sāḷī	wife's sister.
bhaṇūjā	sister's husband.
bhābbī, bharjāī	brother's wife.
jēṭh	husband's elder brother.
jaṭhāṇī	wife of **jēṭh**.

jaṭhuttar	son of **jēṭh.**
deōr	husband's younger brother.
daraṇī	wife of **deōr.**
naṇān	husband's sister.
puttar	son.
dhī	daughter.
pōtrā	son's son.
pōtrī	son's daughter.
bhaṇēwā̃, bhaṇēā	sister's son.
bhaṇēwī̃, bhaṇēī	sister's daughter.
juāī, jawātrā, majmān	son-in-law.
nū̃h	daughter-in-law.
bhatrīõ juāī	brother's son-in-law.
bhatrīõ nū̃h	brother's daughter-in-law.
bhaṇēweõ juāī	sister's son-in-law.
bhaṇēweõ nū̃h	sister's daughter-in-law.

SPECIAL IDIOMS.

The following idioms will, it is believed, be found useful. They are intended merely as references, and the beginner will need to inquire about their usage. In some cases the words bear other meanings also. The list is of course not complete, but the idioms given will suggest others. As very many of them are connected with verbs, an alphabetical list of the verbs is given first.

Verbs.

The infinitive or other part of the verb is understood with each word. The gender is shown in every case as a guide to the agreement of the verb.

auṇā, come, used with various words as nom.; **akkhīā̃,** f. pl., have sore eyes: **sabak,** m., known a lesson: **bōlī,** f., or **zabān,** f., know a language; **jawāb,** m., know the answer: **nafrat,** f., feel disgust; **krīc,** f., feel physical disgust: **sharm,** f., feel shame: **namōshī,** f., feel humiliation: **hōsh,** f., come to one's senses: **jī ūtā̃,** vomit: **yād,** f., or **cētā** m., remember: **jhappē,** m. pl., have stoppage in ears: **dhauḷē,** m. pl., get white hair; **gussā**, m., feel anger; **samajh**, f., understand; **nīndar**, f., feel sleepy: **ubāsī**, f., yawn: **hāssā**, m., laugh: **sufnā**, m., dream: **mũh**, m., have sore mouth (horse, etc.): **kamm**, m., m., be useful.

baihṇā, sit; **wāz (awāz)**, m., become hoarse: **saṅgh**, m., become hoarse; **maṇ (rupayyē) dā kī baiṭhā**, what does it work out at per maund (or rupee): **caul**, m. pl., rice gets soft through overcooking: **suṇtī**, be circumcised: **koṭhā**, m. (etc.), house sinks down: **naṭṭī**, sit long in one place. **baihṇā** is also used for beginning school life or a trade.

bahāṇā, seat; **muṇḍē nū̃**, send boy (to begin school-life, or some trade): **suṇtī**, circumcise: **naṭṭī**, keep sitting long, delay someone.

bhannṇā, break; **ākaṛ**, f., stretch oneself.

bharnā, fill; **muṭṭhīā̃**, f. pl., shampoo: **ghuṭṭ**, m., swallow mouthful (of liquid): **nuksān**, m., recover loss from someone: **kapṛē**, m. pl., clothes get covered (with mud).

caṛhnā, climb; **karz**, m., get into debt: **sill**, f., or **sējjal**, f., get damp: **hāṇḍī**, f., be put on to cook (said of the **hāṇḍī** or pot): **caul**, m. pl., rice be put on to cook: **kass**, f., get fever: **gussā**, m., become angry: **bāzī**, f., lose game.

cāṛhnā, cause to climb, etc.; **hāṇḍī**, f., put on the pot: **salūṇā**, put on vegetables to cook.

cūpṇā, suck, used in preference to **khāṇā**, eat, with the following; **gannā**, m., sugarcane: **amb**, m., mango: **nimbū**, m., lemon: and frequently with **santarā**, m., orange: **māḷṭā**, m., Maltese orange: **miṭṭhā**, m., sweet lime: **khaṭṭā**, m., lime.

dēṇā, give: **duā**, f., invoke blessing on: **bad duā**, f., invoke curse upon: **dhōkhā**, m., or **farēb**, m., deceive: **āṇḍṛā**, m., lay egg: **tā**, m., heat up fire (for cooking).

kaḍḍhṇā, put or bring out; **gāḷ**, f., abuse: **ghuṇḍ**, m., veil oneself to prevent face being seen: **matlab**, m., secure one's end; **kamm**, m., secure one's end: **khaurū**, m., paw ground (of horse, etc.), hence make a fuss: **dand**, m. pl., show teeth, i.e. grin: also show teeth in anger (dog, etc.): used of things daily consumed in sense of "last out," **dō din k.**, last out two days: **khāṇā k**, last out dinner (said of meat, salt, sugar, etc.): **hāḷī (lādū)**, make fit for ploughing (burden bearing): **daddh**, f., affect great style: **ghutkḷā̃**, f. pl., be hypercritical.

kaḍhāṇā, causative of **kaḍḍhṇā**, q.v; **sōh**, m., let a man get a rest (by carrying his load for him). See **sāh**, p. 399.

karnā, do; **rūh**, m., or **jī**, m., or **dil**, m., wish, feel inclined to: **raddī**, throw away as useless: **chuṭṭī**, f., stop work, take leave: **jhāṛ**, f., reprimand: **dō rupaē laiṇē kītē**, agreed to take two rupees: with many nouns and adjectives as **piār**, love: **wall**, make well: **Bānnā Bānnā karkē kuāndē saṇ**, they used to call him Banna: **mārā karkē**, considering it feeble: **māṛī karkē paī hoī e**, owing to being poor is lying fallow: **ēs karkē**, on this account: **ōs nā̃h kītī, hā̃ nehī̃ kītī**, he refused, he did not agree (he said 'no,' not 'yes').

karnā also means have use for, **maī cunjh kī karnī ē (bīṛā kī karnā e)** what use have I for a dib (a button)?

khāṇā, eat; **dhōkhā**, m., or **farēb**, m., be deceived: **dā**, m., be tricked, over-reached: **mār**, f., be beaten: **gahḷā̃**, f. pl., be abused: **jhiṛkā̃**, f. pl., be reproached: **saūh**, f., swear: **ṭhuḍḍā**, m., stumble: **bhambaḷ-bhūsē**, m. pl., wander in difficulties: **cuglī**, f., slander: **kasr**, f., or **ṭōṭā**, m., suffer loss: **waḍḍhī**, f., take bribe: **juttī**, f. (**baint**, m., etc.), be beaten with shoes (cane, etc.).

khēḍnā, play; **shikār**, m., hunt.

laggṇā, begin, be attached, etc.; **patā**, m., get to know; **saṭṭ**, f., get a wound or bruise; **gōḍā**, m., as in **cann nū̃ gōḍā, laggā** see **gōḍā lānā**: **ṭākī**, f., piece be sewn on: **burā (caṅgā**, etc.), dislike (like, etc.), a thing (or rarely a person): **ṭill**, m., force be used: **rupayya**, m., pass, be spent, be charged (rupee, etc.): **cir**, m., or **ḍēr**, f., delay occur: **ākhē**, obey command: **sardī**, f. (**bhukkh**, f., **treh**, f.) feel cold (hunger, thirst): **pāḷā**, m., feel cold: **gallī̃**, get talking: **matthēē**, meet: **muhdṭhī̃**, stand against doorpost: **gaḷ**, m., embrace: **kasr**, f., or **mōs**, f., suffer loss. **kamm**, be at work; **naukarī**, f., be on duty: **dā**, m., succeed in trick; **maukā**, m., get opportunity: **lāggā**, m., get sore on back (horse, etc.): **kunjī**, f., key fit; **julāb**, m., take effect (purgative): **mull**, m., be charged (price): **ōh mērā bhra (etc.) laggdā e**, he is by relationship (practically) my brother, etc.: other meanings are, be engaged in work: cause pain (of medicine, shoe, etc.): hold oneself back from or keep out of.

lāhṇā, bring down; **būhā**, m., open door: **bārī**, f., open window. **izzat**, f, or **pat**, f, dishonour: **juttī**, f. (**kapṛā**. m, etc) take off shoes (garment, etc.): **karz**, m., remove debt (by paying it).

lāṇā, causative of **laggṇā**; **gōḍā lānā**, said of **cann**, moon, rise (for first time) after sunset. **ṭill**, m., use force: **patā**, m., find out; **dā**, m. trick, overreach: **lēkhā**, m., calculate: **ṭākī**, f., sew on patch: **rōṭī**, f., put **capātī** into oven: **cir**, m., or **dēr**, f., delay: **ḍann**, m., fix fine: **mull**, m., fix price: **nishān**, m., affix mark: **rupayyā** (etc.) cause to pass (rupee, etc.), fix price of one rupee (etc.).

laiṇā, take; **ubāsī**, f., yawn: **gāḷ**, f., be abused: **jhiṛkā̃**, f. pl., be reproached: **hūnṭē**, m. pl., take ride upon

luṭṭṇā, rob; **lillā̃**, f. pl., **bullhē**, m. pl., amuse oneself, have a jolly time.

maḷnā, rub; **maḷeā hoeā**, ill: **maḷ geā**, ran away.

mannā, acknowledge; **burā**, feel offended at, be annoyed at.

mārnā, strike, kill; **būha**, m., shut door: **bārī**, f., shut window: **jhūṭh**, m., tell lie: **chāḷ**, f., jump: **wāz (awāz)**, f., shout, call to: **nicch**, f., sneeze: **jānō̃**, kill: **gōḍā**, same as **gōḍā lāṇā**, q. v.; **matt**, f., or **hōsh**, f., or **bā**, f., or **akl**, m. f., **mārī jāṇī**, be confused, lose one's senses: **ṭiṭṇē**, m. pl., kick up hind feet (of donkey, horse, etc.), hence make a fuss: **mār chaḍḍṇā** or **mār suṭṭṇā**, kill: **thā̃**, kill: **kūk**, f., shout: **cīk**, f., scream: **hakk**, m. (**paisa**, etc.), defraud of right (of money, etc.): **tālā**, m., or **jandrā**, m., lock: **cubbhī**, f., dive: **japphā**, m., embrace: **nazr**, f., glance at: **rauḷā**, m., make confusion: **ṭakkar**, f., knock against: **phērā**, m., go a round: **shēkhī**, f.. exhibit pride: **sir**, m., wag head (of priest in incantations): **gapp**, f., make false, exaggerated statements.

milṇā, meet: **majjh**, f. (**gā̃**, f.), permit to be milked, of buffalo (cow, etc.).

nikḷṇā, go out, come out: **cor (badmāsh** etc.), turn out or become a thief (scoundrel, etc.): **haḷī**, m., become fit for ploughing (of bull), hence become able to do any work (of man):

akhbār, f., be published, newspaper (so with books, etc.): **mōh,** f., be sprained.

paiṇā, fall; many uses, some will be best explained by examples For sense of being in the act of or of continuance see under compound verbs. It is used in many compounds as **phull peā** blossomed: **hass peā,** burst out laughing: **akk peā,** got sick of: **guṭak peā,** broke out into a smile: **ṭur peā,** started: **mārn peā sī,** he came at me to strike me: **hatthī peā,** he seized me or struggled with me: **ṭuṭkē peā,** came at me with anger: **bhaira peā,** he got ashamed: **kuttā paindā e,** the dog attacks one: **jīwī paī hoī, e,** the land is lying fallow: **hanēre pae,** at fall of darkness: **kamm pai geā,** work has turned up which must be done: **maī suttā peā uṭṭhea wā,** I have just got up from sleep: **mār,** f., be beaten: **juttī, f. (sōṭī,** f., etc.), be beaten with shoe (stick, etc.): **gāhḷā̃,** f. pl., be abused: **pīṛ,** f., have pain: **shakk,** m., feel doubt: **ṭōṭā** m., or **ghāṭā,** m., suffer loss: **nazrī,** be seen: **pīḷā,** get pale.

pakāṇā, cook; **gall,** f. arrange beforehand, plot.

pakkṇā, be cooked; **gall,** f., be arranged beforehand, be plotted.

paṇa, put in: **khair,** f. give something to beggar: **ṭukkar,** m., give food (to dog. etc.): **ḍanḍ,** f., or **rauḷā,** m., make noise: **arzii** f., bring case against: **hāl hāl,** f., **hālpāhreā,** m., call out for help: **juttī,** f. (**kapṛē,** m. pl. etc.), put on shoes, (clothes, etc.): **bhaṅgṛā,** m., or **dhamāḷ,** m., dance: **acār,** make pickle, etc: **japphī,** f. (of two people) interlace arms over shoulders: **wāstē,** m. pl., beseech: **kahāṇi,** f., tell story: **mahīnā (dō dihāṛē,** etc.), give respite for month (two days, etc.): **rāh,** show the way to.

pīṇā, drink; **gussā,** m., swallow down one's anger: **hukkā,** m. (**sigraṭ,** f., **curuṭ,** f., **tamākū,** m., etc.) smoke huqqa (cigarette, cheroot, tobacco, etc.).

rakkhṇā, place, keep; **dōstī,** f., be friendly with: **mhabbat,** f., love.

wāhṇā, causative of **waggṇā; aṅgrēzī,** f. (etc.), drag in English (etc.) (into speech).

tōṛnā, break; used of reducing someone in rank.

ṭórnā, causative of **ṭurnā; kamm,** m., get work done.

ṭurnā, walk, go: **kamm**, m., work go on: **gāll**, f., be agreed to (of one's suggestion, etc.).

wagṇā, flow; **bhāṇḍā**, m., leak (of vessel): **rāh**, m., be much used of road: **wag jā**, go off quickly.

wagāṇā, causative of **wagṇā**, cause to flow: send off quickly.

waṭṭṇā, twist; **kacīciā**, f. pl., show teeth in anger: **ghurākīā**, f. pl., frown.

wēkhṇā, see, look: **rāh**, m., look out for, wait for someone **wēkhī japēgī**, we shall see.

Other Idioms.

akhē, lit. **ōs ākheā**, he said, also one says, they say, sometimes the Greek hoti, **ohnā̃ kahāṇī pāī akhē**, etc, they told a story to the effect that, etc.

baihṇī; **kehṛī baihṇī baiṭhā e**, in what company is he?

bhā, **waṇḍē**; **mērē bhā** (or **waṇḍē**) **dā ōh ṭur geā**, in my opinion, or so far as I am concerned, he went away: **ohdē bhā** (**waṇḍē**) **dī te tū̃ i dhī ẽ**, in his opinion you are the daughter

bhāṇē; **mērē bhāṇe**, **sāḍḍē bhāṇe**, etc., in my opinion, in our opinion, etc., or for me, for us: **mērē bhāṇē tusī̃ i rājē ō**, for me you are the Raja.

cāh, tea; weak, **patlī**; strong, **saṅhṇī**, **tēz**, **gūṛhī**.

dā, trick, etc.; **kehṛē da dī gall**, what kind of affair (is this)? **lammē dā**, long ways: **cauṛē dā**, crosswise: **kehṛē dā**, in what way (i.e., long ways, crosswise)?

cuṭkī, f., snap of fingers; **cuṭkī wicc**, very quickly or easily.

dil, heart; **dil haulā** or **chōṭā**, (feel) faint, ashamed: **dil chōṭā**, unaspiring.

gizā, f., food; used practically as meaning habit, **gizā pakk gai e**, (he) has got used to it.

hallṇā, move, shake (intrans.); **hallkē**, **hillkē**, **quickly** hurryingly.

hīlā, pretence; **hīlā karnā**, look sharp, hurry up.

hēṭhā̃ utā̃, lit. downwards, upwards: **not very well in** health, in a bad state.

hēṭh uttē, one on top of the other.

jī, person, wish; **cār jī, panj jī**, four persons, five persons, but **dōwẽ jī** always means husband and wife.

makkū, part of cloth of huqqa; **makkū ṭhappṇā**, sit on someone, "go for" someone (slang).

pallā, border of garment; **mēre pallē** (or **mēre piṛ pallē**) **kujjh nehĩ peā**, I did not understand anything, I got no good from it: **mērē palleō̃**, at my expense.

sagō̃, but rather; sometimes means 'extremely,' **sagō̃ i māṛā**, extremely feeble or poor: also **sagō̃**.

sāh, m., breath; **sāh laiṇa**, take breath, rest: **sāh duāṇā**, let man or animal take a rest: **sāh kaḍhāṇā**, let man rest by carrying his burden.

sarfā, expense; **sarfā karnā**, spare expense.

uccā, high; **uccā suṇṇā**, be rather deaf: **uccī ākhṇā**, etc., to speak, etc., loudly: **uccī dittī**, loudly.

waṇḍē, see **bhā**.

wattar, moisture, frequently used of the moisture required for ploughing; **wattar ā geī e**, the land has got dry enough for ploughing (after heavy rain): **wattar hō geā**, moisture has come (to the land): **hēṭhlā utlā wattar raḷ geā e**, the lower moisture (already in the ground) and upper moisture (from rain) have joined, i.e., all the ground is wet through.

Additional Idioms.

laggṇā be attached, etc., **dhupp**, f., the sun to come out, **dhuppā̃ laggnīā̃**, have days of sunshine.

lāṇā, attach, **ṭhuḍḍa**, m., kick.

karnā, make; **patā**, m., find out; **mhabbat**, f., feel affection for. See below **dard, dardī, dukkh, dukkhī**.

khēḍṇā, play; **hāl**, m., move head to and fro as in incantations.

ghaṭṇā, grow less; **dil**, m., feel faint.

mārnā, beat; **ghāh**, m., cut grass: **sannh**, f., commit burglary, break through wall: **ṭhuḍḍā**, m., kick.

paiṇā, lie, etc.; **shām**, f., (**rāt**, f. **hanērā**, m.) come on or fall of evening (night, darkness).

rakkhṇā, place; **mhabbat**, f., love. See below **dukkh**.

bhāī, m., brother, to be contrasted with **whaī**, a term of address which may be used with anyone who is spoken to in the second sing. Thus one might address a servant, a schoolboy or little girl as **whaī**, but not as **bhāī**.

dard, m., pain, grief; **kise dā dard karnā, kise nū̃ kise dā dard hōṇā**, sympathise with.

dardī, sympathiser. Contrast **dard** and **dardī** with **dukkh, dukkhī, dōkhī**, below.

dukkh, m., pain, grief; **dukkh karnā** or **rakkhṇā**, feel jealous of or enmity against: **kise dā dukkh kise nū̃ hōṇā**, feel pain or sorrow in connection with anyone, also feel jealousy or enmity.

dukkhī, adj., feeling pain or grief on account of someone, whether through sympathy or through worry, but **dōkhī** feeling jealousy or enmity.

kakkh, m., piece of straw; **kakkh wī nehī̃**, nothing at all: **kakkh wī patā nehī̃**, no trace at all.

pāskū̃, m., something tied on to one side of uneven scales to make them even: **ohdā pāskū̃ wī nehī̃**, not a patch on him, nothing at all in comparison with him.

Auṇā, baihṇā, bahāṇā, bhannṇā, bharnā, caṛhnā, cāṛhnā, cūpṇā, dēṇā, duāṇā, kaḍḍhṇā, kaḍhāṇā, karnā, khāṇā. Pages 393–395.

1. Pira's eyes have become sore.	1. **Pire diā̃ akkhīā̃ āīā̃ hoīā̃ nē̃.**
2. He does not know the lesson or answer (language).	2. **Ohnū̃ sabak (jawāb) nehī̃ aundā (bōlī, zabān nehī̃ aundī).**
3. I feel disgust (physical disgust, ashamed, humiliated, angry).	3. **Menū̃ nafrat aundī e (kric, sharm, namōshī, gussā).**
4. Now I understand, I remember.	4. **Huṇ samajh ā gaī, gall yād āī.**
5. You are very sleepy, you are yawning.	5. **Tenū̃ nindar baṛī āī, tainū̃ ubāsīā̃ aundīā̃ nē̃.**
6. Last night I had a dream, I laugh to think of it.	6. **Rātī̃ ikk sufnā āeā, sōcke hāssā aundā e.**

7. He vomited, he is not in his senses yet.	7. Jī utā̃ āeā sū, aje hōsh nehī̃ āī.
8. Are your ears stopped, are you deaf?	8. Jhappe ā gae nī? (or lag gae).
9. The mare has a sore mouth.	9. Ghōṛī dā mū̃h āeā hoeā (or pakkā hōeā) e.
10. His hair has become white.	10. Ohnū̃ dhauḷe āe hoe nẽ.
11. Does he not remember yet?	11. Aje nehī̃ cētā āeā sū?
12. Well, what did it come to per maund?	12. Phēr maṇ de kinne rupayye baiṭhe?
13. When will the boy begin reading with the (Muhammadan) priest?	13. Muṇḍā kadõ miyyẽ kōḷ bawhēgā?
14. What did it work out at per rupee?	14. Rupayye dā kinnā baiṭhā?
15. I have become hoarse.	15. Mērā saṅgh (wāz) baih geā e.
16. Their house has collapsed.	16. Kōṭhā baih geā nẽ.
17. Take off the pot, the rice will get soft.	17. Hā̃ḍī lāhī̃, cauḷ baih jāṇīge.
18. You have kept me sitting here.	18. Tū̃ menū̃ ētthe naṭṭī bahā rakkheā e.
19. He has sent his grandson to learn tailoring.	19. Apṇe pōtre nū̃ darzī kōḷ bahāeā sū.
20. The old man is stretching himself.	20. Buḍḍhā ākaṛ peā bhanndā e.
21. I shall just drink a mouthful and come and massage you.	21. Maī̃ zarā ghuṭṭ bhar āwā̃ te āke muṭṭhīā̃ bharā̃gā.
22. My clothes are covered with mud, you will have to make good the loss.	22. Mēre kapṛe bhare hoe nẽ, nuksān bharnā pawīgā.
23. Sister, put on the pot (the vegetables, rice).	23. Bhaiṇ, tauṛī cāṛh (salūṇā cauḷ).

English	Panjabi
24. He got angry and lost the game.	24. Gussā caṛhn nāḷ bāzī caṛh gaī sū.
25. It has got very damp.	25. Baṛī sill (sējjaḷ) caṛhī hoī e.
26. Is the pot on, will rice be cooked to-day?	26. Tauṛī caṛh gaī e, ajj cauḷ cāṛhne nẽ?
27. Do not affect such style, you will get into debt.	27. Ēḍḍī shūkā shākī nā kar, ḳarz caṛh jaīgā.
28. Mashers (swells) suck Indian and Maltese oranges, also limes and sweet limes, but villagers swallow the whole.	28. Jeṇṭalmain te santare te Māḷṭe, te nāḷe khaṭṭe te miṭṭhe, cūp lende nẽ, par jaṭṭ būṭ sāre ragaṛ lende nẽ.
29. You have got fever through eating a lot of mangoes and sugar-cane.	29. Bāhḷe amb te ganne cūpaṇ nāḷ kass caṛh gaī je.
30. Do not curse me, invoke a blessing, do not deceive me.	30. Bad duā nā deī, menū̃ duā deī, dhōkhā (pharēb) nā deī.
31. The hen has laid an egg, heat up the fire and boil it.	31. Kukkṛī ā̃ḍṛā (or ā̃ṇḍā) dittā e, tū̃ tā dēke bail kar sū.
32. Let the horse (or ass) rest, it will break down.	32. Waihtar nū̃ dhūf kaḍhá haṇēk ghattēgā.
33. Why did he come? Because I called him.	33. Ōh kis karke āeā? Ēs karke paī maī ohnū̃ kuāeā.
34. Rub it this way, don't do the work carelessly (badly).	34. Aiñ karke maḷī, aīwẽ nā kamm tarangaṛ chaḍḍī.
35. I do not feel inclined to eat bread made of maize or millet.	35. Ḍhōḍhā khāṇ nū̃ mērā rūh (dil) nehī̃ kardā.
36. Find out and tell me	36. Patā karke menū̃ dassī.

37.	I do not feel inclined to throw it away.	37.	Raddī karn nū̃ mērā jī nehī̃ kardā.
38.	He has agreed to take eight annas, he will stop work at four.	38.	Dhēlī laiṇī kītī sū, cār waje chuṭṭī karēgā.
39.	Make him well, I love him.	39.	Wall karī sū, maī ohnū̃ piār karnā wā̃.
40.	He gave up the field as being poor.	40.	Māṛī karke pailī chaḍḍī sū.
41.	I called him Sardar, still he refused.	41.	Maī ohnū̃ Sardār karke kuāeā, tā̃wī nā̃h kītī sū.
42.	He has attained his end by abuse.	42.	Gāhḷā̃ kaḍḍh kaḍḍhke matlab (kamm) kaḍḍh leā sū.
43.	She veiled herself, what of it? Why are you so critical?	43.	Ghuṇḍ kaḍḍheā, tā̃ kī hoeā? Tū̃ kyū̃ ghutkḷā̃ kaḍḍhnā ẽ?
44.	When the horse paws the ground the dog shows his teeth.	44.	Jad ghōṛā khaurū kaḍḍhdā e, kuttā dand kaḍḍhdā e.
45.	What are you grinning at? The sugar will last out dinner anyway.	45.	Tū̃ kehṛī galle dand kaḍḍhnā ẽ? Khaṇḍ khāṇā te kaḍḍhēgī.
46.	They were teaching him to carry burdens, but he has not learned yet.	46.	Ohnū̃ lādū kaḍḍhde te hai sāṇ, par aje nikḷeā nehī.
47.	Swearing (that he is speaking the truth) he slanders people, but he will in the long run injure himself.	47.	Sauhā̃ khā khāke cuglī khāndā e, tā̃wī chēkṛe apū̃ kasr khāēgā.
48.	He affects great style.	48.	Baṛī daddh kaḍḍhdā e.
49.	In the meantime we are making it fit for ploughing (or fit for work).	49.	Hāli ohnū̃ hāḷī kaḍḍhne ā̃ pae.

50.	He was greatly deceived, tricked.	50.	**Baṛā fareb khādhā, baṛā dā khādhā.**
51.	He wandered about, then he stumbled, he was then abused and reproached and finally beaten, receiving blows with sticks, fists and shoes.	51.	**Bhambaḷbhūse khāndā rehā phēr ṭhēḍḍā khādhā, (lagā) muṛ gāhḷīā̃ te jhiṛkā̃ khādhīā̃, chēkṛe mār khādhī, sōṭīā̃ te hūre te juttīā̃.**
52.	He suffered serious loss, he took a bribe and was caught.	52.	**Tagṛā ṭōṭā khādhā, waḍḍhī khāke phaṛ ghattā.**

Khēḍṇa, laggṇā, lāṇā lāhṇā, laihṇā, laiṇā, mārnā. Pages 395, 396.

1.	He got hurt while shooting.	1.	**Shikār khēḍdeā̃ saṭṭ laggī sū.**
2.	It is very late, you do not obey.	2.	**Baṛā cir laggā, tū̃ ākhe nehī̃ laggdā.**
3.	They learned that the rupee would not pass.	3.	**Patā lagg geā nē̃ paī rupayyā nehī̃ laggdā.**
4.	He feels cold (hungry, thirsty).	4.	**Pāḷā laggā sū (bhukkh, treh laggī sū).**
5.	You have begun talking leaning against the doorpost.	5.	**Muhāṭhī̃ laggke gallī̃ lagg peā ē̃.**
6.	I suffered great loss through his tricking me.	6.	**Ohde dā lāṇ nāḷ menū̃ baṛī kasr laggī.**
7.	He has begun working, now he is on duty.	7.	**Ōh kamm lagg geā e, huṇ ohdī naukarī laggī hoī e.**
9.	Since I fined him he does not come near me (meet me).	9.	**Jadō̃ dā maī̃ ohnū̃ ḍann lāeā, ōh mēre matthe nehī̃ laggdā.**
10.	The tailor is putting on a patch, his wife is plas-	10.	**Darzī ṭākī lāndā e peā, ohdī suāṇī rōṭīā̃ lāndī**

	tering the *capatis* on the sides of the oven (a *capāti* is really finer than a *rōṭi*).		**e paī.**
11.	He is (or may be considered) my sisters's son, but I do not like his talk.	11.	**Ōh mērā bhaṇẽwā laggdā e, tad wī ohdīā̃ gallā̃ menū̃ burīā̃ laggdiā̃ nẽ.**
12.	What did it cost, shall I calculate?	12.	**Kī mull laggā e? Mai lēkhā lā̃?**
13.	Using force he affixed the mark.	13.	**Baṛā ṭill lāke nishān lāeā.**
14.	The mare will get galled.	14.	**Ghōṛī nū̃ laggā laggēgā.**
15.	Are your eyes smarting from the medicine?	15.	**Akkhīā̃ nū̃ duāī laggdī e?**
16.	This key will never fit.	16.	**Ēh kunjī kadī nehī̃ laggaṇ laggī.**
17.	For two days the moon has risen late.	17.	**Cann te dū̃h dinā̃ tõ gōḍā lāeā hoeā e.**
18.	Open the door, brother, or the window.	18.	**Būhā lāh, bhāī, yā̃ bārī.**
19.	He has dishonoured me by taking off my turban.	19.	**Ōs mērī pagg lāhke mērī pat lāhī.**
20.	I will pay your debt	20.	**Mai tērā karz lāh deā̃gā.**
21.	Taking off his shoes and clothes he began to wash.	21.	**Juttī te kapṛe lāhke nhauṇ laggā.**
22.	A patch is required here, why are you delaying?	22.	**Ētthe ṭākī laggdī e, cir kāhnū̃ lānnā ẽ?**
23.	Find out whether he has caught cold.	23.	**Patā lai pai shardī laggī sū ke nehī̃.**
24.	Pass this four-anna bit if you can fool anyone.	24.	**Ēh pauḷī lā lai, je dā lagge te.**
25.	You will suffer loss, they will fine you.	25.	**Tenū̃ mōs laggēgī, ḍann lāṇīge.**
26.	The *capatis* have been	26.	**Rōṭīā̃ lagg te geīā̃, baṛā**

	English		Panjabi
	put into the oven, a lot of force was necessary.		ṭill laggā.
27.	Have the signs been affixed, what did he charge for them ?	27.	Nishān lagg gae? Kī lāeā sū nishānā̃ dā?
28.	Open the lock with a key.	28.	Kunjī lāke jandrā lāhī.
29.	To-day the moon will rise late.	29.	Ajj cann nū̃ gōḍā laggēdā.
30.	If they get an opportunity they will say it.	30.	Maukā laggō nē, tā̃ ākh chaḍḍaṇge.
31.	He wanted to embrace me, but I do not want to embrace him.	31.	Menū̃ gaḷ lāndā sī, maĩ nehī ohde gaḷ laggdā.
32.	Why did they have my shoes taken off? My honour has suffered.	32.	Mērī juttī kyū̃ luhāī nē, mērī pat laih gei e.
33.	Take a breath sometimes (wait a bit, don't talk so fast).	33.	O sāh wī leā kar.
34.	On account of his travelling first class he was much abused and reproached.	34.	Fasṭ klās wicc baihṇ dā sadkā baṛīā̃ gāhḷā̃ te jhiṛkā̃ leīā̃.
35.	He is yawning a lot, he must be ill.	35.	Baṛīā̃ ubāsīā̃ lendā e peā, maḷeā hoeā hōwēdā.
36.	The thief has bolted altogether.	36.	Cōr te ukkā mukkā maḷ geā.
37.	Do not take it amiss, I have told no lie.	37.	Burā nā mannī, maĩ jhūṭh kōī nehī māreā.
38.	Shutting both windows and one door he gave vent to scream after scream.	38.	Dōwe bārīā̃ te ikk būhā mārke baṛīā̃ cīkā̃ mārn lagg peā.
39.	Many make a living by cutting grass.	39.	Bāhḷe te ghāh khōtar khōtarke gujārā karde nē.

	English		Panjabi
40.	You lunatic, why are jumping so much?	40.	Bā mārea, ēḍḍiā̃ chāḷā̃ kāh de jōgā mārnā ẽ peā̃?
41.	Are you out of your senses?	41.	Matt (or hōsh or akl or bā) mārī hoī ā?
42.	They killed him.	42.	Ohnū̃ thā̃ mārеō nẽ, or mār saṭṭeō nẽ or mār chaḍḍeā nẽ, or jānō māreā nẽ.
43.	He had a jolly good time.	43.	Wāh wā lillā̃ luṭṭīā̃ or bullhe luṭṭe sū.
44.	An Indian pony, kicking up his hind feet like an English pony (i.e., aping great airs).	44.	Dēsī ṭaṭṭū Aṅgrēzī ṭiṭ-ṇe (mārdā e).
45.	I will lock it and go round (take a turn, etc.).	45.	Tālā or jandrā mārke phērā mārā̃gā.
46.	He didn't defraud him of his right? He cheated him out of a lot of money.	46.	Ohdā hakk nehī̃ māreā sū? Ohde baṛe rupay-ye māre.
47.	Do not simply call to him, give a good shout.	47.	Aiwẽ wāz nā mār, tagṛī kūk mār.
48.	He seized him in an embrace and dived.	48.	Ohnū̃ japphā mārke cub-bhī mārī.
49.	Just take a look at these papers, he has made a great mess.	49.	Ehnā̃ kāgazā̃ te zarā nazr mār, ōs baṛā rauḷā māreā.
50.	He did not sneeze, he had a hiccup?	50.	Nicch nehī̃ sāsū mārī, hidkī laggī hoī sū.
51.	Why are you knocking up against me?	51.	Tū̃ kāhnū̃ ṭakkarā̃ peā mārnā ẽ?
52.	Has the moon begun to rise late?	52.	Cann aje gōḍā māreā e?
53.	He shows great conceit, he is telling falsehoods.	53.	Shēkhī mārdā e, gappā̃ mārdā e.

54. He wagged his head (in incantations) a long time.	**54. Cōkhā cir sir mārdā rehā.**
55. The buffalo calf butts me.	**55. Jhōṭī menū̃ siṅ (siṇg) mārdī e.**

Miḷṇā, mārnā, nikaḷṇā, raihṇā, pīṇā, rakkhṇā, ṭōrna, ṭurnā, wagṇā, wāhṇā, waṭṭṇā, wēkhṇā. Pages 396–398.

1. To-day neither the cow nor the buffalo permitted herself to be milked.	**1. Ajj nā te gā̃ milī te ṇā majjh (maīh).**
2. If the printer had not turned out a scoundrel the paper would have been published now.	**2. Jē chāpaṇwālā badmāsh nā nikḷe ā akhbār huṇ tīkar nikḷe ā.** (*See* Gram. p. 320.)
3. Has the boy become fit for work? No he has turned out a thief.	**3. Muṇḍā hāḷī nikḷeā e? Sagõ cōr nikḷeā.**
4. You are always grinning, I am sick of it.	**4. Tū̃ jhaṭe binde guṭak painnā ẽ, maī te akk peā wā̃.**
5. When the mother started, the girl laughed.	**5. Jadõ bēbbe ṭur paī, kākī hass paī.**
6. At dusk work turned up to be done.	**6. Hanēre pae kamm peā sū.**
7. First he began to seize me, afterwards he was very much ashamed.	**7. Paihlā̃ te hatthī̃ peā, magarõ ḍāhḍā bhaiṛā peā.**
8. The girl was getting up from being asleep when the dog attacked her.	**8. Kuṛī suttī paī uṭṭhdī sī, te kuttā pai gēō sū.**
9. When he began to get abused he turned very pale.	**9. Gāhḷā̃ jad paiṇ laggīā̃ burā pīḷā peā.**
10. I am afraid (in doubt) that there will be great loss.	**10. Menū̃ shakk paindā e paī baṛā ṭōṭā (or ghāṭā) pawẽdā.**

11. If you had got a good beating, you would not have shown your face again.	11. Tagṛī phanḍ (or mār) paindīo ī muṛ nazrī wī nā paindõ.
12. If you get two or three blows from shoes or sticks do not say anything to *me*.	12. Jē dō cār juttīā̃ yā̃ sõṭīā̃ paīõ nī menū̃ kujjh nā ākhī̃.
13. He came at me to strike me, but I ran away.	13. Menū̃ mārn peā sī par mai uṭṭh nassēā.
14. When I said the banyan had blossomed he rushed at me.	14. Jad mai ākheā pai bōhṛ phull paī (or peā) e ōh menū̃ tuṭṭke peā.
15. The field is uselessly lying fallow.	15. Pailī dhigāṇe paī hōi e.
16. If they plot a thing like that, there will be plots on this side too.	16. Jēkar ehojehī gall pakālō nē, ūddharõ wī gallā̃ pakkṇāgīā̃.
17. If he had entreated would you (f.) have given him alms?	17. Jē wāste pāndā khair pāndiõ sū̃?
18. He was calling out for help, and they were saying why are you making a noise?	18. Ōh te hāl hāl (hāl pāhreā) peā pāndā sī te ōh āhnde sāṇ ḍanḍ (rauḷā) kyū̃ pānnā ē̃ peā.
19. If he dances this dance his father will bring a case against him.	19. Jē bhaṅgṛā (dhamāḷ) pāeo sū̃, peō ohde te arzī pāegā. (*See* Gram. p. 379).
20. We put on our shoes after our clothes.	20. Asī̃ kapṛe pāke juttī pānne ā̃.
21. The two men were going along with their arms over each other's shoulders.	21. Dōwẽ jaṇe japphī pāke lage jānde sāṇ.
22. He told a very interesting story.	22. Ḍāhḍī suādḷī kahāṇī pāī sāsū̃.

23. Very well, brother, I will give a respite of two months.	23. Halā, bhrā, dō mahīne pāẫgā.
24. Have your smoke and make the pickle.	24. Hukkā pīke acār pāĩ.
25. How do you smoke tobacco? Sometimes a cigarette, sometimes a cheroot.	25. Tū̃ kīkaṇ tamākū pīnnā ẽ? Maĩ kade sigraṭ te kade curuṭ pīnnā wā̃.
26. A plague on him, why does he not swallow down his anger.	26. Pīṛ pawe sū, apṇā gussā kāṛ de jōgā nehī pi l..nda?
27. By letting people smoke his huqqa he makes friends with all.	27. Hukkā piā piāke sāreā̃ nāḷ piār pā lendā e.
28. If you love him, he will also be friendly with you.	28. Je ohde nāḷ mhabbat rakkhīō je, ōh tuhāḍḍe nāḷ wi dōstī rakkhēdā.
29. If the work can be done I will get it done.	29. Kamm ṭure te ṭōrā̃gā.
30 The Deputy Superintendent of police reduced him in rank.	30. Kaptān sāhb ohnū̃ trōṛeā sī.
31. His proposal seems likely to be agreed to, he has the knack of getting things agreed to.	31. Gall ohdī huṇ ṭurnwāḷī jāpdī e, ohnū̃ ṭōrn dī jāc jō hoī.
32. Get the leaking vessel patched. Off with you at once.	32. Wagde bhāṇḍe nū̃ ṭāṇkā luā̃; wag jā huṇ.
33 Send him off by that road, it is a great deal used.	33. Ose rāh wagā̃ sū, ōh rāh bāhḷā wagdā e.
34. He is always dragging in Persian.	34. Oh te habbhe (sabbhe) wēḷe Fārsī wāhndā raihndā e.
35. She is always showing her teeth (in anger) or frowning	35. Kaciclā̃ ghurāklā̃ waṭṭdī ī rainhdī e.

36. Will you watch out for him? We shall see.	36. Tusī ohdā rāh wēkkhōge? Wēkhī jāpēgī.
37. No, my good Sir, I have no idea. Get along with you (what nonsense), *you* have no idea?	37. Nā mallā menū̃ kakkh wī patā nehī̃ laggdā. Hēkkhā̃, (for wēkh kh̲ā̃) tenū̃ nehī̃ patā laggdā?

Miscellaneous Idioms. Pages 398–400.

1. They were saying that washermen are very deceitful.	1. Ōh gall pae karde sāṇ ak̲h̲e chīmbe baṛe khuṭṭarī hunde nẽ, ak̲h̲e.
2. I said why are you keeping your mouth open (I said).	2. Tū̃ mak̲h̲e mū̃h kyū̃ aḍḍī rakkhnā ẽ, mak̲h̲e.
3. My son will not stay in this company.	3. Ēs baihṇī nehī̃ mērā puttar baihndā.
4. So far as I am concerned he is dead.	4. Mēre waṇḍe dā te ōh mar geā e.
5. In my opinion it is perhaps a bird.	5. Mēre bhāṇe k̲h̲abare janaur e.
6. In your opinion is he a professional singer?	6. Tēre bhā dā ōh kōī mirāshī e?
7. Look here, my man, don't make the tea so weak, make it stronger than this.	7. Lai whaī, cāh ēḍḍī patlī nā baṇāī, edū̃ saṅhṇī (tēz, gūṛhī) baṇāī.
8. What way shall I place the bed? Put it the long way, not crosswise.	8. Manjī kehṛe dā ḍāhā̃? Cauṛe dā nā ḍāhī̃, lamme dā ḍāhī̃.
9. What way are you talking, have you so little spirit?	9. Kehṛe dā dī gall karnā ẽ, tērā dil ēḍḍā chōṭā e?
10. I feel faint from the blow	10. Saṭṭ laggaṇ nāḷ mērā diḷ hauḷā (chōṭā) hō geā e, or ghaṭṭ geā e.

11. Why does he not hurry? He has got used (to the place, etc.) and is lazy.	11. **Hallke kyū̃ nehī̃ caldā, huṇ te hiḷeā hoeā e. sustī kardā e.**
12. Look sharp about the work, will you?	12. **Hilā karke kamm kar wī.**
13. How are you? Oh, only so so (poorly).	13. **Kī hāl ī? Hēṭhā̃ utā̃ ī ā̃.**
14. They all fell over one another.	14. **Ṣāre jaṇe hēṭh utte ḍigg pae.**
15. We have five mouths to feed, we are two (husband and wife) and we have three little ones.	15. **Asī̃ panj ā̃ khāṇwāḷe, dō jī āp, te trai añāṇe.**
16. Have they gone away, both husband and wife?	16. **Ōh ṭur gae nẽ dōwe jī?**
17. If you touch the edge of my shirt I'll go for you (slang).	17. **Jē jhigge de palle nū̃ hatth lāeō ī makkū ṭhappū̃gā.**
18. The gentleman has spoken so long, have you understood anything?	18. **Sāhb inniā̃ gallā̃ kitiā̃ nẽ, kujjh piṛ palle peā ī?**
19. I have not understood a word (lit. not a straw).	19. **Mēre palle kakkh wī nehī̃ peā.**
20. They bore the whole expense themselves.	20. **Sārā kamm ohnā̃ de palleō̃ hoeā.**
21. This is good indeed.	21. **Ēh te sagō̃ ī caṅgā e.**
22. Just take a rest yourself, and let the animal have a rest. I will carry the boy's load a bit.	22. **Tū̃ zarā sāh lellai te caukhar nū̃ wī sāh duā, te mai muṇḍe nū̃ sāh kaḍhānnā̃.**
23. If he spares expense, nothing will be done.	23. **Jē sarfā kitō sū, kakkh wī nehī̃ baṇēgā.**
24. If he were not somewhat deaf one would not need to speak loudly.	24. **Jē uccā nā suṇea tā̃ uccī uccī kūṇā nā pawe ā̃.**

25. He said loudly, will you not keep quiet ?	25. Ucci dittī ākkhaā laggā amn wī kareā kar.
26. Oh no, the ground is not properly wet yet, there have been just a few drops.	26. Aje kitthe wattar hoeā ? Aje te kaṇī muṇī ī hoī e.
27. There has been heavy rain, now if we get sunshine, in ten days the ground will be the right moisture for ploughing.	27. Tag̱ṛā mīh peā, huṇ dhuppā̃ laggaṇ te dasā̃ dihāṛeā̃ nū̃ jīwī̃ wattar āwedī.
28. The moistures (from the ground and the rain) have met.	28. Huṇ raḷ geā e wattar.
29. The priest was performing incantations last night.	29. Ilmā̃ rātī̃ hāl (ḍōlī) khēḍdā̃ sī.
30. First evening falls, then it gets a little dark, finally night comes.	30. Paihlā̃ shām paindī e, muṛ thōṛā thōṛā hanērā paindā e, ōṛak nū̃ pūrī rāt paindī e.
31. No, my man, do not beseech me.	31. Nā whaī, mēre agge hatth nā bannhī̃.
32. I said "no my man" (or my woman, my boy, my girl), I did not say "no brother."	32. Maī ohnū̃ "nā whaī" ākheā, maī "nā bhāī" te nehī̃ ākheā.
33. He has strong enmity against us.	33. Ōh sāḍḍe nāḷ baṛā dukkh kardā or rakkhdā e.
34. The co-wife always felt jealousy or enmity towards her co-wife.	34. Saukaṇ nū̃ apṇī saukaṇ dā dē̃h rātī̃ dukkh raihndā sī.
35. The mother sorrows much on account of her son.	35. Mā̃ nū̃ apṇe puttar dā baṛā dukkh e.
36. The mother sympathises much with her daughter.	36. Bēbbe apṇī dhī dā baṛā dard kardī e.

Note on Nos. 33—36.—The word **dukkh (dukh)** with **rakkhṇā** or **karnā** implies enmity or jealousy. With **nū̃** and the auxiliary verb (see Nos. 34 and 35) the meaning may be sorrow as well as jealousy or enmity, the context enables one to decide.

37. He stumbled or he got a kick. — 37. **Ohnū̃ ṭhēḍḍā laggā.**

38. The shepherd kicked the lamb. — 38. **Ājṛī lēlle nū̃ ṭhuḍḍā lāeā (mārеā).**

Locative Case, etc.

See Grammar, pages 274, 275, 286, 344, 345.

1. He was to stay a fortnight in Gujrat, he will come now in a week. — 1. **Pandrā̃ dihāṛe Gujrāte raihṇā sāsū, huṇ aṭṭhī̃ dinī̃ āwēdā.**
2. Earthquakes come when doors are shut, burglaries are committed when men are asleep. — 2. **Wajjī̃ būhī̃ bhucāḷ aunde nẽ, suttī̃ bandī̃ cōr sannh mārde nẽ.**
3. At midday he sat in the sun at the tahsil. — 3. **Dopaihrī̃ tasīle dhuppe baiṭhā rehā.**
4. In the evening he was in Kular but he spent the night in Natt. — 4. **Shāmī̃ Kulārī̃ sī, par rātī̃ Nattī̃ jā rehā.**
5. In the morning I shall go to the bazar, and I shall stay in the bazar. — 5. **Fajrī̃ bazār jā̃āgā te bazāre rāhā̃gā.**
6. He has not come yet, but in the morning he was at home. — 6. **Aje ghar nehī̃ āeā, waḍḍewēḷe ghare sī.**
7. He bought ghi at Re. 1-12 for two seers. — 7. **Pauṇī̃ dū̃h rupaī̃ waṭṭī gheō leā.**
8. You come before it is quite light and begin arguing. — 8. **Muhānjhḷe āke dalīlī̃ lagg painnā ẽ.**
9. Why do they sit in other houses? — 9. **Kehṛī galle hōrnī̃ gharī̃ baihnde nẽ?**

English	Panjabi
10. He lives in Bāgṛīā̃ and goes to school in Aujḷe. They study in the sun.	10. Bāgṛī ghar sū par Aujḷī paṛhdā e. Sīye baihke paṛhde nẽ.
11. Look for them in Mardeke, during the day they are in the mosque.	11. Maṛdēkī labbhī ne, dine masītī hunde nẽ.
12. In Gujranwala it sells at eleven annas a seer.	12. Kujrā̃āḷe yāhrī ānnī sēr wikdī e.
13. My wife wears shoes fourteen fingers and I sixteen fingers long.	13. Mērī wauhṭī cauhdī juttī pāndī e, maī sōhḷī pānnā wā̃.
14. A man of his size will wear seventeen or eighteen finger shoes.	14. Ohde jēḍḍā jaṇā k͟haure satāhrī aṭhāhrī pāndā hōwēdā.
15. The donkey which was yours is his and the fat-tailed sheep which was his is mine. (This can have other meanings).	15. Tuhā̃ḍḍe wāḷā khōtā ohdā e te ohde wāḷā dumbā mērā e.
16. The horse connected with me, the buffalo calf connected with him and the buffalo connected with them will be of the same value.	16. Mērewāḷā ghōrā te ōswāḷā jhōṭā te ohnā̃ wāḷī majjh ikkō mull de hōṇge.
17. He is only pretending to agree.	17. Aīwẽ uttõwāḷī hā̃ kardā e.
18. He went out to meet him.	18. Ohnū̃ aggõwāḷī miḷeā.
19. Why did you take the trouble?	19. Kyū̃ taklīf kītī je?
20. Why did you give trouble?	20. Kyū̃ taklīf dittī je?

A few Hints.

I. It is always wrong to omit the words for am, is, are, etc., except in negative sentences. The error is very common with Europeans, who constantly say **muṇḍā kitthe?** for **kitthe we** (where is the boy?): **oh kī āk͟hdā** for **kī āk͟hdā e**, (what is he saying ?) : **kihdiā̃ ciṭṭhiā̃** for **kihdiā̃ ciṭṭhiā̃ ne** (whose letter are they ?) : **māshkī teār** for **teār e** (is the water-carrier ready ?).

II. In English we use "do" to avoid some other verb already used. Thus: put them away. I have *done* so. In Punjabi this can never be **maĩ kītā e.** The two sentences would be **ohnā̃ nū̃ sāhmke rakkh. maĩ rakkh chaḍḍe ne.** The same verb must be used again. In this case it is **rakkhṇā.**

III. Similarly we are fond of an unnecessary "like that." We say:—don't cry like that: don't shout like that. If we translate by **es tarhā̃** it means: do not cry or shout in that particular way, do it in some other way. The words should simply be omitted.

IV. We are addicted to a great use of possessive pronouns. We say: "we read in our Bibles." In parts of the British Isles people say "he's having his tea," "I'm going to my bed." All these must be omitted.

Baibal wicc likheā hoeā e,	we read in our Bibles.
maĩ sauṇ caleā wā̃.	I am going to (my) bed.

V. The future is not much used in negative sentences. The following will show the common usage.

maĩ bawhā̃dā, I shall sit down: **maĩ nehī̃ baihndā** or **nehī̃ baihṇ lagā̃,** I will not sit down.

Yet sometimes we do hear the future with the negative, especially in promises, as—

edū̃ agge maĩ nehī karā̃ karā̃dā, in future I will not do so.

VI. Interrogative words: the position of interrogative words should be noted.

The nominative of the sentence must never come between the interrogative word and the verb. Europeans accustomed to the English order "where are you going ?" "what have you done ?" are apt to say **kitthe tū̃ caleā ẽ, kī tū̃ kītā e.** This is quite wrong. The following show the order:—

oh kāhde jogā kūndā e?	why is he speaking ?
bhrā kadõ āwīdā?	when will your brother come ?

Sometimes conversationally the nominative is brought to the end as: **kūndā kāhde jogā e oh, kadõ āwīdā bhrā,** but this does not violate the rule given above.

APPENDIX.

P. 268, ll. 1–3. The feminine of **geā, peā, leā** is pronounced both **geī, peī, leī** and **gaī, paī, laī.**

P. 276, l. 2. For **paññ̃ī**, locative of **panj**, five, **panjī̃** is commoner.

P. 287, ll. 14–16. The rule that a tonic **h** is inserted in the ordinal numbers from 11 to 99, except those from 69 to 78, should be extended to include all declension of the corresponding cardinal numbers. Any of these numbers when declined, i.e., when occurring in the prepositional or locative case, inserts a tonic **h**. Thus we have—

yārā̃ rupayye, 11 rupees; **yāhrī̃ rupaī̃,** for 11 rupees; **yāhrā̃ rupayyā̃ tõ,** for 11 rupees; **yāhrwā̃ rupayyā,** 11th rupee.

So also **cāḷī rupayye, cāhḷī rupaī̃, cāhḷiā̃ rupayyā̃ nū̃, cāhḷīwā̃ rupayyā.** For this reason it would be better to spell the locatives of 15, 57, 90, **pandhrī̃, satwanjhī̃, nabbhī̃,** and not as spelt on p. 21, ll. 17, 21, 23 and also for the prepositionals and the prepositional of 14, **cauhdā̃,** and not as spelt on p. 287, l. 9.

This tonic **h** is a characteristic also of the numeral adjectives expressing the size of shoes. The size of shoes is given in terms of finger-breadths. We have the following:—

tēhrī juttī, a shoe whose length is thirteen finger-breadths. So also **cauhdī, pandhrī, sōhḷī, satāhrī, aṭhāhrī,** shoes of the length of fourteen, fifteen, sixteen, seventeen, eighteen finger-breadths, respectively.

P. 301, l. 33; 302, l. 3, **rāhī̃** is probably m. pl., not fem. sing.

P. 319, ll. 8–10. In the second form of the past conditional some say **āh** instead of **ā**; in this case we have in place of the forms given, **karẽ āh, kare āh, kariye āh, karo āh.**

P. 319. The future tense. When two verbs are so closely joined as to contain practically one idea it is usual to omit from the first the ending **-gā** or **-dā.**

maĩ tenū̃ mārā̃ kuṭṭā̃gā or maĩ marū̃ kuṭṭū̃gā, I will beat you well. The emphatic particle ī (ī) is frequently inserted before the ending, as rinnh te lāīgā, I will indeed cook.

P. 322, l. 24. When the negative nehī is used it is not generally necessary to insert the present auxiliary. This does not hold for the negative nā.

ōh wall nehī, he is not well.

ōh nehī muṛeā, he has not desisted.

ōh nā muṛeā, he did not desist.

P. 381, l. 14. In the pres. indic. with pronominal suffixes the auxiliary may end in -dā, etc. Thus, maī āhndā je, I say to you; asī āhnde je, we say to you.

P. 372, l. 33 wāḷā. It is worthy of note that when wāḷā is added to the genitive of pronouns it is always added to the prepositional case of the genitive. Thus when it is added to mērā, tuhāḍḍā, ohdā they become mēre, tuhāḍḍe, ohde, giving the forms mērewāḷā, āḍḍewāḷā, ohdewāḷā. As explained on p. 373 the third singular pronouns have two forms ohdewāḷā and ōswāḷā, ehdewāḷā, ēswāḷā, etc., while the third plural pronouns are not found with the genitival construction. They are put in the prepositional case before wāḷā, as in ohnāwāḷā, ehnāwāḷā, kihnāwāḷā.

P. 379, l. 24. In the second sing. past tense of intrans. verbs the -ō may, in negative sentences, be separated from the rest of the word which then takes the ordinary form.

tū nehī ō muṛī, didst thou (f.) not desist?

tū nehī ō geā, thou didst not go.

P. 382, l. 29. *Further Note on the Imperative.* The polite imperative, as contrasted with the ordinary forms, suggests that the action need not be performed at once. Thus ghall sū, ghallo sū, send him (at once): ghallī sū, ghallīo sū, ghalleo sū, send him (but not necessarily at once).

When the infinitive is used as an imperative it generally implies that the nominative is tusī, not tū. The infinitive is, therefore, not the usual form employed with a servant.

Exceptions are found to both these rules.

P. 387, l. 12. The verbs ākhṇā, say, wēkhṇā, see have

present participles formed as if form the roots **āhṇā, wēhṇā** in addition to the regular pres. part. Thus :—

ōh āhndī sī, she was saying: **tū̃ wēhndā saī̃,** you were looking.

jē wēhndō̃, if you had looked: **jē kujjh āhndō sū,** if he had said something to him.

These pres. parts may be employed in all the tenses formed from the pres. part.